SELF-DECEPTION
AND
SELF-UNDERSTANDING

SELF-DECEPTION
AND
SELF-UNDERSTANDING

NEW ESSAYS IN
PHILOSOPHY AND PSYCHOLOGY

Edited by Mike W. Martin

UNIVERSITY PRESS OF KANSAS

Published by the University Press of Kansas (Lawrence, Kansas 66045), which was
organized by the Kansas Board of Regents and is operated and funded by Emporia
State University, Fort Hays State University, Kansas State University, Pittsburg State
University, the University of Kansas, and Wichita State University

Library of Congress Cataloging in Publication Data
Main entry under title:

Self-deception and self-understanding.

Bibliography: p.
Includes index.
1. Self-deception. 2. Self-perception. 3. Personality.
4. Defense mechanisms (Psychology). 5. Values. I. Martin, Mike W.
BF697.S433   1985   155.2   84-27013
ISBN 0-7006-0264-X

Printed in the United States of America

TO
A. I. MELDEN and FRED HAGEN

Contents

Preface

At the turn of the century, not long after psychology separated from philosophy to become an autonomous discipline, Freud proclaimed that all of us constantly hide the truth from ourselves—often with disastrous results. Moralists and ethicists earlier explored how conscience and commitment can be undermined by lying to oneself. Yet self-deception became a major philosophical concern only after the existentialists, especially Jean-Paul Sartre, identified it as the primary avenue for evading honest self-awareness. Recently, psychologists and philosophers have devoted increasing attention to self-deception, to its meaning, causes, effects, tactics, goals, and value implications.

Two convictions shaped this anthology. First, if we are to understand ourselves, we need to understand self-deception and to a significant extent overcome it. Second, an understanding of self-deception should be based on insights from both psychology and philosophy. All the essays included here were written for this volume and are published for the first time. Authors were selected in part because of the significance of their previous work on self-deception or closely-related topics, and in part because they represent a variety of interests and contrasting perspectives.

This book, more than most, evolved because of creative sponsorship by its publisher, who extended to me an invitation to develop this collection of essays, wrote innumerable letters to potential contributors, and supported me at every stage of the project. I am especially indebted to Kate Torrey. For their useful suggestions I wish to thank the contributors and also Jonathan E. Adler, Christopher Boehm, John Flowers, D. W. Hamlyn, William J. McGuire, A. I. Melden, David Pears,

J. Michael Russell, John Sabini, Gerasimos Santas, Jerome L. Singer, Tod S. Sloan, and especially Daryl J. Bem. Chapman College provided aid through its research support program.

Above all I am grateful to Shannon Snow Martin for providing the conditions for meaningful work, and for her love. Together we thank our daughters, Sonia and Nicole, for giving our lives a rich mixture of order and chaos and laughter.

General Introduction

Mike W. Martin

> If the 'searching of our heart and reins' be the purpose of this human drama, then what is sought seems to be what effort we can make. . . . [Heroic individuals] find a zest in it, not by 'ostrich-like forgetfulness,' but by pure inward willingness to face the world.
> —William James, *The Principles of Psychology*

In deceiving ourselves, we are the victims and often the primary objects of the deception. Above all we are the source—the deceivers. Sometimes our own wishes, biases, emotions, or sheer complacency inadvertently mislead our judgment, making us deceivers only in a weak sense. This *nonwillful self-deception* can involve negligence and avoidable ignorance for which we are responsible. Other times, however, we are more active, more like purposeful and intentional deceivers. Such *willful self-deception* frequently proceeds by ignoring the truth, disregarding evidence, manipulating our emotions and attitudes, pretending to ourselves and others, or even persuading ourselves to believe what we know "deep down" is false. Both forms of self-deception constitute potent threats to understanding ourselves. Together they suggest the irony that we may be our own greatest obstacles in a search for self-understanding.

Acquiring self-understanding is a genuine achievement in overcoming at least much self-deception. It demands considerably more than merely memorizing assorted facts about ourselves, such as the circumference of our big toes or the astrology charts for the day we were born.

1

We must gain insights into important aspects of ourselves, based on significant explanations, which lead to appropriate changes in our lives. For this reason, recommendations about how to achieve self-understanding presuppose value judgments. Counselors who refer us to particular psychological theories and therapies, to philosophical standpoints and skills, or to religious precepts and practice, are not describing preordained paths to self-discovery; they are *prescribing* how (in their views) to develop a justifiable and meaningful perspective on our lives.

For the same reason, self-understanding entails more than disinterested self-analysis, just as understanding the plight of others entails more than detached observation. There must be appropriate adjustments in attitude, emotion, and conduct. Not infrequently these adjustments emerge from a foundation of suffering, which compels insight and confronts us with new demands. Freud had this in mind when he remarked, ''Knowledge is not always the same as knowledge: there are different sorts of knowledge, which are far from equivalent psychologically.''[1] Like Socrates, Freud located the test for genuine self-knowledge in a creative inner transformation and a more meaningful life.

Psychologists and philosophers have had three main interests in exploring the relationship between self-deception and self-understanding. First, they have seen the topic of self-deception as fertile ground for describing and explaining what it is to be a ''self''—that is, a person who is aware of himself or herself. Second, they have assessed the role of self-deception in undermining a life based on values. Third, and especially during the past three decades, they have sought to clarify the paradoxical aspects of willful self-deception, to explain whether and how it occurs, and to determine how much self-deception can be viewed as nonwillful. All these interests are pursued, often in tandem, by the authors of this book. I will comment briefly on each of the interests in setting a context for the essays and then provide an overview of the volume. More detailed introductions to the essays appear at the beginning of each section of the book.

SELF

Views about what it means to be a self-aware person are frequently embedded in theories of human nature. These theories give systematic perspectives on the enduring properties, possibilities, realistic prospects, and proper aims of human beings. One example is Freud's interpretation of self-deception as unconscious defense against fundamental biological instincts like sex and aggression. A second example is

Sartre's interpretation of self-deception as the evasion of the radical freedom he viewed as defining human beings. Yet a third example is the insistence of some theologians that self-deception is the primary avenue for rejecting God through camouflaged hubris.

It will suffice to allude to such theories as we proceed, focusing instead on narrower aspects of the self. Yet it is worth noting that when perspectives on self-deception are wedded to general theories of human nature, there arises an irresistible temptation to defend the theories by accusing their critics of self-deception. This is unfortunate, for the concept of self-deception is generally abused within the rhetoric of such sweeping accusations.

For instance, the existence of Freudian unconscious defense processes cannot be supported by ascribing unconscious anxieties and evasions to the critics of psychoanalysis. Sartre's insistence on the freedom of consciousness cannot be defended by his charge that self-deception underlies the belief in universal causal determinism. And it is something of a spectacle to watch theists ascribe self-deceiving pride to atheists, and then atheists (like Sartre, Freud, and Marx) dismiss belief in God as a self-deceiving soporific. More often than not, when the concept of self-deception is invoked to defend a theory of human nature, it generates ad hominem rhetoric that should be replaced by cogent argument and intellectual tolerance.

Self-Awareness

Persons are "selves" to the extent that they are aware of themselves, and hence some degree of self-awareness is a prerequisite for being a self at all. But just what is involved in becoming conscious of specific characteristics of ourselves, and how does self-deception function to impair this awareness?

Descartes was confident that through immediate reflection on our stream of consciousness we can know our own minds with greater certainty than we can know anything else. Similarly, later introspective psychologists assumed that we can best learn about our mental states by attending inwardly to them, as if they were displayed on an inner screen waiting to be observed. In this view, self-deception would consist primarily of a refusal to introspect with due care. Most twentieth-century movements in psychology and philosophy of mind, however, have begun by renouncing the Cartesian picture of immediate access to mental states.

One of these movements, of course, was initiated by Freud. His two familiar triads, conscious-preconscious-unconscious and id-ego-super-

3

ego,[2] are part of everyday discourse. Roughly, Freud regarded something as conscious when it is attended to, whether intensely and fully, or indistinctly and partially. It is preconscious if the person is readily able to attend to it under normal circumstances when awake. It is unconscious if the person cannot readily attend to it, and it is "dynamically unconscious" if unconscious "mechanisms of defense" keep it unconscious. "Repression" is the primary defense process, and it consists of preventing something from being conscious or preconscious. It occurs unconsciously and should be sharply distinguished from "suppression," which is the act of consciously ignoring something. Freud's central thesis, contrary to that of Descartes, is that many mental states are unconscious.

"Id," "ego," and "superego" refer to mental systems. The id encompasses instinctual biological drives, especially sex and aggression, as well as ideas, desires, and attitudes based on them. The superego comprises personal values, primarily culturally conditioned attitudes and commitments. The ego includes all functions of perceiving, reasoning, and responding to the environment while simultaneously reconciling the demands of the id and the superego. At first Freud equated the id with everything kept dynamically unconscious. Since he thought of the id as supplying the primary topics for repression, this was understandable. Later on, beginning with *The Ego and the Id*, he rejected this equation as a major mistake. Since psychological defense is conducted by the ego and since we are unconscious of that psychological defense, it follows that part of the ego is unconscious, just like those aspects of the id that do not reach consciousness.

Many thinkers have rejected Freud's notion of unconsciousness, for reasons such as those given by Kenneth Gergen. Most notably, and with striking similarities, Alfred Adler and Jean-Paul Sartre attacked the idea of an unconscious censorship that mechanically prevents self-consciousness. Sartre abandoned the term "unconscious" altogether. Adler redefined it to apply to those aspects of ourselves that we do not understand. Both of them urged that self-ignorance and self-deception are essentially failures of courage to recognize the goals we are pursuing and to understand them within the wider context of our lives. Self-deception is conscious in the sense that we act with systematic evasion. We avoid confrontation with the full implications of our choices. It is nonconscious in that we do not reflect upon the evasion itself. Yet, as Timothy Wilson suggests, there might by plenty of room for both unconscious and conscious forms of self-deception.

Complex mental states, such as beliefs, attitudes, intentions, and emotions, involve behavioral dispositions. Behaviorists, like B. F.

Skinner in psychology and Gilbert Ryle in philosophy, carried this truth to an extreme by equating mental states with behavioral tendencies. Yet they had the insight that self-awareness is often best attained by looking outward to our behavior and the context in which it occurs, rather than by monitoring our immediate stream of consciousness. John Dewey, George Herbert Mead, and the social psychologists they inspired avoided behaviorist dogmas and allowed a looser connection between mental states and behavior; their concern was to emphasize how self-knowledge is mediated by awareness of other people and of others' awareness of us. Daniel Gilbert and Joel Cooper explore ways in which self-deceivers may manipulate this interpersonal dimension of self-awareness. Benzion Chanowitz and Ellen Langer contend that self-deceivers are heedless in routine interpersonal contexts.

SELF-IDENTITY

In some contexts the term "self-identity" refers to the objective features that distinguish persons, but here it refers to individuals' subjective sense of who they are—to their own self-images. In the nineteenth century, Friedrich Nietzsche and Søren Kierkegaard identified the intimate connection between self-deception and self-identity, especially as related to inner unity, self-acceptance, and individuality. Genuine inner unity involves a heightened sensitivity to the diverse aspects of oneself that are accepted, without self-deception, as complementary dimensions of a single personality. As Nietzsche saw, failure to accept oneself generates self-deceiving *ressentiment:* "For one thing is needful: that a human being attain his satisfaction with himself . . . only then is a human being at all tolerable to behold. Whoever is dissatisfied with himself is always ready to revenge himself therefor; we others will be his victims."[3]

For Nietzsche and Kierkegaard a unified personality emerged around central commitments chosen autonomously. Nietzsche stressed artistic and intellectual commitments, while Kierkegaard emphasized moral and religious commitments. Kierkegaard explicitly linked those commitments to self-understanding: "The ethical individual knows himself, but this knowledge is not a mere contemplation . . . it is a reflection upon himself which itself is an action, and therefore I have deliberately preferred to use the expression 'choose oneself' instead of know oneself."[4] Both Nietzsche and Kierkegaard inveighed against self-deceivers who refuse to confront themselves as they are at present in order to initiate self-transformation, it being "far easier and safer to be like the others, to become an imitation, a number, a cipher in the crowd."[5]

In our own time it was Herbert Fingarette, in his book *Self-Deception*, who made the theme of self-identity central in thinking about self-deception. Fingarette envisaged self-identity as the product of inner acts of "avowing" our experiences, actions, beliefs, or other "engagements" in the world. Self-deception arises when individuals are strongly tempted to pursue an engagement that conflicts with the current "guiding principles" around which they have constructed their present self-identity. Rather than forgoing the engagement or creating inner conflict by consciously pursuing it, they pursue it without avowing it. Self-deception is essentially a refusal to acknowledge an engagement as one's own, both by systematically avoiding explicit consciousness of it and by not making appropriate adjustments in attitude, emotion, and behavior. In his essay Fingarette develops his perspective further and applies it to the enigmas of alcoholism.

Self-Esteem

Many of the authors in this book premise their discussions on the belief that people generally value themselves. This belief need not be bolstered by a postulate of innate egoism. Instead, some affirmation of our worth seems to stem from the very nature of human life. To live is to act; to act (without whim) is to act for reasons; to view our actions as based on good reasons is to see them as endowed with some degree of worth; and to identify ourselves with such acts is tacitly to regard ourselves as having some worth.

A healthy degree of self-esteem, however, is notoriously difficult to maintain. Failure to do so, according to Alfred Adler, underlies neurosis. (Freud, by contrast, believed that neurosis arose from a failure to manage biological instincts.) Neurotics lack the courage to change the world or themselves in a way that warrants increased self-esteem: "Instead of overcoming obstacles he will try to hypnotize himself, or autointoxicate himself, into *feeling* superior. Meanwhile his feelings of inferiority will accumulate, because the situation which produces them remains unaltered. . . . Every step he takes will lead him farther into self-deception."[6] Thinking along similar lines, Robert Solomon in *The Passions* argued that ultimately all emotions are attempts to give worth to ourselves. Phony feelings of inferiority and superiority merely illustrate irrational self-deceptive avenues for creating our worth.[7]

Yet there is another side to the relationship between self-deception and self-esteem. The British pragmatist Ferdinand Canning Scott Schiller, a contemporary of Adler, insisted that some self-deception is "an essential requisite of human life" in bolstering self-esteem: "For the ordinary man could hardly carry on, could he not delude himself into the belief that, in some ways at least, he was more than ordinary. A certain amount of self-deception, therefore, is universal and salutary."[8] In drama, Henrik Ibsen and Eugene O'Neill also explored this idea. In *The Wild Duck*, Ibsen portrays self-deception as "the stimulating principle" or "vital lie" that enables us to avoid self-contempt and despair: "Take away the life-lie from the average person, and you take his happiness along with it."[9] In *The Iceman Cometh*, O'Neill has his protagonist exclaim, "To hell with the truth! . . . The lie of a pipe dream is what gives life to the whole misbegotten mad lot of us, drunk or sober."[10] Both playwrights warn us of the dangers of removing illusions in the name of honesty, without sensitivity to how the illusions may form a basis for self-esteem.

COPING

In bolstering self-esteem, self-deception may provide the confidence necessary for coping effectively. It might also help us in other ways to cope with difficult realities. Like blinders on a horse, self-deception sometimes enables us to move forward unhampered by distress. By narrowing vision, it may prevent us from being overwhelmed by the sheer multiplicity of stimuli. In sustaining our hopes, it can evoke our energies. And in fostering our faith in other people, it can support friendship, love, and community. These considerations led Amélie Rorty to praise selective uses of self-deception:

> Like programs for eradicating the vices, attempts at doing away with self-deception would damage habits that are highly adaptive. Those incapable of self-deception are probably also incapable of romantic love, certain sorts of loyalty, and dedication to causes that require acting slightly larger than life. While these gifts have their dangers, they have on occasion served us well. What we need is not the wholesale substitution of self-knowledge for self-deception, but the gifts of timing and tact required to emphasize the right one in the appropriate place.[11]

"Timing and tact" are necessary because self-deception also has the potential to facilitate avoidance of love and the responsibilities it brings,[12] or to spawn destructive fanaticism in the pursuit of loyalty.[13]

The role of self-deception as a psychological coping technique is examined by all the authors in Part II, and its rationality or irrationality by the authors in Part III. Here we might mention one further example of where coping self-deceptively can be beneficial or harmful depending

7

on its circumstances and duration. Each of us on occasion finds it necessary to dampen the harshness of death via temporary self-deception. We are like medical students who might otherwise be unable to watch their first autopsy if they did not freeze their emotions and distract their reflections about death for a short time.[14] Some people, however, systematically evade acknowledging their mortality (and that of their loved ones) throughout much of their lives. As in *The Death of Ivan Ilych*, this may generate phoniness and inauthenticity as well as preclude appreciation of the humane values possible within an all-too-finite existence. Or so it has been argued by Martin Heidegger, Albert Camus, Ernest Becker, and many other thinkers who have criticized systematic self-deception about death.[15] This brings us to our next main topic.

VALUES

Earlier we commented on the intimate connection between self-understanding and values. It comes as no surprise that self-deception is a fundamental concern whenever it is believed to undermine insight into genuine values and action based on them. Four categories of value have been given special attention: rationality, morality, religion, and health. All these categories are discussed in relating self-deception to weakness of will.

RATIONALITY

By "rationality" I mean what might be called truth-centered or "epistemic" rationality, that is, living according to norms aimed at truth, rather than "pragmatic" rationality—acting so as to attain one's goals efficiently. Our grasp of self-deception has been vastly enriched since the time of the Greeks, but Socrates was no stranger to it. When he condemned the unexamined life as not worth living, he was chastising his peers for avoiding reflection aimed at important truths and for mindlessly pursuing pleasure, wealth, or honor. Socrates' life symbolizes for us the attitudes and standards of intellectual honesty and courage, respect for evidence, impartial reasoning, clarity of thought, freedom and tolerance of inquiry, and dedication to disciplined argument. Insofar as self-deception subverts these "values of reason,"[16] Socrates condemned it as a paramount corruption: "there is nothing worse than self-deception—when the deceiver is always at home and always with you—it is quite terrible."[17]

With the growth of modern science, commitment to a life based on truth became partially institutionalized. The ideal arose of grounding all beliefs about the world in the hard evidence provided by observation and testing. When evidence is lacking, beliefs should be replaced with tentative hypotheses that await examination by the scientific community. In the nineteenth century W. K. Clifford aggressively defended this scientific ethos, urging that it is our sacred "duty to mankind" to guard the purity of beliefs tested through scientific inquiry. Clifford concluded that "it is wrong always, everywhere, and for anyone, to believe anything upon insufficient evidence."[18]

Nowhere is the life of reason more vulnerable than in politics, as George Orwell so forcefully showed us in *1984*. The totalitarian party he describes has many familiar weapons at its disposal: destruction of free speech; government censorship; obfuscation through secrecy, deception, and gobbledygook language; torture; behavioral control; and sabotage of privacy and personal intimacy. Yet its most important tactic was to mold the consciousness of party members in order to prevent alternative ideologies from emerging. That was accomplished by systematically fostering "doublethink," an egregious form of self-deception:

> *Doublethink* means the power of holding two contradictory beliefs in one's mind simultaneously, and accepting both of them.[19]
> . . . .
> To know and not to know, to be conscious of complete truthfulness while telling carefully constructed lies, to hold simultaneously two opinions which cancelled out, knowing them to be contradictory and believing in both of them, to use logic against logic . . . to forget, whatever it was necessary to forget, then to draw it back into memory again at the moment when it was needed, and then promptly to forget it again, and above all, to apply the same process to the process itself.[20]

MORALITY

Self-deception is especially inviting when we want to do something we know is immoral, or when we seek to avoid an onerous task we have reason to think is our duty. In the eighteenth century Joseph Butler was a keen observer of this phenomenon. He suggested that people usually have suspicions of where their faults and neglected obligations reside, but they disregard them, it being "as easy to close the eyes of the mind, as those of the body: and the former is more frequently done with wilfulness, and yet not attended to, than the latter."[21] This enables them to avoid painful feelings of guilt and shame. It also corrupts conscience and makes them "inner hypocrites," who culpably enjoy a higher estimate of themselves than their characters warrant. Self-deceit about wrongdoing, Butler concludes, "is essentially in its own nature vicious and immoral. It is unfairness; it is dishonesty; it is falseness of heart: and is therefore so far from extenuating guilt, that it is itself the greatest of all guilt in proportion to the degree it prevails."[22]

Immanuel Kant went further in claiming that all self-deception (about wrongdoing *and* other topics) constitutes insincerity before oneself.[23] He held that it is a contemptible violation of human dignity, even when it merely involves exaggerating the good qualities of friends and lovers. In our own century the philosopher-sociologist Max Scheler explored how self-deception can warp entire value perspectives. Developing insights of Nietzsche, he studied how *ressentiment* leads to a systematic warping of genuine values in directions laid down by unacknowledged hatred, frustrated anger, and smoldering envy. The values of health and freedom, for example, become transformed into suffering and slavish obedience, even though an appreciation of the genuine values is not altogether lost: "The *ressentiment* experience is always characterized by this 'transparent' presence of the true and objective values behind the illusory ones—by that obscure awareness that one lives in a sham world which one is unable to penetrate."[24]

Jean-Paul Sartre rejected Butler, Kant, and Scheler's notion of objectively justifiable values. In fact he charged that belief in objectively justifiable values is founded on a self-deceiving evasion of recognizing that we create our own values through our commitments. In making this charge, he shifted attention to the decision-making process and away from traditional duties. Influenced by Heidegger, Nietzsche, and Kierkegaard, Sartre set forth as his supreme ideal authenticity, which is a combination of intellectual honesty and personal autonomy: "Authenticity, it is almost needless to say, consists in having a true and lucid consciousness of the situation, in assuming the responsibilities and risks that it involves, in accepting it in pride or humiliation, sometimes in horror and hate."[25] By "responsibilities" Sartre did not mean objectively defensible duties but the implications of our commitments, whatever they may be. He viewed us as constantly refusing to acknowledge that we are authors of our actions and interpretations of the world, continually trying to excuse ourselves with cowardly self-deceits about the extent of our freedom.

RELIGION

A long tradition of Christian thinkers (including Bishop Joseph Butler) regarded self-deception as a "cover" for sin, understood as rebellion against God. The New Testament admonishes, "If we say that we have no sin, we deceive ourselves, and the truth is not in us."[26] Saint Thomas Aquinas observed that "ignorance is sometimes directly and intrinsically voluntary, as when one freely chooses to be ignorant so that he may sin more freely."[27] Reverend Daniel Dyke, who to my knowledge wrote the first book on self-deception, invoked the idea of self-deception in explaining why sinners turn away from God, misunderstand His commandments, conceal sins in order to avoid the agony of repentance, and refuse to accept responsibility by blaming others for everything that goes wrong.[28] And Søren Kierkegaard, the greatest religious thinker of the nineteenth century, filled his voluminous writings with discussions of self-deception. In his most systematic work, *Sickness unto Death*, he interpreted sin as 'despair' in the special sense of failing to affirm oneself as a unique individual in relationship with God, and then portrayed despair as the self-deceiving evasion of one's individuality.[29]

Health and Responsibility

Surely it is a mistake to say that self-deception always renders a person guilty and blameworthy. Even when it is harmful there may be extenuating circumstances, including mental illness, which invite forgiveness. Some thinkers have gone further in generalizing that the responsibility of all self-deceivers is unclear or ambiguous. Robin G. Collingwood, for example, urged that self-deception (or "corrupt consciousness") is "the worst disease of mind": "In so far as consciousness is corrupted, the very wells of truth are poisoned. Intellect can build nothing firm. Moral ideals are castles in the air. Political and economic systems are mere cobwebs. Even common sanity and bodily health are no longer secure."[30] Yet because we are not fully conscious of the self-deception and its consequences (while engaged in it), we are not clearly culpable. Nor are we clearly innocent, since we are the source of the deception. We are in an unhealthy state of moral limbo, neither clearly guilty nor innocent.

Herbert Fingarette reached a similar conclusion: self-deception is morally ambiguous because full voluntariness and consciousness are lacking. Self-deceivers' personal and moral agency is subverted in a way that often makes it impossible to assess their responsibility or blameworthiness accurately.[31] And M. R. Haight, in *A Study of Self-Deception*, argued that the expression "self-deception" is applied metaphorically to puzzling forms of behavior in which we cannot tell whether people are able to help themselves enough to be held morally accountable.[32]

It is Freud, of course, whom we first think of in connection with how unconscious self-deception can cause illness: "The division of the psychical into what is conscious and what is unconscious is the fundamental premiss of psycho-analysis; and it alone makes it possible for psycho-analysis to understand the pathological processes in mental life."[33] Freud thought that refusing to acknowledge our sexual, aggressive, and other anxiety-creating impulses merely gives them license to operate in unhealthy ways without conscious supervision. The result is a more or less drastic restriction of capacities for meaningful work, human interaction, and pleasure. This link between neurotic behavior and self-deception has been explored in many "self-help" books intended for the wider public, such as Nathaniel Branden's *Disowned Self* and Gardner Murphy's *Outgrowing Self-Deception.*

While Freud focused on neurosis, other social scientists have used the concept of self-deception in trying to understand some psychotic disorders. In *The Divided Self*, R. D. Laing described schizophrenics as acting purposefully in hiding themselves from a hostile and horrifying world.[34] The anthropologist Jules Henry likewise traced many psychoses to self-directed sham.[35] And Erving Goffman agreed that psychotics are sometimes self-deceivers who "frame" their experience in ways that go against their own ability to interpret it realistically.[36]

WEAKNESS OF WILL

Self-deception is often discussed in connection with weakness of will.[37] In its widest sense, "weakness of will" means voluntarily acting against one's better judgment about what ought to be done (morally, prudentially, as a matter of etiquette, etc.). In a narrower sense it refers to voluntarily acting against one's better judgment specifically because of a lack of strength, whether due to momentary weakness or to the enduring effects of poor habits.

But is weakness of will really possible? Socrates denied its possibility when he insisted that "Knowledge is Virtue": to genuinely know what is right, good, or reasonable entails acting accordingly unless physically prevented. If one is literally unable to act on one's better judgment, then one is not acting voluntarily. This view has some basis in the dictum that "actions speak louder than words" in determining what people really believe, judge, or are committed to. Thus we say "Sunday-only believers" are not genuinely convinced of (or committed to) the doctrines to which they pay lip service. At the same time, however, common sense allows that people may lack the requisite endurance or fortitude to do what they honestly believe ought to be done. The integrity of their convictions (or commitments) may be shown by subsequent feelings of guilt or attempts to make amends for harm done. To this extent Socrates' view represents a paradoxical departure from common sense.

The notion of self-deception is invoked in this connection to explain how we often fail to implement our values and our better judgment by blurring our awareness of relevant facts. This may involve temporary ignoring and distraction, or longer-term persuasion into holding false beliefs that conflict with what our rational capacities would lead us to see (if we exercised those capacities without self-deception). Furthermore, much self-deception can itself be viewed as a form of weakness of will insofar as it constitutes a failure to exercise one's rationality in implementing one's values.

In this volume the moral issues surrounding self-deception are given special attention by John King-Farlow and Richard Bosley, David Kipp, C. R. Snyder, and Béla Szabados. Robert Audi and Béla Szabados study the relationship between self-deception and rationality. The pathological dimensions of self-deception are discussed by Herbert Fingarette, Benzion Chanowitz and Ellen Langer, M. R. Haight, and C. R. Snyder, among others. David Kipp, Béla Szabados, John King-Farlow, and Richard Bosley discuss weakness of will.

PARADOX

Most recent discussions of self-deception begin by referring to one or more paradoxical aspects of willful self-deception. "Paradox" can mean two different things. Literary critics use the term to refer to seemingly contradictory or absurd statements that upon deeper examination turn out to be true or at least plausible. In contrast, logicians use the term to refer to statements or ideas that really are contradictory or imply absurdities. Willful self-deception (and even some nonwillful self-deception) can certainly be puzzling and seemingly absurd at first glance, and hence it is paradoxical in the literary sense. But is it paradoxical in the logician's sense? A number of writers have charged that it is. They have argued that intentional self-deception in any literal sense does not exist and that the expression "self-deception" is at most a metaphor for other phenomena like nonwillful bias, wishful thinking, or deception of other people.

The air of paradox arises when we try to understand self-deception by modeling it strictly after interpersonal deception (that is, the deception of one person by another). In a typical case of interpersonal deception an individual, aware that something is false, intentionally gets another individual to believe it is true (either by lying, withholding appropriate information, or pretending). If we attempt to understand self-deception as happening in exactly the same way, a cluster of interlocking puzzles arises. The puzzles concern psychological unity, contradictory beliefs, knowledge, willful belief, consciousness, intentions, and moral responsibility. Let us consider them in turn.

UNITED AND DOUBLED SELVES

The idea of deceiving oneself seems to imply that one person is transformed into two selves, a deceiver and a victim of deception. But how can one self be two selves? Immanuel Kant raised this problem long ago: "It is easy to show that man is, in fact, guilty of many *inner* lies, but to explain the possibility of an inner lie seems more difficult. For a lie requires a second person whom one intends to deceive, and intentionally to deceive oneself seems to contain a contradiction."[38] Kant suggested that in fact we do think of ourselves as double when we make avowals before our own consciences, whether sincerely or insincerely. We regard ourselves both as the judge of our behavior and the defendant who sometimes tries to con the judge. In contrast, M. R. Haight insists that reflexive deception requires that one self deceive itself, and such literal self-deception cannot really occur. If there were actually two selves embedded in one body, we would be confronted not by self-deceivers, but by split personalities (where one personality may be able to deceive another by having one-way access to its consciousness).[39] The general issue raised by Kant and Haight is how to make literal sense of the idea of one person's simultaneously playing the two distinct roles of deceiver and deceived.

BELIEVE AND NOT BELIEVE

Normally when I deceive another person I get that person to believe the opposite of what I believe. In a widely discussed essay, Raphael Demos argued that something just like this occurs in self-deception, even though there is a genuine problem about how it occurs: "Self-deception entails that B [a person] believe both p [a proposition] and not-p at the same time. Thus self-deception involves an inner conflict, perhaps the existence of a contradiction. . . . Believing and disbelieving are pro and con attitudes; they are contraries and therefore it is logically impossible for them to exist at the same time in the same person in the same respect."[40] Demos's view becomes clearer if we distinguish several different kinds of statements about conflicting beliefs:[41]

14

(1) The person believes p and also believes not-p (that is, the person believes that a given proposition is true and also believes its negation is true);

(2) The person believes p and disbelieves p (that is, the person believes that a given proposition is true and also believes the proposition is false);

(3) The person believes p-and-not-p (that is, the person believes that an explicit contradiction is true);

(4) The person believes p and it is not the case that the person believes p.

Only in asserting statements of the last kind would we patently contradict ourselves and affirm the existence of an impossible state of affairs. According to Demos, the first two statements describe self-deceivers who manage to hold their conflicting beliefs in different respects. Self-deceivers, he contends, are willing to attend in explicit consciousness to the belief they are happy with, but unwilling to attend to the contrary unpleasant belief, which they keep latent (or "preconscious" as Freud would say). There has been (and still is) wide disagreement over whether Demos's account is satisfactory and over whether statements of the first three types describe actual self-deceivers.[42]

KNOW AND NOT KNOW

When I deceive another person, I both believe and know the opposite of what I get the other person to believe. That is, my belief is both true and warranted, whereas my victim is ignorant of the truth. Now surely it is impossible for self-deceivers to both know and not know the same thing at the same time in the same respects. Nevertheless, we do sometimes speak of them as knowing "deep down" or "in their hearts" what they refuse to acknowledge, fully accept, or know with full conviction. Could it be that knowledge is a complex state, and that in some respects persons might act, talk, think, and feel as if they knew something which in other respects they do not know? If so, the language of knowing and not knowing might express this with literary paradox.

WILLFUL vs. PASSIVE BELIEF

The interpersonal deceiver causes false beliefs in another person, often simply by uttering certain words. But can self-deceivers willfully create and manipulate their own beliefs in any similar manner? Surely if we know something is false, we cannot make ourselves believe it just by saying it to ourselves (unless aided by drugs, hypnosis, or other special techniques). But then is belief something that we cannot control at will, something that just happens to us? We do seem able to influence our beliefs indirectly via our actions and omitted actions. For example, we search for evidence and weigh it carefully, or we willfully ignore facts and evidence either by distracting attention from them or by discounting their implications. Again, we actively try to restrain our biases or passively allow them to operate unchecked. Are such maneuvers sufficient to make sense of the idea of self-deceivers' persuading themselves into holding false beliefs?[43]

CONSCIOUS AND NOT CONSCIOUS

Interpersonal deceivers are normally quite ready and able to attend explicitly to the truths they are trying to conceal from others. Their victims, by contrast, are precluded by their ignorance from becoming conscious of the truths (as long as the deception is effective). Plainly, self-deceivers cannot be readily able and willing to attend to the truth while at the same time unable and unwilling to attend to it. Nevertheless, couldn't some self-deceivers be psychologically able to become conscious of the truth but simply refuse to do so? Or couldn't they have intermittent moments of partial or even clear consciousness of what they are deceived about, and then lapse back into the self-deception? Indeed, do not some interpersonal deceivers likewise refuse to be altogether explicit with themselves about the truths they are concealing from others?

INTENTIONAL AND UNINTENTIONAL

To deceive others, as opposed to inadvertently misleading them, is to act intentionally. Interpersonal deceivers draw upon their knowledge of the truth in order purposefully to mislead others into believing falsehoods. This fact raises two problems about deceiving oneself. Sartre identified both of them. First, how can one *use* one's knowledge (or suspicions) of the truth in the very act of concealing that knowledge from oneself without the knowledge subverting the attempt? In Sartre's provocative words, "I can in fact wish 'not to see' a certain aspect of my being only if I am acquainted with the aspect which I do not wish to see. This means that in my being I must indicate this aspect in order to be able to turn myself away from it; better yet, I must think of it constantly in order to take care not to think of it."[44]

16

Second, if the concealment is intentional, the self-deceiver apparently knows something about the intention or purpose of deceiving. Why doesn't *that* knowledge thwart the activities involved in the concealment? If the reply is that the intention is unconscious, then we need to understand how an unconscious intention can be pursued effectively by a conscious being. Sartre believed that a scrutiny of self-deception should lead us to reject the entire notion of an unconscious mind. According to him, "that which affects itself with self-deception must be conscious (of) its self-deception since the being of consciousness is consciousness of being" what it is (even though the consciousness may be diffuse, fragmented, and intermittent).[45] Is Sartre right, or couldn't there be both unconscious and more conscious forms of intentional self-deception?

RESPONSIBLE AND NOT RESPONSIBLE

The interpersonal deceiver, it might be alleged, is insincere, hypocritical, guilty, blameworthy, and responsible; the victim of the deception is sincere, not hypocritical, innocent, blameless, not responsible.[46] If so, the self-deceiver would seem both sincere and insincere, hypocritical and not hypocritical, guilty and innocent, blameworthy and blameless, responsible and not responsible. But surely not all interpersonal deceivers are culpable. Lying to others is morally warranted on some occasions, such as when it is the only way to counter malicious intrusiveness into our privacy. Similarly, self-deception might be morally wrong or permissible depending on its circumstances, motives, and effects. Nevertheless, it remains problematic how far self-deceivers can be held responsible for their self-deception and its effects, if they are not complete masters of the knowledge hidden from them (even though they hid it in the first place).

THE INTERPERSONAL MODEL

We noted that all these paradoxes arise from an attempt to view self-deception on the model of interpersonal deception. Accordingly, our response to the paradoxes will be shaped largely by how appropriate we find the model. Three different reactions to the interpersonal model are important methodologically: jettison it altogether; embrace it without qualification; explore it cautiously, neither wholly accepting it nor entirely renouncing it.

We might be inclined to jettison the model because it seems to blind us to a phenomenon (or set of related phenomena) we are sure exists.

17

Ludwig Wittgenstein warned that models embedded in our language sometimes mislead us: ''A picture held us captive. And we could not get outside it, for it lay in our language and language seemed to repeat it to us inexorably.''[47] The preceding paradoxes would dissolve if we rejected the interpersonal model built into expressions like ''deceiving oneself,'' ''lying to oneself,'' ''conning oneself,'' and ''duping oneself.'' Yet surely it is not a freak linguistic accident that such expressions have acquired currency in our language. An overhasty rejection of the interpersonal model may itself handicap us by blinding us to some close analogies between self-deception and interpersonal deception.

The second reaction to the interpersonal model is to embrace it wholeheartedly. Doing so would open several options. On the one hand, we might view some or all of the paradoxes as expressing genuine contradictions and conclude that literal self-deception is logically impossible; it simply could not occur. The next move might be to try to understand why we use a literally self-contradictory and incoherent notion in describing human beings. In their contributions to this volume, Kenneth Gergen, M. R. Haight, and David Kipp adopt this tack and seek to provide such an understanding. Another move would be to refocus attention on various metaphorical uses of ''self-deception,'' interpreting the metaphors as gestures toward interesting forms of behavior. This path is pursued by David Kipp, M. R. Haight, and (with qualification) by Benzion Chanowitz and Ellen Langer.

On the other hand, while at least in part embracing the model, we might be convinced that some or all of the paradoxes are only superficially puzzling and, on close examination, can be understood. This is the approach of John King-Farlow and Richard Bosley with respect to doubled selves, C. R. Snyder and Timothy Wilson with respect to conflicting beliefs and states of consciousness, and Herbert Fingarette with respect to responsibility.

A third reaction to the interpersonal model is to explore it both sympathetically and critically in the course of studying the mental states and behavior that expressions like ''self-deception'' typically describe. Patrick Gardiner once estimated what the results of such an exploration would be:

> We shall (I suspect) find analogies and similarities [between cases of self-deception and cases of interpersonal deception] . . . that are sufficient to make the reflexive extension of the concept [of deception] appear, within limits, reasonably appropriate. But the instances themselves will form a variegated spectrum, and the analogies can in any event never be more than partial ones. Which we select, which we find it most natural to press, will no doubt be partly determined by our particular moral viewpoint or conception of human nature.[48]

This approach to some of the paradoxes is found in several of the essays already mentioned, and in others as well. Robert Audi, for example, concludes that self-deceivers do not hold full-blown contradictory beliefs but are in the closely analogous state of sincerely avowing something they know is false. And Béla Szabados implies that self-deceivers pervert rational standards for getting at the truth in a manner analogous to how interpersonal deceivers violate standards for conveying truth. Needless to add, one could adopt any of the above approaches with respect to some of the paradoxes while having a different approach for other paradoxes.

It seems to me that the relationship between "deceiving others" and "deceiving oneself" will turn out to be somewhat like the relationship between "teaching others" and "teaching oneself."[49] Obviously if we tried to treat literal self-teaching as precisely like interpersonal teaching, then self-teaching would be impossible: one cannot first as a teacher know and be conscious of what one as a student is simultaneously ignorant and unaware. At the same time, teaching others and teaching oneself are not wholly unrelated, for in both forms of teaching there is intentional activity directed toward the acquisition of knowledge and understanding. Self-deception and interpersonal deception, by analogy, may often involve purposeful and intentional activities aimed at disguising and concealing truth, or evading its full acceptance and acknowledgment. But many different kinds of activities may be employed in any given instance: for example, ignoring what we suspect is true, disregarding evidence, avoiding inquiries, blocking appropriate emotional responses, avoiding suitable attitudinal adjustments, pretending to ourselves and others, and so on. The ways of evading self-acknowledgment are as varied as the ways of coming to acknowledge and understand ourselves and our world.

OVERVIEW

The following essays are grouped thematically rather than segregated by discipline. In part this is because understanding any dimension of self-deception requires insights from both philosophy and psychology. In part it is because there are few sharp boundaries to be drawn between the two disciplines, a point that bears emphasis.

We may agree that psychology is a science that seeks explanations grounded in experimentation and spawns therapeutic arts like counseling and behavior modification. Philosophy, by contrast, is a branch of the humanities that pursues questions about concepts and values not amenable to the laboratory. Nevertheless, the essential subject matter of psychology is shared with philosophy of mind: action, emotion, belief, consciousness . . . and self-deception. Many basic aims are also shared: to clarify key concepts and distinctions, remove confusion, develop unifying perspectives to yield new insights into minds and social interactions. Furthermore, the procedures of the two disciplines are often similar and should not be stereotyped with familiar shibboleths: for example, that philosophy is armchair reflection that disregards science, or that psychology is purely value-neutral description. Much psychology, after all, consists of ''armchair'' reflection on the results of experiments, clinical encounters, everyday experience, and indeed the work of philosophers. Much of it, especially humanistic psychology, is as value-centered as philosophy. In turn, philosophy of mind is enormously enriched when it draws on the work of psychologists. Even when the specific aims and approaches of the two disciplines differ markedly, the results are more often than not complementary and mutually enriching. Or so the following essays would suggest.

Part I centers on the everyday role of self-deception in making excuses designed to defend a relatively unified person against threatening aspects of the personality or environment. Part II explores the role of self-deception in shaping a sense of personal identity amidst psychic and social disunity. Part III focuses on how self-deception undermines or occasionally supports the values of rationality and morality. Part IV raises skeptical objections to the idea of willful self-deception but also constructively explores related forms of behavior and the social function of the expression ''self-deception.''

Never is self-deception more tempting than when it serves to camouflage our own errors, weakness, or wrongdoing. Here its most ready-made avenue is the ubiquitous practice of making excuses in order to defend one's self-esteem and current self-image. C. R. Snyder provides a systematic overview of the ''collaborative'' relationship between self-deception and self-directed excuse making. Not all excuses, of course, are vehicles for self-deception. Willful self-deception is present only when a person holds an unacknowledged belief, with lessened awareness, which conflicts with the belief constituting the excuse. After exploring how excuse making serves to bolster our preferred self-images, Snyder distinguishes several types of excuses, identifies some social influences that encourage self-deceptive excuse making, and surveys the good and bad effects of it. Some of his concluding observations concern culturally sanctioned excuses that support harmful behavioral tendencies like alcoholism—the focus of the next essay.

Herbert Fingarette challenges the widespread assumption that alcoholism per se is a mental disease (while allowing that its devastating effects make it a major health concern). This assumption, he contends, is not established by experimental evidence and is actually a socially endorsed basis for long-term heavy drinkers to deceive themselves. The loss of personal control over the use of alcohol results largely from alcoholics' muddled interpretations of their behavior. Developing the influential perspective set forth in his book *Self-Deception*, Fingarette portrays self-deception as the disavowal of an engagement, that is, the refusal to identify oneself as the person making certain responses to the world. Disavowal entails a refusal to become explicitly conscious of (to spell out) the engagement, but it also implies diminished control over the engagement that is pursued in isolation from avowed aspects of the personality, precisely the main element present in alcoholism.

Part II begins with Daniel T. Gilbert and Joel Cooper's study of self-deceiving strategies used to maintain self-esteem. The authors discuss motivated distortion of perception, but most of their essay deals with the complex interpersonal behavior that facilitates the smoke screens of self-deceivers. Since we shape our self-conceptions by our perceptions of what other people think about us, we can to some extent present ourselves in a manner that will encourage them to perceive us as we would like to be perceived. Self-deceivers take advantage of this "feedback loop" by misleading others in order to maintain overly favorable evaluations of themselves. They may also render their behavior ambiguous, so as to invite ego-boosting excuses.

Timothy D. Wilson presents experimental evidence about how we fail to achieve accurate awareness of our own mental states. Contrary to the views of both Descartes and introspective psychologists, we do not have immediate and certain access to these states. Beliefs, attitudes, emotions, and intentions involve behavioral tendencies that we must sometimes learn about by making inferences from our behavior, past, and surroundings. Wilson hypothesizes that there are two general mental systems, one of which functions largely without conscious supervision and one of which comprises conscious activities like interpreting, inferring, and verbal expression. He introduces a wide conception of self-deception encompassing virtually all self-caused failures to have accurate self-awareness, especially those involving slanted inferences, while allowing for unconscious repression of unpleasant realities as one special case.

Like the authors in Part IV, Benzion Chanowitz and Ellen Langer question whether the expression "self-deception" helps us understand the forms of behavior to which it is typically applied. They suggest that much of it is better described as "mindless" (uncritical, inattentive) behavior, which we display most of the time in routine everyday life. Drawing on the work of John Dewey and on their own experiments, they develop a view of persons as lacking unity and consistency, indeed as being clusters of loosely confederated selves. A unified self or character is the result of acts of "self-inception" that interconnect otherwise semiautonomous social selves bent on protecting themselves. So-called self-deception is best viewed as a failure to have unification occur, rather than as a unified personality purposefully fending off a threatening subself.

Part III focuses on the connections between self-deception, rationality, and moral responsibility. Béla Szabados argues that willful self-deception amounts to a perversion of the standards for rational belief. Like wishful thinkers, self-deceivers are motivated to hold beliefs that are unwarranted by evidence. Unlike wishful thinkers, however, self-deceivers distort reasonable assessments of the evidence available, whether by disregarding it or by rationalizing away its implications. Szabados argues against attempts to reduce self-deception to interpersonal deception, nonpurposeful bias, or weakness of will. He suggests that deceiving oneself presupposes having rational abilities, and that, ironically, self-deceivers undermine their own general commitments as rational beings.

Robert Audi also explores whether and why self-deception is irrational. He defines it as the disposition to affirm sincerely something that contradicts knowledge held unconsciously because of some motivating want. Thus it constitutes a mental state analogous to interpersonal deception, without involving the paradox of directly contradictory beliefs. Audi develops a conception of rationality as well-groundedness and applies it to the beliefs, wants, acts, and overall states involved in self-deception. He concludes that, with some exceptions, self-deception and self-deceivers tend to be irrational.

John King-Farlow and Richard Bosley explore the moral dimensions of self-deception by invoking the idea of the Golden Mean, the balance between too much and too little. They argue that self-deception is a human power that can serve good or bad, right or wrong. Its role in moral development is explored within the contexts of childhood, adolescence, and adulthood. Two species of willful self-deception are distinguished: ignorance due to ignoring (a kind of defect of appropriate attending) and getting oneself to hold false or misleadingly clustered beliefs (a kind of excess). Which of the two is worse forms the culminating topic in a dialogue between Aristotle and Confucius, the two classic theorists of the Golden Mean.

In Part IV Kenneth J. Gergen launches a sweeping attack on the alleged coherence and applicability of the concept of willful self-deception. He urges that there is no solid experimental evidence establishing the kind of unconscious mental defense postulated by Freud, and that the idea of directly contradictory beliefs and impulses is absurd. How did a concept with such difficulties arise? Essentially it is the product of unwarranted folk beliefs about human psychology and has survived because it continues to function as a culturally useful myth. It enables us to hold people responsible for acting as they do (since self-deception is presumably voluntary) and simultaneously to excuse them as blameless (since self-deception supposedly entails the absence of consciousness about the content of the deception).

M. R. Haight develops a skeptical attack based on her book *A Study of Self-Deception*. Some of her conclusions match Gergen's. Haight emphasizes that knowledge can be "buried" in the sense of not recalled or readily invoked ("freely") in consciousness on appropriate occasions, and she surveys a range of behavior to which the expression "self-deception" can be applied metaphorically. Nevertheless, self-deception in any literal sense is impossible since it requires a deceiver who has "free" knowledge (knowledge that is easily available to consciousness) and also a victim of deception who lacks free knowledge of the same thing at the same time in the same self. Moreover, since there are almost always alternative interpretations of the behavior of 'self-deceivers,' their minds are ultimately indecipherable black boxes. As a result their moral responsibility is ambiguous and opaque, which is why we use a literally self-contradictory expression to refer to them.

David Kipp concurs that the idea of intentionally deceiving oneself is contradictory because it suggests that a person could both know and not know the same thing at the same time. The expression "self-deception" is best viewed as referring to instances of either ignorance or purposeful pretense before others. Kipp develops his thesis with a study of the pressures to conform and engage in pretense when a given ideology dominates, in particular when Christianity and more modern mass movements became culturally dominant. He draws on Nietzsche, Scheler, and especially Heidegger's insights into authenticity, while suggesting that Sartre's indictments of self-deceivers are based on resentment and sham.

Each of these essays is self-contained, and although a few of them could just as well appear in other parts of the book, I believe that studying them in the order presented is one way to augment overall coherence and cumulative impact. However, readers familiar with the literature on self-deception might prefer to begin with Part IV and then

23

consider the preceding essays as responses to the skeptical challenges. Another option is to approach the essays as dialectical pairs, in various combinations: for example, Kipp and Szabados (to study the relationships between self-deception, interpersonal pretense, and weakness of will); Snyder and Fingarette (to study the contrast in a "two-belief" approach and an identity-avowal approach to self-deception); Gergen and Wilson (as challenger and defender, respectively, of a conscious-nonconscious duality of mental systems); Chanowitz/Langer and Gilbert/Cooper (for contrasting views on identity formation); Fingarette and Chanowitz/Langer (for contrasting views on the unity of self-deceivers); Szabados and Audi (for contrasting views on rationality and irrationality of self-deceivers); and Haight and King-Farlow/Bosley (for opposing views on the possibility of cogent moral assessments of self-deceivers).

NOTES

1. Sigmund Freud, *The Complete Introductory Lectures on Psychoanalysis*, Lecture 18 (New York: Norton, 1966), 281. Cf. Søren Kierkegaard: " 'if they truly had understood, their lives would have expressed it, they would have done what they understood.' To understand/and to understand are therefore two things? Certainly they are." *Fear and Trembling* and *The Sickness unto Death*, trans. Walter Lowrie (New York: Anchor Books, 1954), 221.

2. Interpretations of Freudian defense mechanisms as tied to self-deception are given by Herbert Fingarette in *Self-Deception* (New York: Humanities Press, 1969) and Roy Schafer, *A New Language for Psychoanalysis* (New Haven, Conn.: Yale University Press, 1976). With increasing degrees of technicality the following sources are useful for approaching Freud's key distinctions: Henri F. Ellenberger, *The Discovery of the Unconscious* (New York: Basic Books, 1970); Charles Brenner, *An Elementary Textbook of Psychoanalysis* (Garden City, N.Y.: Anchor Books, 1974); Anna Freud, *The Ego and the Mechanisms of Defense* (New York: International Universities Press, 1966); Merton M. Gill, *Topography and Systems in Psychoanalytic Theory* (New York: International Universities Press, 1963).

3. Friedrich Nietzsche, *The Gay Science*, in *The Portable Nietzsche*, ed. Walter Kaufmann (New York: Viking Press, 1954), 99.

4. Søren Kierkegaard, *Either/Or*, vol. 2, trans. Walter Lowrie (Princeton, N.J.: Princeton University Press, 1959), 263.

5. Kierkegaard, *Fear and Trembling* and *The Sickness unto Death*, 167. Cf. José Ortega y Gasset, *The Revolt of the Masses*, (New York: Norton, 1932), 156–157.

6. Alfred Adler, *The Individual Psychology of Alfred Adler*, ed. Heinz L. Ansbacher and Rowena R. Ansbacher (New York: Harper and Row, 1964), 257–258.

7. Robert Solomon, *The Passions: The Myth and Nature of Human Emotion,* pt. 3 (Notre Dame, Ind.: University of Notre Dame Press, 1983). Also see Nathaniel Branden, *The Disowned Self* (New York: Bantam, 1980).

8. Ferdinand Canning Scott Schiller, *Problems of Belief* (New York: Doran, 1924), 124.

9. Henrik Ibsen, *The Wild Duck,* trans. Dounia B. Christiani (New York: Norton, 1968), 64.

10. Eugene O'Neill, *The Iceman Cometh* (New York: Vintage Books, 1957), 9–10.

11. Amélie Oksenberg Rorty, "Adaptivity and Self-Knowledge," *Inquiry* 18 (1975): 22.

12. Cf. Stanley Cavell, "The Avoidance of Love: A Reading of *King Lear,*" in *Must We Mean What We Say?* (New York: Scribner, 1969).

13. In this connection consider Albert Speer, Hitler's powerful minister of arms, who reports being ignorant about Auschwitz because "I did not investigate—for I did not want to know what was happening." Albert Speer, *Inside the Third Reich,* trans. Richard and Clara Winston (New York: Avon Books, 1971): 481.

14. Cf. Richard S. Lazarus, "Cognitive and Coping Processes in Emotion," in *Stress and Coping,* ed. Alan Monat and Richard S. Lazarus (New York: Columbia University Press, 1977), 150.

15. A good starting point for the wide literature on self-deception and death is Ernest Becker's *Denial of Death* (New York: Free Press, 1973).

16. This expression is borrowed from R. S. Peters, "The Justification of Education," in *The Philosophy of Education,* ed. R. S. Peters (New York: Oxford University Press, 1973), 251–253.

17. Plato, *Cratylus,* in *The Collected Dialogues of Plato,* ed. Edith Hamilton and Huntington Cairns, and trans. Benjamin Jowett (Princeton, N.J.: Princeton University Press, 1971), 462.

18. William Kingdon Clifford, "The Ethics of Belief," *Lectures and Essays of W. K. Clifford,* ed. Leslie Stephen and Frederick Pollock (London: Macmillan, 1879), 186.

19. George Orwell, *1984* (New York: New American Library, 1983), 176.

20. Ibid., 32.

21. Joseph Butler, "Upon Self-Deceit," *The Works of Joseph Butler,* vol. 2, ed. W. E. Gladstone (Oxford: Clarendon Press, 1896), 179.

22. Ibid., 177–178. For two recent insightful discussions along this line see Mary Midgley, *Wickedness: A Philosophical Essay* (Boston: Routledge and Kegan Paul, 1984); and Ronald D. Milo, *Immorality* (Princeton, N.J.: Princeton University Press, 1984).

23. Immanuel Kant, *The Doctrine of Virtue,* trans. Mary J. Gregor (Philadelphia: University of Pennsylvania Press, 1964), 92–95.

24. Max Scheler, *Ressentiment,* ed. Lewis A. Coser, trans. William W. Holdheim (New York: Schocken, 1972), 60.

25. Jean-Paul Sartre, *Anti-Semite and Jew,* trans. George J. Becker (New York: Schocken, 1948), 90. Sartre's analysis of self-deception is given in *Being and Nothingness,* trans. Hazel E. Barnes (New York: Washington Square Press, 1975), 86–116. His condemnation of self-deceivers as "cowards and scum" is in "Existentialism Is a Humanism," *Existentialism from Dostoevsky to Sartre,* ed. Walter Kaufmann (New York: New American Library, 1975), 366.

26. 1 John 1:8.

27. St. Thomas Aquinas, *Summa Theologiae*, vol. 25 (New York: McGraw-Hill, 1964), 155.

28. Reverend Daniel Dyke, *The Mystery of Selfe-Deceiving, or a Discourse and Discovery of the Deceitfulness of Man's Heart* (London, 1630). Dyke adopts as his main text Jeremiah 17:9: "The heart is deceitful above all things, and desperately wicked: who can know it?" I am grateful to the Department of Special Collections, A 1713 University Research Library, University of California, Los Angeles, for making Dyke's book available to me.

29. Closer to our own time, the Protestant theologian Reinhold Niebuhr claimed that the fundamental sin of pride in rebelling against God is grounded in self-deception. *The Nature and Destiny of Man*, vol. 1 (New York: Scribner, 1964), 203–207.

30. Robin G. Collingwood, *The Principles of Art* (New York: Oxford University Press, 1958), 284. Also see 215–224, 282–285, 336.

31. Herbert Fingarette, *Self-Deception*, 141. Cf. 136–150.

32. M. R. Haight, *A Study of Self-Deception* (Atlantic Highlands N.J.: Humanities Press, 1980), 120. Also see 120–132 and 142–149. Haight expresses doubts about whether we are ever free in a sense that makes it appropriate to hold us morally responsible.

33. Sigmund Freud, *The Standard Edition of the Complete Psychological Works of Sigmund Freud*, vol. 19, trans. James Strachey (London: Hogarth, 1961), 13.

34. R. D. Laing, *The Divided Self* (Baltimore, Md.: Penguin, 1965).

35. Jules Henry, *Pathways to Madness* (New York: Vintage Books, 1973), 99–108; and *On Sham, Vulnerability and Other Forms of Self-Destruction* (New York: Vintage Books, 1973), 120–127.

36. Erving Goffman, *Frame Analysis* (New York: Harper and Row, 1974), 112–115.

37. An especially interesting discussion is Arthur E. Murphy, "The Moral Self in Sickness and in Health," *The Theory of Practical Reason*, ed. A. I. Melden (La Salle, Ill.: Open Court, 1964), 134–161. Also see Raphael Demos, "Lying to Oneself," *Journal of Philosophy*, 57 (1960): 588–595; and David Pears, *Motivated Irrationality* (Oxford: Clarendon Press, 1984).

38. Kant, *The Doctrine of Virtue*, 93–94.

39. Haight, *A Study of Self-Deception*, 24–26.

40. Demos, "Lying to Oneself," 588 and 591.

41. Cf. John Canfield and Patrick McNally, "Paradoxes of Self-Deception," *Analysis*, 21 (1961): 140–144.

42. The literature on this problem is vast. As a sample, see the bibliographical entries for Kent Bach, John Canfield and Don Gustavson, Jeffrey Foss, Ruben Gur and Harold Sackeim, D. W. Hamlyn, H. O. Mounce, Stanley Paluch, David Pears, Terrence Penelhum, David Pugmire, Richard Reilly, Amélie Rorty, Frederick Siegler, and contributors to this volume.

43. See, for example, Bernard Williams, "Deciding to Believe," in *Problems of the Self* (Cambridge: Cambridge University Press, 1973); and Barbara Winters, "Believing at Will," *Journal of Philosophy*, 76 (1979): 243–256.

44. Sartre, *Being and Nothingness*, 83.

45. I am using the slightly altered translation given by Walter Kaufmann in *Existentialism from Dostoevsky to Sartre*, rev. ed. (New York: New American Library, 1975), 302. A helpful discussion of the paradoxes of intention is given by

David Pears, "Freud, Sartre and Self-Deception," in *Freud*, ed. R. Wollheim (Garden City, N.Y.: Anchor Books, 1974), 97–112.

46. Cf. Herbert Fingarette, *Self-Deception*, 1 and 136.

47. Ludwig Wittgenstein, *Philosophical Investigations*, 3d ed., trans. G. E. M. Anscombe (New York: Macmillan, 1953), remark 115.

48. Patrick Gardiner, "Error, Faith, and Self-Deception," in *The Philosophy of Mind*, ed. Jonathan Glover (New York: Oxford University Press, 1976), 51–52.

49. Cf. T. S. Champlin, "Double Deception," *Mind* 85 (1976): 102.

PART I
DEFENDING THE SELF:
SELF-ESTEEM AND EXCUSES

Introduction

Mike W. Martin

Each of us insists on being innocent at all cost, even if he has to accuse
the whole human race and heaven itself.

—Albert Camus, *The Fall*

No assessment of ourselves is dearer to us than our own. Even
when we passively submit to other people's appraisals, viewing ourselves through their eyes, our resulting self-appraisal remains decisively
significant. Ultimately it establishes the core of the 'self' we take
ourselves to be—the self that is fashioned by our self-interpretations. In
turn, our sense of self-worth undergirds whatever personal meaning we
find in life, and it generates the vigor or apathy with which we pursue
our commitments. Yet sustaining a sense of self-worth is notoriously
difficult, given the seemingly inevitable gap between aspiration and
accomplishment. The practice of making excuses is ready-at-hand to
help conceal or minimize the significance of this gap.

Frequently excuses are intended as a defense against other people's
recriminations. In this role they can help preserve respect from others or
prevent penalties for poor performance. Just as often, however, excuses
are intended primarily for our own consumption. In this capacity they
can relieve us of the onerous burdens of making amends for wrongdoing or errors. Most often they help us sustain self-esteem by mitigating
or preventing painful emotions such as guilt for having hurt others,
shame for failing to meet our standards of excellence, anger over our
stupidity, or depression over our weakness. Self-deception frequently

proceeds by way of self-directed excuse making, as C. R. Snyder shows in his opening essay.

Snyder notes that not all self-directed excuses involve self-deception. An excuse is simply an explanation of an action, which is intended to lessen its appearance of being the fault of the agent. Many such explanations are fully justified and accurately assess responsibility. Self-deception enters, according to Snyder, when individuals somehow know or believe that the explanation is not really appropriate, even though they also believe that it is appropriate. Thus, self-deceivers hold conflicting beliefs about the action they explain to themselves. The self-deceiving belief constituting the excuse is held with fuller awareness and may be of the form "I am a good person," "I have done nothing wrong," or "I am not responsible for the harm." The other belief is held with lesser awareness and may be of the form "I have acted improperly" or "I am responsible for the harm my act caused." Furthermore, the conflicting beliefs result from a motivated or purposeful strategy to keep one belief less conscious, rather than from sheer stupidity or absence of insight. The primary motive is the preservation of a positive self-image (and sometimes, we might add, the avoidance of burdens involved in making amends for harm done and of making changes in our character).

Snyder distinguishes between two major types of strategies in making excuses. "Reframing performance strategy" consists of dismissing an apparent failure or diminishing the degree of harm done. Here self-deception often involves an inappropriate attempt to justify one's action or inaction. For example, we might claim that we were not really obligated to help someone in distress, or we might insist that we did not seriously hurt the person to whom we were rude. By contrast, "transformed responsibility strategy" involves acknowledging a failure, hence not trying to justify the act, but downplaying responsibility for it. In this case we deceive ourselves in claiming that most other people would also have failed as we did ("consensus-raising excuses"), or that the failure was a temporary and uncharacteristic lapse ("consistency-lowering approaches").

Next Snyder identifies four general conditions that nurture self-deception in excuse making. First, the greatly enhanced options afforded by contemporary society bring with them dizzying new expectations and accompanying pressures of responsibilities for shortcomings. In order to escape those pressures, we selectively endorse a belief in causal determinism that has prevented us from acting appropriately. Second, our friends and peers are often eager to encourage our excuse making in order to put us at ease (if not to invite indulgence of their own excuses). In general, sanctioning excuse making in others serves as a "social lubricant" enabling peaceful coexistence. Third, there is almost always some ambiguity or vagueness about what our standards and values require of us in specific situations, providing leeway for self-deceptive interpretations of actions and responsibility. Fourth, and underlying all the others, is the powerful drive to preserve our self-esteem.

Is self-deceiving excuse making always bad? Snyder suggests not. By bolstering self-esteem, it can improve effective social functioning. It can also help us accept our limitations and thereby cope without a paralyzing sense of unmanageable responsibilities or an anxious drive to perfectionism. Self-deception in excuse making becomes bad when it is used to support preventable wrongdoing or when it exposes us to ridicule from those who see through our ruses. It is especially dangerous and seductive when it proceeds by an appeal to mental illness, an appeal standardly made by or on behalf of alcoholics, for example. Snyder draws on his clinical experience to offer some recommendations about replacing harmful forms of self-deceiving excuses with greater self-understanding.

Herbert Fingarette shifts the topic of alcoholism to center stage. In recent decades the view that alcoholism is a disease has become an official tenet among health-care professionals. Fingarette launches a sweeping attack on this dogma, contending that it amounts to little more than a tailor-made rationalization for self-deception on the part of alcoholics. Decades of experimentation have failed to reveal that heavy long-term alcohol use is the direct causal effect of physiological dependency or environmental conditioning. Nor have studies even defined features of alcoholism or shown any one therapeutic procedure to be preferable to others. The only unifying thread in the vast scientific literature is that alcoholics lose control over their drinking, and Fingarette proposes that often this loss can best be understood in terms of self-deception.

For centuries drunkards were regarded as having chosen a socially unacceptable life style based on overindulgence in the pleasurable activity of drinking. While there is a partial truth to this, a more accurate view is that heavy drinkers are seeking to cope with aspects of their lives that are unacceptable to them—so unacceptable that they typically refuse to acknowledge them to themselves. What easier way to avoid the inner conflict that honest self-confrontation would entail than to rely on the consciousness-blurring effects of alcohol at a time when health-care experts are telling them that they are the unfortunate victims of a disease!

Fingarette develops and applies the seminal theory about willful self-deception set forth in his 1969 book, *Self-Deception*. According to that theory and in contrast to Snyder's view, self-deception has no necessary connection with holding conflicting beliefs. Essentially it is the activity of disavowing some "engagement," that is, refusing to avow or acknowledge as one's own some aspect of one's life or the world. To disavow is to reject identification as the person pursuing an engagement (whether an act, emotion, attitude, perception, belief, or whatever) that is inconsistent with one's values or "guiding principles," and as such would be distressing and internally disruptive to admit to oneself.

Disavowal is a multifaceted act. It involves a systematic refusal to become explicitly conscious of what one is deceived about—a refusal to "spell it out." Yet it also involves refusing to integrate the disavowed engagement into parts of the personality that are acknowledged as aspects of one's identity. The result is that the disavowed engagement is pursued in an isolated or alien manner, typically without conscious supervision by the more reasonable aspects of the personality. In particular, one does not assume moral responsibility for it. Moreover, in order for self-deception to occur, the activity of disavowing an engagement must itself be disavowed. In this sense, to deceive oneself entails deceiving oneself about the fact that one is deceiving oneself. All of this leads to a loss of control over the engagement: precisely the element present in the alcoholic.

Actually there are two engagements that the alcoholic often flees through disavowal. First, there is some primary aspect of the individual that would cause inner conflict if explicitly acknowledged. This aspect provides the original motive for alcohol abuse: for instance, to flee a nagging sense of failure, to subdue anger toward a family member, to express frustrated resentment toward an employer. Second, one deceives oneself about the role alcohol plays in one's life, that is, about the strategy of using alcohol as an escape. This second disavowal is directly encouraged by the intellectual rationalization that alcoholism is a disease that happens to unfortunate victims, rather than a conduct in which one engages. The twofold disavowal merely intensifies the loss of control involved in self-deceiving alcoholism.

Fingarette does not suggest that either alcoholism or self-deception is fully voluntary or can be surmounted by a simple act of will. The very genuine loss of control involved makes it unclear just how voluntary the disavowed engagements are. For this reason moralistic preaching to alcoholics is worse than useless and may cause further harm by intensifying the inner conflicts being fled, thereby intensifying the motives for engaging in self-deception. Alcoholics need compassion and supporting discipline to help them achieve self-understanding. Moreover, even after removing their self-deception, alcoholics remain free not to make the effort to regain control over their drinking; some alcoholics are not self-deceivers, and overcoming alcoholism is a personal achievement.

Collaborative Companions:
The Relationship of Self-Deception and Excuse Making

C. R. Snyder

In the eyes of laypersons and professionals alike, excuses have typically been conceived as mechanisms for deceiving *other* people. Although other people undoubtedly play an important part in excuse making, excuses are also aimed at the internal audience of oneself. In this relatively unmapped inner turf, it will be argued that self-deception often works through excuse-making strategies. This essay will first pose a definition of self-deception and then elaborate on how excuse making serves to fulfill this definition. Next, the focus will shift to the societal and personal factors that serve to nourish excuse making. The essay will close with an examination of the pros and cons associated with self-deceptive excuse making.

DEFINITION OF SELF-DECEPTION

For purposes of the present essay, self-deception is the process of holding two conflicting self-referential beliefs, with the more negative belief being less within awareness.

Several points are worthy of elaboration in regard to this definition, especially since it may differ from the way in which others have conceptualized self-deception. First, it is assumed that self-deception occurs principally in circumstances where the self-deceiver is very ego-involved. In this sense, the conflicting beliefs employed in the definition represent pieces of information that pertain to important aspects of the way a person sees himself or herself. It takes the weight of such self-referential information to generate the conflict that characterizes self-deception. Thus, the probability of self-deception should be in direct proportion to the magnitude of the relevance of the conflicting beliefs to one's personal image. The greater the discrepancy (or conflict) between the self-referential beliefs, the greater the potential for self-deception. This definition emphasizes the purposeful or motivated nature of the self-deception process. Indeed, the roots of the word *deceive* suggest a purposeful activity. Although one could build a model of self-deception that includes nonmotivated action, such descriptors as errors in self-perception or lack of self-insight appear to capture this latter definition more accurately. Additionally, the theoretical and empirical case for motivated self-deception appears compelling.

Finally, it should be noted that the present self-deception definition merely assumes a differential awareness between the two conflicting self-referential beliefs; this stands in contrast to definitions of self-deception that postulate that one of the beliefs is within awareness and the other is beyond awareness. Thus, the definition employed in the present essay may entail instances wherein both self-referential beliefs are within awareness, but one is clearly more recessive at any given point or points in time. The greater the degree to which one relative to another self-referent belief is in awareness, however, the more effective should be the self-deceptive process.

EXCUSE MAKING
AS A SELF-DECEPTIVE STRATEGY

Self-deception often appears in the process of excuse making; furthermore, excuse making often fits the previous definition of self-deception. In order to understand the relationship between self-deception and excuse making, it is necessary to describe this latter concept in some detail.

EXCUSE MAKING DEFINED

"Excuses are explanations or actions that lessen the negative implications of an actor's performance, thereby maintaining a positive image for oneself and others."[1]

Positive Image Motive. The aforementioned definitions of excuse making and self-deception rest on the assumption that human beings are motivated to preserve a positive image of themselves. This motive is, of course, a widely assumed one, and it has been advocated by a variety of psychologists. William James called it a "fundamental instinctive impulse";[2] Gordon Allport suggested that it was "nature's oldest law";[3] and Carl Rogers spoke of the "need for positive regard."[4]

Likewise, more recent theory echoes the importance of the self-image or self-esteem motivation.[5] Although some persons may not exemplify this self-esteem maintenance pattern, most persons are described in William Saroyan's words, "Every man is a good man in a bad world—as he himself knows."[6]

Positive Images for Whom? The typical conceptualization of excuse making emphasizes how a person aims an excuse at external audiences.[7] Although impression management for an external audience may play a role in excuse making, excuses often are aimed at the internal audience of oneself. The major theories of moral development illustrate how this occurs. Whether in the Freudian psychoanalytic framework,[8] the Piaget or Kohlberg cognitive approach,[9] or the Bandura social-learning perspective,[10] the developing child is portrayed as internalizing the rules and standards of important external audiences. This "socialization" process eventuates in internal guidelines that people seek to uphold. In other words, the audience increasingly becomes one's self over the years.

The Bad Performance Conflict. The two conflicting self-referential beliefs that ignite the excuse-making process are (a) that one is responsible for a negative outcome, and (b) that one is a good person. In this vein, a negative outcome "represents any action or behavior on the part of the person that falls below the standards that have been established as being typical for that person or people in general."[11]

The bad act–good person clash represents a cognitive/emotional conflict that the individual must resolve. (This logic is reminiscent of recent reinterpretations of the phenomenon known as cognitive dissonance, wherein the individual's perceived inconsistencies are "resolved" so as to maintain a sense of self-esteem.)[12] Excuse making is a common strategy for dealing with this conflict in order to preserve a benign view of oneself. Excuse making accomplishes this goal in at least two major ways. First, an individual can attempt to lessen the negativity of the "bad" act and thereby diminish the conflicting information about the good self; this type of excuse is called a *reframing performance strategy.* Second, the person can seek to lessen the degree of responsibility for the bad act and thus dampen the conflict; this type of excuse is called a *transformed responsibility strategy.* The reframing and transforming excuses are treated next.

Reframing Performance Strategies

The self-deceptive resolution inherent in reframing excuses involves attempts to diminish the negativity of the action for which one is responsible.

C. R. Snyder

Reframing strategies often emphasize the fact that the person does not perceive or comprehend the badness of his or her action. A first example of this "see no evil, hear no evil" tactic could be called the Kitty Genovese phenomenon. In 1964, a young woman named Kitty Genovese was stabbed to death in Queens, New York. Although 38 witnesses observed the slaying, none called the police or became "involved." Surely, this lack of helping was a bad act. This was not the case, however, in the eyes of the witnesses. They were convinced that they did not see anything that warranted their intervention; "It was just a lovers' quarrel" or "It wasn't my responsibility."[13] This murder generated an enormous amount of interest in American society, and prompted several social scientists to examine the process that has come to be called "bystander apathy."[14] It is revealing to examine the logic of those persons who did not render aid in laboratory tests. For example, those persons who did not report smoke that was billowing into a room suggested that it was just smog or steam;[15] similarly, persons who did not render aid to a woman who had suddenly fallen off a ladder noted that they were not sure she had really fallen, while others expressed the view that "it really wasn't serious."[16]

In contrast to the scenario in which the lack of (helping) action constitutes a bad performance, there are many times when one performs an action that requires reframing. Experimental studies show that persons who willfully engage in an action that harms another person will tend to underestimate the harm that they have done. Whether it is painful electric shocks,[17] or attitudes that may have aversive effects on another person,[18] the perceived negativity of these actions is diminished by the purposefully behaving transgressors. These studies suggest that for many "ill deeds" that we choose to perform, there may be a lessening of the negativity of our actions.

Another type of reframing is victim derogation. History, like the laboratory, documents sad instances in which people derogate those persons they believe they have harmed.[19] Thus, the victim is transformed into an "object" that is "less than human."[20] Implicitly, the aggressor reasons that it is not a negative act to hurt a "bad" or "worthless" person.

Reframing can also occur when a person derogates the source of the negative feedback. Since the badness of an action may in part reflect an appraisal that another external agent has made of one's words or deeds, a way of diminishing the negative evaluation is to undermine the source. This source may be an instrument or a test that generates the feedback, or an external evaluative person. In regard to evaluative instruments, research shows that feedback recipients are more prone to devalue the accuracy, validity, and reliability of tests when the feedback becomes more negative. This is the case when the test is a psychological one given by a mental health professional,[21] or an achievement or scholastic one given by a teacher.[22] In a similar view, the person who gives negative feedback is evaluated very poorly by the feedback recipient; this has been found when teachers,[23] mental health professionals,[24] or peers[25] give the feedback.

Before leaving the present section on reframing performance excuse strategies, it may be useful to highlight how these maneuvers fit the definition of self-deception posited at the beginning of this essay. The two conflicting self-referential beliefs that are central to reframing excuses are that (a) the good person has (b) committed a bad act. Reframing excuses are purposeful in the sense that they do not appear unless the person is held responsible for a bad action of some sort.[26] Further, given the enduring positive self-images that people hold, and the empirical and real-life robustness of reframing excuses as maneuvers to upgrade the positiveness of a particular negative act, it is logical to assume that the positive self-referential belief supersedes the awareness of the situation-specific negative self-referential belief. In the extent to which the reframing has lessened the personal appraisal of the negativity of one's action, then the self-deception has also been accomplished.

TRANSFORMED RESPONSIBILITY STRATEGIES

Whereas reframing excuse strategies focus on lessening the negativity of the particular bad act, transformed responsibility excuse strategies focus on a diminution of responsibility for the bad act. In the theater of the mind, the person recounts a series of "Yes, buts" that serve to transform one's sense of responsibility for an ill deed. Borrowing from social psychologist Harold Kelley's attributional framework of how people assign causality or responsibility for an action,[27] I will examine the role of *consensus* and *consistency* information. Depending on the nature of the consensus or consistency information pertaining to a particular bad performance, a person may be held less responsible. Consensus information represents the extent to which many people behave in the same fashion in a given situation. Because of the attributional logic that the situation must have impelled the people to behave thus, nobody will be held responsible under conditions of high consensus in which almost everyone behaves in a similar (bad) manner. Consistency information represents the extent to which a person is seen as behaving similarly over time in the same situation. Because of the attributional logic that something in the particular situation must have elicited the bad behavior, a person is not held responsible under conditions of low consistency in which he or she has *not* behaved in a (bad) fashion in previous similar circumstances.

Consensus-Raising Approaches. A person reduces the "psychological" responsibility for a bad action if he or she can raise consensus by showing that others would behave similarly under the same circumstances. Failure in achievement-related tasks gives us a glimpse of consensus raising in action. Following such experiences, research consistently reveals that persons attribute their failure to two external factors, task difficulty and bad luck.[28] If the task is extremely difficult, then the person can rationalize that almost anyone would fail; it is the fault of the task, not the person. Likewise, bad luck can rear its ugly head and undermine any of us on occasion; we are powerless against such a powerful foe as fate.

Another consensus-raising excuse involves the suggestion that a person was coerced. Within psychology, the best-known example of this phenomenon is found in Stanley Milgram's classic studies on obedience.[29] In these studies, research participants were willing to deliver exceedingly high levels of electric shock to another person in order to get that person to learn some word pair associates. (The learners did not, of course, actually receive any electrical shocks, but the research participants were under the impression that they were delivering the shocks.) Of the 40 research participants, 65% went all the way to the top of the shock-generating machine (450 volts!) in order to get the person to learn the material. Although the research participants pressed the shock buttons, they did not take responsibility for the action; they usually asserted that "the experimenter made me do it." Subsequent studies have further delineated this phenomenon by showing that the more harmful the electric shocks appear to be, the less the perpetrators believe that they had any choice in delivering the shocks.[30]

The clinical phenomenon of projection provides yet another example of consensus-raising excuses. Projection is generally defined "as the process whereby the person ascribes personal shortcomings to others in order to avoid a psychological threat."[31] Relevant research on projection reveals that when people are given negative rather than positive feedback about themselves, they consistently depict other people as also possessing the negative characteristics that constitute the feedback.[32] Furthermore, there are at least four studies that suggest that such projection after a failure-like experience serves to reduce the sense of personal stress.[33] These projection results, along with the aforementioned consensus-raising appeals to task difficulty, luck, and coercion, all attest to the data base for the old adage of "misery loves company."

Consistency-Lowering Approaches. The excuse-making person may also assert that he or she does not always behave so badly in the same circumstances. This adoption of a temporary inconsistency mutes the responsibility for the one bad act. There are at least two versions of such consistency-lowering excuses. The first is the intentionality plea, where the person asserts to himself or herself that "I didn't really mean to do it." A considerable amount of literature illustrates how *external* audiences find unintentional acts to be less culpable.[34] Certainly, the legal system gives a good deal of weight to the intentionality factor in assigning culpability.[35] The recent furor over the "temporary insanity" plea of John Hinckley, Jr., in the attempted assassination of President Reagan is a prime example. In the present context, however, it should be emphasized that the excuse maker intuitively knows how external audiences employ intentionality in assigning responsibility, and thus the same lack of intentionality mechanism probably is used to convince the internal audience of oneself that the responsibility for a bad action should be lessened.[36]

A second consistency-lowering excuse pertains to effort-lowering assertions of "I didn't really try." Here, the person implicitly reasons that the "one bad performance" was the result of not trying on that particular occasion; moreover, if the person were to try in future similar circumstances, he or she reasons, success would follow. The research relevant to this issue clearly reveals that people will employ the lowered-effort strategy after experiencing failure.[37] Whether through intentionality or effort strategies, therefore, it appears that the excuse maker seeks to soften the responsibility for the poor performance.

As with the earlier discussion of reframing, it may be useful to close the present section on transformed responsibility strategies by emphasizing the self-deceptive role of such excuses. The two conflicting self-referential beliefs inherent in transformed responsibility excuses are that (a) the good person is (b) *responsible* for a bad act. Unlike the reframing strategies that focus on a recasting of the bad act, the transformed responsibility excuses work on the responsibility linkage. The purposeful nature of transformed responsibility maneuvers is supported by the fact that they occur after bad rather than good acts;[38] moreover, some studies demonstrate that these excuses lessen the sense of personal distress associated with having committed a negative act. Finally, the stable image of oneself as a good person who *is not the author* of bad actions is the belief that predominates in awareness if the transformed responsibility excuse has actually lessened one's personal responsibility for a bad performance. The more that a personal sense of responsibility for a negative outcome is lessened, the greater the degree of self-deception achieved.

41

Although for purposes of exposition, the reframing and transformed responsibility excuses have been presented separately, in reality
these self-deceptive excuses may operate simultaneously. For example,
by invoking a high-consensus rationale, it may be reasoned that in
addition to lessening the sense of responsibility, the negativity of the
action should be diminished. If "everyone is doing it," the act must not
be so bad. Related research supports the reasoning that the more
prevalent any characteristics and behaviors are in the population generally, the less negatively these behaviors are viewed.[39] When a person
convinces himself or herself of the diminished negativity of an action, as
well as the lessened responsibility for that action, the self-deception is
more complete.

WHY SELF-DECEPTIVE EXCUSE MAKING THRIVES

At least four complex, interrelated factors provide the precursors to,
and reinforcement of, the self-deceptive excuse-making process. The
theater of one's mind and society together provide arenas that nurture
self-deceptive excuse making.

THE CHOICE-DETERMINISM DILEMMA

Excuses are related to a basic philosophical question: do we have
choices in our human existence? Determinism holds that there are
factors largely outside of human control that drive our behavior.[40]
Although this perspective is well-anchored in history, it has always had
an equally viable alternative among those who advocate the constant
existence of choice. Indeed, the existentialists have built their view-
points around the concept of choice.[41] Although the existence of choice
has been a question that has captured the imagination of thinkers
throughout the ages,[42] the practical reality is that society operates as if
we have choices that influence our lives.[43] Indeed, the concept of
responsibility for our actions appears throughout the written legal codes
and the unwritten mores of society.

Our modern world gives more freedom to people than it did in past
ages. With this enhanced freedom, our choices have undergone an
increase. This sense of choice brings with it an accompanying responsibility, not only for our own lives, but also for events in other parts of the
world and in the future. Paradoxically, the individual within this context
may feel less ability to determine his or her fate. This is a catch-22: we
increasingly feel as if we have choice and responsibility, but we do not

feel we can exercise it. Excuse making offers a solution to this dilemma. While we can embrace the societal view of responsibility for our actions, when we find ourselves in a predicament in which we have done something bad, we can make excuses to get ourselves off the hook and to maintain our positive image.

SOCIETAL FACILITATION OF EXCUSE MAKING

As noted in the previous section, society has a set of rules reflecting excuse making. Our legal system represents a complicated system of evaluating the acceptability of excuses for bad actions. It is not surprising, therefore, that we implicitly and explicitly teach our children the basic and advanced principles of excuse making.[44] Little nine-year-old Ian, for example, does poorly on a spelling test and his teacher tells him "Now, I know you didn't study for this because you normally do much better." Ian has just received an important lesson in effort-lowering excuse making. Or, suppose eight-year-old Stephanie is caught slugging her four-year-old brother. Mom says, "Surely you didn't mean to hit Bobby that way, so what was going on?" Here, the real lesson is in lack of intentionality as an excuse. Although society holds that individuals have a sense of choice and responsibility for their actions, at the same time it allows and trains its inhabitants to lessen responsibility by making excuses.

Another example provides an additional view of the social aspect of excuses. Suppose fifteen-year-old Terry does not hand in his term paper. To compound matters, he does not give an excuse, but merely says, "I didn't feel like doing it!" This response is especially threatening to the system because it assaults the authority of the teacher's rules and assignments. If Terry were to have given an excuse, at least he would have been recognizing the continued status of the teacher's role. Excuses are a social lubricant that the society often expects. Having given an excuse, the transgressor can continue within the particular social framework. That society rewards and almost demands excuses suggests an other-deception rather than a self-deceptive process. It is likely that these same societal forces enhance the excuse-making process to such an extent that the maker of excuses often comes to deceive himself or herself.

VAGUENESS OF BAD PERFORMANCE AND ONE'S RESPONSIBILITY

A further force that serves to nurture the use of self-deceptive excuses is that we often do not have an objective yardstick for how badly we have behaved, nor do we know how responsible we are for our behavior. The definition offered for self-deceptive excuse making suggests that people will often bias their interpretation of an activity (i.e., hold the more positive self-referential belief in awareness relative to the less positive one), but it does not always follow that the interpretation is absolutely *false*. Although excuses are always biased, they are not necessarily errors. Given the literature on the imperfection of the human memory for events, especially if those events pertain to potentially negative information about oneself,[45] it is easy to see how self-deceptive excuses operate in these gray areas.

ESTEEM MAINTENANCE OF EXCUSE MAKING

A major reason that self-deceptive excuses thrive is that they preserve our sense of personal worth. Because of excuses, the precious positive self-image remains less tarnished by the failures that visit our lives. This process is undoubtedly a powerful reinforcer for excuse making.

A RELATIONSHIP FOR BETTER OR FOR WORSE?

To this point, the intimate relationship between excuse making and self-deception has been explored. In this section, I shall consider the positive and negative implications of the relationship between self-deception and excuse making.

FOR BETTER

Two important advantages to self-deceptive excuse making have been described in the previous section. Beyond the role of excuses in garnering self-esteem and providing social grace, however, are two additional benefits. Although it may seem paradoxical, excuse making can help an individual to recognize his or her limits. It is easy to imagine the frustration that accrues to persons who take full responsibility for any and all events in which they are even remotely involved. By refusing to recognize the limitations that we all face, the burden of responsibility becomes awesome. In this sense, excuses are not pernicious and loathsome maneuvers engaged in by "weak" people, but rather they allow us to accept our human imperfection.

Closely related to the way in which excuses may allow us to recognize limitations is the fact that excuses can facilitate risk taking. We live in a world in which we know that personal failures of various sorts will occur inevitably, and yet we may proceed in our daily activities with the assurance that in a scrape we can call upon excuses. Without excuses, we may attempt only those activities in which we are certain of success. With excuses, we can truly push our goals to the limits of our talents.

FOR WORSE

The darker side of self-deceptive excuse making is characterized by excesses. When they are too extreme, extensive, and intractable, excuses begin to cause more problems than they solve. In extreme excuse making, the very obviousness of the excuse making subjects a person to social ostracism. If the subtlety vanishes, the effectiveness of excuses as an image-maintaining self-deceptive strategy will be undermined. In such extreme excuse making, society may shatter the self-deceptive value of the excuse. For example, consider the members of the Charles Manson "family." They asserted that they had murdered because Manson ordered them to do so. Furthermore, they implicitly reasoned that they were doing their victims a favor by involving them in their "holy mission."[46]

As excuse making is applied across a greater number of situations, it may become so obvious to others that the excuse maker is confronted with his or her "explanations." Perhaps this phenomenon can be illustrated by an experience of a psychotherapy client of the author. When Tom W. did not perform well in his high-school math course, he invoked the rationale that he "hadn't really tried." This appeared to have gained him some sense of personal solace for his poor performance, whereupon he began to employ the "not trying" excuse in his other courses. Not surprisingly, his classmates called him on this maneuver as it became more prevalent in different arenas. In fact, he was given the mocking nickname of "Too-Tired Tom."

When excuses become irreversible, then the excuse maker's sense of freedom is limited. If the excuse-making person accepts some particular label (e.g., test-anxious, shy, addicted smoker, alcoholic, etc.), then the excuse not only becomes very salient to others, but it becomes obvious to the excuse maker. The person literally can become stuck to his or her self-label. A brief examination of how the label of mental illness represents just such a circumstance is appropriate at this point.

The basis of mental illness as an excuse relates to its supposed involuntary underpinnings (i.e., the disease model). In reality, however, there is mounting evidence that the manifestation of psychological symptoms is in many cases a purposeful rather than an involuntary process; that is, people in many instances will initially evidence psychological symptoms as a way of protecting their self-esteem (e.g., "I'm test-anxious" rather than "I'm dumb").[47] If society and the person agree that his or her symptoms warrant a particular diagnostic label, then an unfortunate cooperative illusion may result. Both society and the person may mistakenly believe that mental illness prevents the person from coping. The unfortunate part of this process from a personal and societal view is that many people become needlessly entrenched in their "sick role" behavior.[48] Thus, the worker who is performing poorly on the job notes that he has been "drinking too much." Later, he and his social network of family and friends hear that he "has a drinking problem." Eventually, he may be an "alcoholic" who no longer is expected to work. In this instance, the original excuse to protect self-esteem in the work setting has become more extreme, extensive, and intractable. Although our "alcoholic" may be absolved from many responsibilities, by adopting the "sick role" behavior, he has to endure the stigma attached to his label. The life of our "alcoholic" in this example becomes the epitome of the "for worse" side of excuse making.

A Vital Balance

Self-deceptive excuses, when used in moderation, serve a useful role. Too little as well as too much excuse making, both have their disadvantages. The person who uses excuses too infrequently often accepts an undue amount of responsibility for his or her failures. At the other end of the spectrum, the extreme excuse maker often may find his or her "excuses" to be more trouble than they are worth.

For the client who takes undue responsibility for his or her behavior, one of the therapeutic tasks can be to teach the person *how to become a better excuse maker*. For example, when one of my psychotherapy clients reported that his shyness was becoming more and more debilitating, and that he felt very different from his fellow college students because of this shyness, the therapeutic homework assignment implicitly fostered excuse making! That is, the client was asked to go to a party and inform any new person that he met that he was shy and rather uncomfortable at parties. When he tried this, it proved to be a good way of initiating a conversation and it turned out that one or two other people also felt shy and awkward at parties. (Since estimates suggest that a large proportion of the population evidences some shyness,[49] the chance of meeting other shy people at a party is relatively high.) In this case, the unrealistically special sense of isolation and responsibility that this client felt was alleviated through a consensus-raising excuse strategy. At the close of treatment, the client reported that he still felt some discomfort at parties, but he was able to tolerate them more easily because "everyone feels uneasy at parties." (This latter cognition that everyone feels this way is, of course, probably not true, but its consensus-raising self-deceptive excuse sentiment appeared to serve the client well.)

Unlike the shy client who profited by increased excuse-making skills, there are many instances in which the clients need to decrease excuse making. "Too-Tired Tom" had increasingly used the "I-didn't-try" excuse to the point that he had been given the painful nickname of "Too-Tired Tom." In fact, Tom had become the living testimony to his nickname; he not only verbalized the "not trying" excuse, but he actually did not try. He came to believe that he *was* lazy. The treatment in this case initially involved a discussion of how Tom actually did have control over his effort expenditure. This resulted in his abandoning his view of himself as somehow inherently lazy. The next phase of treatment involved detective work pertaining to how the lack of effort concept first appeared. Tom had first used it in an area (mathematics) that was especially difficult for him; over time, he began to employ it in other courses where he actually had natural talent. This phase of treatment enabled Tom to "exert no effort" only in the math courses, and thus he did not have to "use" lowered effort in his other courses. Eventually, when he was able to get outside tutorial aid, he stopped using the lowered effort concept even in the mathematics course.

In neither instance did the therapist make the client highly aware that he was either engaging in deficient (the shyness case) or excessive (the lowered effort case) excuse making. In these and other therapy cases involving excuse-making components, it may be best to refrain from explicitly describing the process as excuse making; this may merely serve to "label" the person. Also, people do not want to see themselves as excuse makers. This assertion illustrates yet another twist on excuses: society trains and rewards us for excuse making, we use excuses and profit from them, *but we prefer to believe that we are not using them.* Therefore, not only is excuse making self-deceptive in the sense of maintaining the more positive self-referential belief in awareness (as has been argued throughout this essay), but excuse making is self-deceptive in that we often do not perceive that we are engaging in it. We may be giving explanations, or better yet, reasons for our misbehaviors, but we do not see ourselves as making excuses.

SUCH GOOD FRIENDS

For better or worse, the relationship between self-deception and excuse making appears to play an important role in the lives of people. Although they are not constant companions, self-deception and excuse making often are found working together in the theater of the mind. They are, to borrow an apt phrase, "such good friends."

NOTES

1. C. R. Snyder, Raymond L. Higgins, and Rita J. Stucky, *Excuses: Masquerades in Search of Grace* (New York: Wiley, 1983), 45.

2. William James, *The Principles of Psychology,* vols. 1 and 2 (New York: Holt, 1890).

3. Gordon W. Allport, *Personality: A Psychological Interpretation* (New York: Holt, 1937).

4. Carl R. Rogers, *Client-Centered Therapy: Its Current Practice, Implications, and Theory* (Boston: Houghton Mifflin, 1951).

5. L. Edward Wells and Gerald Marwell, *Self-Esteem: Its Conceptualization and Measurement* (Beverly Hills, Calif.: Sage, 1976); and Ruth C. Wylie, *The Self-Concept: Theory and Research on Selected Topics,* vol. 2, rev. ed. (Lincoln: University of Nebraska Press, 1979); S. C. Jones, "Self and Interpersonal Evaluations: Esteem Theories vs. Consistency Theories," *Psychological Bulletin* 79 (1973): 185–199; and C. R. Snyder, Randee J. Shenkel, and Carol R. Lowery, "Acceptance of Personality Interpretations: The 'Barnum Effect' and Beyond," *Journal of Consulting and Clinical Psychology* 45 (1977): 104–114.

6. Donald G. Myers and J. Ridl, "Can We All Be Better Than Average?," *Psychology Today* 12 (1979): 89–98.

7. James T. Tedeschi, ed., *Impression Management Theory and Social Psychological Research* (New York: Academic Press, 1981); Erving Goffman, *The Presentation of Self in Everyday Life* (Garden City: Doubleday-Anchor, 1959), *Interaction Ritual: Essays on Face-to-Face Behavior* (Garden City: Doubleday, 1967), and *Relations in Public* (New York: Basic Books, 1971).

8. Sigmund Freud, *The Ego and the Id* (London: Hogarth, 1927).

9. Jean Piaget, *The Moral Judgment of the Child* (1932; reprint, New York: Free Press, 1965); and Lawrence Kohlberg, "Moral Development and Identification," in *Child Psychology:* 62d Yearbook of the National Society for the Study of Education, ed. H. Stephenson (Chicago: University of Chicago Press, 1962).

10. Albert Bandura, *Aggression: A Social-Learning Analysis* (Englewood Cliffs: Prentice-Hall, 1973), and *Social Learning Theory* (Englewood Cliffs: Prentice-Hall, 1977).

11. Snyder et al., *Excuses: Masquerades in Search of Grace,* 39–40.

12. Elliot Aronson, "The Theory of Cognitive Dissonance: A Current Perspective," in *Advances in Experimental Social Psychology,* vol. 4, ed. Leonard Berkowitz (New York: Academic Press, 1969); and Leonard Berkowitz, *Social Psychology* (New York: Holt, Rinehart, and Winston, 1980).

13. A. M. Rosenthal, *Thirty-Eight Witnesses* (New York: McGraw-Hill, 1964).

14. Bibb Latané and John M. Darley, "Bystander Apathy," *American Scientist* 57 (1969): 244–268, and *The Unresponsive Bystander: Why Doesn't He Help?* (New York: Appleton-Century Crofts, 1970).

15. Bibb Latané and John M. Darley, "Group Inhibition of Bystander Interventions in Emergencies," *Journal of Personality and Social Psychology* 10 (1968): 215–221.

16. Bibb Latané and Judith Rodin, "A Lady in Distress: Inhibiting Effects of Friends and Strangers on Bystander Interaction," *Journal of Experimental Social Psychology* 5 (1969): 189–202.

17. Timothy C. Brock and Arnold H. Buss, "Dissonance, Aggression and Evaluation of Pain," *Journal of Abnormal and Social Psychology* 65 (1962): 197–202.

18. Marc Riess and Barry R. Schlenker, "Attitude Change and Responsibility Avoidance As Modes of Dilemma Resolution in Forced-Compliance Situations," *Journal of Personality and Social Psychology* 35 (1977): 21–30.

19. Snyder et al., *Excuses: Masquerades in Search of Grace*, 85–86; M. B. Scott and S. M. Lyman, "Accounts," *American Sociological Review* 33 (1968): 46–62; and Leonard Berkowitz, James A. Green, and Jacqueline R. Macaulay, "Hostility Catharsis and the Reduction of Emotional Tension," *Psychiatry* 25 (1962): 23–31.

20. Gresham M. Sykes and David Matza. "Techniques of Neutralization: A Theory of Delinquency," *American Sociological Review* 22 (1957): 664–670.

21. C. R. Snyder and Mark S. Clair, "Does Insecurity Breed Acceptance? Effects of Trait and Situational Insecurity on Acceptance of Positive and Negative Diagnostic Feedback," *Journal of Consulting and Clinical Psychology* 45 (1977): 843–850; and C. R. Snyder and Randee J. Shenkel, "Effects of 'Favorability,' Modality, and Relevance on Acceptance of General Personality Interpretations Prior to and after Receiving Diagnostic Feedback," *Journal of Consulting and Clinical Psychology* 44 (1976): 34–41.

22. C. R. Snyder and Mark S. Clair, "Effects of Expected and Obtained Grades on Teacher Evaluation and Attribution of Performance," *Journal of Educational Psychology* 68 (1976): 75–82; and Mark S. Clair and C. R. Snyder, "Effects of Instructor-Delivered Sequential Evaluative Feedback upon Students' Subsequent Classroom-Related Performance and Instructor Ratings," *Journal of Educational Psychology* 71 (1979): 50–57.

23. Clair and Snyder, "Effects of Instructor-Delivered Sequential Evaluative Feedback"; and Snyder and Clair, "Effects of Expected and Obtained Grades."

24. Snyder and Shenkel, "Effects of 'Favorability.' "

25. Paul Skolnick, "Reactions to Personal Evaluations: A Failure to Replicate," *Journal of Personality and Social Psychology* 18 (1971): 62–67.

26. Snyder et al., *Excuses: Masquerades in Search of Grace*, 82–93.

27. Harold H. Kelley, "Attribution Theory in Social Psychology," in *Nebraska Symposium on Motivation*, vol. 15, ed. D. Levine (Lincoln: University of Nebraska Press, 1967); *Attribution in Social Interaction* (New York: General Learning Press, 1971); and "The Process of Causal Attribution," *American Psychologist* 28 (1973): 107–128.

28. Miron Zuckerman, "Attribution of Success and Failure Revisited: or The Motivational Bias Is Alive and Well in Attribution Theory," *Journal of Personality* 47 (1979): 245–287.

29. Stanley Milgram, "Behavioral Study of Obedience," *Journal of Abnormal and Social Psychology* 67 (1963): 371–378, and "Some Conditions to Obedience and Disobedience to Authority," *Human Relations* 18 (1965): 57–76.

30. Timothy C. Brock and Arnold H. Buss, "Effects of Justification for Aggression and Communication with the Victim on Postaggression Dissonance," *Journal of Abnormal and Social Psychology* 68 (1964): 403–412; John H. Harvey, Ben Harris, and Richard D. Barnes, "Actor-Observer Differences in the Perceptions of Responsibility and Freedom," *Journal of Personality and Social Psychology* 32 (1975): 22–28.

31. Snyder et al., *Excuses: Masquerades in Search of Grace,* 97.

32. David S. Holmes, "Dimensions of Projection," *Psychological Bulletin* 69 (1968): 248–268; and "Projection as a Defense Mechanism," *Psychological Bulletin* 85 (1978): 677–688.

33. David H. Bennett and David S. Holmes, "Influence of Denial (Situation Redefinition) and Projection on Anxiety Associated with Threat to Self-Esteem," *Journal of Personality and Social Psychology* 32 (1975), 915–921; Thomas G. Burish and B. Kent Houston, "Causal Projection, Similarity Projection, and Coping with Threat to Self-Esteem," *Journal of Personality* 47 (1979): 57–70; David S. Holmes and B. Kent Houston, "The Defensive Function of Projection," *Journal of Personality and Social Psychology* 20 (1971): 208–213; Robert Zemore and T. Greenough, "Reduction of Ego Threat Following Attributive Projection," *Proceedings of the 81st Annual Convention of the American Psychological Association* 8 (1973): 343–344.

34. K. Rotenberg, "Children's Use of Intentionality in Judgments of Character and Disposition," *Child Development* 51 (1980): 282–284; M. E. Shaw, "Attribution of Responsibility by Adolescents in Two Cultures," *Adolescence* 3 (1968): 23–32; M. E. Shaw and H. T. Reitan, "Attribution of Responsibility as a Basis for Sanctioning Behavior," *British Journal of Social and Clinical Psychology* 8 (1969): 217–226.

35. Snyder et al., *Excuses: Masquerades in Search of Grace,* 103.

36. Ibid.

37. Miron Zuckerman, "Attribution of Success and Failure Revisited."

38. Snyder et al., *Excuses: Masquerades in Search of Grace,* 93–106.

39. Snyder and Shenkel, "Effects of 'Favorability.'"

40. Joseph Rychlak, *Discovering Free Will and Personal Responsibility* (New York: Oxford, 1979), 33.

41. J. Lachalier, *Psychologie et Metaphysique* (Paris: Universitaire de France, 1949); and Jean-Paul Sartre, *Being and Nothingness* (New York: Philosophical Library, 1956).

42. Gilbert Ryle, *The Concept of Mind* (New York: Barnes and Noble, 1949), and *Dilemmas* (1954; reprint, Cambridge: Cambridge University Press, 1980).

43. J. G. Kemeny, *A Philosopher Looks at Science* (Princeton, N.J.: Van Nostrand, 1959).

44. Margaret Schadler and Beverly Ayers-Nachamkin, "The Development of Excuse-Making," in *Excuses: Masquerades in Search of Grace.*

45. Snyder et al., *Excuses: Masquerades in Search of Grace,* 27–34; and Ulric Neisser, "John Dean's Memory: A Case Study," *Cognition* 9 (1981): 1–22.

46. Ernest Becker, *The Denial of Death* (New York: Free Press, 1975), 138.

47. Snyder et al., *Excuses: Masquerades in Search of Grace,* 221–223; C. R. Snyder and Timothy W. Smith, "Symptoms as Self-Handicapping Strategies," in *Integrations of Clinical and Social Psychology,* ed. Gifford Weary and Herbert L. Mirels (New York: Oxford, 1982); Timothy W. Smith, C. R. Snyder, and Mitchell M. Handelsman, "On the Self-Serving Function of an Academic Wooden Leg,"

Journal of Personality and Social Psychology 42 (1982): 314–321; and Timothy W. Smith, C. R. Snyder, and Suzanne Perkins, "The Self-Serving Function of Hypochondriacal Complaints: Physical Symptoms as Self-Handicapping Strategies," *Journal of Personality and Social Psychology* 44 (1983): 787–797.

48. Thomas J. Scheff, *Being Mentally Ill: A Sociological Theory* (Chicago: Aldine, 1971).

49. Philip G. Zimbardo and Shirley Radl, *The Shy Child* (New York: McGraw-Hill, 1981).

Alcoholism and Self-Deception

Herbert Fingarette

This paper has two specific, closely related aims. First, I want to correct some misconceptions of my book *Self-Deception*,[1] by placing into sharp focus the most central theme of that book—avowal and disavowal. Then, against that background, I want to show how the widely believed but unwarranted concept that alcoholism is a disease serves to encourage self-deception. More generally, in doing these things I hope to illustrate the practical relevance of the analysis of self-deception that I gave in the book; but of at least equal importance, I hope to provide fundamental substantive insight into the human problems so often denoted by the label "alcoholism."

GETTING THE MODEL OF SELF-DECEPTION
BACK INTO FOCUS

In *Self-Deception* I offered a model of consciousness, *explicit* consciousness, as "spelling out."[2] Correlatively, I proposed that absence of explicit consciousness by reason of refusal to spell out is distinctive of self-deception. This model of consciousness was presented early in the order of the book's exposition, and it had enough that was novel or controversial about it to have fixed the attention of many readers. As a result it has often been discussed as if it were the core of the book's analysis of self-deception. This view is definitely incorrect. The theme of consciousness as spelling out is distinctly secondary to the theme of avowal and disavowal.

In the book I argued[3] that the disavowal of an engagement creates an inner split: The totality of what I called the individual's actual

52

engagements in the world remains unchanged, but the personal self disavows identity with those engagements in some respect(s), thus establishing self-deception. The policy of not spelling out an engagement—and in that way not being explicitly conscious of it—is then a derivative, though important, consequence of the disavowal. It is a consequence because, if I disavow my personal identification with engagement X, then it follows as part of the very sense of this move that I am abdicating authority to speak *for* X, or to speak *as* X.

Another important consequence of disavowal—often overlooked in discussions of the book—is the establishment of impairment or defect in capacity as a responsible actor.[4] Because of the inner split created by disavowal, personal agency is compromised, and so the voluntariness of conduct is compromised, the relevant conduct being no longer either straightforwardly voluntary or straightforwardly involuntary.

The concept of disavowal was not invented ad hoc to account for self-deception; I showed its roots—and that of its corollary, avowal—in Freud,[5] Sartre, and Kierkegaard.[6] I also discussed at length the familiar external analogues, avowal or disavowal of allegiance, of loyalty, of oneness with persons, families, groups, nations, ideals, social movements.[7] When we avow identity with something, we do not bring that thing into being, but we adopt a certain distinctive stance toward it. And when we disavow something, its existence is not taken from it, but our stance as one with it is abandoned.

There is a natural connection, however, between avowing or disavowing some engagement, and, respectively, actually acting or not acting as one who is so engaged. Normally, if I disavow love for her, she finds no love in me. If I inwardly disavow a desire for X, it will also be the case (normally) that no such desire exists in me. But, though normal, these are by no means inevitable connections. A person may earnestly disavow love, and yet we may see that love is still there in the individual—and we see how it brings the individual to act in ways that the person does not understand or quite control. Disavowed desires that in fact continue to exist are experienced as "alien," as "forces" that press us, drive us, or overcome us. In these cases, the disavowed engagements are like all engagements we once had—in the period of infancy and early childhood, prior to the emergence of personhood.

In our first years, before any true sense of a single personal identity or a personal *self*-consciousness exists, the infant individual is already engaging in a wide variety of complexly organized actions. Playing "train" at one time, eating lunch at another, being dressed at another, building sand piles at another—each of the infant individual's engagements is a complex, purposive, intelligently conducted project, but each proceeds in psychic isolation from the other. The crucial point to notice is that each isolated engagement is more or less effectively carried on, and yet there is no inner sense of a single, continuous self whose one life and one identity are realized through these many engagements.

The normal process of human maturation is the movement toward integration of these many engagements, by means of successive avowals, as the conjoint activities of one single personal identity. Whence comes this emerging personal self and its capacity for avowal? This seems to be a constitutional given that arises after a couple of years or so of life. This self or person defines itself to itself by the distinctive inner avowals of self-identification, in effect acknowledging, *This* I am, and this, and this, but *not* that, or that.

A person is not a mere collection of engagements, of course; there is a degree of unity, harmony, coherence among the elements that go into a person's make-up. It may be a looser or tighter unity, a greater or lesser harmony and coherence. Perfect coherence is impossible; but substantial coherence, or at least compatibility of the elements, is essential, for where there is great inner discord, there is great inner distress, often manifested as guilt, remorse, self-criticism, indecision and ambivalence, or anxiety. It is this distress that is the generic motive for disavowal. When an individual does not in fact give up a certain engagement with the world, but when avowal of it would engender inner discord, and thus acute distress, the engagement may be disavowed; the person is then in self-deception. We do not deal here with simple error, though self-deception may engender errors, nor with simple insincerity, though it may engender insincerities. These are categories, along with "voluntary" and "involuntary," that apply paradigmatically to a person as integrated agent whose avowals and disavowals actually reflect that individual's engagements and non-engagements. But self-deception is precisely what dis-integrates personal agency, thereby confusing understanding and compromising action.

THE CONCEPT OF ALCOHOLISM AS A DISEASE

The notion of "alcoholism" raises a host of complex problems, most of which cannot be touched in this paper. What follows is not intended as a proof, either scientific or philosophical. It is aimed at developing a way of seeing the phenomena. Since it is a different way of seeing them than is fashionable today, and since the problems are substantively addressed here, and are not merely used as source material for illustrating a philosophical point, I will use this section of the paper to develop a few basic critical theses about the prevailing concept of alcoholism as a disease. Then, in the following section, I will turn to the self-deception aspect.

Inasmuch as I will set the theses out flatly, I will say this in their defense: (1) On the basis of a comprehensive analysis of the literature,[8] I am convinced that what I say is scientifically sound and (2) in any case, these theses merit discussion because they reflect major new ideas that have become important in the recent research and scholarly literature on the topic.[9]

The widely held but scientifically unfounded belief that alcoholism is a disease is easily confused with other and better-founded beliefs. It is necessary, therefore, briefly to identify the latter in order to isolate and clearly identify the nature of the genuinely unfounded belief in question.

It is well established that even moderate amounts of alcohol can directly impair perceptual, motor, and cognitive functioning during the period that the alcohol is in the system (i.e., during actual intoxication). Though not what one would normally call "disease," still this is physical and mental impairment. In any case, it is not the so-called disease of alcoholism; after all, many people get intoxicated, whereas only a small minority of them are classified as alcoholics and considered to be suffering from the disease of alcoholism.

More closely related to the supposed disease of alcoholism are the physical ailments that result from frequent and heavy use of alcohol over a period of years. The probability rises ominously that a heavy drinker will develop one or more of a wide variety of grave physical pathologies (e.g., organ damage, neurological damage, or physiopathology). Mortality rates rise significantly if drinking stays at high levels for a long period. In the long-run consequences of heavy drinking we encounter disease with a vengeance! And yet we should note that many of these diseases are not peculiar to those who are diagnosed as alcoholics; they are ailments well known and fully identifiable independently of alcohol use, though in some instances alcohol happens to be a significant etiological factor. Thus, we still have not arrived at a specific disease that warrants the special name of "alcoholism."

We come upon the relevant specific phenomenon when we ask whether there is a way of preventing the increased risks of catastrophic illness to which long-term heavy drinkers are so vulnerable. There is a highly effective preventive measure, and it is childishly simple: Stop drinking!

And there's the rub: What is so very distinctive, and what seems to justify a special label and the notion that there is a highly specific disease involved, is that a certain number of long-term heavy drinkers *don't*, *won't*—some would say *can't*—take the simple and obvious step, namely to stop (or even cut down on) their drinking.

Given what seems the enormous weight of considerations against such drinking, and what often seems the absence of remotely comparable considerations in favor of drinking, the inference almost forces itself on one: Something has gone awry in connection with such a drinker's ability to make choices about drinking. We look at the drinker—drinking again and again and again—and there comes to seem a kind of inevitability about it. Paradoxically, however, on particular occasions the person may seem able to choose—and often does choose—not to drink, or to drink relatively moderately. Few of those labeled "alcoholic" get drunk all day, every day, no matter what the situation.

Any account of what is at issue when the label "alcoholism" is used must come to grips with the question of self-control, and with these distinctive, paradoxical data in regard to it.

The concept that there is a specific disease, whose distinctive symptom is loss of control over drinking, has come to seem in the public mind the plausible and scientifically proven explanation of the phenomena. Two basic questions arise: (1) Has the theory that there is a specific disease of alcoholism been scientifically substantiated? (2) Does the theory account for the paradoxical phenomena? I turn, first, to a summary of the facts in answer to question 1.

What is supposed to be the etiology or cause of this disease? In 1946, when E. M. Jellinek published his classic article on the phases of alcoholism[10] and effectively energized the modern alcoholism movement, he explicitly disclaimed offering any theory explaining the causes of the disease. What he did offer was a highly specific description of sets of symptoms that follow one another in a standard sequence among "habitual inebriates." By 1960, however, in his book, *The Disease Concept of Alcoholism*,[11] he explicitly claimed the existence of alcoholism as a specific disease, and he discussed 150 theories as to its cause, all of them speculative, and a number that could be dismissed. Since his book appeared, additional theories have been proposed and widely discussed. A number of the theories have intuitive appeal as explanations: drinking is a conditioned learned response, or a means of tension relief, or an irresistible desire caused by chemical dependency, or an effect of genetic or neurophysiological abnormalities. Such theories are widely familiar in one form or another, and each year brings its quota of new "breakthroughs." The amount of scientific effort devoted to the problem has been enormous.

In the end there is little or no controversy among researchers about the result to date: No theory of a single cause of alcoholism is generally accepted by the scientific community, nor has any specific causal hypothesis, however complex, satisfactorily explained for scientists the etiology of alcoholism.[12] Thus there never was, and still is not, a scientifically established causal explanation of the supposed disease.

Some authorities who have held to a disease theory have tried to minimize the significance of this situation by asserting that there are probably many factors, indeed *very* many factors, that go into causing the supposed disease. We are told that one must look at the question of etiology in a "wholistic" or "multi-disciplinary" way.[13] But since no one can specify the exact factors, or the specific structure of the "whole," or the precise pattern for integrating the work of the multiple disciplines, this amounts to saving the jargon but saying nothing.

If science has never known the cause of the disease, how could science describe the syndrome itself? This was indeed the goal of Jellinek's original work, which gave the impetus to the modern disease concept.[14] Jellinek presented an elaborate and highly specific description, the first such account in the modern literature. It was cast in the form of a scientific study. Jellinek has remained a respected scholar.

All the more potent, then, was the dramatic, impressive, and by now widely familiar tragic tale; it begins with the first innocent social drink, then proceeds insidiously until life centers on drinking, and finally develops into that wreckage of a life called "hitting bottom."

Unfortunately Jellinek's account is now generally acknowledged to have been derived from a scientifically utterly inadequate data base.[15] Subsequent, more adequate research by others has failed to confirm any such uniform sequence, and in fact has revealed that drinking patterns among so-called alcoholics vary widely.[16]

All of this raises the question: What, then, *is* an alcoholic? If the patterns of drinking vary, and if there is no known unitary causal process, what are we talking about when we talk about "alcoholics" and "alcoholism"?

From the early days of the movement there have been a variety of definitions and diagnostic schemes in use, and they differ substantively and significantly. In fact, it is widely recognized that a basic handicap in scientific interpretation of the enormous research literature on alcoholism is noncomparability; the lack of uniform terminology and methods hinders accumulation of data on well-defined issues.

Some definitions emphasize the development of bodily chemical reactions to alcohol, such as withdrawal symptoms and increased tolerance. But many heavy drinkers show such reactions and yet are not diagnosed as "alcoholics." Nor do all who are so diagnosed show these reactions. And since persons diagnosed as alcoholics do not necessarily drink when having these reactions, it is unclear why these phenomena—objective though they be—are relevant enough to be definitional.

But don't these people have something exceptionally distinctive in common in their behavior? Can't we define the terms by reference to the way they drink so heavily, so frequently, with such terrible imprudence, and at such a cost?

After all, we *selected* only those who have that set of traits. And we excluded from our grouping any who do not have these traits. Should we be surprised that each member of the group turns out to have exactly those exceptional characteristics? But have we any reason to think that all alcoholics behave this way for the same reason rather than for many different reasons?

Many of those who maintain that alcoholism is a disease claim to see one ubiquitous, genuinely unique, and distinctive phenomenon over and above the mere fact of extremely heavy drinking—it is customarily referred to as "loss of control." It is not always clear whether "loss of control" is supposed to be a common element that we *see* in the behavior of all these people, or whether it is supposed to be a hypothesized, underlying causal factor whose effect is the observed heavy drinking. But the centrality of this notion in the alcoholism literature is plain: "Loss of control" has been characterized as the "pathognomonic" symptom of alcoholism, and of course the concept is intended to capture that element of apparent intractability in the drinking pattern that I mentioned earlier as being so central and so puzzling in the context of long-term heavy drinking.

Discussions, studies, and experiments over the past decade or two have established that it is false that persons diagnosed as alcoholics, once having had one drink, will continue to drink uncontrollably.[17] As a result, the very concept of "loss of control" has by now had to be so qualified and redefined by its advocates that it has become essentially void of content.

In spite of the lack of a causal or descriptive account, and in spite of the lack of an adequate concept of what is to be explained or described, it may seem that a kind of pragmatic approach might yet save the concept that alcoholism is a disease. Should we not consider the practical success that medicine can now achieve in the cure of alcoholism? And, by contrast, should we not consider the dismal failure of the more traditional legal, moral, and religious approaches? So, at least, the advocates of the disease concept might phrase the rhetorical questions. We, however, have to ask more ingenuously, how much more successful, in fact, have medical approaches been than have other approaches?

A number of comprehensive analytical reviews of the literature on success rates of alcoholism therapies have been published. In these reviews, program design, data and statistical adequacy, and interpretations of program data are subjected to scientifically and mathematically sophisticated scrutiny. The reviews have all come up with essentially the same overall assessment: no medical therapy for alcoholism—indeed no sort of therapy for alcoholism—has demonstrated superiority over any other sort. Nor is it proven that therapy for alcoholism, of whatever kind, adds any significant improvement to what might have occurred anyway without it. While the impact of therapy programs is at best dubious, such program-independent factors as age, and family and job status of the individual, are significantly associated with differential rates of improvement.

As with many of the explanatory theories about "alcoholism," so, too, with many of the therapeutic approaches to "alcoholism": the doctrines that rationalize the programs are often plausible, and the statistics offered look impressive to those who are unsophisticated in handling statistics. Many of the active workers in this field are scientifically unsophisticated, so it may often be with good faith that they continue to present the numbers they collect, and to make claims of success for their program and for its superiority over other types of programs (which, of course, make correspondingly confident claims of superiority, all in the name of "science").

The idea that alcoholism is a disease is now widely discounted in the sociological literature and is increasingly watered down in the medical literature. It is still very much the dominant view in the enormous alcohol health "establishment," however, and in the public mind. Indoctrination of drinkers and nondrinkers is pervasive.

What is the effect of such indoctrination and public opinion on the drinker? Having now set out the background of confusion underlying this doctrine, we are in a position to see how it tends to markedly exacerbate and further complicate the problems posed by long-term heavy drinking. Specifically, the disease concept of alcoholism is now an endemic source of self-deception for long-term heavy drinkers; it offers a moral bargain—under the guise of moral neutrality—that subverts autonomy and self-respect in those who accept it.

SELF-DECEPTION AND THE
DISEASE CONCEPT OF ALCOHOLISM

Knowing now how widely drinking patterns vary, even among the heaviest of drinkers, we should expect explanations of drinking to be various, i.e., specific to the individual whose drinking is to be explained. Limited generalizations may well be possible, but it becomes implausible to expect one basic explanation as to why these people live as they do. I shall offer here no alternative to the disease concept of alcoholism by way of a general explanation of heavy drinking, nor indeed do I even offer any individualized explanations. What I do try to suggest is a different general perspective on such lives, a general perspective that is compatible with the known facts.

In the seventeenth and eighteenth centuries in this country, people generally liked to drink; they thought it was salutary, and they drank a lot. It was acknowledged, however, that some folks made too much of a good thing; they were habitual drunkards. This was considered unfortunate and objectionable. Was there a "cause"? One widely held view was that drunkards were people who hung around taverns, and tavern life and society were bad influences, encouraging gossip, gaming, and drinking with the gang rather than sweating to earn one's daily bread.[18]

We need not wholeheartedly accept that explanation, or the sermonizing that went with it, but we should notice an underlying simplicity and directness with regard to the phenomena themselves. What people saw was that a human being had come increasingly to adopt a way of life that was generally disapproved as immoral and destructive, a way that consisted of a complex pattern of social behavior, one of the elements of which was very heavy drinking. There was no occasion for the unfortunate person to engage in self-deception by denying what was going on, or to be encouraged by others to do so. The person had come to prefer, for any of a variety of reasons, a certain way of life, and that was that—a simple but sad fact.

Something new is imported into the life of the habitual heavy drinker, however, as soon as the idea of "disease" or "illness" takes over. The usual modern claim has been that the disease concept of alcoholism at last introduces reason and reality into the picture, a breath of fresh air that clears the atmosphere of archaic moralism and punitive tactics. The opposite is the case, however; the acceptance of the "disease" concept has created a generalized encouragement of self-deception, and of covertly intensified, rigid moralizing.

What is usually overlooked is that the disease concept of alcoholism presupposes it to be self-evident that the drinker's way of life is both pernicious and senseless. Instead of encouraging those concerned to see the drinking in the context of the person's way of life, and thus to discern what role or roles it may play for that person in coping with life, the logic of the disease concept does the contrary. It leads all concerned, including the drinker, to deny, to ignore, to discount what meaning that way of life may have. Seen as an involuntary symptom of a disease, the drinking is isolated from the rest of life, and viewed as the meaningless but destructive effect of a noxious condition, a "disease." The disease concept leads one logically, if tacitly, to the basic assumption that the alcoholic's way of life ought to be abandoned if at all possible—a devastating moral judgment on that life. It is as if we say to the drinker, "We will absolve you of personal blame if you will in turn surrender all claim to any human meaning in your drinking and the life linked to it; as a condition of receiving help and moral support, you must come to see all this as waste, as emptiness."

But what if this is totally wrong? What if that life reflects, perhaps unwisely and obscurely, the drinker's attempts to cope with feelings, emotions, attitudes, relationships that are not acceptable to others—perhaps not fully acceptable even to the drinker—but that are, for better or worse, those that surge up in the drinker's soul? The drinker may be striving to express deep needs and genuine feelings—but how tempting to be freed of guilt and turmoil if only one will accept the bargain offered by the disease concept advocates!

But how can the drinker accept that bargain without *belief*? The disease doctrine may seem intellectually appealing and persuasive—but how can people believe themselves to be driven uncontrollably by alien forces, when, if I am right, no such thing is really true? Must they not know inwardly of this falsehood?

The answer is, of course, that indoctrination with the disease doctrine gives the needed intellectual license and social encouragement to disavow the desire to drink, and thus to experience it as alien to self. Combined with the motive of evading inner conflict—the motive that is generic to self-deception—the proselytizing of the disease concept becomes a prime incentive to self-deception in the long-term heavy drinker.

The drinker is encouraged not only to disavow the desire for drink, but also to avow the "decent" values, which may in fact have become uncertain or even been rejected by the drinker. "I care for my wife, my children, my job; I care for the decent and proper way of life—but I am a victim of some force that is not me." The drinker may in fact have deep feelings of resentment, or anger, or rebellion, or disillusionment, and these may be generalized or be directed to specific objects—for example, spouse, job, or competitive pressures. These are to be disavowed: "I do not hate my wife, nor resent my children, but I am driven to do things that hurt them." The drinking may well be only one element in a strategy for expression of these attitudes and in the attempt to cope with the inner conflicts engendered. But the disease concept smothers it all, and encourages focusing on the drinking in isolation, applauding the self-deceptive disavowals and avowals, though not, of course, under their true guise as such.

There is then a kind of self-fulfilling truth to seeing a person as an alcoholic and as one who suffers impaired self-control. Impaired self-control is inherent in all self-deception. A genuine inner split arises: the *individual* has strong and complex feelings and attitudes associated, among other things, with the desire to drink; but the *person* has disavowed identity with such desires, thereby undermining personal agency in regard to them. The *person* avows the "proper" feelings and attitudes, but even if they really exist, the picture is fatally distorted because of the contrary feelings that are disavowed and thus not explicitly conscious.

Self-deception is a form of self-compromise that systematically sows confusion and disorder within the self.

Even though there is that element of self-fulfilling truth in the feeling that one has been conquered by an alien desire (because of the complex inner division created), this should not obscure for us the strong element of untruth in it. For the desire is not alien, in the sense that it *is* the individual who desires to drink and who has the associated feelings and attitudes.

Moreover, these desires, feelings, and attitudes must all be avowed by the person if they are to come within that person's powers of rational understanding and fully autonomous self-control. The inner split and the impairment of control associated with it represent, not a fait accompli, but a task, a deed that must be undone. To avow, of course, is not necessarily to approve; it is merely to acknowledge that for better or worse this *is* who I am, and that it is for *me* to take action in the matter if needed. To avow identity with an engagement is to accept the role of thinking and acting rationally and responsibly as the agent who is engaged.

Against this background one is not surprised to learn that the current therapeutic regimens for the "disease of alcoholism" commonly require as basic that there be an authentic decision by the drinker to take responsibility for abstaining from drink during the program and for willingly cooperating with the program's regimen in general. The irony is, of course, that this appeal to the drinker's own decision and self-discipline is made by those who insist that the alcoholic's drinking is the symptom of a disease, and hence is *not* voluntary conduct and not subject to personal self-control. This radical inconsistency between diagnosis and therapeutic expectations is typically ignored.

It is not enough, however, merely to avow what was disavowed. One must then come to terms personally with it all. For after all, the person's problems in life are not resolved by avowal; avowal is only the condition that makes it possible to confront life with candor, clarity, and autonomy. It is here, in the task of coming to terms candidly with life, that we come upon another phenomenon of major importance, one that is easily confused with impairment of self-control. One who is inwardly whole in confronting life finds that difficulties still abound in seeking to understand oneself and one's life more deeply, and in seeking to figure out ways and means of coming to better terms with life. Even more central to the theme of control over one's life is the enormous difficulty that so often lies in seeking to actually *make* major changes in one's way of life if that seems desirable.

Such difficulties are not peculiar to the heavy drinker's life. They are difficulties that have at times proven too much for very many of us. After a certain time in life, a fairly early time, we have grown into activities, motivations, sensitivities, desires, habits, social associations, conditioning, skills, all interwoven and interdependent with one another to form a way of life. Any relatively isolated judgment or decision to change, no matter how well supported by reasons, is very often a weak reed indeed on which to lean as a basis for effecting major change. All of the already established propensities conspire against an effective follow-through of such a resolution.

Thus, even without self-deception and the confusion and illusions it introduces, paradoxical "self-control" phenomena in the life of long-term heavy drinkers remain. We may see each individual choice to drink or not to drink as a genuine choice; and yet we still see the larger *pattern* of frequently choosing to drink as having a kind of intractability; we see the will to choose drink as itself reflecting a powerful impetus having a deep source, deeper by far than the moment of choice.

But this difficulty in changing the large pattern is not an "impairment" of self-control; it is a normal feature of anyone's way of life. It is one of the conditions of being human, of being a person whose identity has psychic continuity and stability through time. This is no mystery or puzzle, no rarity, no pathology or disease needing a special explanation. Self-deception is a special phenomenon that complicates and confuses the situation, and thus exacerbates the difficulties in making rational change in one's way of life. And the disease concept of alcoholism elicits precisely this additional complication and confusion.

The analysis I have presented up to this point suggests a few things that might be said, finally, about strategies for dealing with long-term heavy drinkers.

Practical experience often teaches the futility of direct appeals to long-term heavy drinkers to stop drinking or to change their way of life.

But now we can see two very different sorts of reasons for this refractoriness to appeals.

When self-deception plays a role, the first and essential step to be taken before the person can appropriately respond to rational appeals to stop the drinking is to avow what was self-deceptively disavowed. Moralistic appeals to change one's conduct, however, tend to intensify the very motives that evoke self-deception. This is because the generic motive for self-deceptive disavowal lies in the tensions and conflict that are aroused within the person when there is avowal of engagements that clashes with other major values and propensities avowed by the person. These tensions to a great extent manifest themselves in the form of feelings of guilt and remorse, of self-hatred or self-contempt. Thus, in the case of the self-deceiver, any direct appeal, but especially a moralistic one, will intensify the very feelings that motivate the self-deception in the first place. Advocates of the disease concept of alcoholism never tire of pointing out the futility of preaching to alcoholics, but they explain the futility in terms of the drinker's disease and "loss of control," which purportedly makes compliance with the appeals as impracticable as an appeal to a sufferer of influenza to stop sneezing. It can now be seen, however, that this explanation for the frequent futility of direct moral appeals to the drinker can be replaced by the explanation in terms of self-deception. It follows from the latter account that any realistic and morally constructive tactic must aim at undoing self-deception, i.e., at bringing about conditions that encourage and facilitate candid avowal rather than self-deceptive disavowal. This becomes a ubiquitous necessity in a period when the disease concept of alcoholism has so captured the public imagination. I have no therapeutic program or grand strategy to offer; I have only tried to provide a conceptual framework within which to approach the problem.

Where self-deception is not an issue, it still remains true that *mere* preaching (or nagging) is unlikely to bring about a change in the long-term heavy drinker's way of life, any more than a mere "decision" to change is likely to suffice to actually change that person's way of life. But these things are true, as I have noted, for all of us, and are not peculiar to drinkers. Nevertheless, moralizing—or at least moral reflection and discourse—is less specifically contraindicated than in the case where self-deception does exist. For where there is candid avowal, moral comment is simply one of many kinds of possibly relevant comment, and is in general no more legitimate, but no less legitimate, than any other.

More than words and preaching, however, the concerned empathy and sympathy of others, their thoughtful and practical support and aid, and their judicious and commonsense use óf carrot and stick, are likely to have a greater impact in effecting appropriate objective changes in the drinker's way of life. To say this is to speak no more than common sense—and that is the upshot of this analysis, which aims to clear the air of pretense and deception and misinformation, but not to present a new theory of alcoholism. The argument is that we should eliminate the pseudoscientific proselytizing that induces self-deception. This should then leave us free to do all the things we usually would do to aid people in candidly exploring their life, and to aid them in changing how they live if that is what they want.

NOTES

1. Herbert Fingarette, *Self-Deception* (London: Routledge and Kegan Paul; New York: Humanities Press, 1969). See also the following works by the author on specific aspects of alcoholism: "The Perils of *Powell*: In Search of a Factual Foundation for the 'Disease Concept of Alcoholism,'" *Harvard Law Review* 83 (February 1970): 793–812; "How an Alcoholism Defense Works under the ALI Insanity Test," *International Journal of Law and Psychiatry* 2 (1979): 299–322; (with Ann F. Hasse) *Mental Disabilities and Criminal Responsibility* (Berkeley: University of California Press, 1979); and "Legal Aspects of Alcoholism and Other Addictions: Some Basic Conceptual Issues," *British Journal of Addiction* 76 (June 1981): 125–132.

2. Fingarette, *Self-Deception,* chap. 3.

3. Ibid., chap. 4.

4. Ibid., chap. 7, especially 141 ff.

5. Ibid., chap. 6.

6. Ibid., chap. 5.

7. Ibid., chap. 4, 67–71.

8. Herbert Fingarette, "Philosophical and Legal Aspects of the Disease Concept of Alcoholism," in *Research Advances in Alcohol and Drug Problems,* vol. 7, ed. Reginald G. Smart et al. (New York: Plenum Press, 1983), 1. This paper, with its extensive bibliography, provides a thorough and up-to-date analytical review of the relevant scientific and legal literature on the disease concept of alcoholism. The reader who is interested in the factual background for the claims made in the present paper is directed to the above paper, hereafter cited in brief as, Fingarette, "Disease Concept." There will be no attempt here to provide independent citation of the medical literature. Rather than intruding on the present text in a pedantic fashion by constant reference to the above article, I will simply state here that each factual claim in the present paper is specifically supported, and placed in the context of the relevant literature, pro and con, in Fingarette, "Disease Concept." Thus one can follow the logic of my present argument by reading the present paper; and if one wishes, one can also examine the primary sources for the scientific issues by referring to Fingarette, "Disease Concept," and to the full bibliography in it that is keyed to the specific issues.

9. For an excellent recent analytical survey of the literature from a primarily sociological standpoint (rather than the medical and legal standpoints of the work cited in note 8, above), see: Robin Room, "Sociological Aspects of the Disease Concept of Alcoholism," in *Research Advances* (cited in note 8, above), 47.

10. E. M. Jellinek, "Phases in the Drinking History of Alcoholics: Analysis of a Survey Conducted by the Official Organ of Alcoholics Anonymous," *Quarterly Journal of Studies on Alcohol* 7 (June 1946): 1.

11. E. M. Jellinek, *The Disease Concept of Alcoholism* (New Haven, Conn.: Hillhouse Press, 1960).

12. A major medical text contains the following opening paragraph on "Etiology" in the section on "Alcohol Abuse and Alcohol Related Illness": "No specific biologic, psychologic, or social variable has been shown to have high predictive value for determining which individuals are at high risk to develop and sustain problem drinking behavior. There are no known psychologic tests which can reliably differentiate alcohol abusers from normal drinkers. Many theories have purported to explain the causation of alcoholism in terms of psychodynamic factors, personality profiles, psychosocial developmental and growth characteristics, nutritional idiosyncrasies, allergic disorders, and specific and nonspecific metabolic derangements. To date, none of these theories of the causation of alcohol abuse or alcohol addiction have significant support from well-controlled laboratory and clinical investigations. The contribution of specific genetic and environmental factors which may enhance the risk for development of alcohol-related problems has not been clarified. . . . at present it appears reasonable to conclude that both genetic and developmental factors may contribute to the genesis of alcohol-related illness." Jack H. Mendelson, in *Textbook of Medicine*, ed. Paul B. Beeson and Walsh McDermott, 14th ed. (Philadelphia: W. B. Saunders, 1975), 597.

13. See, for example, the text on p. 310, and note 24 on pp. 310–311, in Fingarette, "How an Alcoholism Defense Works under the ALI Insanity Test."

14. See note 10, above.

15. He used a survey-questionnaire that had been printed on the first page of the *Grapevine*, the organ of Alcoholics Anonymous. This publication, as he reported, was typically subscribed to by groups rather than individuals; thus there were not anywhere near enough copies of the questionnaire distributed to give each individual member of AA a chance to reply. In fact, of about 1,000 copies distributed in toto, 98 were returned. Jellinek reduced this 10% response even further; he eliminated several questionnaires that had group answers stated in averages, and he eliminated all the women's responses because they did not fit the patterns he saw in the men's responses. Thus his analyses were based on the responses of a small, wholly male group, a self-selected small minority of the highly selective membership of one single organization!

16. Room's work in this area is highly informative. See note 9, above.

17. In general, these studies and experiments consist either (a) of making it possible for a person diagnosed as an "alcoholic" to have access to drink, or even inducing drinking, under conditions that significantly differ—e.g., a hospital program—from that person's usual life circumstances, or else (b) of "double-blind" tests where alcoholics are asked to drink, and allowed access to further drink, under a variety of conditions of knowledge or ignorance as to whether what they are drinking contains alcohol or not. The double-blind

experiments consistently show that alcoholics will drink more of the liquid that they *believe* to be alcoholic, even if in reality it is nonalcoholic, and will drink less of what they believe to be nonalcoholic, even if in reality it contains alcohol. Thus it is the *belief* rather than the actual chemical substance that seems to induce greater drinking. Moreover, in these, as in the other type of experiments mentioned, the alcoholics do not simply drink up all they can get, but control and moderate their drinking voluntarily. It is therefore plainly false that once an alcoholic takes a drink, an uncontrollable bout of drinking is triggered. It has been objected that the conditions of these experiments are different (''artificial,'' or ''supportive'') as compared to ''real life.'' This, of course, is irrelevant to the main point: Alcohol per se does not trigger uncontrollable drinking. Plainly, environment is a crucial factor, over and above whether alcohol is taken or not. Since the term ''alcoholic'' is used selectively to apply only to those who drink excessively in their everyday life, we naturally enough find, as noted in the text above, that when released from the hospital program and placed back into their usual life circumstances again, many of them do again drink excessively. The moral of this would seem to be that there is something about their everyday way of life, and not about the chemical alcohol per se, that engenders the heavy drinking.

    18. See Harry Levine, ''The Evidence from History: Good Creature of God—Demon Rum,'' *Proceedings* of Conference on Alcohol and Disinhibition, NIMH monograph, in press.

PART II
SHAPING THE SELF: INNER DISUNITY AND SOCIAL COPING

Introduction

Mike W. Martin

> Every ego, so far from being a unity, is in the highest degree a manifold world, a constellated heaven, a chaos of forms, of states and stages, of inheritances and potentialities.
>
> —Hermann Hesse, *Steppenwolf*

Consciousness is rife with conflicting desires, ambivalent emotions and attitudes, competing value commitments, and clashing inclinations to believe and disbelieve. Moreover, if Schopenhauer is right, "consciousness is the mere surface of our mind, and of this, as of the globe, we do not know the interior, but only the crust."[1] Fully attentive consciousness operates within wider contexts of mental activity and social interaction, which carry their own potential for discord. Amidst this welter, self-deception contributes to shaping our sense of identity, in addition to defending the unified aspects of our personalities via excuse making and disavowal.

The essays in Part I explored the extent to which self-deception helps preserve self-esteem and inner unity as we cope within society, and the next three essays develop this theme further, while emphasizing inner disunity. They proceed from the fundamental premise of social psychology that self-conceptions are largely shaped by how we interpret other people's interpretations of us. As social creatures we function as mirrors, one to another. Yet we are rarely altogether passive reflections of each other. We manage to select and adjust the social mirrors of the 'significant others' in our lives, thereby modifying our reflected appearances.

Daniel T. Gilbert and Joel Cooper set out to identify some of our subtle and intricate skills in this process. While their main interest is in interpersonal self-deceptive strategies used to form unduly generous self-appraisals, they begin by discussing "intrapersonal" strategies employed in directly distorting our own perceptions. Perceiving is not just something that happens to us; we actively interpret the raw data of experience by making inferences guided by "cognitive schemas." Cognitive schemas are sets of concepts, beliefs, and expectations about the world through which we filter experience, and our self-image can be regarded as such a schema. Experiments reveal that we have a marked tendency to select and emphasize information consistent with our preferred self-image. Nevertheless, this perceptual distortion operates only within narrow limits (so long as we are not psychotic), and although pervasive it is relatively mild.

Far more dramatic is the impact of self-deceptive strategies involving other people. The sheer complexity of social interaction operates as a smoke screen concealing our attempts to restructure the social environment in ways that sustain our self-esteem. A wide range of experiments reveals that we can influence other people's reactions to us by altering the manner in which we present ourselves before them. Via self-deception this "self-presentational feedback loop" becomes completed by reshaping or confirming typically generous self-conceptions in accordance with the reactions of those people we influence.

When confronted with situations that threaten our self-esteem, we can employ the further tactic of rendering our behavior ambiguous in ways that invite excuses. As we also saw in Part I, alcohol and drugs serve this purpose. Another tactic is to lessen the effort we put forth on a task in order (ironically) subsequently to defend our sense of competence: "The failure means nothing. I know I am able to do better; I just didn't try." Alternatively, we may seek to lower the standards by which we are judged and compared to others, even resorting to sabotaging friends' performances when we are being compared with them.

Timothy D. Wilson focuses on internal, intrapersonal, means of deceiving ourselves. He introduces a wide conception of self-deceptive strategies that encompasses virtually all self-caused failures to identify our own mental states. This enables him to locate willful self-deception and repression (unconsciously blocking a threatening truth from entering consciousness) along a wide spectrum of self-generated obstacles to self-knowledge. Like Gilbert and Cooper, Wilson begins with a brief consideration of self-deception in perception, suggesting that it is a special instance of selective attention and 'selective inattention' (to use a phrase made popular by Harry Stack Sullivan). The bulk of his essay, however, concerns self-deception about more complex mental states such as emotions, desires, and attitudes, which involve behavioral dispositions not always immediately visible through introspection. Learning about them is often akin to learning about other people, and unlike peering into a private box to which only we have access.

In order to explain our lack of self-awareness, whether purposeful or not, Wilson presents a model of the human mind as divided into two mental systems. One system is biologically primordial and enables us to react to the world largely without deliberation or "regulation" by consciousness. The other system is reflective or deliberative and functions by consciously regulating behavior and communicating with others. It also includes our ability to interpret and make conscious inferences about the nonconscious mental system. Wilson cites an array of experimental evidence, much of it from his own laboratory, suggesting that the two systems often act independently and inconsistently.

Because the conscious system often proceeds by basing its inferences on our chosen assumptions and self-images, it frequently generates biased interpretations, for example, our conscious beliefs about our affection and disaffection for other people, beliefs that are heavily influenced by our stereotypes about how we ought to feel. Our actual emotions may remain largely untouched by and quite different from what we infer about them. Another example is how monetary incentives generate alterations in our behavior without accompanying changes in our conscious beliefs about the behavior. And surprisingly, sometimes encouraging self-reflection ("priming the conscious explanatory system") can actually lessen accuracy in self-awareness by prompting rationalization and slanted intellectualizing: self-examination is sometimes inimical to self-understanding.

Throughout, Wilson is preoccupied with methodological questions about reliably testing his hypothesis of two distinct mental systems. The central problem is how to select behavioral manifestations of complex mental states so as to facilitate the accurate identification and diagnosis of them. Not only do such states involve a vast range of possible behavioral expressions, but each element of human behavior is susceptible to interpretation by reference to different kinds of mental states. As we shall see in Part IV, this problem of ambiguous behavior can generate skepticism about the possibility of willful self-deception, and for that reason Wilson devotes special care to it.

Benzion Chanowitz and Ellen J. Langer regard the expression "self-deception" as misleading insofar as it suggests that one unified self defends itself against a threatening aspect of the personality. The difficulty confronted by 'self-deceivers' arises precisely because people are not consistent, unified, selves. Each of us is composed of many "social selves," which function in semi-independence within particular social roles or types of circumstances. For example, there is the professional self, which functions at work, and the private self, which functions at home, and each of these selves may be composed of many more specialized subselves.

Within its native context, a given social self operates to preserve its essential inner coherence by expressing itself in conformity with the standards appropriate to that context. To a large extent it manages to pursue its self-expression and "self-protection" in the absence of special deliberation, conducting itself "mindlessly," that is, without attention to many of the details of its familiar environment and without attending to the other social selves loosely confederated to form one's character.

Of course the social selves are not completely insulated from one another. Even as they express themselves automatically they may retain some "dim awareness" of the other selves, and the person has a large general capacity for relating various social selves together in order to create a consistent unity. Such acts of incorporation or "self-inception" typically require explicit reflection and "mindful activity." A central problem of life—the problem confronted by individuals we misleadingly call self-deceivers—is when and how to allow two social selves to operate independently ("self-protection") and when and how to incorporate them into a higher synthesis as coordinated aspects of one more unified self ("self-inception").

Chanowitz and Langer develop their perspective by presenting some results of their experiments. People, they have found, tend to behave mindlessly (inattentively, uncritically) insofar as they interpret their social environment as routine and stable. By contrast, they act more mindfully (attentively, critically) when they view their circumstances as containing prospects for change and novelty ("labile contexts"), thereby increasing the prospects for self-inception. As they explore some of the factors that encourage or discourage mindful behavior, Chanowitz and Langer provide fresh commentary of topics dealt with in the preceding essays: alcoholism, self-handicapping behavior, self-esteem, and feelings of inferiority and superiority.

In different ways these three essays tend to deemphasize willful self-deception, which has been the focus of most philosophical discussions (such as those in Part III). Only Wilson explicitly defends the existence of purposeful self-deception, and he does so in the course of widening the topic of self-deception to include many other forms of limited access to our mental states. Gilbert and Cooper specify early in their essay that in speaking of "strategies" of self-deception, they do not mean to imply that self-deceivers act deliberately or with advance conscious planning of any kind. For them, "purposeful" self-deception means "serving a purpose" rather than acting with a purpose in mind. Again, in emphasizing mindless behavior, Chanowitz and Langer leave the impression that sheer ignorance and the sheer absence of purposeful acts of self-inception suffice to understand self-deception.

Yet it is worth asking whether the strategies described by Gilbert/Cooper and Chanowitz/Langer might sometimes be used in more intentional, voluntary, and even partially conscious ways that would warrant speaking of willful self-deception. After all, the social selves described by Chanowitz and Langer are supposed to retain some dim awareness of the person's other social selves, possibly sufficient for forming a tacit strategy to not engage in self-inception. And self-inception is supposedly an intentional act which we can to some degree purposefully choose to engage in or not engage in. If so, some of the differences they emphasize with Fingarette may turn out to be partly matters of emphasis (with Fingarette emphasizing the more unified self's decision not to incorporate a subself, and Chanowitz and Langer emphasizing the ability of subselves to pursue their own ends independently).

Furthermore, it would seem that the subtle interpersonal strategies identified by Gilbert and Cooper might sometimes by employed by self-deceivers who are more voluntary and intentional, less conditioned and determined. Sartre would insist on this. He would also recognize a more nearly literal meaning to Gilbert and Cooper's remark that "people may deceive themselves in deceiving others." Because of the direct relevance of purpose and willfulness to evaluating self-deceivers, one's response to these concerns will affect one's approach to the issues raised in Part III.

NOTE

1. Arthur Schopenhauer, *The World as Will and Representation*, vol. 2, trans. E. F. J. Payne (New York: Dover, 1966), 136.

Social Psychological Strategies of Self-Deception

Daniel T. Gilbert and Joel Cooper

O, what a tangled web we weave,
When first we practise to deceive!
—Sir Walter Scott, *Marmion*, Stanza 17.

The purpose of the present essay[1] is to explicate some of the strategies people use to deceive themselves about themselves—specifically, how they come to subscribe to overgenerous conceptions of themselves as competent, well-loved, and virtuous.[2] Although numerous psychological perspectives on self-deception may be drawn, we plan to sketch but one: a social psychological perspective founded in experimental research. Rather than attempt an exhaustive portrait, we shall try to explore the relevance of several currently important research topics for an understanding of self-deception. In so doing we shall return several times to different instances of the same set of assumptions, and thus it may be useful to try to spell them out here.

First, we assume that people are often egocentric and self-serving in their self-assessments, attempting to highlight their positive features and deemphasize their flaws, and ultimately coming to believe these somewhat optimistic portraits of themselves. Moreover, we assume that this tendency is functional, from both an information-processing and a motivational perspective. Greenwald's[3] conceptualization of the self as an information system that will sometimes distort information in order to maintain a coherent and stable view of the world seems particularly appropriate in this first regard. Greenwald argues that the ''beneffectance bias'' (the perception of responsibility for desired but not un-desired outcomes) is a fundamental and necessary process: information systems require information selection and distortion in order to preserve cognitive organization, and we conceive of self-deception as helping attain such ''systems benefits.'' Self-deception also helps a person attain the more obvious ''ego benefit'' of enhanced self-esteem, a crucial factor in most conceptualizations of normal personality functioning. The moral ramifications of such self-deceptive processes are adequately discussed in other essays in this volume, and as experimental psychologists, we shall try to leave such discussion in the more capable hands of philosophers. Nonetheless, it will probably become apparent that we do not necessarily construe self-deception as morally onerous but are prone to view it as a critical and adaptive part of both cognitive systems and social behavior.

Second, we assume that although people are deceived often, they are not deceived easily. To extend our first assumption, people may be self-serving and egocentric, but they do not like to think of themselves as such. If we are to put stock in our overgenerous self-assessments, we must see them as objectively derived, for while we are sometimes willing dupes, we are at the same time insightful ''naive psychologists,'' well aware of human tendencies to be self-serving. This knowledge of our own capacity for duplicity means that self-deceptive strategies must do more than merely produce inflated self-assessments; they must produce these outcomes in ways that seem reasonable, accurate, and fair. As we hope to convince the reader, social interaction is a fertile context for self-deception because its very complexity often acts as a ''smoke screen,'' keeping the self-deceptive process from becoming obvious. We do not doubt that powerful intrapsychic mechanisms operate to exile information from consciousness, and we shall consider some such mechanisms in our discussion of intrapersonal strategies. Our primary interest, however, is in the ubiquitous *social* strategies that people have developed to derive positive self-assessments that pose as accurate information.

Third, we assume that all of the self-deceptive procedures that we shall describe can be effected without benefit of consciousness. It is abundantly clear that behavior can be affected by information that is itself not available to conscious scrutiny.[4] People can enter a situation, extract its features, behave appropriately, and receive feedback about their behavior, all without a significant contribution from awareness.[5] In what sense is such behavior ''strategic''? We use the word strategic simply to indicate our belief that these behaviors serve a larger goal (cognitive organization, ego strengthening, etc.), but not to imply deliberation or planning. Rather, as we will argue later, the psychological benefits of self-deception act as reinforcers that sustain these behaviors in the person's repertoire, independently of his or her awareness. Throughout this essay we shall describe self-deceptive strategies as though the person were indeed behaving with calculated insincerity, but this narrative convenience should not obscure our conviction that self-deceptive strategies are complex but overlearned behavioral procedures that are conditioned and maintained by the contingencies of the social world and the needs of the individual.

The plan of the essay is first to discuss intrapersonal strategies of self-deception—how people accomplish the restructuring and reinterpretation of information that threatens to damage their self-esteem. Second, we will discuss interpersonal self-deceptive strategies—how people structure their social environments and social interactions such that the information produced by these environments and interactions is likely to be less ego-threatening. Again we caution that we have not attempted an even-handed representation of *the* social psychological perspective of self-knowing. Such an attempt would require that we also discuss research concerning strategies for *accurate* self-understanding—how people structure their perceptions and actions so that information achieves its maximum diagnostic value. Suffice it to say that we are interested, at present, in focusing our attention on but one aspect of human behavior: self-deception.

INTRAPERSONAL STRATEGIES

The most fundamental of self-deceptive strategies is the motivated distortion of perception itself. How an individual interprets the world logically depends upon how the world appears; however, experimental evidence suggests that perception is itself an inferential process. In attempting to understand how such processes operate, the notion of "cognitive schema" has been particularly useful. Typically, schemas are described as knowledge structures—a set of rules or expectations about the nature of a stimulus—that functions primarily as an "unconscious theory," preparing an individual to apprehend the stimulus in a particular way, just as scientific theories guide the scientist's research and thus condition the "facts" that he may find. A useful scientific theory will draw the scientist's attention to predicted, rather than anomalous, aspects of his inquiry, and will supply educated estimates when critical pieces of information are missing. Similarly, our schema for a stimulus causes us to search for expected features, and thus draws our attention to aspects of the stimulus that confirm our preconceptions. We may indeed "see what we expect to see" simply because our expectations have guided our attention to precisely these features of the stimulus. Too, when critical features of the stimulus are ambiguous or unknown, we may *infer* their probable values from knowledge contained within the schema. For example, when we see a dark, shadowy object atop the mantelpiece in our ill-lit study, we *know* that it is our old-fashioned clock, not a cat. This knowledge enables us to *see* the long, thin strand that hangs over the edge as an electrical cord, not a tail, and the triangular protrusions at the top as carved figurines rather than ears. This perception, born of expectation, is so compelling and complete that we are quite startled to see the "clock" spring from the mantelpiece and begin preening itself on the Oriental rug—until we remember that the clock is away for repair and the cat is not. Similar experiences underlie an entire family of powerful and familiar perceptual illusions that occur only because we *see* what we know *must* be. For both illusions and other schematic products, the expectations that condition these perceptions are not conscious; rather, because schemas operate at a preconscious stage in the perceptual process, the incoming information has a "given" quality to it. One does not *infer* a clock; one *sees* it.

Recently it has proved of some heuristic value to conceive of the self-concept as a schema.[6] This is not simply the same as saying that persons have a set of beliefs about themselves (i.e., a self-conception); it also implies that these beliefs have the capacity to affect perception in the ways we have mentioned. If schemas act to distort our perceptions of a stimulus so that they more closely resemble the schematic representations of that stimulus (i.e., what the stimulus is expected to be like), then we can easily imagine how these cognitive operations might afford perceptions of a world that confirms our already positive opinions of ourselves.

Swann and Read[7] have studied these confirmatory biases under the rubric of "self-verification." These investigators hypothesized that people maintain their stable self-conceptions by verifying them through social interaction. In an initial study, subjects who were classified as either "self-likers" or "self-dislikers" were led to believe that a future interaction partner probably (but not certainly) held a favorable or unfavorable expectancy about them. Subjects were later given an opportunity to study the future partner's evaluation of the subject (based on the subject's reported attitudes and values). Of course, the interaction partner was entirely fictitious. Subjects were in fact given an evaluation that contained both positive and negative items, each on a separate slide. Swann and Read measured the amount of time each subject spent considering the evaluation, and found that self-dislikers spent more time studying the evaluation of the partner whom they suspected disliked them, whereas self-likers spent more time considering the evaluation of the partner whom they suspected liked them. Thus, people spent more time considering information from sources whom they thought would confirm rather than disconfirm their self-conceptions.[8]

It is a common experience to come away from a seminar in which a proposed research project has been publicly thrashed, only to hear the author of the proposal reiterating to an absent colleague the modest praises of a lone dissenting voice. Is this merely a matter of public face saving? Possibly not. If the author, like most of us, came into the meeting with a positive conception of himself, we can expect that he spent more time considering the comments of the lone dissenter who praised the project (and confirmed his self-conception) than of the colleagues who disliked it, thus mercifully "softening" the cavalcade of criticism. Schemas may operate to focus the perceptual experience on such "schema-congruent" sources of information, which may lead information from such sources to be overrepresented in perceptual products (percepts, judgments, memories, etc.), thus perpetuating a person's positive self-conception.[9]

Self-schemas verify positive self-conceptions not only by drawing attention to selected aspects of the feedback we receive, filling in gaps with self-enhancing information, or by assimilating ambiguous information to a positive self-conception, but also by undermining disconfirming information. Lord, Ross, and Lepper[10] have shown that people who were asked to evaluate research studies on the effects of capital punishment found more technical flaws in the methodology of studies that disconfirmed rather than confirmed their private beliefs—regardless of how the study was actually conducted. If the self-concept is a theory that we hold about ourselves, then we might expect similar effects in the domain of self-assessment. Such effects have been found; people place less faith in the *validity* of information that disconfirms rather than confirms their self-conception.[11] As we have noted, theories about the self may serve much the same function for the individual that Kuhn[12] suggests scientific theories serve for scientists—they may preserve the *status quo* by labeling disconfirming evidence "anomalous," thus allowing the progress of normal functioning (or normal science, as the case may be).[13]

Thus, people may deceive themselves about themselves by assimilating what they perceive to the expectations they hold, paying greater attention to instances that confirm rather than disconfirm their expectations, and by being hypercritical of disconfirming information. In what sense, though, are these biased perceptions products of a process that warrants the label of self-deception? There has been a great deal of debate in social psychology recently about whether perceptual distortion of this kind is engendered by motivational concerns (the need to see oneself in a positive light, etc.) or whether it is simply a byproduct of normal cognitive processes.[14] It seems to us, however, that this "Hobson's choice" risks missing an important point, namely, that the kinds of cognitive processes in which people engage are only some among the many kinds in which they *might engage*. Therefore, it is reasonable to ask why people think the way they do rather than in some other, equally plausible way. A thinking system does not *demand* schematic operations, and yet schematic operations seem aptly to characterize human information systems. One reason (among many) that people may engage such cognitive processes is because they culminate in self-enhancing products. We have already mentioned that self-enhancement can have functional consequences, and it seems quite possible that these benefits serve to reinforce the use of cognitive processes such as schematic operations. The point here is that if we can explain the use of particular cognitive operations by virtue of their benefits, including self-enhancement, then schematic biases are no less examples of self-deception than are more clearly motivationally induced biases. Motivation may well exert its influence on perception by selecting for certain cognitive operations (i.e., those that result in self-enhancing perceptions) and against others (i.e., those that do not). In this sense, motivational and cognitive accounts of information-processing bias constitute different *levels* of description rather than competing explanations.

The purpose of this section has been to argue that self-deception functions at a very basic, perceptual level. Yet, we cannot help but think that the value of these conceptions lies mainly in the light they shed on cognitive process, but that in terms of self-deception they must account for a rather small portion of the variance inherent in self-enhancement. The author whose research proposal was criticized may hold somewhat more charitable beliefs about the proceedings than do his critics, but essentially all parties will agree that the proposal was not well received. That is, the *magnitude* of perceptual bias must be limited (except in some unusual cases) to slight variation on the facts. Were this not so, people would perceive reality in such idiosyncratic ways as to eliminate the potential for social interaction. We are often asked by perplexed students how people can navigate through their everyday affairs if their most basic cognitive processes conspire to produce a distorted, autistic picture of the world. One answer (the one we have touched on) is that there are benefits to seeing things as they are not. The other answer is, of course, that perceptual bias, though systematic and pervasive, is really quite mild. The cat is mistaken for a clock only in a shadowy room and only for a moment, and never is it mistaken for a goat, a television set, or a locomotive. This realization acknowledges an essential tension between accurate perception and gratifying perception that we suspect is resolved largely (though by no means completely) in favor of accuracy.[15] Is self-deception then limited to minute effects that are significant only under conditions designed to inspect them? We do not think so, and the next section seeks to corroborate this belief.

INTERPERSONAL STRATEGIES

Imagine a person who is wired to a machine capable of diagnosing, without error, his true personality, and that at his request, the machine will accurately reveal his standing on a number of characterological dimensions. There is a chance, of course, that the machine will inform him that he is hopelessly incompetent and unintelligent. In order to avoid the unpleasantness associated with these revelations, the person might distort the information as it is imparted—coming to believe, for instance, that *most* of what the machine revealed was flattering, or that the machine actually said *"exceptionally considerate,"* not *"you're an idiot."* As we have noted, however, there are pressures on the individual to perceive information accurately, and accomplishing such distortion may require on optimal set of circumstances that are not currently in force. There is, however, a second strategy the person might follow in order to temper the unwelcome evaluation: the individual may choose to unfold his pocket knife and "fix" the machine so as to increase the probability that the machine's evaluation will be flattering rather than deprecating.

The point of this allegory is that people may find it easier to operate on their environments in ways designed to structure the information that the environments produce, than to distort the information after it has already been produced. As we hope to demonstrate, the "fixing" that people do is often routed rather tortuously through the social milieu and, as a result, is sufficiently removed from the resultant "fixed" information as to keep the connection from becoming obvious. Too, these strategies may be able to accomplish much larger self-deceptive ends for the individual, operating as they do at the inferential, rather than perceptual, level.

SELF-PRESENTATIONAL FEEDBACK LOOPS

In a complex social network, people govern each other's outcomes, acting as gatekeepers who control rewards and mete out punishments. Such mutual interdependence requires people to arrive at a shared conception of social reality, including that aspect of social reality known as the self. In a popular work, Goffman[16] explored this symbolic interactionist notion with his dramaturgical approach to the negotiation of social identity, arguing that people present themselves in particular ways in order to convey to others a definition of both themselves and the situation, thus negotiating with the other "players" a mutual understanding of both the players' roles and the play. Jones and Pittman[17] also have recognized the consequences of social interdependence for the presentation of self but have instead emphasized the power augmentation motive that such interdependence promotes for the individual. Jones and Pittman have developed a taxonomy of self-presentational strategies, each designed to elicit from the target of the self-presentational attempt a specific attribution about the self-presenter that will act to increase his interpersonal power.

There is, at first blush, something puzzling about theories of self-presentation. If we are prone to present ourselves in ways that are at odds with our true dispositions, should we not be aware of this tendency in others, thus disarming them in their self-presentational gambits? Indeed, the basic postulates of attribution theory, a theory that deals with the naive attempts of people to understand the causes of behavior, suggest that behavior elicited by self-presentational concerns should not be used to infer the existence of an underlying disposition that corresponds to the observed behavior, because the self-presentational demands on the actor are sufficient to explain the behavior without recourse to such dispositional attributions.[18] Yet, a consistent finding of attributional research is that people do in fact infer correspondent dispositions from observations of behavior that could easily be attributed to external demands, such as the self-presentational demands of the situation. Jones and Harris[19] asked students to read speeches said to have been prepared under highly constraining conditions (i.e., written at the instruction of a debate coach who determined the position to be advocated) and then to estimate the disposition of the essay writer. Although the external constraints on the essay writers were sufficient to explain the positions advocated in the speeches they had supposedly written, subjects inferred that the essay writers held mildly correspondent opinions. Essay writers instructed to write speeches in favor of Castro's regime were rated as being more pro-Castro than were essay writers who were assigned to write anti-Castro speeches. Similar results have been obtained in many attributional domains, including the attribution of attitudes, abilities, and personality characteristics.[20] This tendency to overestimate the role of dispositions in the genesis of behavior has been implicated as the fundamental source of many other attributional errors,[21] but for our purposes, it is simply important to note that people may present themselves to others in ways that are blatantly aimed at power augmentation, and yet leave others with the impression that these actions are diagnostic of underlying attitudes, values, or features of personality.

Of what relevance is this to self-deception? Initially, we would suggest that the relative ease with which our self-presentational behaviors become others' conceptions of us is of particular importance in that the targets of our self-presentations may reciprocally convince us of the validity of their impressions. As many theorists have noted,[22] our self-conceptions hinge upon others' conceptions of us. In jointly constructing social reality, people mutually determine each other's identities—we become, in a sense, what others believe us to be. In their study of "behavioral confirmation," Snyder, Tanke, and Berscheid[23] showed subjects photographs that led them to believe that a future interaction partner of the opposite sex was either physically attractive or unattractive. Given only this expectation of their partner's appearance, subjects were allowed to interact with the partner (another naive subject) via an intercom while (unbeknownst to the subjects) the conversation was recorded. It is perhaps not surprising that subjects came to conclude that their partners were more sociable, poised, and humorous when the subject expected the partner to be attractive rather than unattractive. We have already discussed how expectations can come to influence perceptions. However, some time after the experiment, a new set of student-judges, listening only to the partner's half of the recorded conversation, concluded the same thing. In other words, the subject's belief in the partner's attractiveness not only influenced the subject's conclusion, but actually caused the partner to behave in a manner consistent with these expectations.

In one sense, then, people may deceive themselves by deceiving others. We may present ourselves in ways that underscore our best traits and obscure our worst, and because of the tendency to draw correspondent inferences from behavior, others may credit us with these characteristics. In the course of interaction, the people we know may somehow cause us to behave as they expect us to behave. Yet, is it reasonable to assume that having behaved this way, we will ourselves conclude that we possess these characteristics? Bem's[24] work on self-perception suggests that we will. If our behavior is shaped by subtle social forces, we may fail to recognize these as the true causes of our actions, concluding that we do indeed possess the dispositions we were once merely pretending to possess.[25] There are several links in this "self-presentational feedback loop," any one of which might fail to occur, thus obviating the net result of self-deception. However, each of the phenomena we have discussed is a reliable effect, readily produced in the laboratory, and it thus seems reasonable to assume that such loops do, at least occasionally, make their final connection.

SELF-PRESENTATION AND COGNITIVE DISSONANCE

Let us return for a moment to our mention of self-presentational strategies. As Jones[26] notes, there is often a somewhat distasteful ambience that pervades the notion of self-presentation, probably because of our cultural emphasis on genuineness and sincerity in our public dealings. Yet, the mutual interdependence of individuals in social systems places a premium on disingenuity and insincerity, at least with some of the people some of the time, thus subtly coercing self-presentational behavior. What might be the result of subtly coercing people to behave in ways that are at once both strategically advantageous and culturally disdained? A classic social psychological theory speaks to just such a situation. Festinger's[27] theory of cognitive dissonance maintains that simultaneously held beliefs that are logically inconsistent will result in a psychological tension state—a state of cognitive dissonance—that can only be attenuated by rectifying the inconsistency. Zanna and Cooper[28] have shown that this notion of cognitive tension or arousal is more than a mere metaphor: when inconsistent beliefs are induced in subjects, physiological arousal is demonstrably present, and under some circumstances, measurable.[29]

Typically, dissonance is produced by inconspicuously coaxing subjects to behave in ways that are at odds with their basic beliefs. If subjects perceive themselves as having a modicum of choice (although they are in fact coerced by the experimenter to engage in these behaviors), their basic self-conceptions will change to accommodate their new behavior. College students who are artfully induced to write an editorial in favor of the campus police will come to hold more favorable opinions of the police. According to dissonance theory, the simultaneous beliefs that the person is both ill-disposed toward policemen and has written an editorial in their support are logically inconsistent, and since the behavior cannot be "undone," the attitude must be changed. The subtlety of the coercion is paramount; Linder, Cooper, and Jones[30] have shown that if dissonance is to be produced, subjects must feel that the experimenter's carefully phrased request constitutes an insufficient justification for writing the editorial. When the experimenter's request is blatant and powerful, neither dissonance nor subsequent attitude change occurs. Evidently, a request that cannot be refused is a sufficient justification for engaging in the counter-attitudinal behavior, and thus there is no logical inconsistency to be remedied.

In what way does this "insufficient justification" paradigm shed light on the present concerns? Given the cultural disapproval of insincere behavior, people should feel somewhat anxious about promoting a false persona simply in order to augment their power in interpersonal relations. Their simultaneous beliefs that they are good people, that they are presenting themselves falsely, and that good people do not present themselves falsely constitute a trio of incompatible cognitions, one of which must be altered in order to achieve a degree of intrapsychic harmony. In this case, both cultural norms and core self-conceptions may be relatively immune to change, and thus the least resistant member of the threesome ("I am presenting myself falsely") may be modified ("I am presenting myself as I really am"). In this way, people may come to believe their own self-presentations, simply in order to alleviate the dissonance associated with disingenuous behavior.[31]

Thus far, we have suggested that people may accomplish self-deceptive goals simply by attempting to deceive others. Yet, shouldn't others be able to follow this line of reasoning themselves, thus rendering such strategies transparent and impotent? We suspect that the links in the self-presentational feedback loop are sufficiently numerous, complex, and counterintuitive as to make such reasoning unlikely. Furthermore, we suspect that the conditioning techniques that people use to shape our behavior to their expectancies are every bit as subtle as the experimenter's request in the insufficient justification paradigm and, as such, do not facilitate their identification as the actual causes of behavior. In this volume and elsewhere (cf. note 4), Wilson argues that people do not *identify* the causes of their behavior at all; rather, they select a likely causal agent from among a set of culturally approved candidates. Until the notion of "behavioral confirmation" becomes an accepted part of the cultural wisdom, we can expect that people will continue to misidentify their actions as dispositionally produced.

Similarly, the elements of social interdependence that mandate ingenuous behavior and that might thus serve as a reasonable justification for its performance are equally difficult to identify and thus do not adequately quell the intrapsychic tension of cognitive dissonance. Again we would rush to reiterate our earlier claim that none of these strategies need function at the level of awareness. People may *incidentally* learn that self-presentation is a useful way to "fix" the information they receive about themselves as well as a potent trigger for dissonance-reducing mechanisms. If there are, as we claim, significant psychological benefits to seeing oneself in a positive way, then strategic self-presentation should be adequately reinforced to sustain itself as a permanent feature of social behavior.

SELF-HANDICAPPING AND ATTRIBUTE AMBIGUITY

Just as the need for accuracy places a limit on the degree of perceptual distortion that can be tolerated, performance requirements may hold self-presentational misrepresentation in check. We are not permitted drastically to misrepresent ourselves without ultimately coming to be asked to support our self-advertisements with verifiable behavior. Often, too, we may suspect that the outcomes of such acid tests will not speak well of our capacities and talents, that they will lower others' opinions of us and, more importantly, our opinion of ourselves. We have seen how people may attempt to structure the information they receive about themselves through actions designed to increase the likelihood that the information will be positive, but what do people do in situations in which the information is likely to be negative and unalterable? Given that self-presentations demand occasional supporting performances, how might people use performance opportunities to deceive themselves about their abilities?

Berglas and Jones[32] suggest that if the individual considers it likely that his performance will provide negative feedback about his competence in some domain, he will attempt to *ambiguate* the meaning of this potentially negative performance feedback by creating credible alternative explanations for his poor performances. Under some circumstances, this quest for ambiguity will actually necessitate the individual's sabotaging his own performance simply to muddy the meaning of its outcome. Berglas and Jones asked subjects to complete an initial series of insoluble problems and then gave them feedback indicating that they had done extremely well. Unbeknownst to these subjects, success was not contingent upon their performance, and presumably this created anxiety about whether they would continue to do as well on an expected second experimental task (another series of similar problems). Prior to completing the second task, subjects were told that the experimenter was testing the effects of two new drugs—Pandocrin and Actavil—which supposedly had the respective effects of either inhibiting or facilitating performance on the test. Subjects were then given a choice about which drug they would like to take before embarking upon the second task. As Berglas and Jones's notion of "self-handicapping" would predict, the majority of (male) subjects chose to take Pandocrin, the performance inhibitor, undermining their likelihood of success in service of ambiguity.

How does this finding translate into more usual social behavior? Jones and Berglas[33] suggest that the appeal of performance-inhibiting drugs such as alcohol may be at least partially understood in terms of self-handicapping strategies. Alcohol, like the fictitious Pandocrin, is reputed to interfere with performance. Thus, alcohol consumption prior to a performance allows one to externalize potential failures, blaming one's poor showing on the drug and thus protecting one's self-conception of competence. In addition, should the performance somehow result in success, an "augmentation effect"[34] should occur such that self-competence beliefs are actually enhanced beyond what a non-handicapped performance might provide ("I did well in *spite* of being drunk").

Jones and Berglas suggest that underachievement may also be conceived of as a self-handicapping strategy that utilizes the withdrawal of a facilitative agent (effort) rather than the imposition of an inhibitory agent (alcohol). The classic attributional model of the causes of behavior argues that the individual's effort combines multiplicatively with his abilities to determine his outcomes. Thus the well-known conceptual equation: $(E \times A) \pm TD = B$, in which effort times ability, plus or minus task difficulty equals the behavioral outcome.[35] There is no claim, of course, that these are the true determinants of behavior; rather, the assertion is that people *believe* these to be the determinants of behavior. The equation is meant to represent a phenomenological conceptualization of action.

Working with this action equation, Jones and Berglas note that when the effort component for the equation is brought to zero, the equation cannot be "solved" for ability, i.e., behavior does not have clear diagnostic value. Thus, although the withdrawal of effort may have dire social consequences of its own,[36] it can function to protect beliefs in one's own competence and ability. There is some evidence that students classified as academic underachievers pursue just such a strategy.[37] Working with a different component of the action equation (TD), Frankel and Snyder[38] demonstrated that subjects were more likely to expend effort on a difficult task rather than an easy one after a noncontingent experience of failure, which usually inhibits later effort expenditure, presumably because failure on a difficult task does not have clear and damaging implications for ability, whereas failure on an easier task does.

The work of Jones and Berglas deals primarily with the protection of competence images. In their work on attribute ambiguity, Melvin Snyder and his colleagues have explored the use of similar strategies by people seeking to deceive themselves about their own beliefs and social motives.[39] Snyder, Kleck, Strenta, and Mentzer[40] brought subjects into a large room that was partitioned at one end. The subject could see that on each side of the partition was a video monitor and two chairs. A handicapped person (actually an experimental confederate) sat on one side of the partition and a "normal" person (also a confederate) on the other. In one condition of the experiment, the two video monitors displayed different movies, whereas in the other condition they displayed the same movie. Subjects were told that they could choose to sit on either side of the partition and watch either monitor. They were told that their task was simply to complete a questionnaire about the movie they chose to watch.

This unique situation presents subjects with an interesting attributional problem. If we assume that subjects wish to avoid the handicapped person but do not wish to think of themselves as bigoted or unkind, the "different-movie" condition provides an opportunity to shun the handicapped person while leaving the *reason* for that choice unclear (Did he want to avoid the handicapped person, or did he *prefer* to watch *Slapstick* rather than *Sad Clowns*?). For subjects who found the same movie displayed on both monitors, the situation generates no such alternative explanation—avoidance of the handicapped person clearly indicates a corresponding motive, because this is the only thing that differentiates the seating choices. In line with this reasoning, subjects in the "same-movie" condition chose to sit with the handicapped person significantly more often than did subjects in the "different-movie" condition.

As the work on self-handicapping and attribute ambiguity clearly demonstrates, people are adept at structuring the contexts within which their performances occur so that the information gleaned has uncertain implications that are not likely to damage self-esteem. Performances have consequences beyond the merely informational, however. Social interdependence means that others will be affected by our behavior, and that we may exert some control over their performances as well as our own. Our last section seeks to address this issue.

SOCIAL COMPARISON AND THE SEM MODEL

Of what use is it to know that we can run a six-minute mile, publish five articles in three years, or score seventy-two out of one hundred points on an intelligence test? By itself, such information is virtually worthless, because its meaning can be assessed only with regard to the relative normality of these accomplishments. Only when we compare our lap time, vita, or test score with the outcomes of others do we gain insight about our abilities. Festinger's[41] theory of social comparison formalizes many of the principles presumed to guide this process by which people seek comparative information. These postulates assume that people seek to understand themselves, and thus the theory explicates a rational program for the acquisition of accurate information about the self. There seems little doubt that the theory is generally correct under many circumstances, but in the years since its appearance, it has become apparent that acquiring accurate comparison information can have painful consequences for self-esteem (e.g., when we find that our grandmother runs the same course in five and a half minutes or that the national norm on the intelligence test we took is eighty-nine).

Tesser and Campbell[42] have recently offered their Self-Evaluation Maintenance (SEM) model to predict the circumstances under which other people's achievements will make us feel good or bad, and what we will do to invite the former and avoid the latter. Essentially, Tesser and Campbell postulate that the successfulness of the other person's performance, the psychological closeness of the other to oneself, and the relevance of the performance dimension to one's own self-definition will interact in a systematic fashion to determine whether we will compare ourselves with another, and if so, how pleasurable or painful that comparison will be. When the dimension is of little relevance to our self-definition (e.g., athletic ability to a librarian), we will engage in a *reflection* process, by which the achievements of a person close to us cause us to feel proud and satisfied. However, when the dimension is highly relevant to our self-definition (athletic ability to a basketball player), a *comparison* process is invoked, by which the achievements of a close other cause us to appear to ourselves incapable, thus promoting jealousy and recrimination.

The SEM model makes specific predictions for behavior relevant to one of the three critical factors (closeness, performance outcome, relevance of dimension) when the other two are held constant. In an intriguing study, Tesser and Smith[43] brought subjects in groups of four into the laboratory to complete a word identification task. For each subject, one of the four persons was known to be his close friend. Each subject was given feedback indicating that he was not particularly adept at the word identification task, which was described to half of the subjects as a measure of an important verbal skill, and to the remaining subjects as a mere game. Subjects were then given the opportunity to give clues to the other people in their group as these members tried to complete the same word identification task. Under these circumstances, the SEM model predicts that comparing oneself to a close other (a friend) on a relevant dimension (when the task is an important skill) will be painful to the extent that one is outperformed by the other individual. What can subjects do to ensure that such painful comparison is not possible?

It would seem somewhat difficult to alter either the relevance of the task or the closeness of the other individual, but in this situation subjects *can* influence the other individual's performance, increasing the likelihood that he, too, will do poorly. This is precisely what Tesser and Smith found. Subjects gave less useful clues to strangers than to friends when the task was described as a mere game (i.e., the dimension was irrelevant to self-definition), but they gave less useful clues to friends than to strangers when the task was described as an important test of verbal ability. In other words, subjects sought to interfere with their friends' performances, presumably in order to reduce the likelihood that they would be forced to compare themselves with someone who outperformed them and thus made them feel incompetent.

In a related experiment, Tesser and Paulhus[44] held constant the performance of a close other and found that subjects did indeed lower the self-relevance of the dimension when the other individual performed well, and also demonstrated that this effect was not simply a matter of public face saving but, rather, a strategy designed to prevent loss of self-esteem. These and several other studies attest to the general utility of the SEM model. If the performances of others serve as a context that provides meaning for our own performances, then we may deceive ourselves about our competence by lowering the standards of comparison (e.g., sabotaging the other person's performance). The SEM model, then, provides a systematic picture of the ways in which people may alter the meaning of the self-relevant feedback they receive by influencing the behavior of others.

CODA

The purpose of the present essay has been to present a social psychological perspective on self-deception. We have argued that in order to maintain their positive self-conceptions, people may distort the information they process about themselves, paying greater attention to information that confirms their self-conceptions or more critically scrutinizing information that disconfirms it. Alternatively, people may act upon their environments so that self-relevant information is likely to be self-enhancing or, at worst, ambiguous, and they may actively influence the performances of others in order to provide a more gratifying yardstick against which to measure themselves. Too, the demands of social interaction may instigate a psychological tension state that can be alleviated only through self-deceptive practices.

The portrait of people as self-deceivers provides an underlying dynamic for a vast body of social psychological thought, and in general, the experimental data attest to the validity of this conception. At the same time, the experiments we have discussed tell us only that these types of processes *can* occur; they do not supply us with any actuarial information about the *frequency* with which such behaviors occur. Throughout, we have tried to caution that inferential irrationality— whether in the form of informational distortion or situation "fixing"— cannot be the whole picture. Rather, there is a delicate balance struck between rational information seeking and self-enhancing goals, permitting us to avoid some, but only some, of the painful sequelae of accurate self-knowledge. The point to extract from this essay is that people are quite able to deceive themselves about their own inner qualities by altering the information they receive, choosing performance settings inappropriate to diagnostic ends, or by lowering the standards against which they must be measured. There are also a significant number of studies, however, that demonstrate conceptually opposite effects: people can be rational, willing to accept blame for their poor performances, and may seek situations in which their true mettle will be tested. Which of these perspectives is the right one? We suspect that each is true under its own special set of circumstances. As McGuire[45] argues, human behavior cannot be made to fit the Procrustean bed of a single psychological perspective; neither the rational nor the irrational can by itself capture the richness and complexity of human behavior. Our burden is to separate those circumstances that promote a quest for self-understanding from those that promote self-deception.

NOTES

1. The authors wish to thank Ned Jones, Abe Tesser, and Bill Swann for their valuable comments on an earlier version of this essay.

2. The current essay construes as self-deceptive those processes by which self-assessments are enhanced. Of course, the depressive who mercilessly derogates himself may also be engaging in self-deception, but for the purposes of this essay we shall restrict ourselves to the former definition.

3. Anthony G. Greenwald, "The Totalitarian Ego: Fabrication and Revision of Personal History," *American Psychologist* 35 (1980): 603–618.

4. Richard E. Nisbett and Timothy D. Wilson, "Telling More Than We Can Know: Verbal Reports on Mental Processes," *Psychological Review* 82 (1975): 231–259.

5. Ellen J. Langer, "Rethinking the Role of Thought in Social Interaction," in *New Directions in Attribution Research*, vol. 2, ed. John H. Harvey, William Ickes, and Robert F. Kidd (Hillsdale, N.J.: Erlbaum, 1978).

6. Hazel Markus, "Self-Schemata and Processing Information about the Self," *Journal of Personality and Social Psychology*, 35 (1977): 63–78.

7. William B. Swann and Stephen J. Read, "Self-Verification Processes: How We Sustain Our Self-Conceptions," *Journal of Experimental Social Psychology* 17 (1981): 351–372.

8. It is important to note that subjects did not spend more time considering *information* that confirmed their self-conceptions—all subjects spent more time considering negative than positive items. Rather, subjects spent more time considering items from suspected confirming *sources*.

9. Of course, in some situations, schemas will lead to better memory for schema-*incongruent* information (see, for example, Reid Hastie, "Schematic Principles in Human Memory," in *Social Cognition: The Ontario Symposium*, vol. 1, ed. E. Tory Higgins, C. Peter Herman, and Mark P. Zanna [Hillsdale, N.J.: Erlbaum, 1981]). Also, for people with low self-esteem, positive feedback about the self *is* schema-incongruent.

10. Charles G. Lord, Lee Ross, and Mark R. Lepper, "Biased Assimilation and Attitude Polarization: The Effects of Prior Theories on Subsequently Considered Evidence," *Journal of Personality and Social Psychology* 37 (1979): 2098–2109.

11. For a review see J. Sidney Shrauger, "Responses to Evaluation as a Function of Initial Self-Perceptions," *Psychological Bulletin* 82 (1975): 581–596.

12. Thomas S. Kuhn, *The Structure of Scientific Revolutions* (Chicago: University of Chicago Press, 1962).

13. See John M. Darley and Charles Huff, "Person Perception as a Kuhnian Process: A Paradigm-Based Model of Attribution," unpublished manuscript (Princeton University, 1983).

14. See, for example, Dale T. Miller and Michael Ross, "Self-Serving Biases in the Attribution of Causality: Fact or Fiction?" *Psychological Bulletin* 82 (1975): 213–235. See also Philip E. Tetlock and Ariel Levi, "Attribution Bias: On the Inconclusiveness of the Cognition-Motivation Debate." *Journal of Experimental Social Psychology* 18 (1982): 68–88.

15. See the discussion of "basic antinomy" in Edward E. Jones and Harold B. Gerard, *Foundations of Social Psychology* (New York: Wiley, 1967).

16. Erving Goffman, *The Presentation of Self in Everyday Life* (Garden City, N.Y.: Anchor Books, 1959).

17. Edward E. Jones and Thane Pittman, "Toward a General Theory of Strategic Self-Presentation," in *Psychological Perspectives on the Self*, vol. 1, ed. Jerry Suls (Hillsdale, N.J.: Erlbaum, 1982).

18. See. Edward E. Jones and Keith Davis, "From Acts to Dispositions: The Attribution Process in Person Perception," in *Advances in Experimental Social Psychology*, vol. 2, ed. Leonard Berkowitz (New York: Academic Press, 1965). Also see Harold H. Kelley, "Attribution Theory in Social Psychology," in

Nebraska Symposium on Motivation, vol. 15, ed. David Levine (Lincoln: University of Nebraska Press, 1967).

19. Edward E. Jones and Victor A. Harris, "The Attribution of Attitudes," *Journal of Experimental Social Psychology* 3 (1967): 1–24.

20. For a review see Edward E. Jones, "The Rocky Road from Acts to Dispositions," *American Psychologist* 34 (1979): 107–117.

21. For a forward-looking discussion of this phenomenon see (especially chap. 4 of) Gustav Ichheiser, "Misunderstandings in Human Relations: A Study in False Social Perception," *American Journal of Sociology* 55 (1949): pt. 2. For a more up-to-date discussion see Lee Ross, "The Intuitive Psychologist and His Shortcomings: Distortions in the Attribution Process," in *Advances in Experimental Social Psychology*, vol. 10, ed. Leonard Berkowitz (New York: Academic Press, 1977).

22. For example, Charles H. Cooley, *Human Nature and the Social Order* (New York: Scribner's, 1902); George H. Mead, *Mind, Self, and Society* (Chicago: University of Chicago Press, 1934); Harry Stack Sullivan, *The Interpersonal Theory of Psychiatry* (New York: Norton, 1953).

23. Mark Snyder, Elizabeth D. Tanke, and Ellen Berscheid, "Social Perception and Interpersonal Behavior: On the Self-Fulfilling Nature of Social Stereotypes," *Journal of Personality and Social Psychology* 35 (1977): 656–666.

24. Daryl Bem, "Self-Perception Theory," in *Advances in Experimental Social Psychology*, vol. 6, ed. Leonard Berkowitz (New York: Academic Press, 1972).

25. The reader will note that this is another example of persons underestimating situational contributions to behavior. In this case, however, the perceiver and the perceived are the same person.

26. Edward E. Jones, *Ingratiation* (New York: Appleton-Century-Crofts, 1964).

27. Leon Festinger, *A Theory of Cognitive Dissonance* (Stanford: Stanford University Press, 1957).

28. Mark P. Zanna and Joel Cooper, "Dissonance and the Pill: An Attributional Approach to Studying the Arousal Properties of Dissonance," *Journal of Personality and Social Psychology* 29 (1974): 703–709.

29. Robert T. Croyle and Joel Cooper, "Dissonance Arousal: Physiological Evidence," *Journal of Personality and Social Psychology* 45 (1983): 782–791.

30. Darwin E. Linder, Joel Cooper, and Edward E. Jones, "Decision Freedom as a Determinant of the Role of Incentive Magnitude in Attitude Change," *Journal of Personality and Social Psychology* 3 (1967): 245–254.

31. Barry R. Schlenker makes a similar point, though from a different perspective, in his interesting chapter, "Translating Actions into Attitudes: An Identity-Analytic Approach to the Explanation of Social Conduct," in *Advances in Experimental Social Psychology*, vol. 15, ed. Leonard Berkowitz (New York: Academic Press, 1982).

32. Steven Berglas and Edward E. Jones, "Drug Choice as a Self-Handicapping Strategy in Response to Non-Contingent Success," *Journal of Personality and Social Psychology* 36 (1978): 405–417.

33. Edward E. Jones and Steven Berglas, "Control of Attributions about the Self through Self-Handicapping Strategies: The Appeal of Alcohol and the Role of Underachievement," *Personality and Social Psychology Bulletin* 4 (1978): 200–206.

34. Harold H. Kelley, "Attribution in Social Interaction," in *Attribution: Perceiving the Causes of Behavior,* ed. Edward E. Jones et al. (Morristown, N.J.: General Learning Press, 1971). See also Jones and Davis, "From Acts to Dispositions."

35. See, for example, Fritz Heider, *The Psychology of Interpersonal Relations* (New York: Wiley, 1958). See also John M. Darley and George R. Goethals, "People's Analyses of the Causes of Ability-Linked Performances," in *Advances in Experimental Social Psychology,* vol. 13, ed. Leonard Berkowitz (New York: Academic Press, 1980).

36. Edward E. Jones and Richard deCharms, "The Organizing Function of Interaction Roles in Person Perception," *Journal of Abnormal and Social Psychology* 57 (1958): 155-64. See also Darley and Goethals, "People's Analyses."

37. Janet M. Riggs, "The Effect of Performance Attributions on the Choice of Achievement Strategy" (Ph.D. diss., Princeton University, 1982). See also Elizabeth A. Preston, "The Role of Effort Expenditure in Academic Achievement" (Ph.D. diss., Princeton University, 1983).

38. Arthur Frankel and Melvin L. Snyder, "Poor Performance Following Unsolvable Problems: Learned Helplessness or Egotism?" *Journal of Personality and Social Psychology* 36 (1978): 1415-1423.

39. Snyder and his colleagues do not present their research in this way. Rather, their stated concern is with how individuals seek to ambiguate the causes of their own behavior in order to make themselves unpredictable to others. However, this interesting work clearly lends itself to interpretation as self-deception as well as "other-deception."

40. Melvin L. Snyder, Robert E. Kleck, Angelo Strenta, and Steven J. Mentzer, "Avoidance of the Handicapped: An Attributional Ambiguity Analysis," *Journal of Personality and Social Psychology* 37 (1979): 2297-2306.

41. Leon Festinger, "A Theory of Social Comparison Processes," *Human Relations* 7 (1954): 117-140.

42. Abraham Tesser and Jennifer Campbell, "Self-Definition and Self-Evaluation Maintenance," in *Social Psychological Perspectives on the Self,* vol. 2, ed. Jerry Suls and Anthony Greenwald (Hillsdale, N.J.: Erlbaum, 1983).

43. Abraham Tesser and Jonathan Smith, "Some Effects of Task Relevance and Friendship on Helping: You Don't Always Help the One You Like," *Journal of Experimental Social Psychology* 16 (1980): 582-590.

44. Abraham Tesser and Del Paulhus, "The Definition of Self: Private and Public Self-Evaluation Management Strategies," *Journal of Personality and Social Psychology* 44 (1983): 672-682.

45. William J. McGuire, "A Contextualist Theory of Knowledge: Its Implications for Innovation and Reform in Psychological Research," in *Advances in Experimental Social Psychology,* vol. 16, ed. Leonard Berkowitz (New York: Academic Press, 1983).

Self-Deception without Repression: Limits on Access to Mental States

Timothy D. Wilson

The topic of self-deception can be viewed as the Chinese dish of psychology. Its ingredients are improbable and seemingly contradictory, yet they combine to form what is to many a savory topic. To others, however, the topic is far too spicy and exotic. The contradictions are glaring: people are said to possess a mental state, yet at the same time the claim is made that they do not recognize this state. The oldest method of psychology, introspection, is used to assess the contents of consciousness, yet the limits of introspection are recognized, and behavioral measures are used to tap inaccessible mental states. The study of self-deception has been very much an empirical enterprise. At the same time, many of the views of one of the most nonempirical areas of the field, psychoanalysis, have been adopted.[1]

Self-deception has been defined as the simultaneous possession of two contradictory beliefs, with one belief held outside of awareness because of its unpleasant or threatening nature.[2] Though some writers object to the characterization of self-deception as the simultaneous existence of incompatible beliefs, there is agreement that it is a purposeful act, whose goal is to avoid knowing some "unpleasant truth to which [the person] has already seen that the evidence points."[3]

My intent is to broaden the topic of self-deception, by demonstrating that it is not always a means of avoiding unpleasant truths. Undoubtedly people can deny the existence of an internal state that is threatening. There may be, however, many reasons why mental states fail to reach consciousness.

In one area of psychology this argument is noncontroversial. As will be seen in a brief discussion of research on perceptual defense, people were once thought to fail to perceive external stimuli because of the threatening nature of the stimuli, whereas today perceptual defense is accepted as one example of the broader phenomenon of selective attention. This essay will focus primarily on a more controversial topic, namely the conscious recognition of higher-order mental states such as evaluations and attitudes. It has traditionally been thought that mental states that fail to reach consciousness must pose a threat to the individual. I will argue, with a tentative model and some empirical evidence, that people may also misperceive mental states that are not threatening.

PERCEPTUAL DEFENSE

The perception of external stimuli, according to advocates of the ''New Look'' in experimental psychology, is very much influenced by a person's needs, wishes, and defenses. The case of perceptual defense became the best-known experimental demonstration of this phenomenon, in part because of the merging of experimental psychology with psychoanalytic ideas. In the classic paradigm, subjects were presented with words at very brief exposure times, and required to say (or guess) what the word was.[4] The exposure time was gradually increased until subjects correctly identified the word. Early studies found that subjects took more trials to report words that were threatening or anxiety-provoking (such as obscene words) than they did neutral words, but heightened galvanic skin responses (a measure of emotionality) to the threatening words indicated that subjects appeared to ''perceive'' the words before consciously recognizing them.

Early research on perceptual defense generated considerable criticism on both theoretical and methodological grounds, leading to a hiatus of research in this area. Chief among the theoretical objections was the apparent paradox of hypothesizing that people could perceive something but not know that they had perceived it. At about the same time, however, the information-processing revolution was fermenting in cognitive psychology, which rendered obsolete many of the objections to the study of perceptual defense. The logical paradox was resolved by new models that viewed perception not as a unitary process in which something is either perceived or not perceived, but as a multilevel, multistage process in which a preconscious filter determines what enters consciousness.[5] The concept of preconscious selection has become an integral part of most current theories of perception and is used to explain how people decide what to attend to from the vast amount of stimulus information that is encoded at any given moment.

Exactly how these selection processes operate is a subject of much debate (and research). It is clear, however, that the threatening nature of a stimulus is but one reason why it might not be selected to enter consciousness, and probably a minor reason at that. Such variables as the novelty of a stimulus, the expectations of the perceiver, and the intensity and duration of the stimulus are at least as important in determining what is selected for consciousness.

ACCESS TO MENTAL STATES

Thus, what started out as an exotic, psychoanalytic phenomenon, perceptual defense, is now viewed as a special case of a central, more general perceptual mechanism, selective attention. I will argue that a similar state of affairs may exist with what is more commonly thought of as self-deception, namely the case in which people fail to recognize a mental state such as an attitude or desire. As with perceptual defense, the fact that a feeling is threatening may be a sufficient but unnecessary cause of a failure to recognize it.

One reason there is relatively little research on access to mental states is because of several arduous definitional and methodological problems with the idea that people can be incorrect in their belief about how they feel. I will first outline these problems (with no claim to have completely solved them). I will then discuss evidence from social-psychological research, which suggests that access to mental states can be limited, even in the absence of repression. Next I will present a rather preliminary model that explains why such limited access might occur. Finally, several experiments from my laboratory will be described that have tested various aspects of this model.

BELIEFS ABOUT MENTAL STATES:
DEFINING ACCURACY

The states with which I will be concerned are those psychological dispositions that exert a causal influence on behavior. Examples include most attitudes, desires, moods, traits, affects, and evaluations. This definition corresponds closely to what philosophers refer to as intentional states. These states can exist in relation to a specific stimulus ("I like the movie"), or as a more general disposition ("I feel happy"), with the assumption that they usually guide behavior in some way.

It is not a simple matter to demonstrate that a belief about a mental state is inaccurate. Indeed, such beliefs are often said to be incorrigible precisely because there is no means of verifying their accuracy. This presents a major difficulty that will leave a cloud of ambiguity over all attempts to investigate access to mental states. In this section I will discuss ways of cutting through this fog as much as possible, though, as will be seen, it cannot be completely dispelled.

Mental states often have behavioral indicants that can be publicly observed. As argued by Rorty,

> our subsequent behavior may provide sufficient evidence for overriding contemporaneous reports of [mental states]. . . . If I say that I believe that *p*, or desire *X*, or am afraid, or am intending to do *A*, what I go on to do may lead others to say that I couldn't *really* have believed *p*, or desired *X*, or been afraid, or intended to do *A*. . . . Statements about beliefs, desires, emotions, and intentions are implicit predictions of future behavior, predictions which may be falsified.[6]

The objection might be made that people sometimes suppress any overt sign of their feelings. An employee might loathe her boss but behave as if they were long-lost friends. There is evidence, however, that even when people try to disguise their feelings, their true feelings "leak" through some nonverbal channels.[7] This raises an important issue concerning behavioral indicants of mental states. Since verbal reports are themselves a form of behavior, it is necessary to become more specific about which kinds of behaviors are the best indicants of mental states. To do so, a distinction must be made between behaviors that are consciously regulated and those that are not. Verbal reports and many other behaviors (such as facial expressions) are usually under conscious control and typically reflect people's *beliefs* about how they feel (barring attempts to be deceptive). To test the accuracy of these beliefs, behaviors should be measured that are not normally under conscious control, and thus have the potential to leak quite different feelings. Thus, the behaviors must not be ones that people deliberately control to correspond with their verbal reports, but ones that are diagnostic of other, hidden feelings.

Of course, one cannot use just any unregulated behavior as a criterion for accuracy. Unregulated behaviors must be used that have been demonstrated to be diagnostic of the feeling in question. Diagnosticity is not easy to establish; nevertheless, considerable evidence in support of the diagnosticity of a behavior can be gathered by seeing how the behavior varies under different stimulus conditions. For example, several researchers have used the amount of time people spend on an activity (such as a game or puzzle), in an unconstrained, "free-time" period, to test predictions about intrinsic interest made by self-attribution and other theories.[8] One hypothesis that has been heavily researched is that people who engage in interesting activities for extrinsic reasons will lower their interest in the activity. This hypothesis has received substantial support, as indicated by the fact that people given an extrinsic reason subsequently spend less time with the activity, in a free-time period, than people not given extrinsic reasons. Interestingly, a different conclusion would be reached if only self-report measures of liking for the activity were used. However, since the amount-of-time behavioral measure has proved to be very sensitive to experimental manipulations, and has generally responded as predicted by major theoretical positions, it is accepted as a valid measure of people's liking for the activity.

It is possible, of course, that the theories are wrong, and that free-time activity reflects something other than liking. This is the residual fog of ambiguity that is impossible to eliminate from any behavioral measure. I will plunge forward, however, and assume that free-time activity and other well-established behavioral measures are valid reflections of mental states. In all of the research reviewed and reported below, well-established behavioral measures were used. As we shall see, these measures often conflict with beliefs about the mental states the behaviors are said to measure. This will lead to one of two conclusions: Either the behavioral measures are invalid, which will necessitate a reinterpretation of several major theories in social psychology, or, as I will argue, there is a margin of error in people's beliefs about their mental states.

EVIDENCE FOR
LACK OF ACCESS TO MENTAL STATES

A striking finding in social psychological research over the past several decades has been the tendency for people to behave inconsistently with their attitudes, emotions, and evaluations. This finding has occurred regularly in two of the major areas of the field, attitude research and self-attribution research. For example, in a review of research on attitudes and behavior, Wicker concluded that "it is considerably more likely that attitudes will be unrelated or only slightly related to overt behaviors than that attitudes will be closely related to actions."[9]

A similar lack of correspondence between verbally reported mental states and behavior is commonly found in self-attribution research. According to attribution theory, people often infer their mental states from observations of their behavior and the conditions under which the behavior occurs.[10] Attempts to demonstrate this process usually involve a manipulation of external factors that might be influencing behavior (e.g., offering people money to perform an interesting activity, to see if they infer that they are "doing it for the money"), and then measuring the effects of this manipulation on people's inferences about their internal states (e.g., seeing if people infer that they enjoy the activity less when they are paid to do it). Often both verbal and behavioral measures of internal states are included, for example, questionnaire items about how much people enjoy the activity versus observations of how much time they spend with it in an unconstrained, "free-time" period.

A curious pattern of results has emerged from self-attribution research. If we look only at the behavioral indicants of the process, such as people's tendency to play with a puzzle in a free-play period after being rewarded for playing with it earlier, we find substantial evidence that the self-attribution process occurs as predicted. If we look at the verbal report measures (such as people's reported liking for the puzzles), however, we often find no difference between those who received the experimental manipulations (e.g., the reward) and those who did not. A recent review of forty self-attribution studies that included both self-report and behavioral measures of changes in internal states revealed that most of these studies found behavioral evidence for state change in the absence of changes in self-reports.[11]

There are many possible reasons why such an inconsistency between verbal reports and behavior has been found in social psychological research. For example, perhaps our self-report instruments and methods of observing behavior are so poor that we have been unable to detect the vast amount of mental state-behavior consistency that exists. I certainly do not deny that this and other problems contribute to the inconsistency between reported mental states and behavior. This is particularly true in the attitude literature; recent studies show that attitudes are more apt to predict behavior when variables such as how confidently the attitudes are held are taken into account.[12]

As discussed elsewhere,[13] however, the vast amount of inconsistency between reported mental states and behavior that has been found, particularly in the self-attribution literature, has yet to be fully explained by problems such as measurement error. I believe that a major contributing factor to this inconsistency is that people often have imperfect access to their mental states, and thus do not report these states accurately.

Reasons why there may sometimes be poor access to mental states are discussed in the next sections. It should be noted, however, that the states investigated in the attitude and attribution literatures are often of a nonthreatening nature, such as liking for a puzzle or a film. Thus, it is unlikely that people in all these studies deliberately misperceived their attitudes to avoid "unpleasant truths."

TWO MENTAL SYSTEMS

If it is true that access to mental states is sometimes limited, the question arises as to what people are doing when attempting to report their attitudes, beliefs, and evaluations. A preliminary model will be offered to explain the origins of beliefs about mental states. Issues involving consciousness are exceedingly complex; thus this model is presented more as a heuristic for generating research than as a theory with firm empirical underpinnings.

Following Bem's self-perception theory and previous arguments of Nisbett's and mine, it is argued that people often attempt to *infer* their internal states with the use of a conscious, verbal, explanatory system. This verbal system involves conscious attempts to estimate one's feelings, independently of cognitive processes mediating behavior. This position can be understood best by making a distinction between conscious attempts to examine one's thoughts and feelings and cognitive processes that typically do not occur in consciousness. As stated cogently by Mandler, "Cognition and conscious thought are two different concepts."[14] Many cognitive processes appear to be unavailable to conscious scrutiny. When asked to report these processes, people are unable to examine them directly and thus rely on a conscious explanatory system to describe them. The present analysis extends this argument to reports about mental *states*. Cognitive processes and resulting changes in internal states can sometimes occur unnoticed. In self-attribution studies this appears to happen often. Processes that lead to changes in attitudes are triggered, yet people are unable to report either the cognitive processes or the resulting internal states. When asked to report these states, people rely on the conscious, verbal system.

In essence the argument is that there are two mental systems. One system mediates behavior (especially unregulated behavior), is largely nonconscious, and is, perhaps, the older of the two systems in evolutionary terms. The other, perhaps newer system, is largely conscious, and attempts to explain and communicate mental states. Undoubtedly people often have direct access to their feelings, and in these cases the verbal system can make "direct contact" and report feelings easily and accurately. When there is limited access, however, the verbal system makes inferences about what these processes and states might be.

This position is very similar to what Wason and Evans, in a somewhat different context, have called Type 1 and Type 2 cognitive processes. The former processes underlie behavior and are generally nonconscious, and thus can be deduced only by observing people's behavior in response to different stimulus conditions. The latter process is described as a conscious thought process that involves the "tendency for the subject to construct a justification for his own behavior consistent with his knowledge of the situation."[15]

A parallel can also be drawn between the present view of two mental systems and research on the role of hemispheric differences of the brain in mental functioning. There has been a tendency to equate virtually all dualist concepts in psychology with right- versus left-brain functions, resulting in an unfortunate state of "dichotomania."[16] I do not wish to add to this trend by making extreme claims about the location in the brain of what I have referred to as the verbal explanatory system. It is worth mentioning, however, that there are some striking similarities between the arguments made here about the role of the verbal explanatory system and the role played by the left hemisphere in mental functioning. After years of study of people who have had the connecting tissue between the hemispheres surgically removed, Gazzaniga and his colleagues make the following conclusions about the left hemisphere in normal people:

> We feel that the conscious verbal self [in the left hemisphere] is not always privy to the origin of our actions, and when it observes the person behaving for unknown reasons, it attributes cause to the action as if it knows but in fact it does not.[17]

> The emerging picture is that our cognitive system is not a unified network with a single purpose and train of thought. A more accurate metaphor is that our sense of subjective awareness arises out of our dominant left hemisphere's unrelenting need to explain actions taken from any one of a multitude of mental systems that dwell within us.[18]

Gazzinaga's conclusions are consistent with social psychological research indicating that under certain conditions, people appear to possess a mental state that influences their behavior, but the verbal, conscious self infers the existence of a different mental state.[19]

The Verbal Explanatory System

Nisbett and I have outlined the manner in which the verbal explanatory system operates when individuals try to describe and justify their responses. When trying to decide why they performed a certain action, people call upon culturally learned and idiosyncratic theories about "why I perform behavior X." Similarly, since access to internal states is sometimes limited, people may call upon the explanatory system to infer how they feel. These conscious inferences are influenced by theories about themselves and about what feelings seem like plausible reactions to a stimulus.

This view bears some similarity to the sociologist Hochschild's discussion of what she terms "emotion work."[20] She argues that people often engage in an active attempt to evoke a new emotion or suppress an existing one. People make such attempts according to "feeling rules," namely what the culture and situation demand we should feel. For example, a person feeling happy at a funeral or sad at a wedding will attempt to change his or her feelings in a more appropriate direction. In my view, emotion work may often occur only at a conscious level; that is, it may involve attempts by the verbal explanatory system to change a belief about how one feels. Thus, a bride who feels sad on her wedding day may convince herself that it is really the happiest day of her life, and genuinely believe that she is happy. It is very difficult to change the actual feeling, however. Thus the bride's sadness is apt to remain and be expressed behaviorally, even though she has convinced herself that she is not sad.

A further example comes from the following excerpt from a story by Mary Kierstead, where two people, when children, consciously adopted the "feeling rule" that children love their pony. It was not until much later that they realized their true feelings were quite different:

> "You know, it wasn't until I was about thirty that I realized that I'd always hated that goddamn pony. He had a mean disposition, and he was fat and spoiled. He would roll on me, and then step on my foot before I could get up."
>
> "And he bit you when you tried to give him lumps of sugar," Kate added. It wasn't until Blake said it that Kate realized that she, too, had always hated Topper. For years they had been conned into loving him, because children love their pony, and their dog, and their parents, and picnics, and the ocean, and the lovely chocolate cake.[21]

If beliefs about feelings are often inferences generated by an explanatory system, they may be incorrect. A child may assume that he loves his pony, for example, when he actually hates it. If so, the child's report of liking should conflict with his *unregulated* behaviors toward the pony, which would leak his true feelings. Inferences about feelings may also be accurate, however, producing spuriously correct reports, spurious because the accuracy is not the result of direct access to the feeling but to the coincidental correspondence between the feeling and the inference made by the explanatory system. Thus, the characters in Kierstead's story eventually realized that their theory about their liking for Topper was incorrect, and made what were presumably more accurate inferences about their feelings.

PRIMING THE EXPLANATORY SYSTEM

This analysis suggests that the origins of how we feel and how we think we feel can be quite different. For example, the fact that a pony steps on our feet and bites us may produce genuine dislike, but due to the cultural theory that children love their ponies, we overlook this data and infer that we love our pony. If so, one ought to be able to manipulate self-reports independently of actual feelings by altering what theories and data are salient to people.

I conducted three laboratory experiments to test this hypothesis. Each experiment used attributional manipulations to produce changes in internal states. Both self-report and behavioral measures of state change were included in each study. As in most previous research, subjects were expected to behave as if they possessed a new internal state, but to fail to report these states. The major purpose of the studies was to see if priming the verbal explanatory system produced new self-reports independently of the manipulations influencing behavior. Each study included a "reasons analysis" manipulation in which subjects were asked to reflect consciously on the reasons for their behavior. By making people take a closer look at themselves and the situation, inferences about how they felt were expected to change. Since the verbal explanatory system is hypothesized to be relatively independent of the feelings mediating behavior, the reasons analysis manipulations were not expected to influence behavioral measures of internal states.

For example, in study 2 by Wilson, Hull, and Johnson, college students were either paid $1 or not paid to work on an interesting puzzle.[22] Their subsequent interest in the puzzle was assessed with standard self-report measures, as well as with a behavioral measure— the amount of time subjects played with the puzzle in an unrewarded, "free-time" period. A reasons analysis manipulation cross-cut the attribution manipulation (in this case, the reward). Just before the dependent measures were administered, some subjects were asked to think about why they had initially played with the puzzle.

The results were generally as predicted. When no reasons analysis was performed, subjects behaved as if their internal states had changed, but did not report these new states. That is, subjects who were rewarded played with the puzzle significantly less in the free-time period than did subjects in the no reward condition, but rewarded subjects did not *report* that they liked the puzzle any less than did nonrewarded subjects. A different pattern of results, however, occurred in the reasons analysis conditions. When people were induced to reflect on the reasons for their behavior, behavioral evidence for changes in attitudes toward the puzzle were still found, but now significant self-reported differences were found as well. Similar results were found in study 1 of Wilson et al.

DIRECT ACCESS OR INDIRECT INFERENCE?

The two experiments of Wilson et al. showed that when subjects reflected on reasons for their behavior, they reported internal-state changes that were consistent with their behavior. It is important to consider in detail why this pattern of results occurred. One possibility is that subjects do not normally exert much effort to discover what their current internal state is, but when made to look more carefully, as in the reasons analysis conditions, they are able to examine their internal states directly. According to this view, the reasons analysis manipulations caused subjects to introspect more carefully and thus achieve direct access to internal states. This view is very similar to self-awareness theory, which argues that focusing attention on the self produces more valid reports about mental states.[23]

In contrast, the reasons analysis variable in the studies of Wilson et alia was conceived, not as a manipulation of self-awareness, but as a means of priming the verbal explanatory system, which changes people's inferences about their internal states in a direction that may or may not correspond to their behavior. Several sources of evidence support this view. First, a reasons analysis manipulation in a study by Wilson and Linville significantly changed subjects' mood reports, but not in a more accurate direction.[24] That is, subjects who analyzed reasons made different inferences about their moods, but the mean of their mood reports did not become uniformly more consistent with behavioral measures of their internal states, as would be expected if the reasons analysis were increasing the accuracy of their reports.

Second, if analyzing reasons increases access to one's mental states, then the correlation between self-reports and behavior should be higher in the reasons analysis conditions. Correlational differences in the studies of Wilson et al. and Wilson and Linville are difficult to interpret, since there were differences in means across conditions that could influence correlations for artifactual reasons. Nonetheless, it should be noted that there were no significant differences in correlations between the reasons analysis and no reasons analysis conditions in any of the three studies. More convincingly, we have found in three studies discussed below that analyzing reasons can actually reduce self-report/ behavior correlations.

The three priming experiments can be summarized as follows. The first major finding to emerge is that in each study people reported internal states that were at variance with their behavior. As discussed earlier, one explanation of this pattern of results is that under some circumstances, people have poor access to the internal states that mediate their behavior.

The second major finding was that in each of the three studies, inducing subjects to reflect on the reasons for their responses changed their self-reports of internal states but did not influence their behavior. The failure of the reasons analysis manipulations to affect behavior is consistent with the view that there is substantial independence between the verbal system that makes conscious inferences about states and the processes mediating behavior. Priming the conscious system led to changes in self-reports, apparently because this caused subjects to examine more carefully their behavior and its implications, or because it caused certain aspects of the situation to become more salient (e.g., extrinsic reasons for playing with a puzzle). It is not yet entirely clear in what direction a particular reasons analysis manipulation will influence self-reports. In all likelihood this depends on which aspects of the situation become salient as a result of reflecting upon reasons. It is clear, however, that the changes in self-reports that occur are not necessarily more accurate (that is, more consistent with behavior).

CONDITIONS FOSTERING IMPERFECT ACCESS TO MENTAL STATES

It is very unlikely that people always have poor access to their mental states. It is thus important to specify the conditions fostering good versus imperfect access. Several such conditions, some speculative, have been identified.

MOTIVATED SELF-DECEPTION

As discussed earlier, one reason why people might have poor access to a mental state is due to the threatening nature of the state. In Freud's words, such a state is similar to "the legendary Titans, weighed down since primaeval ages by the massive bulk of the mountains which were once hurled upon them by the victorious gods."[25] The present model acknowledges that motivated self-deception can occur. The presence of a motive to self-deceive, however, is not viewed as a necessary condition for poor access to mental states. Under some conditions the verbal, conscious system may possess mistaken beliefs about one's attitudes and evaluations, even in the absence of a motive for self-deception. I shall now discuss three conditions that promote poor access and that do not necessarily involve a motive to avoid knowing how one feels.

EFFECTS OF SELF-ANALYSIS

Self-reflection is often considered a beneficial exercise, leading to greater insight about one's feelings. We have obtained recent evidence, however, that analyzing the reasons for one's feelings can, under some conditions, actually lower the accuracy of people's beliefs about their feelings. In the words of Theodore Roethke, "Self-contemplation is a curse/That makes an old confusion worse."[26]

As seen earlier, we found in three priming studies that inducing subjects to analyze reasons changed their reported mental states more than it did their behavior, though it was not entirely clear whether this change was in a more or less accurate direction. Two of the studies found greater consistency between mean reported feelings and mean behavior in the analysis conditions, but given that there was no increase in self-report/behavior correlations in these conditions, the correspondence between means could have been fortuitous.

Fortunately, this rather cloudy picture on the issue of accuracy has been cleared considerably by three studies better designed to assess self-report/behavior correlations.[27] In the first study of this series, subjects were given several minutes to familiarize themselves with five different types of puzzles, e.g., a letter series task where people guessed the next letter that logically followed a given progression, and a Gestalt completion task, where people guessed on the basis of an incomplete portrayal of an object what object was depicted. In one condition subjects were instructed to think about why they felt the way they did about each puzzle while working on it. After working on the puzzles, they wrote down reasons why they found each one interesting or boring. They then rated how interesting they thought each puzzle was, and were left alone with several examples of each puzzle during a "free-play" period. Subjects in the control condition were treated identically, except that they completed a filler task after initially working on the puzzles and were not instructed to analyze reasons.

Correlations were computed for each subject between his or her interest ratings and the time spent in the free-play period working on each of the five puzzles. In the control condition the average correlation was .54, demonstrating a fair degree of correspondence between the interest ratings and behavior. When subjects first analyzed reasons, however, the average correlation was only .17, indicating little or no correspondence between the interest ratings and subsequent behavior.

Two other studies in this series replicated the finding that analyzing reasons reduces self-report/behavior correlations. In one study, subjects either analyzed or did not analyze their reactions to a slide show of vacation pictures, and in the analysis condition there was a significantly lower correlation between reported liking for the slides and ratings made by hidden observers about how much subjects appeared to enjoy the slides. In the final study, couples involved in a steady dating relationship analyzed or did not analyze why their relationships were going the way they were. Couples who analyzed their relationships had a significantly lower correlation between their responses about how well-adjusted the relationship was and whether they were still dating several months later.

Evidence that analyzing reasons affected self-reports but not behavior in our studies comes from the puzzle study and the dating couples study. In the puzzle experiment, the relative mean amounts of time spent with the different puzzles were nearly identical in the analysis and control conditions, yet the relative interest ratings of the puzzles were quite different. Also, the liking expressed in the reasons given by subjects who analyzed correlated with their subsequent interest ratings but not with their behavior. Finally, it is unlikely that the analysis manipulation in the experiment with couples affected the decision to break up several months after the study, and more likely it influenced their reported adjustment, measured right after the manipulation. In support of this argument, the liking expressed in the couples' reasons correlated more with their reported adjustment than with their decision to break up.

When people dissect and analyze their responses, at least in the short-term fashion that occurred in our studies, they appear to convince themselves that their attitudes are something other than what they really are. In terms of the model outlined earlier, analyzing reasons seems to prime the explanatory system, producing incorrect inferences about one's attitudes. The precise mechanism by which this occurs is not apparent at this time, but two possibilities can be mentioned. First, the aspects of one's feelings and reasons for them that people can verbalize may not accurately represent their actual feelings. For example, when analyzing a relationship, a person might find the fact that her dating partner shares most of her beliefs and attitudes easier to put into words than the fact that he is sometimes cold towards her. This may convince her that she likes him more than she really does, since what is easy to verbalize about the relationship is primarily positive.

Second, if people have prior experience with the attitude object, as in the study of dating couples, then analyzing reasons for one's feelings might cause people to focus too much on stimulus characteristics that are available in memory. For example, when asked to analyze their relationship, a couple who had just had a fight might focus on the negative aspects of their relationship (since the fight was on both of their minds), when in fact as a whole their relationship is going well. In other words, what is available in memory is not always a representative sample of the "population" of good and bad aspects of the stimulus.[28]

Adoption of Feeling-Rules

The verbal explanatory system may sometimes operate according to feeling-rules independently of one's actual feelings, as in the earlier example of the bride who convinces herself that her wedding day is the happiest day of her life, when in fact she is miserable, or the child who adopts the rule that "children love their pony" when in fact he cannot stand his pony. If people become convinced by consciously adopting a feeling-rule that they feel something they do not, then their self-reported feelings and their regulated behaviors should be consistent with the feeling rule, while a different feeling should be expressed with unregulated nonverbal behaviors.

Evidence consistent with this view has been obtained by Snyder and Endelman[29] and by Wilson, Lassiter, and Stone.[30] The feeling rule investigated in both studies has been well studied in social psychology, namely, that similarity causes attraction. Dozens of studies have found that people like others who have similar attitudes. Interestingly, by far the majority of research in this area has relied on self-report-dependent measures of liking. In the standard paradigm, developed by Byrne, subjects fill out a series of attitude scales, are shown responses on the same scales supposedly made by another subject, then report their liking for this subject. The larger the overlap between the subject's attitude responses and those of the other person, the greater the liking reported by the subject for this person.[31]

Occasionally researchers have included behavioral measures of liking, typically how close the subject places his or her chair to another person. The results on these measures have been mixed, though they are often at odds with self-report measures of liking. For example, Snyder and Endelman manipulated three levels of similarity (slight, moderate, and extreme), and found that as similarity increased, so did self-reported liking. A curvilinear relationship was found between similarity and interpersonal distance, however, such that subjects placed their chairs closest to the moderately similar other, but kept their distance from both the slightly and extremely similar other.

Consistent with the present viewpoint, Snyder and Endelman argued that self-reported liking is "susceptible to the expectations placed upon [people] as members of a society that make certain assumptions about the merits of similarity."[32] Interpersonal distance, they argued, revealed people's actual feelings, which reflected concerns about uniqueness. That is, people may actually prefer moderately similar others the most, since they are rewarding but do not challenge one's sense of uniqueness.

Wilson, Lassiter, and Stone first established more definitively which nonverbal behaviors are regulated in social interaction. Subjects were instructed either to hide or reveal their feelings toward a likable confederate while interacting with him. Three behaviors were much more negative when subjects were expected to hide their feelings (facial expression, body lean, and talking time), suggesting that these are regulated channels. Three other behaviors did not differ across condition (interpersonal distance, body orientation, and eye contact). Since each of these channels has been identified as a measure of attraction,[33] but was not controlled by subjects in our first study, we labeled them as unregulated indicants of attraction.

In Wilson, Lassiter, and Stone's second study, the similarity-attraction feeling rule was investigated from an individual difference perspective. Subjects reported whether they preferred moderately or extremely similar others better. Several weeks later they came to the laboratory, where they met a confederate whose attitudes were either moderately or extremely similar to their own. As hypothesized, subjects' reported preferences for moderate versus extremely similar others predicted their self-reported liking for the confederate several weeks later, as well as their regulated behaviors in her presence (facial expression, body lean, talking time). Consistent with the idea that the reported preferences reflected a conscious feeling rule that may not have corresponded to actual preferences, subjects' initial reports did not predict their unregulated behaviors in the presence of the confederate (interpersonal distance, eye contact, body orientation). The unregulated behaviors were unaffected by either initial preferences or the similarity of the confederate to subjects.

Despite the fact that the unregulated behaviors we assessed have been shown to be sensitive to situational manipulations of attraction in other studies, the possibility that they were invalid measures in our experiment, rather than signs of inaccessible feelings, cannot be completely ruled out. A conservative summary of the results of the Wilson, Lassiter, and Stone and the Snyder and Endelman studies is that there are two possible interpretations, both very interesting. First, the unregulated behaviors may have been invalid measures of attraction, in which case a substantial part of the literature on nonverbal communication will have to be revised. What we view as a more compelling interpretation is that people sometimes adopt feeling rules at a conscious level (e.g., ''I like extremely similar others''), which do not correspond to their actual reactions. When this occurs, self-reports and regulated behaviors will reflect the feeling rule, but be at odds with unregulated behaviors.

Amount and Accessibility of Processing Preceding Attitudes

The attitudes usually studied by social psychologists are the result of substantial information processing by subjects, such as the inferences made by people in self-attribution studies, or the processing of persuasive communications in attitude change experiments. In contrast, many affective states appear to be preceded by minimal processing of stimulus information.[34] It is interesting to note that it is the former type of states—those that are the result of substantial processing—that have been found to be poor predictors of behavior. Perhaps there is something about the preceding processing of attitudes in attribution and attitude change experiments that reduces the accessibility of the attitudes. For example, the processes themselves are often unavailable to conscious scrutiny, which might reduce the accessibility of the resulting mental states. In contrast, states that are more immediate, and not the result of complex, inaccessible processing, may be much more accessible.

Such a hypothesis is tentative; in fact I can offer only a thought experiment to support it. Suppose subjects were introduced to a confederate who preceded to punch them in the nose. Subjects would then be given a questionnaire asking how much they like the confederate. Several behavioral measures of their liking would also be gathered, including their tone of voice while talking with the confederate, their aggressiveness toward the confederate, and the likelihood of their initiating future interactions with him. All of these responses would be compared with those of a different group of subjects to whom the confederate was warm and friendly.

There seems to be little doubt that the subjects who were punched in the nose would have immediate, negative reactions to the confederate, and that they would have good access to this reaction. Both their reported liking and their behavioral reactions to the confederate should be very negative, compared with those of the group to whom the confederate was warm and friendly. In addition, compared with self-attribution and attitude change studies, the self-report/behavior correlations in our punch-in-the-nose study would probably be high. Why? One possibility is that the more processing subjects have to do to form an attitude, the more apt they are to lose track of what that attitude is, especially if the processes themselves are inaccessible. (Other possible interpretations of the thought experiment are of course possible, i.e., that the more extreme the attitude is, the more accessible it will be.)

THEORETICAL AND METHODOLOGICAL IMPLICATIONS

Theoretically, the present arguments may help to organize the self-attribution literature. Light can be shed on some of the conflicting results in this area by looking at whether behavioral or self-report-dependent measures were used. For example, there has been some controversy over when and how children learn the discounting principle, which is the tendency to downplay the significance of a causal agent when other plausible causal agents are present. There have been two chief paradigms to study the discounting principle in children. In one, children of various ages are read a story describing people who perform an activity either in the presence or absence of an external causal agent (e.g., playing with a toy and receiving or not receiving an ice cream cone for doing so), and are asked how much the people like the activity. It has generally been found that children do not use the discounting principle (i.e., inferring that people who played with the toy without receiving ice cream liked it more) until approximately age nine.[35]

In the other, overjustification, paradigm children are either rewarded or not for performing an attractive activity, and then interest in the activity is assessed by seeing how much time they spend on it in a "free-play" period. If children use the discounting principle, they should downplay their interest in the activity when another plausible reason for doing it, the reward, is present. This result has been repeatedly found in children as young as three to five years of age.[36] Thus, children do not give verbal responses that reflect the discounting principle until approximately age nine, but behave as if they were utilizing it as young as age three.

There are many differences between the two paradigms that might account for this conflicting pattern of results, such as the fact that one involves other-perception and the other self-perception. One possibility, however, is that the two types of studies are tapping different systems. The story-reading paradigm, by using self-reports as dependent measures, may have been investigating the development of the verbal explanatory system. The overjustification paradigm, by using behavioral measures, may have been investigating processes that are less verbal and, perhaps, nonconscious. If so, the two systems may well develop at different rates, accounting for the discrepancy between the ages at which discounting effects are found in the different types of studies.[37]

Another implication of the present analysis is a distressing one: It is even more difficult to investigate cognitive processes than generally believed. Though it is recognized by cognitive psychologists that many mental processes cannot be accurately reported and must be studied indirectly with the use of converging operations, social psychologists rely heavily on self-report measures of attributions, attitudes, and moods. If it is true that people sometimes lack access to higher-order mental phenomena, then social psychologists should be more inclined to study them with the use of behavioral dependent measures.

This is distressing, because behavioral measures themselves are often ambiguous, and it makes it all the more difficult to rule out competing interpretations of one's data. For example, the exact interpretation of the overjustification effect is still controversial, despite ten years of voluminous research. Imagine how much easier it would be to explore this issue if people could verbalize the exact cognitive processes they underwent in one of these studies, or even if people could verbalize the feelings towards the task they end up with. Since it appears they cannot verbalize their thoughts or feelings very well, it is all the more difficult to determine what the mediating processes of the overjustification effect are.

I am not suggesting that psychologists abandon the long-trusted self-report questionnaire. People often can make very accurate reports about their attitudes, moods, motives, and evaluations. Often they cannot, however, and it is under these conditions that behavioral measures of internal states are useful. Though I have outlined several possible conditions under which reports will be inaccurate, it is clear that considerably more work is necessary to confirm and add to an understanding of these conditions. In the meantime, researchers should adopt the safe course of including both self-report and behavioral dependent measures. If it is established that the two measures correlate (particularly if self-report measures correlate with both regulated and unregulated behaviors), then the self-report measures can be trusted. If such correlations are not found and one has reason to believe that the behavioral variables are valid measures of the mental phenomena under study, faith in people's access to these phenomena should be reduced. The more this result is found, as it has been so many times in self-attribution research, the more apt will be an observation by a British character in a novel by Shirley Hazzard: "Americans might be the only people left who asked how one felt—still imagining one might know."[38]

NOTES

1. I leave it to the reader to decide which of these ingredients is sweet and which sour.

2. Cf. Ruben C. Gur and Harold A. Sackeim, "Self-Deception: A Concept in Search of a Phenomenon," *Journal of Personality and Social Psychology* 37 (1979): 147–169.

3. Herbert Fingarette, *Self-Deception* (London: Routledge and Kegan Paul, 1969): 28.

4. See, for example, Elliot McGinnies, "Emotionality and Perceptual Defense," *Psychological Review* 56 (1949): 244–251.

5. See Matthew Erdelyi, "A New Look at the New Look: Perceptual Defense and Vigilance," *Psychological Review* 81 (1974): 1–24; and N. F. Dixon, *Preconscious Processing* (New York: Wiley, 1981).

6. Richard Rorty, "Incorrigibility as the Mark of the Mental," *Journal of Philosophy* 67 (1970): 419–420.

7. Cf. Paul Ekman and Wallace V. Friesen, "Nonverbal Leakage and Clues to Deception," *Psychiatry* 32 (1969): 88–106; P. Ekman and W. V. Friesen, "Detecting Deception from the Body or Face," *Journal of Personality and Social Psychology* 29 (1974): 288–298; Miron Zuckerman, Bella M. DePaulo, and Robert Rosenthal, "Verbal and Nonverbal Communication of Deception," in *Advances in Experimental Social Psychology,* vol. 14, ed. Leonard Berkowitz (New York: Academic Press, 1981): 1–59; and Miron Zuckerman, D. T. Larrance, N. H. Spiegel, and R. Klorman, "Controlling Nonverbal Cues: Facial Expressions and Tone of Voice," *Journal of Experimental Social Psychology* 17 (1981): 506–524.

8. Cf. Edward L. Deci and Richard M. Ryan, "The Empirical Exploration of Intrinsic Motivational Processes," in *Advances in Experimental Social Psychology,* vol. 13, 39–80; Russell H. Fazio and Mark P. Zanna, "Direct Experience and Attitude-Behavior Consistency," in *Advances in Experimental Social Psychology,* vol. 14, 161–202; and Mark R. Lepper and David Greene, eds., *The Hidden Costs of Reward* (Hillsdale, N.J.: Erlbaum, 1978).

9. A. W. Wicker, "Attitudes versus Actions: The Relationship of Verbal and Overt Behavior Responses to Attitude Objects," *Journal of Social Issues* 25 (1969): 41–78.

10. Daryl J. Bem, "Self-Perception Theory," in *Advances in Experimental Social Psychology,* vol. 6, pp. 1–62.

11. Timothy D. Wilson, "Strangers to Ourselves: The Origins and Accuracy of Beliefs about One's Own Mental States," in *Attribution in Contemporary Psychology*, ed. J. H. Harvey and G. Weary (New York: Academic Press, 1985).

12. Russell H. Fazio and Mark P. Zanna, "Direct Experience and Attitude-Behavior Consistency," 161–202.

13. Wilson, "Strangers to Ourselves: The Origins and Accuracy of Beliefs about One's Own Mental States."

14. George Mandler, *Mind and Emotion* (New York: Wiley, 1975), 13.

15. P. C. Wason and J. St. B. T. Evans, "Dual Processes in Reasoning?" *Cognition* 3 (1975): 149.

16. Cf. Sally P. Springer and Georg Deutsch, *Left Brain, Right Brain* (San Francisco: Freeman, 1981).

17. Michael S. Gazzaniga and J. E. LeDoux, *The Integrated Mind* (New York: Plenum Press, 1978): 149–150.

18. Michael S. Gazzaniga, "Right Hemisphere Language Following Brain Bisection: A 20-Year Perspective," *American Psychologist* 38 (1983): 525–536.

19. See Fingarette, *Self-Deception*, for a related discussion.

20. Arlie R. Hochschild, "Emotion Work, Feeling Rules, and Social Structure," *American Journal of Sociology* 85 (1979): 551–575.

21. Mary D. Kierstead, "The Shetland Pony," *New Yorker*, 6 April 1981, 48.

22. Timothy D. Wilson, Jay G. Hull, and Jim Johnson, "Awareness and Self-Perception: Verbal Reports on Internal States," *Journal of Personality and Social Psychology* 40 (1981): 53–71.

23. Cf. Charles S. Carver and Michael F. Scheier, *Attention and Self-Regulation: A Control-Theory Approach to Human Behavior* (New York: Springer-Verlag, 1981); and R. Wicklund, "Self-Focused Attention and the Validity of Self-Reports," in *Consistency in Social Behavior: The Ontario Symposium*, vol. 2, ed. Mark P. Zanna, E. Tory Higgins, and C. Peter Herman (Hillsdale, N.J.: Erlbaum, 1982): 149–172.

24. Timothy D. Wilson and Patricia M. Linville, "Improving the Academic Performance of College Freshmen: Attribution Therapy Revisited," *Journal of Personality and Social Psychology* 42 (1982): 367–376.

25. Sigmund Freud, *The Interpretation of Dreams*, ed. and trans. J. Strachey (1900; reprint, New York: Avon, 1972): 592.

26. Theodore Roethke, *The Collected Poems of Theodore Roethke* (Garden City: Anchor, 1975), 249.

27. Timothy D. Wilson, Dana Dunn, Jane Bybee, Diane Hyman, and John Rotondo, "Effects of Self-Reflection on Attitude-Behavior Consistency," *Journal of Personality and Social Psychology* 47 (1984): 5–16.

28. Cf. Amos Tversky and Daniel Kahneman, "Judgment under Uncertainty: Heuristics and Biases," *Science* 184 (1974): 1124–1131.

29. C. R. Snyder and J. R. Endelman, "Effects of Degree of Interpersonal Similarity on Physical Distance and Self-Reported Attraction: A Comparison of Uniqueness and Reinforcement Theory Predictions," *Journal of Personality* 47 (1979): 492–505.

30. Timothy D. Wilson, G. Daniel Lassiter, and Julie I. Stone, "Regulated versus Unregulated Nonverbal Behavior in Social Interaction: Evidence for Limited Access to Mental States," unpublished manuscript, University of Virginia, 1983.

31. Cf. Donn E. Byrne, *The Attraction Paradigm* (New York: Academic Press, 1971).

32. C. R. Snyder and J. R. Endelman, "Effects of Degree of Interpersonal Similarity on Physical Distance and Self-Reported Attraction: A Comparison of Uniqueness and Reinforcement Theory Predictions," 494.

33. Cf. D. Byrne, G. D. Baskett, and L. Hodges, "Behavioral Indicators of Interpersonal Attraction," *Journal of Applied Social Psychology* 1 (1971): 137–149; R. V. Exline, "Visual Interaction: The Glances of Power and Preference," in *Nebraska Symposium on Motivation*, ed. James K. Cole (Lincoln: University of Nebraska Press, 1971): 163–206; Edward T. Hall, *The Hidden Dimension* (New York: Doubleday, 1966); and Albert Mehrabian, *Nonverbal Communication* (Chicago: Aldine-Atherton, 1972).

34. Robert B. Zajonc, "Feeling and Thinking: Preferences Need No Inferences," *American Psychologist* 35 (1980): 151–175.

35. Cf. E. A. Cohen, D. N. Gelfand, and D. P. Hartmann, "Causal Reasoning as a Function of Behavioral Consequences," *Child Development* 52 (1981): 514–522; B. DiVitto and L. Z. McArthur, "Developmental Differences in the Use of Distinctiveness, Consensus, and Consistency Information for Making Causal Attributions," *Developmental Psychology* 14 (1978): 474–482; M. Guttentag and C. Longfellow, "Children's Social Attributions: Development and Change," in *Nebraska Symposium on Motivation*, ed. C. B. Keasey (Lincoln: University of Nebraska Press, 1977): 305–341; R. Karniol and M. Ross, "The Development of Causal Attributions in Social Perception," *Journal of Personality and Social Psychology* 34 (1976): 455–464; A. Kun, "Development of the Magnitude-Covariation and Compensation Schemata in Ability and Effort Attribution of Performance," *Child Development* 48 (1977): 862–873; M. Morgan, "The Overjustification Effect: A Developmental Test of Self-Perception Interpretations," *Journal of Personality and Social Psychology* 40 (1981): 809–821; T. R. Shultz, I. Butkowsky, J. W. Pearce, and H. Shanfield, "Development of Schemes for the Attribution of Multiple Psychological Causes," *Development Psychology* 11 (1975): 502–510; and M. C. Smith, "Children's Use of the Multiple Sufficient Scheme in Social Perception," *Journal of Personality and Social Psychology* 32 (1975): 737–747.

36. E.g., Mark R. Lepper, David Greene, and Richard E. Nisbett, "Undermining Children's Intrinsic Interest with Extrinsic Reward: A Test of the 'Overjustification' Hypothesis," *Journal of Personality and Social Psychology* 28 (1973): 129–137.

37. For related discussions, see Saul M. Kassin and Mark R. Lepper, "Oversufficient and Insufficient Justification Effects: Cognitive and Behavioral Development," in *The Development of Achievement Motivation*, ed. J. Nicholls (Greenwich, Conn.: Jai Press, in press); and D. Wells and T. R. Shultz, "Developmental Distinctions between Behavior and Judgment in the Operation of the Discounting Principle," *Child Development* 51 (1980): 1307–1310.

38. Shirley Hazzard, *The Transit of Venus* (New York: Playboy Paperbacks, 1981), 136.

Self-Protection and Self-Inception

Benzion Chanowitz and Ellen J. Langer

Diversity does not of itself imply conflict, but it implies the possibility of conflict.

—John Dewey, *Human Nature and Conduct*

INTRODUCTION

You would be hard pressed to find persons who act with more sincerity and conviction than the anorexic woman who starves herself into shapely beauty. In her own way, she is guided by the professed goal of improving the situation. For the outsider who witnesses such moments and is pained by them, there can be no doubt that something is wrong. For the observer, the pain most deeply arises because the woman also intrinsically cherishes the values of health and life that are at odds with other values that have taken up residence in her. Most painful for all is the torturous effect of the war that is going on *within* the woman. This inner restlessness can be publicly evident in the initial stages of the battle, when the two ends that are in internal conflict are explicitly and contemporaneously valuable to the person. Then, a calm may settle in; a resolution has been found. In many cases, however, this pacific solution has all the appearances of lunacy. The anorexic woman may blithely assure all that everything is fine. She barely shows the effects of strain. All we now see is the aftereffect of a dramatic conflict that has manifested itself as a perverse coherence, whereby she maintains a stake in the value of both sides of the contradiction. The battle is

117

over, but the war still goes on. For those who assert the reality of self-deception, the calmer moments of such instances constitute evidence that both ends of a contradiction can be pacifically maintained within a person. That person's actions indicate belief in one proposition while we can see quite clearly that she knows it is the opposite. She sees no problem in what she is doing. (She might quite "honestly" say, for example, that she has no eating problem.) Her untroubled action shows that she does not know. Yet we clearly see that she "must" know. We therefore infer that she is engaging in self-deception.

Many cases of "self-deception" do not occur within the dramatic settings portrayed in such an example. Often, there is no storm before the calm, and often, the process is played out with much less at stake. Even when the pain is evident, it is not a problem for those who attempt to decipher the puzzle of self-deception. Rather, their interest centers on the resources that persons have on hand for achieving the apparently unachievable. We draw attention to the pain because it signifies that there is more underfoot when a painless, uneasy calm has been achieved.

Knowledge, truth, and pain are not unrelated. Sometimes it hurts when we must forsake one truth and incorporate another. Why does the truth hurt? In some cases, this process of exchange stops and stabilizes midway between what was and what will be so that two truths uneasily and "immorally" coexist within the person. The occasionally evident pain points to the fact that there is some actuality that must be addressed, even when no pain is evident. The incorporation of certain uncomfortable truths and the subsequent calm in which the discomfort is "resolved" indicate the existence of something distinct that requires our special attention. Therefore, we cannot accept the alternative approach that tries to "resolve" the problem of self-deception by denying its existence.[1] Such an approach asserts that because the purported act is too paradoxical, persons are incapable of engaging in self-deception. For them, self-deception is an impossible event that defies logic; one cannot both affirm and deny a proposition in a single gesture. If this were admissible, it would render fruitless all of the results that the processes of logic have yielded. Anything and its contradiction would be acceptable at the same time, and no proposition could be asserted to the exclusion of others.

On psychological grounds, too, self-deception is an implausible event. Picture a person playing both sides of a chess game. The opponent's strategy is immediately evident when the player switches sides and gazes at the board. It is implausible that the player could put out of mind the opponent's strategy while playing the game with all the resources that are at hand as he attempts to counter the other's moves. Such a game is possible, but the possibility of an enduring strategy that is sustained across turns on either side of the table is rendered nil since each "player's" move is informed by "intimate" knowledge of the other's strategy. Each must therefore adjust in light of the other's informed countermove. From this perspective, the attempt that some have made to posit self-deception and to unpack its practical implications is misconceived and quixotic.

We, too, are uncomfortable with the given name for self-deception, but not because of its intolerable epistemological implications. There is a bind, but the name misconceives that character of the bind that the person must solve. Morally, the problem of self-deception cannot be dismissed simply because our conception of that problem apparently yields logical nonsense. This would be an unconscionable response to persons who must live through this problem. The apparent absence of pain does not diminish this problem. But moral problems also intrude if we admit the existence of self-deception. In part, this is because the name implies that the state is achieved, not by somehow sliding into it unwittingly, but by the active initiation of the self-deceived persons. The *moral* implications of the name "self-deception" are intolerable, since this enables one to attribute wholesale moral responsibility to persons for their current self-deceived state. They intended to get into it. They should get out of it on their own. Further, its existence as a common-sense "thing" in the social world provides one with a vehicle with which to "accuse" disagreeable others. The accusation can unjustifiably induce a corrosive self-reflection in others that serves, by the route of doubt, to undermine their integrity. And from the self-deceiver's perspective, this process supposedly allows for the possibility of telling lies without needing to take responsibility. Moral security is not easily achieved in this domain.

We are uncomfortable both with the assertion and with the denial of the reality of self-deception. Either approach involves implications that we find unacceptable. Instead, we sketch out the framework for a different approach that we believe makes it easier to grapple with the problem. Certainly, from a philosophical perspective, more questions are raised than are settled by our proposal. But in the long run, the route we propose seems to offer a better chance for solving the philosophical dimensions of this problem. From a psychological perspective, the problem becomes more manageable. We bring to bear some of our research that should make this approach intelligible. We hope that this approach will better help one to understand, and even to know what to do, when confronted with another who is entangled in this problem.

THE WRONG PARADOX

Ironically, both those who assert and those who deny the existence of self-deception depend on a certain set of presuppositions about the person. The coherence of either position relies on the assumption that the healthy, sane person is already marked by a unity of character in which all facets are in conformity with each other and with some supra-situational standard of rationality. Any traces of disunity, inconsistency, or mixed feeling are symptoms of an organismic irrationality that is to be avoided at any cost. For those who assert the reality of self-deception, it is just these standards and the inability of "inconsistent" persons to face themselves that set in motion the processes of self-deception. Self-deception consists of a compromised attempt to recoup consistency within this flawed unity. The problem for philosophers and psychologists, then, is to understand how this unbalanced coherence is preserved over time. For those who deny the reality of self-deception, it is just this sort of unbalanced coherence that cannot exist in time. There can be no inconsistency precisely because by definition there is no disunity to the self. Unity precludes inconsistency and, so, for them, there cannot be self-deception. It is inconceivable that the self can honestly know (or affirm or believe) what it knows to be untrue. Both sides of the dispute hinge on this relation between unity and inconsistency where one side responds to the relation's purported existence with fascination while the other side responds with disbelief. One could say that their dispute centers on whether this requirement for consistency within the unified self is conventionally normative or logically necessary.

Both approaches are couched in the presumption that the "right" status of the self is in unity. As an issue to be considered, inconsistency and self-deception make definable though problematic sense only when the two propositions that are at odds reside within a single entity. Otherwise, the "inconsistency" is between two entities, and no single entity is inconsistent. But are these assumptions a necessarily adequate account of the person's character? Do the words "self-deception" accurately reflect the person's quandary? Do these two positions address the worldly problem that is named with words? If the answer to these questions is "no," then neither interlocuter offers a satisfactory approach to the problem that is named by "self-deception." In that spirit, we assert the unreality of self-deception as a problem. However, there is a problem that requires resolution.

The issue of paradox *per se* is not what we find problematic about making reference to self-deception. The problem of self-deception amounts to one in which transparency and opacity must be exhibited at the same moment so that each part of the person can operate with sensitivity to and yet in ignorance of other parts of the person. Some reject this problem because of its intolerably paradoxical character. But what is so unacceptable about paradox? Hiding behind logic is often no better than defying logic. The problem is not how to eliminate paradox; the problem is how to manage it. And in this case, we have been dealing with the wrong paradox.

There is no need to fall back on ungenerous metaphors of thievery or deceit in order to understand the problematic process. The problem involves a more mundane mystery of social life once we consider that the unity of the person may not be presumed. The problem, then, has its roots in the puzzle of routine social behavior. How can persons routinely act with competence in social circumstances without conscious reference to the conventional norms that give appropriate shape to behavior in those situations? How do people engage in ''roles'' and ''social habits'' when they are not minding the social manners that are their sole guidelines? We propose that the resources used by persons to act routinely in uncontroversial situations are also used by persons in more controversial situations, when others judge that these persons *do* know when they act as if they *do not* know (i.e., that these persons are self-deceived). Thus, it is not the process itself that is problematic or suspect but the particular circumstances under which it is invoked.

Consider the man who expertly drives his car down the highway without paying much attention to the road and then mindlessly puts his foot on the brake when there is a red light up ahead. How can he mindlessly abide by the social force of that sign if he is not paying attention to it? How can persons be sensitive to, *and yet unaware of,* the social stimuli in a situation that give direction to their behavior when they are acting in role? We know that such things are done routinely when persons are deeply embedded in any single, particular context. This recognition then introduces a more complex problem, once we appreciate that any one person is capable of routinely enacting a number of social roles from time to time as a function of circumstance. How are the standards that are routinely available to the person within one context kept out of sight and mind when an alternative context has been invoked? The person's dumbness to detail within the context that we initially posited is different from this current numbness to standards that are a part of currently unused contexts. Consider the easy distinction that we make between our personal lives and our professional lives and the distinctive set of skills and norms that we use in each case to give shape to our conduct. A person can mindlessly use one set of norms in business, untroubled by any actual conflict with the other set of norms. Conversely, too, there would be hell to pay if the person used those business norms as a basis for conduct in the home. How are these distinctive sets of social behavior routinely accomplished within their distinctive settings without awareness of the other setting? (This question is distinct from but, we will assert, related to the question of unawareness in detail of the actively used context.)

Supposing for the moment that we can distinguish between the moral and the technical features of this situation, we see two problems. A person is morally untroubled by the problem of double standards and double-dealing. The person is technically untroubled in that it is possible to reduce awareness in any one situation so as to abide routinely by the set of norms that is appropriate to these rather than other circumstances. Neither the moral nor the technical "conflict" ever becomes an issue. There is no interference. How does this happen without any qualms on the person's part? Under the supposition of unity to the person, this could be proposed as a benign example of self-deception. But we do not presume the unity of the person. Nor do we presume that the person is actively forestalling awareness of those other sets of norms and skills that are appropriate only in other contexts.

For each social environment, a socially situated identity of the person (i.e., a social "self") emerges that exhibits a knowledge of the skills and conventional standards that are appropriate for action in that environment. A loose confederation of selves (each of which has a semblance of coherence that is ready to identify with a particular environment) cohabit the person. Each is ready to emerge when the person is surrounded by the corresponding social environment, while the other "irrelevant" selves have retreated into the background. Without relying on the dreaded homunculus, whose existence we do not endorse, the problem then consists of understanding how these different selves do and do not relate to each other, how they influence each other, and how each contributes to the make-up of the person's character.[2] Character is constituted by the mosaic of these selves, and the nature of character itself must also be examined in coming to grips with self-deception. John Dewey's views on habits and on how they interpenetrate in the production of character are useful in this context. For Dewey,

> every habit contains an unconscious expectation. It forms a certain outlook.[3]

> The essence of habit is an acquired predisposition to ways or modes of response. Habit means special sensitiveness or accessibility to certain classes of stimuli.[4]

> Were it not for the continued operation of all habits in every act, no such thing as character could exist. . . . Character is the interpenetra-

tion of habits. . . . Of course such interpenetration is never total. It is most marked in what we call strong characters. Integration is an achievement rather than a datum.[5]

A person's character is the result of the confederation of selves. But only observers see the character of a person. The person is acting in context, in a particular social self that has thrown the other selves into background relief. Awareness is couched in terms of this self and not in terms of the character. And when the person is deeply embedded in any one routine and self, he is doubly unaware. He is unaware of the detail in the relevant social environment as he responds automatically to its structure; and he is unaware of the resources that lie fallow in other selves within his character. For example, the significance of the red light is absent from the routine driver's awareness in a way that is different from the absence in his mind while on the road of the way in which he should treat his children in his role as father.

Our research has focused on how persons can remain mindless to the details within context even as they routinely accomplish behavior that demonstrates knowledge of those details. But for any one person, we maintain that there is a relationship between this within context mindlessness and the person's insensitivity to other selves across contexts when a particular self is in control. This is our route to the problem of "self-deception." But the same process can persist under either benign or malignant circumstances. How is it that these selves are and are not connected to each other? How and when do they exercise more or less influence over each other? Dewey, again, made some relevant remarks.

> If each habit existed in an insulated compartment and operated without affecting or being affected by others, character would not exist. That is, conduct would lack unity being only a juxtaposition of disconnected reactions to separated situations. But since environments overlap, since situations are continuous and those remote from one another contain like elements, a continuous modification of habits by one another is constantly going on.[6]

Perhaps. But we will contend that there are specifiable circumstances under which this "continuous modification" reliably will not amount to significant changes in any one self over time—to wit, when persons are particularly mindless. In this case, when knowledge from another context remains out of reach with malignant results, then we may speak of "self-deception."

Recall the person who easily distinguishes between his personal life and his professional life and who comfortably acts in routine conformity with each setting despite the fact that the conventional standards of the two settings contradict each other. The untroubled action in either setting was offered as an example of what might come under the rubric of self-deception, since we have here a person whose actions endorse one standard while "covertly" endorsing another, contradictory standard. However, in coming to grips with this problem, the focus should not be on how the man does and does not *know* his personal standards while he is acting professionally, as is encouraged by framing the problem as one of self-deception. Instead, the focus should be on how, when the person is acting professionally, the personal self has its effect. How is it both connected to and separated from the professional self that is acting out?

Notice, too, that the problematic aspects of the situation hang together differently once we do not presume the unity of the person. For those who have asserted the reality of self-deception, it is the total *character* (using our terms) who has the problem that is "resolved" by self-deception. In some fashion, he maneuvers to keep a part of his character at bay, knowing full well that this is necessary in order that the other part operate successfully. From the perspective of our reformulated paradox, it is *one of the selves* that is in the "quandary" as it continually consolidates its position. It does not necessarily see that it is threatened by the contradictory standards of the other (i.e., the personal) self. Does it or doesn't it? From a distance, the situation might seem quite similar to what is purportedly going on during self-deception, but the dynamics of the situation are quite different. The self is not involved in its own deception by keeping a part of itself at bay. The self is wholly involved in its own protection by keeping tabs on all of itself with never a mind to what is "out there," even if it is dimly aware that there is something out there (within character). The self is involved in keeping everything about itself the same. Its attention is turned inward rather than both inward and outward at the same time as self-deception would have it be. At least this seems to be what is going on when the self is involved in what is better named as *self-protection*. This problematic process has been regarded from the outside in when, to appreciate it truly, it should be regarded from the inside out.

Notice, too, that given this account, a person's life project becomes told in different terms. Under the presumption that there is a given unity to a person, any inconsistency in the person is regarded as a flaw in the character. Diverse parts of the person must be commensurate with each other. They retain their legitimacy and rationality because they are rooted in and consistent with one transcendent, all-purpose set of values that guarantees their commensurability. Any inconsistency is a sign of pathology and life's project consists of recouping the perfect state of grace.

Under the presumption that there is no necessary unity to the person, however, each self cultivates an appreciation for the context-specific values that are native to its setting. The person whose character is less than perfectly consistent is not a sick person. What looks like an inconsistency in *character* from the outside observer's view does not necessarily pose a conflict for any one of the selves on the inside. The problem of life becomes how to incorporate and/or keep at a distance the disparate sets of standards that each have value in their distinct settings. When two different selves join together in a fashion that is more intricate than that which either possessed alone, we have observed what could be called the process of *self-inception* as the two earlier selves are dissolved. Life's project then becomes a matter of surpassing the present with a character that reflects a more encompassing, co-ordinating, and satisfying integrity. Within this framework, the alternative response to approaching conflict is self-protection, where the person is statically involved in preserving one self. Under desperate circumstances, when the person shuts out the rest of the world, this action takes on the appearance of what is called self-deception. Life's tale is told in terms of the distinct selves that a person cultivates and the growing closeness or remoteness of these selves over time. The key to the problem at hand involves sorting out the distinctive conditions that foster one sort of growth or another (i.e., self-protection or self-inception).

Under normal circumstances, the socialized person competently responds in different social settings. Each social environment stimulates the emergence of the appropriate social self. There is no question of which social self "should" emerge since, under routine circumstances, any one social environment is relevant to and recognizable by only one social self. In simple terms, it is merely a case of stimulus and response. This social self is the response to that social environment. No other self responds. In these cases, the process of self-protection operates quite productively. It seals off from awareness all irrelevant details of this domain and all other domains as it is oriented toward achieving certain goals and purposes. Much of this is done unwittingly as this self is single-mindedly attuned to growing more at home with this context.

Consider a more complicated version of an earlier example. The person sustains diverse selves including social identities as a son, husband, executive, golfer, father, student, and man. Each self has its own skills and conventional standards. These context-specific skills and standards that are embodied in each identity are not necessarily consistent with those embodied in other identities. How is each done so skillfully without reference to the cohabiting standards that would appropriately emerge in other social environments? Or is it really done without that reference? This is the crux of the issue that we see as basic to the management of life.

The problem assumes new and more personally urgent dimensions when confusion reigns and it is not clear which self or corresponding skills and standards are now appropriate in the social environment that surrounds the person. It becomes a more troubling, personal problem when two identities may equally "claim" to be the relevant one that should assume control in the situation. Reconsider our example and see the person as husband and father. The gesture of tenderness that this husband embodies for his wife is different from the gesture of tenderness that this father embodies for his daughter—even when those gestures are initiated by the "same" character. But are those two gestures different? The man is becoming confused. He is beginning to see his daughter in a new light, and an uneasy feeling has settled in. Are we seeing the first traces of an incestuous situation? The mechanism has broken down, and the paradoxical equilibrium has been disturbed. How is the person going to respond? A dramatic episode is potentially in sight. Conflict and contradiction are possibilities now that the mysterious relation between two selves has been unbalanced and the two have come in view of each other. How does the person handle approaching conflict and contradiction? Does he respond with self-protection or with self-inception? And what would either response look like? Which would be the better response?

These are the difficult problems that have traditionally been addressed under the rubric of self-deception if, for example, the father is seen to act towards his daughter as if she were his wife while he claims to be treating her as his daughter. But they may be more adequately dealt with in this framework we have been setting forth, even if all its problematic features cannot be completely resolved. Research that we have been conducting can provide insight into these issues. In that work, we have distinguished between mindful and mindless activity. Most of the work has focused on how a person's behavior can become mindless when one self is operating within one context. But we will articulate how mindless versus mindful activity within context does have clear implications for the way in which one self will respond to others across contexts in these possibly conflictual situations.

AN ALTERNATIVE APPROACH

As a species, humans do not set out with purpose to deceive themselves. Rather, from time to time and from place to place, they find themselves exposed to new social environments. As they grow more familiar with any one environment and as it takes on more detail, a corresponding social self is cultivated that grows attached to the recognizable sight. In many cases, they stake themselves to certain contexts and commit themselves to the skills and values necessary for operating in that context while remaining oblivious to the consistency of this commitment with their other commitments. In fact, they are liable to remain oblivious to the whole question of consistency. (Picture, for example, the Nazi soldier who has had a tiring day at the concentration camp and who returns to his off-base home in order to enjoy a restful evening with his family eating dinner and listening to Mozart. This "whole" situation may be the upshot of this person dutifully consolidating the commitment to each context while remaining unwitting of the other.) Laudable or not, this is an accurate reflection of the way persons operate as they move from scene to scene in their social world. Responsible or not, the issue of consistency often does not arise until there is a promise of conflict. Without this promise, persons continue to consolidate their commitments from context to context, while "isolating" from each other the different selves that have taken root in the distinctive contexts. This isolation can be seen more as a function of the desire to grow near to what is present than to become distant from what is absent.

Given the absence of conflict, this is a reasonable approach to take when one is operating in the world. It leads to concentrated, focused attention to the task at hand without any distractions from the external environment or the internal conventional standards that are irrelevant to this goal-directed activity. But it also leaves the person blind to the storm clouds of contradiction that are on the horizon, clouds that are more easily visible from the perspective of an outside observer who can see the person's whole character. There are two distinguishable ways in which any one of the person's selves can be prepared to respond in the event that the conflict breaks out. He can be prepared to respond self-protectively if he has produced too rigid a definition of all of the elements that constitute this social environment including its social self. His rigid perceptions represent every object in the environment as if they could be no other way. From this perspective, the alteration of any object's shape amounts to its destruction, and this cannot be allowed. Or he can be prepared to respond self-inceptively if he has produced a labile definition of all the elements that constitute the social environment including the social self. His labile perceptions represent every object in the environment as amenable to an alteration that would not necessarily destroy the identity of the whole.

The former case has advantages in that operations can take place more quickly and efficiently given that conditions remain the same, but it may leave the door open to inefficiency if conditions change significantly. We have called this form of activity a mindless engagement with the environment. The other case has advantages in that operations can flexibly adjust to changing conditions in the environment, but it may leave the door open to significant inefficiency by some criteria if conditions remain radically unaltered; a great deal of effort will have been put to no useful purpose in maintaining the person's readiness to change. We have called this form of activity a mindful engagement with the environment.

In any case, the person's obliviousness to "internal" contradictions obvious to the outside observer should not be taken as definitive evidence that self-deception is occurring. A great deal of recent social psychological research indicates that the views offered by an actor's perspective and by an observer's perspective yield radically different sights.[7] The observer may infer that all of the actor's beliefs that are available to the observer are equally available to the actor's awareness. But the awareness of one's own beliefs and perceptions is unevenly distributed. Other research shows that as persons gaze at the environment, they are more liable to pick up on and process self-relevant information.[8] Given such circumstances, the observer might note that the actor is "endorsing" two contradictory propositions, one by his actions and one in some more covert fashion; and he might infer that the person is engaging in self-deception. But such a view of the process may be evident only from the observer's perspective. Unlike the actor, he presently has access to both contradictory propositions. And so when he sees the actor choosing one and "ignoring" the other, he presumes that a process of cogitation preceded the action—a process that amounts to continuing self-deception. The actor, however, does not see this and perhaps never engages in the process of rejection of the other proposition. He is intent on self-relevant action, oblivious to all irrelevance and anything other than its presence.[9] As we remarked, this self-protective behavior may often be quite benign and useful. In these cases, if the person is troubled, then it is with the pragmatic problem of what to do rather than with the logical and cognitive inconsistencies.

Perhaps this, in part, was why Fingarette shifted the emphasis in analyzing self-deception from "cognition-perception" terms to "volition-action" terms.[10] His analysis relies on the assumption of a unified person who maneuvers to cover up his flawed coherence. For the reasons that have been detailed, we find this to be an unsatisfactory approach. The person is not occupying himself with a *refusal* to spell out or avow, so as to avoid possible inconsistency. The person is occupied with a different self that is intent on moving in its own direction.

Initially, it has no bearing on the other selves that may or may not sustain contradictory beliefs or actions. Later, perhaps, it senses the burden. In order to understand how the self might prepare itself, for better or worse, when the system is unbalanced and drawn into unexpected contact with another self, we must examine how the one self operates when it is singularly involved within its own context.

MINDLESS AND MINDFUL ACTION

In attempting to understand the nature of routine social activity, we have been conducting an ongoing research program that distinguishes between mindless and mindful action. Mindlessness refers to a state of reduced cognitive activity where the meaningful cues of the surrounding environment are processed in a relatively automatic fashion. The environment assumes a relatively rigid structure, and behavior proceeds according to a well-defined and unchanging routine. Mindfulness, on the other hand, refers to a more active state of cognitive activity during which the meaning of the environment is currently being shaped. The environment is represented as having a more labile structure; behavior, in this context, is much less regular than it is under mindless conditions. The structure that organizes mindless activity usually emerges over time as the person is repeatedly exposed to and engaged with a certain social environment. Under certain conditions, however, mindless activity can be induced by means of a single exposure to a structured environment. Therefore, it should be distinguished from the associationist grasp of habit which pictures the routine as something that is built up over time.

Much of the research that we will describe focuses on determining how any one social self operates under either mindless or mindful conditions. As we said earlier, other selves persist in the background. The relation between these and the self that is in person remains indeterminate. We maintain that the self is reliably prepared to relate in one way or another with the other selves depending on whether that self is operating mindlessly or mindfully within any one context.

A study performed in a field setting experimentally documented the character of mindless activity.[11] We used the Xerox machine in a university library as a prop. When subjects approached the machine and placed their material on it, the experimenter asked for a favor. Could he or she use the machine before the subject used it? We hypothesized that the levels of compliance would be higher when the request was accompanied by a reason. In that light, experimenters articulated one of three forms of request for a favor: (1) a request alone ("May 1 use the

Xerox machine?''), (2) a request and a reason with sufficient information (''May I use the Xerox machine? I'm in a rush''), or (3) a request accompanied by what we called placebic information because it had only the structure of added information but in reality added no extra meaning (''May I use the Xerox machine? I have to make copies''). Why else would one want to use the machine? ''I want to make copies'' adds the structure of a reason to the request that might stimulate a response of compliance under mindless conditions, but it does not add meaningful information that would stimulate a higher level of compliant response under mindful conditions.

We reasoned that if the placebic subjects were responding mindlessly (to the structure), then their levels of compliance would resemble those of subjects who were given a meaningful reason along with the request. If they were responding mindfully (to the meaning), then their levels of compliance would resemble those of subjects who were given a request only, since both groups received the same amount of meaningful information—just a request. In fact, we created experimental conditions to demonstrate both mindless and mindful responses in the placebic subjects—the former where a small effort was called for by the subject and the latter where a large effort was required. In the former case, mindless response to the structure of the request was exhibited by placebic subjects in their compliance levels that were comparable to those of the subjects with sufficient information. In the latter case, mindful response to the meaning of the request was exhibited by placebic subjects in their compliance levels that were comparable to subjects who had been given no reason at all. These data demonstrated the distinction between mindless and mindful activity where, on the one hand, a person responds routinely to the structure of the environment and, on the other hand, the person is actively involved in processing the meaning of the situation.

Often the structures that organize mindless behavior emerge and take force over time with repeated exposure. Elsewhere, we recount the different ways in which this might occur and the distinctive effects that these processes have on the self that participates.[12] However, as we have said, repeated exposure is not a necessary prerequisite for mindless behavior. If upon initial exposure to new and unqualified information the person, for whatever reason, uncritically accepts that information, that person might later be forced to behave mindlessly within the confines of the conceptual scheme that was implied in that information. He has accepted the rigid definition of the environment with each structural element of the environment rigidly meaning just one thing. Now, when he has to use that information, he is busy applying it uncritically rather than critically reexamining it—if he is operating under mindless conditions. The situation would be different if the information presented had been qualified in some way or if the information was initially relevant and thereby warranted cognitive effort. Then, the environment would be represented as a labile structure that could be seen in any number of ways and that did not necessarily dictate a single course of action.

We examined these proposals regarding premature cognitive commitments using one set of conditions where persons might accept information uncritically—where the information is presented as irrelevant to them. In one study we exposed four groups of subjects to identical information about a purported cognitive defect, a visual incapacity that we called "field dependence."[13] In pamphlets that introduced them to this information for the first and only time, we likened field dependence to dyslexia and color blindness. Since people rarely talk to each other about the details of their perceptions, this long-standing visual problem had been discovered only recently.

The conditions under which this information was given were manipulated in two ways so as to vary the perceived relevance of the information and the amount of independent thinking that they performed. All subjects took an assessment test and "discovered" that they had field dependence. When subjects were subsequently given another assessment, however, only the group that had initially perceived the information as irrelevant and had not been encouraged to think showed severe performance decrements once the information became relevant. This mindlessness can be learned on the basis of a single experience with information. It does not require repeated exposure.

This self-handicapping aspect of premature cognitive commitment has been used to understand how certain alcoholics are unable to benefit from therapeutic treatments. We hypothesized that these alcoholics were exposed to one dysfunctional model of alcoholism when they were children. At the time, they represented the possibilities of recovery from alcohol in rigid, pessimistic terms. Since they had no exposure to alternative models, they mindlessly accepted that this was the way to be alcoholic. They did not appreciate the lability of the environment that would offer the means for alternative responses to their problem. On the other hand, those alcoholics who had experienced alternative modes of adjustment in others during their own childhood would be in a position to recover when support was offered. They would not represent the environment in a rigid manner that leaves no leeway for an alternative response. Preliminary data that we have gathered bears out this hypothesis. Of those alcoholics tested who successfully completed therapy, 100% were not from the single negative model group.[14]

In general, the self is set up to engage in what we observers perceive to be self-handicapping behavior whenever two conditions are satisfied. First, the person has come to appreciate that the environment is composed of a set of rigid elements that can entertain only one meaning. This mindlessness can be the result of either repeated or single exposure. Second, the world has conspired in such a way that the single, rigid meaning of the environment that is available happens to signify and promote a relatively dysfunctional mode of operation. The mindless person is stuck there as he attempts to hold his ground self-protectively, and the alternative response is not recognized as a possibility. Mindlessness or self-protection is not necessarily a pathological activity. However, if the person slips too easily into mindless engagements with the environment, then that person becomes entirely vulnerable to any misleading signs from the environment that "rigidly" signify the person's inferiority.

This was clearly demonstrated in a series of studies that examined what we call self-induced dependence.[15] We explored the role that situational factors play in cuing the person into his relative status in an interaction and what effect this would have on his performance. The cue could connote relative inferiority or superiority in the situation. If the target of that cue was mindless, then his performance should respectively decline or rise as he follows the rigid signification of that cue. If, on the other hand, the person was acting mindfully, then his response to the cue would not necessarily involve him in reducing the efficiency of his prior performance. In fact, the experiments yielded results that supported these hypotheses.

This framework has been applied to understanding the situation of elderly persons who reside in nursing homes. Perhaps, some of the disabilities and dependencies that they display are a function of their mindless endorsement of situational cues that signal their helplessness. If this were the case, then an experimental strategy that either provoked mindfulness or transformed the cue to indicate the elders' superiority would result in their improved performance. The latter strategy was used in one study, and it yielded results that supported these hypotheses.[16] Two groups of elders were taught a psychomotor task. The group that was "helped" was given extensive assistance in completing the task, while the group that was "only encouraged" was given verbal encouragement but minimal assistance. Relative to a control group that received no experience with the task, the performance of the "helped" group deteriorated over the experimental period, while the performance of the group of "encouraged" persons improved. Further, the "helped" group saw the task as more difficult and was less self-confident than the "encouraged" group. The findings indicate that elders were responding to the tacit cues that the situation was providing about their status and competence.

The process of self-deception does not best capture the dynamics through which the subjects in all these experiments were induced to perform at a level that systematically fell short of their capacities. It is true that from an outsider's perspective we may have all the material that is required in order to make the inference of self-deception. This analysis of routine action within context, however, presumes that a person would clearly know what he is capable of, regardless of where that skill is deposited within his person. It posits a set of machinations that somehow hides this knowledge in plain view. These mundane instances bespeak a different process. They present situations in which cognitive activity is almost entirely absent. To the degree that it is present, the self in person is devoted to maintaining equilibrium in the corresponding social environment. In the routine situation, when the self uneasily senses some undefined trouble, it seems more accurate to represent its actions as efforts to grasp what it knows rather than efforts to push away what it knows not. Perhaps the routine example provides us with general lessons about the character of a more dramatic episode of "conflict" that seems to present itself indubitably to others as an example of self-deception. You can interpret it as self-deception, but from the self's perspective, crawling into a hole is better seen as self-protection.

CONCLUSION

When one self is in control, the person is acting under the sway of the social context that is currently shaping the environment. When the outsider notices a conflict between what the person truthfully says and what the person knows but is not saying, the outsider infers self-deception. In that light, he sees a conflict *within* the person. But it is better to say that this is conflict between contexts. These two contexts are personified by two facets of the character. These two facets never necessarily play catch with each other. Because each may be appropriate to a certain set of social circumstances that is radically irrelevant to the other, the two selves may never be interlocutors. That diversity does not dictate conflict. Sometimes, it is an invitation to productive reformulation. At other times, though, the situation is confusing. It is not clear which of two sets of standards that have developed orthogonally is the more appropriate one. In that situation, the two are uneasily aware of one another. It is more of a quandary than a conflict. How does the person handle approaching conflict? It depends. In the final analysis, it is an indeterminate affair. We have sketched two alternative responses. Self-protection can occur, whereby each of the two selves turns into itself as the two grow farther apart. Each is interested in its own preservation and therefore focuses its efforts on rigidly retaining the identity of all its parts. When a person is acting mindlessly, the person is conditioned for a self-protective response. All of the elements of the ascendant self are in a rigid guise. Of course, it is not clear which of the two selves is ascendant, and this is part of the problem. But in the paradoxical way in which the selves are separated and connected, they inject a mindless orientation into the character that is produced by their juxtaposition. And this again mysteriously increases the chances of a self-protective response that may take on the appearance of self-deception.

The other alternative is self-inception, whereby each of the two turns toward something—toward *what?* is the question. But each is ready for something else. This recognition induces in each self a sensitivity to the lability of its own parts. Each self is ready for change. When acting mindfully, the conditions are set for a self-inceptive response where two earlier selves might be left behind. All of the elements are open to alteration in form. Something new is about to happen, and each is sensitive to this through the paradoxical way in which all selves are separated and connected. They inject a mindful orientation into the character that is produced by their juxtaposition. And this again mysteriously increases the chances of a self-inceptive response. Finally, the response is indeterminate. There may be complications. One self may lean toward self-protection while the other leans toward self-inception or vice-versa. As Dewey said, "Diversity does not of itself imply conflict, but it implies the possibility of conflict."[17] But it also implies the possibility of integration.

NOTES

1. See, for example, Kipp (1980) and those whom he cites as contributing to the minor-stream approach to self-deception that solves the problem by dissolving all of its epistemologically problematic aspects. David Kipp, "On Self-Deception," *Philosophical Quarterly* 30 (1980): 305–317.

2. Another problem that we will not consider, even though perhaps we should, consists of the problematic nature of these selves. We are not partisans of a "homunculus account" of human behavior, and we would not want to be

misunderstood as redressing the discussed issues by positing a horde of homunculi. Without getting into the many problems of continuing personal identity, we would use "self" as a metaphor for that socially situated semblance of coherence "within" the person that exhibits a knowledge of skills and conventional standards appropriate to an environment. The issue remains to be resolved, but we do not think that the argument is materially affected by it. Similar problems are at hand about the nature of the self whether one is talking about the one or the many.

3. Dewey, *Human Nature and Conduct* (New York: Modern Library, 1957), 87.

4. Ibid., 42.

5. Ibid., 38.

6. Ibid.

7. Edward E. Jones and Richard E. Nisbett, "The Actor and the Observer: Divergent Perceptions of the Causes of Behavior," in *Attribution: Perceiving the Causes of Behavior,* ed. E. E. Jones et al. (Morristown, N.J.: General Learning Press, 1972), 79–94.

8. Hazel Markus, "Self-Schemata and Processing Information about the Self," *Journal of Personality and Social Psychology* 35 (1977): 63–78.

9. One difficulty in all of this that generally seems to have been glossed over is the presumption that all persons share the same criteria for what is considered relevant; and therefore "it" must have been ignored or rejected if one notes its relevance and notes that it has not been acted upon. Perhaps the actor and the observer do not share a single standard for what is relevant in any one situation.

10. Herbert Fingarette, *Self-Deception* (London: Routledge and Kegan Paul, 1969), 35.

11. Ellen Langer, Arthur Blank, and Benzion Chanowitz, "The Mindlessness of Ostensibly Thoughtful Action: The Role of Placebic Information in Interpersonal Interaction," *Journal of Personality and Social Psychology* 36 (1978): 635–642.

12. Benzion Chanowitz and Ellen Langer, "Knowing More (or Less) than You Can Show: Understanding Control through the Mindlessness-Mindfulness Distinction," in *Human Helplessness: Theory and Applications,* ed. J. Garber and M. E. P. Seligman (New York: Academic Press, 1980), 97–129.

13. Benzion Chanowitz and Ellen Langer, "Premature Cognitive Commitment," *Journal of Personality and Social Psychology* 41 (1981): 1051–1063.

14. Ellen Langer, Lawrence Perlmuter, Benzion Chanowitz, and Robert Rubin, "Two New Applications of Mindlessness Theory: Aging and Alcoholism," unpublished manuscript, Harvard University, 1984.

15. Ellen Langer and Anne Benevento, "Self-Induced Dependence," *Journal of Personality and Social Psychology* 36 (1978): 886–893.

16. Jerry Avorn and Ellen Langer, "Induced Disability in Nursing Home Patients: A Controlled Trial," *Journal of the American Geriatrics Society* 30 (1982): 397–400.

17. Dewey, *Human Nature and Conduct,* 52.

PART III
COMMITMENT TO VALUES:
RATIONALITY AND MORALITY

Introduction

Mike W. Martin

This self-deceit, this fatal weakness of mankind, is the source of half the disorders of human life.
—Adam Smith, *The Theory of Moral Sentiments*

Traditional moralists like Adam Smith criticized self-deception insofar as it serves to camouflage wrongdoing and prevent improvement in character. In this role they regarded it as a derivative and compounding wrong—a wrong that derives from its support for some primary wrong and that serves to double one's guilt. By contrast, existentialist ethicists like Sartre made more sweeping condemnations of self-deceivers as hypocritical, phony, and inauthentic for evading truth and responsibility. Yet another tradition, the mental health tradition, tended to view self-deceivers as unfortunate victims of ignorance and compulsions. And common sense adds its voice in insisting that at least some self-deception has little to do with morality or mental health. I am not immoral or sick just because I deceive myself into believing that my cat is exceptionally talented. The moral status of self-deception is complex and open to alternative ethical interpretations. In their contribution to this part, John King-Farlow and Richard Bosley offer a fresh approach to understanding it.

A further and perhaps equally complicated issue is when and why self-deception is unreasonable or irrational in a pejorative sense. Responding to this issue requires answering three more questions. What is meant by self-deception? What is meant by "irrational"? And what value should be placed on rationality? Béla Szabados and Robert Audi provide contrasting approaches to these questions, emphasizing the first two.

Béla Szabados defines self-deception as entailing the violation of standards of rationality used to establish truth and falsehood. Self-deceivers hold beliefs that go against the evidence in their possession, or refuse to acknowledge truths that they would recognize if they respected rational procedures. Unlike psychotics, they retain the ability to be reasonable, and in fact they undermine their own general commitments to being rational. Their distorted pseudo-rationality relies upon two major strategies: "evasion" of evidence by diverting attention from it or disregarding its implications, and "rationalization" in the sense of allowing desires and fears to bias reasoning. Self-deceivers are motivated by some personal stake, such as love, which is linked to their sense of personal identity. At the end of his essay Szabados illustrates how this explains the profound difficulty in attaining self-knowledge.

Self-deception differs from mere wishful thinking. While both involve holding a motivated belief that is not well-grounded in evidence, only self-deception entails distorting evidence while reasoning. Self-deception is also distinct from (although it can help facilitate) weakness of will, which is the failure to live up to one's values in situations where one is capable of doing otherwise. Most importantly, self-deception is not reducible to mere deception of others, whether in the form of lying or pretense.

At the beginning of the essay and later, Szabados responds to earlier writings of M. R. Haight and David Kipp. Kipp had contended that so-called self-deception is typically a form of conscious pretense before others, and Haight had held that the expression "self-deception" in a literal sense implies a contradiction. Szabados dubs these views "The Conspiracy Theory of Self-Deception"; he interprets them as suggesting that people who employ the concept of self-deception are engaged in a kind of tacit agreement to use an incoherent notion. He urges that we can always ask whether deceivers are willing to admit to themselves their pretenses. If so, they are not self-deceivers. If not, they may be literal self-deceivers if they also distort the proper procedures used in assessing evidence.

Robert Audi also begins by sharply contrasting self-deception and interpersonal deception by invoking the illustration of Iago's deception of Othello. He asks whether self-deception is paradoxical (or impossible) since on the surface it seems to imply getting oneself to believe something that one simultaneously knows and believes is not true. In his view the air of paradox is removed once we introduce a subtle redescription. Self-deceivers sincerely avow what they unconsciously believe is false, where both the avowal and the unconscious belief are explained by a want linked to their self-image or values. The appeal to unconscious beliefs—that is, beliefs not readily accessible to consciousness without special help or self-scrutiny—explains how a person can sincerely avow a proposition that contradicts the unconscious belief. Moreover, sincere avowal is not identical with, nor does it entail, full-blown belief (even though the two usually go together when self-deception is absent).

Audi's conception of self-deception differs in several respects from Szabados's. Audi views the *state* of self-deception (composed of the elements of sincere avowal, contrary unconscious knowledge, and a motivating want) as logically primary. Self-deceiving *acts* must be defined by reference to this state, whether as causing, supporting, or expressing it. This stands in contrast to Szabados's emphasis on the self-deceiving activities of ignoring and rationalizing evidence. Also, Audi de-emphasizes the activity of distorting evidence in generating self-deception. He develops a conception of rationality according to which no distortion of the standards of rationality need occur in self-deception.

Roughly, states of mind are rational when they are well-grounded, and persons are rational to the extent they do not have irrational states of mind or engage in behavior producing them. In particular, beliefs are well-grounded by reference to experience, whether directly via appropriate perceptions or indirectly via sound inferences. Basic wants are well-grounded in terms of their intrinsic desirability or because they would be affirmed after scrutiny in light of relevant facts and logical norms like consistency. And actions are well-grounded when they are based on and contribute to rational beliefs and wants. Audi systematically applies these criteria to the beliefs, wants, and actions involved in self-deception, and concludes that while most self-deception is irrational, not all of it is. Self-deception is rational when it advances reasonable wants better than other available options, does not embody or produce irrational beliefs, wants, or acts, and does not undermine the ability to deal with evidence reasonably.

At the end of his essay Audi comments on the role the concept of self-deception plays in explaining and predicting behavior. The concept only indirectly explains actions by alluding to the more directly explanatory beliefs and wants involved in the state of self-deception, and it has very limited use in predicting specific behavior.

John King-Farlow and Richard Bosley focus on the moral dimensions of self-deception. They begin with several illustrations from literature intended to establish an important thesis: self-deception is a potent force that can serve either good or bad. Much of it is harmless, much of it is creative in bringing about self-fulfillment (as Audi also shows with an example of a timid speaker), and some of it constitutes a prudent escape from a potentially disastrous dilemma. Just as surely, self-deception can be immoral in as many ways as there are contexts of human conduct, and these immoral varieties quickly become the focus of the essay.

In order to delineate some order among the immoral forms of self-deception, King-Farlow and Bosley invoke the Aristotelian-Confucian concept of the Golden Mean: that is, the appropriate or virtuous balance residing between the faults of too much (excess) and too little (defect). Acknowledging and expressing truth is itself a means lying between the extremes of withholding relevant facts (defect) and introducing irrelevant and misleading information (excess). Correspondingly, undesirable self-deception may take the form of either defect—refusing to face or admit the truth—or excess—lying to oneself by fabricating or concealing the truth with phony rationalization.

English idioms of sight and hearing reflect this duality. We speak of being blind to the facts (defect) or blinded by a pleasant illusion (excess), and refusing to listen (defect) or deafening oneself with distracting chatter (excess). These idioms are essentially metaphors, however, since self-deceit proceeds via thought and language instead of mere perceptual distortion. In a culminating dialogue between Confucius and Aristotle it is suggested that self-deception tends to be worse when it involves the excess of embracing rationalization (putting a false face on reality) rather than defect (not facing reality) since the former tends to be more entrenched and difficult to replace with self-enlightenment.

The three parts of the essay following the introduction sketch the main ways self-deception is damaging within the contexts of childhood, adolescence, and adulthood. These contexts represent idealized stages of human development and correspond only roughly to the chronology of any individual's life. The primary moral task in childhood is to emerge from one-way dependence on one's parents ("single dependence") into increasing social interaction based on communal values, beginning with appreciation of the contributions others have made to one's nurturing. The child's liabilities, often mediated by self-deception, are unrestrictive pleasure seeking (excess) or failures to show responsive love and prudently develop talents (defects). With the gradual mastery of language comes increasing subtlety in ways to con, gull, confuse, and manipulate oneself and others via self-deception.

Adolescence is characterized by intense inner disunity, which is aptly described with the metaphor of multiple selves. A morally disciplined Master Self struggles to integrate conflicting passions around a unifying "collective mean" for the subselves. Harmful forms of self-deception enter as a means to evade the difficult task of reconciling competing claims of the subselves. Finally, adulthood represents the age of struggle toward self-enlightenment. There is a gradual increase in the ability to balance conflicting values so as to reach the Golden Mean between moral excess and deficiency: for example, neither stinginess nor extravagance; neither callous indifference nor obsequious subservience. This requires cultivating disciplined passions with increasing sensitivity to situations where each of four types of relationships are warranted: single dependence, mutual dependence, single independence, and mutual independence.

The Self,
Its Passions and Self-Deception

Béla Szabados

> Working in philosophy—like work in architecture in many respects—is
> really more a working on oneself. On one's own interpretation. On
> one's own way of seeing things. . . . Nothing is so difficult as not
> deceiving oneself.
>
> —Ludwig Wittgenstein, *Culture and Value*

THE CONSPIRACY THEORY OF SELF-DECEPTION

There is an interesting heresy in the recent literature on self-
deception. The tradition has been to affirm the coherence of the concept
in spite of seeming contradictions.

In sharp contrast with this, the heretical view begins by affirming
that 'self-deception' is impossible. It is claimed that the sustained
analytical efforts have only succeeded to show that if a case is to count as
a putative case of self-deception, then its description is contradictory;
and if its description is not contradictory, then the case is correctly
described as something else. This gesture towards "something else"
seems to give us the promise of a new direction for exploration. So to
this extent at least, the heretical view is optimistic even though it is
deeply pessimistic about the idea of self-deception itself.

But why is 'self-deception' impossible? Briefly: if self-deception is
really *deception*, then it has to satisfy certain conditions for *deception*. A
necessary condition for 'A deceives B' is that 'A knows that p, and A
keeps B from knowing that p.' Or to put it less strongly: 'A believes that

p and A makes B believe that not-*p*.' So, in a case of self-deception we would have a subject who both knows and does not know the same proposition, at the same time and in the same respect. Or to put it less strongly, we would have a subject who both believes and disbelieves the same proposition, at the same time and in the same respect. And this is contradictory. The upshot is that literal language has failed us here. The idea of self-deception is incoherent and is never more than a mere metaphor. It is always an incorrect way to refer to or describe certain phenomena.

But if 'self-deception' is a metaphor, then we should be able to say, in literal language, what it really means. How are those pieces of conduct and frames of mind that are widely supposed to be cases of self-deception to be correctly described? The heretical view is that self-deception is in fact no more than wishful thinking, gullibility, and misplaced good intentions; or more strongly, self-deception is really a lie only to other people.[1] The self-deceiver is well aware of the truth that he is trying to deny, but he acts as though he were not. "It is to behave as though some manifest truth were false, because this allows one to act in a way that otherwise seems impossible."[2] Lying or pretending is said to be the simplest explanation. There is no paradox about a lie. Hitherto so-called self-deceivers are either wishful thinkers, mere liars and deceivers of other people, hypocrites, or simply weak-willed people.

If self-deception could not possibly exist, then why did we nevertheless have to invent it? To put it paradoxically: Why do we deceive ourselves into believing in 'self-deception'? The answer given is that self-deception is really a game we play with and for other people. We all partake in a conspiracy by having made an unspoken treaty with each other to play this game. The aim of the game is to confuse people so as to make them unsure how to judge us. To deceive oneself is really to pretend that one is self-deceived in order to confuse others so that one gets away scot-free or with little blame for what is a blatant lie or pretense. Consider M. R. Haight's statement of the heretical view of self-deception:

> Its suggestion that the man's contrary behaviour is due to ignorance, to being deceived, will quiet the Judge in us somewhat, and will give Socratic hope to the Social Worker. The claim that such ignorance is self-induced will at least pretend to explain its often very obvious look of means to an end. And once we call a man a self-deceiver we can stress whichever point of view suits us at the time. He is an agent or a victim. He is an ingenious deceiver or strangely deceived. He is sincere or muddled, or he is worse than an ordinary liar. We can do all this only because 'self-deception' is contradictory and so never more than a mere metaphor.[3]

Here the alleged function of 'self-deception' is to confuse others so as to evade or diminish responsibility. Another alleged function of the concept is that of a face-saving device in front of others. In this variation of the heretical view, the self-deceiver is really a deceiver of other people, "who tries to fend off, through deceptive pretense, what they regard as defeat, or loss of face, in a not entirely unreal socially staged power struggle, or status seeking contest, whose goal is to appear in the eyes of others, a maximally enviable existential success."[4]

Is this really what people whom we most unhesitatingly suspect of self-deception are really up to? Can these descriptions be correctly regarded as direct descriptive confrontation with the phenomenon itself? My answer to both of these questions is: No. The conspiracy theory is an extreme stance, which denies the possibility of self-deception. The other extreme stance is the stance of those philosophers who think that self-deception is a pervasive and ineluctable feature of consciousness.[5] Between these two extremes is the robust position of common sense: that men, sometimes but not always, deceive themselves. And that when they do deceive themselves, they do something that is distinctive and different from wishful thinking, weakness of will, self-conscious hypocrisy, or the mere deception of others.

KIN CONCEPTS: WISHFUL THINKING

Suppose that 'self-deception' is a metaphor, as the conspiracy theory suggests. Then we should be able to say what it really is in literal language. According to the weak version of the heretical view, what has hitherto been taken for self-deception is just wishful thinking, weakness of will, and the like. Now, if this proposal to reduce 'self-deception' to these other "unproblematic" notions is to be convincing, then it is a legitimate expectation on our part to be provided with at least a sketch of these other notions. But no such sketch or account has been forthcoming from these heretical philosophers. It seems to me that there are differences between these notions, on the one hand, and self-deception on the other. In this section I shall depict 'wishful thinking' and try to distinguish it from 'self-deception.' Then I shall offer some brief comments on the difference between 'weakness of will' and 'self-deception.'

In the concluding remarks of his stimulating paper "Error, Faith and Self-Deception," Patrick Gardiner suggests that it might even be argued . . . that self-deception really comes down to no more than being mistaken with a motive: a self-deceiver is simply a man who wrongly believes something to be true which he would not have believed to be true in the absence of the particular interest in the matter concerned that he has.[6]

Gardiner immediately proceeds to voice a worry about this suggestion, viz., that the analysis of 'self-deception' in terms of "being mistaken with a motive" blurs the distinction between 'wishful thinking' and 'self-deception.' The implication of what Gardiner says here is that 'wishful thinking' can also be analyzed in terms of "being mistaken with a motive." Now, notice that Gardiner's explication of "being mistaken with a motive" is ambiguous. It can be taken to imply any or all of the following: (1) that a man wrongly believes something to be true because what he believes is really false, (2) that a man wrongly believes something to be true because his belief is not warranted by the evidence, (3) that a man wrongly believes something to be true because he believes it in the teeth of evidence. (a) In the first interpretation we have a man who believes something to be true, which is in fact false, and which he would not have believed to be true in the absence of the particular interest in the matter. It is true that this interpretation will not differentiate 'self-deception' from cases of wishful thinking where the belief held happens to be false. In this connection it is perhaps worth remarking that ascriptions of wishful thinking are not comments about the truth value of the belief held; but rather, they are comments about the lack of well-groundedness of someone's belief. From asserting correctly, "Ah, that is wishful thinking," where this is, of course, an assessment of a certain belief of some person, it does not follow that what he believes is false. Note, however, that if it is correctly said of someone that he is self-deceived in believing some proposition, it follows that the proposition in question is false. (b) The second way of understanding the assertion that a person wrongly believes something to be true is that the person's belief is not warranted by the evidence. It is also true to say that this interpretation will not distinguish 'self-deception' from 'wishful thinking,' for in both cases the belief is held without good reason. Note, however, that the holding of a belief without good reason is perhaps a necessary but certainly not a sufficient condition for self-deception. (c) Interpretations (1) and (2) can be combined to express what appears to be Gardiner's view: that the self-deceiver is a man who believes something to be true that is in fact false and not warranted by the evidence, and that he would not have believed to be true in the absence of his particular interest in the matter. Gardiner is certainly right in

146

thinking that this interpretation does not distinguish self-deception from cases of wishful thinking where the belief held is false. (d) It seems to me that it is interpretation (3) that is essential to consider if we are to understand the difference between the notion of self-deception and the notion of wishful thinking. Surprisingly it is this sense of "believing wrongly," viz., "believing in the teeth of evidence," that Gardiner appears to have overlooked when asking the question, "What then is the distinction between self-deception and mere wishful thinking?"

To begin with, we do well to remind ourselves that 'wishful thinking' is *not* merely the expression of a wish or a hope. To say of someone that he indulges in wishful thinking is often to assess some belief(s) of his from the point of view of rationality. Suppose that a young man, Y, is passionately in love with Miss X. He, naturally enough, yearns to be loved in return. She smiles at him on occasion, chats about the topics in the course they both attend, and even invites him, along with others, for tea and cookies. He jumps to the conclusion that his love for her is reciprocated. In spite of moments of gloom involving thoughts of unrequited love, he is, he tells his friend, convinced that she loves him too. This, it seems to me, is an example of wishful thinking. It is worth stressing that Y quite genuinely believes that he is loved by her. He is cheerful and happy, muttering content-edly, "She loves me." He does not say, "I wish she would return my love," or "Would that she loved me," or "I hope she loves me." These sentences are expressions of wishes and hopes, and it is logically odd to wish for something that one thinks one has or hope for something that one is quite certain that one has. "She loves me," he asserts to his friend, expressing his *belief*.

Consider now the following additions and changes to this story. Suppose his friend, sympathetic but tough-minded, says when he hears this, "Ah, that is wishful thinking." Suppose he continues by pointing out that the young lady keeps frequent and close company with Z, and they have been observed to be quite intimate. Our man is quite unshaken and tells the friend that surely this is mere friendship between Z and Miss X. They have probably been brought up together and are fond of each other. Furthermore, Miss X tends to be quite outgoing. In any case, the "intimacies" do not really bear upon their relationship. He persists in his belief, yet we detect signs of worry in his conduct and the occasional giveaway in his conversation. Sometimes he is on the verge of coming to terms with the mounting evidence, but then, through an effort of will, he continues to explain it away and reassure himself. This, it seems to me, is a case that is properly called 'self-deception' and not simply 'wishful thinking.' It is worth noting that our young man has fallen into self-deception through wishful thinking.

There may be points where we find it impossible to distinguish the wishful thinker from the self-deceiver. On the other hand, there are points where we *can* make a distinction, and this is important. What are the points of resemblance between the two notions? Both the person who indulges in wishful thinking and the person who is self-deceived can be correctly described as holding a belief—for their believing something and expressing this belief are among the reasons for describing them in this way. Both believe as they do largely because they *want* to believe that their love is reciprocated. The truth of the belief would make them happy. In the absence of the motives that we ascribe to them, neither would believe what they presently believe. Both have motives, subjective reasons for their beliefs.

One of the points of dissimilarity is that the man who indulges in a piece of wishful thinking does not *rationalize*, does not engage in the exercise of pseudorationality that is a characteristic of the self-deceiver. Our young man engages in a complicated piece of rationalization for something that he wants very much. ''Surely she loves me, she smiles at me often, talks to me and cheers me up when I feel depressed.'' He gives reasons for thinking that he is loved by her. He jumps to conclusions from shreds of evidence motivated by his desire to be loved by her. We point out that by parity with his ''reasoning'' Miss X could be said to be passionately in love with half of the campus. In fact, she is merely friendly towards him. Moreover, we say, she is known to be involved with Z, and we produce evidence. It is at this point that wishful thinking can be clearly distinguished from self-deceit. The person to whom we ascribe wishful thinking does not pervert the procedures whereby we establish truth and falsehood. When he finds evidence that conflicts with his belief, he will, perhaps reluctantly, acknowledge it as counting against his belief. Thus, a crucial point of dissimilarity between wishful thinking and self-deceit is that in self-deceit the evidence is against the belief held. Once this is pointed out to the person involved, if he then proceeds to resist, by more or less ingenious tactics, the natural implications of the evidence, we feel that he is self-deceived.

This account of the difference between 'wishful thinking' and 'self-deception' helps us to explain why we speak of the self-deceiver in ways that have seemed paradoxical to some, while no one seems to have thought that there is anything paradoxical about our talk about the wishful thinker. It is natural to say of our young man who deceives himself into believing that Miss X loves him, that ''deep down inside,'' he knows that she does not really love him. There is not the least temptation to speak of 'knowledge' in connection with the wishful thinker. The self-deceiver has good grounds for thinking that he is not loved by Miss X, while the wishful thinker does not have such grounds. Now we are inclined to speak of the self-deceiver's knowledge with qualification, never *sans phrase*, because certain conditions essential for full-blooded knowledge do not obtain in his case. A man who is properly said to know some proposition takes the evidence he has for that proposition as grounds for its truth. The self-deceiver does no such thing. Prompted by some deep-seated emotional need, he proceeds to explain away and reinterpret the evidence. That he is prompted by such needs does not occur to him; and if it does, he explains it away. Thus, self-deception tends to breed further self-deception much as lies tend to breed lies.

My account of 'wishful thinking' is not exhaustive. There are other types of phenomena to which ordinary speakers of English apply the words 'wishful thinking.' A person can certainly cultivate thoughts and imaginings that he knows are in conflict with what is the case. A young woman may imagine that her father is alive and nurture warm comforting thoughts to this effect. Such thoughts are prompted by her desire that her father be alive. But she knows that her father is dead and, if appropriate, will say so. This sort of wishful thinking is much like daydreaming or reverie, a momentary escape from a painful but well-known and acknowledged reality. In such cases, some of the salient marks of self-deception are missing, for in daydreams there is no need for false beliefs. It is therefore a mistake to regard wishful thinking of this sort as a species of the genus of self-deception.[7] This is not to deny that a capacity is exhibited in this kind of phenomena that is also exercised in self-deception, namely, the capacity to cultivate and nurture thoughts and imaginings that are in conflict with what is believed.

KIN CONCEPTS: WEAKNESS OF WILL

Recently it has become fashionable to run the concepts of weakness of will and self-deception together as "just one affliction in the end."[8] No doubt there are similarities between these concepts. One important similarity is this: although the weak-willed person acts against his "better judgment," and the self-deceiver believes against his "better evidence," both are motivated by desire. This observation is useful, for it makes us see affinities and connections between the two concepts. But it should not blind us to the conspicuous differences between the two phenomena. Consider Tolstoy's pursuit of chastity, as recounted by Aylmer Maude:

> When he was nearly seventy he one day expressed to me his conviction that, despite difficulties and repeated failures, one should never cease to aim at chastity; and he added: "I was myself a husband last night, but that is no reason for abandoning the struggle; God may grant me not to be so again."[9]

Here is a classic case of weakness of will, where a person who professes to believe in chastity is put to the test and fails. Tolstoy succumbs to sexual desire, but he is apprised of the facts and does not attempt to misrepresent them to himself or to others. Weakness of will need not be blind. In self-deception, however, there is eventual blindness. There is a deliberate attempt to subvert one's own understanding; there is knowledge of the facts, coupled with an attempt to obscure that knowledge or its import: "I must know the truth very exactly in order to conceal it more carefully."[10] Admittedly, this is a provocative formulation of one central difference between weakness of will and self-deception. How this formulation is to be cashed in and understood is the burden of the section titled "The Strategies of Self-Deception."

Initially it is tempting to say that another salient difference between the two phenomena is that self-deception is intentional, while weakness of will is accidental. On reflection, however, one might be puzzled by the assumption that weakness of will is always something that happens to one and not something that is voluntary or partially intentional. It seems excessively strong to say that in weakness of will the intentional project of the mind to practice an ideal or carry out a resolution is frustrated by causal mechanisms. A person who occasionally falls short of his resolution not to have a second helping of dessert is not necessarily a compulsive eater. Nor was Tolstoy a sex maniac. Tolstoy acted voluntarily and intentionally, even though a strong desire was involved. The desire upon which he acted cannot be reasonably dismissed as external and alien to him. Such a dismissal may involve self-deception, for the desire was normal enough, and it was no one else's desire but his own. So, the weak-willed person has the psychological power to act on his principle; he has the physical power and the opportunity to do so.

It could be argued that since Tolstoy tries not to succumb to sexual desire, yet fails, it was not in his "psychological power" to resist. But this is not convincing; it might be responded: "It was in his psychological power to restrain himself; he just did not try hard enough." I believe that someone can sincerely hold a moral belief and yet not act in accordance with it on some, perhaps critical occasions. In this connection Tolstoy's case is revealing. The fact that Tolstoy struggles to be chaste is some evidence of his sincerity; that he recognizes and confesses that he was acting as he should not be acting is also a relevant part of the evidential picture. Furthermore, by referring to Tolstoy's retrospective feelings of guilt, remorse, twinges of conscience, we can say that he genuinely believed that one ought to be chaste, yet he failed to live up to his ideal. These are typical features of weakness of will but not of self-deception. Weakness of will can, and self-deception cannot, speak its name without destroying itself.

This is not to say that the former cannot pass over into the latter. If the weak-willed man tries to blind himself to the fact that he was weak-willed, he may well pass over into self-deception. And self-deception can also facilitate weakness of will. If weakness of will is to be understood as failure to live up to one's values in a situation where one is able to do so, and if previous to the occasion for acting, one can persuade oneself that one's values are not really violated in such a situation, then the akratic action or inaction is relatively smooth and easy.

I hope that what I have said here shows that the idea of self-deception cannot be correctly reduced to the ideas of wishful thinking and weakness of will.

FURTHER REFLECTIONS ON THE CONSPIRACY THEORY

I believe that there are cases of self-deception in which the similarities between self-deception and the deception of others are so striking that we are apt to be incredulous when someone proposes that 'self-deception' is a mere metaphor. Here the conspiracy theory assimilates self-deception into the simple deception of others. This seems too simple to me. If I deceive myself, I may in fact also deceive others. But surely I may do the former without doing the latter, and vice versa. If I deceive others but not myself about being in love with my wife, I know that I am not in love with her, but they do not. If I deceive myself about it successfully, then I knew at one time that I no longer loved her, but I no longer know this, even though I may have glimmerings of the truth from time to time. To deceive oneself, it is essential to have obscured this former item of knowledge and to have persuaded oneself to believe the opposite. To remain self-deceived, it is necessary to explain away or evade recurring glimmerings or thoughts of the truth.

The conspiracy theory exaggerates the role of other people in self-deception. What the self-deceiver is said to dread above everything else is *having to admit to us* that *p*. The self-deceiver thinks it crucial to appear *in the eyes of others* an existential success. His characteristic desire is to save face in front of us. My question is: Does he admit it to himself that *p*? If he does, then what is he deceived about? A person who admits to himself that *p* and knows that *p* but asserts not-*p* to us in order to save face in front of us, is a good candidate for other-deception but hardly for self-deception.

Again, suppose that the alleged self-deceiver may have clear moments in which he spells out the fact that he is lying, but what is he deceived about then and there? The natural description is that such a person emerged from self-deception if only for a short period, and then deceived himself back again into his former condition. To save face is indeed essential to the logic of self-deception. But the dominant feature is to look good in one's own eyes, rather than merely in the eyes of others.

This is not to say that there are not moments in self-deception when the thought of *p* occurs to one. But the mere thought of *p*, or glimmerings of the truth do not amount to a belief that *p* or to an acceptance of the truth. If one is to remain self-deceived, one must exercise the techniques of self-deception: evasion, rationalization, selective focus, myopic attention, willful ignorance, embellishment, distortion, exaggeration, and so on.

This leads me to a further difficulty with the conspiracy theory: Is self-deception really a game that we always or even typically play with others? No doubt sometimes it is tempting to say that it is. There are people who facilitate self-deception. We all know about sycophants and about the fact that both love and hatred can often be blind. But if the conspiracy theory is true, how are we to make sense of the case of the shipwrecked person on a deserted island who deceives himself by believing that he will be rescued? There is no other person to deceive. With whom did he make a pact? Whom is he trying to confuse and why? He cannot deceive anyone but himself into thinking that he is an existential success.

Advocates of the conspiracy theory tend to assert that the self-deceiver is a clumsy, incompetent deceiver of others. Consider this passage from M. R. Haight's book: "Here is A professing not-p, when p is obviously true; and we have reason to think that A knows that p is false. A is so very far from competent."[11] But to me this seems more like a barefaced lie, a case of blatantly irrational belief, rather than typical self-deception. We need not worry about this though, for in other passages this author seems to say quite the opposite; namely, that self-deceivers are good liars who will try to find a story that the other person would like best. And self-deception is alleged to be that story.[12]

Another author, David Kipp, insists that "the element of blind obsession, or desperate grotesqueness characterizes the typical self-deceiver."[13] But persons who suffer from blind obsessions are unable to recover through their own efforts. In such cases some more serious condition is to be attributed to them—some form of mental derangement. In contrast with such cases, the self-deceiver has the capacity for self-correction.

I am also somewhat bewildered about the rationale given for our alleged need to invent 'self-deception.' The aim of the self-deceiver is to confuse us so that "We may therefore not know how to judge him morally and we almost certainly will not be sure how to treat him! While we hesitate, he gains more time."[14]

The reason for my bewilderment is that, to begin with, we are inclined to look upon self-deceit and deceit of others as prima facie bad things; so, if someone has done something monstrous, it is natural to condemn him twice: once for his monstrous deed, and once for his self-deceit. Self-deception does not necessarily exculpate, so I cannot see how the device of 'self-deception' is supposed to prevent us from knowing how to treat and judge the self-deceiver.

Nor is it clear how it could be the self-deceiver's aim to appear an existential success in the eyes of others, while obviously an existential failure. Such a person is not self-deceived. He is just stupid. This strategy collapses beneath anyone's gaze.

Finally, various authors express momentary doubts about the idea that 'self-deception' is a metaphor. Why should 'self-deception' seem a better idea than anything else? Could it be that self-deception is "too good a metaphor to be a metaphor"?[15] Why is it that the term "matches what we feel about self-deceivers?" My view is that 'self-deception' is *not* a metaphor but a literal and descriptive use of language. From the fact that it is a reflexive use of 'deceive,' it does not follow that it is metaphorical. "Jones killed himself" is not metaphorical, yet killer and killed are the same person.

Concerning the alleged contradictory nature of self-deception, it is acknowledged that "no single description of the self-deceiver is a contradiction; it is that too many descriptions might fit, and we cannot have it all ways, and their implications clash."[16]

But let us not worry about what descriptions might fit. Let us look and see what descriptions do fit. That a person has been deceived by someone into believing that *p* cannot be determined by looking and describing his present state of mind. One has to, *inter alia*, find out how he has come to acquire his belief. Someone, through some tactic or another, brought him to believe *p*. Juggling the evidence, making him focus on some parts rather than on others, explaining away these other parts, rationalization, evasion: these are some of the tactics of deception. But these have their recognizable analogues in self-deception. So if we distinguish between the state of self-deception and the process or activity of which this state is the result, we can, I believe, describe the self-deceiver without contradictions but not without tension. 'Self-deception' is not incongruous: it is the consistent description of an inconsistent stretch of one's mental life and conduct.

THE STRATEGIES OF SELF-DECEPTION: RATIONALIZATION AND EVASION

It seems to me that some essential features of self-deception merit further attention. First, belief is, quite literally, involved in self-deception. Secondly, self-deception involves actions. Philosophers in general have been so preoccupied with self-deception as a problematic mental state that they have neglected what might be called the strategies of self-deception. It is this latter feature we have in mind when we describe someone as engaged in the activity of deceiving himself or when we tell someone to stop deceiving himself.

Both of these features are brought out in the example of the young man in love. At first (t_1) he has a comfortable conviction that Miss X loves him. The fact that his belief is naive and inadequately based is not a good reason for denying that it is a belief. Naive or inadequately based beliefs are none the less beliefs. If he just *likes to think or entertain the thought* that he is loved by Miss X, then daydreaming would be a more felicitous description. It is when our young man's cherished belief is challenged, when evidence is brought forth that is against his belief that p and supports the contrary belief, not-p, that the "strategic" aspects of self-deception are most clearly seen. By resisting the natural implications of the evidence, by forcing an unnatural interpretation on the evidence, he obstinately clings to his belief.

So self-deception is not merely being mistaken, nor is it just motivated error; it involves the manipulation or twisting of evidence on the level of inference. The psychoanalyst Ernest Jones makes the following interesting observations concerning 'rationalization':

> Everyone feels that as a rational creature he must be able to give a connected and continuous account of himself, his conduct and opinions and all his mental processes are unconsciously manipulated and revised to that end. No one will admit that he deliberately performed

an irrational act, and any act that might appear so is immediately justified by distorting the mental processes concerned and providing a false explanation that has a plausible ring of rationality. This justification bears a special relation to the prevailing opinion of the circle of people who are most significant to the individual concerned, and two different groups of false explanations can be distinguished according as they are formed mainly for private or mainly for public consumption. The former of these I would term ''evasions,'' the latter ''rationalizations''; there is however no sharp line dividing the two.[17]

It is true that most of us have a picture of ourselves as rational agents, and as a consequence, we are inclined to give an account of ourselves, our beliefs, attitudes, and emotions. However, we give such an account only on those occasions when we are challenged—no remark without remarkableness. When our integrity is at stake, when the truth or reasonableness of our beliefs is questioned, when the appropriateness of our emotions or attitudes is attacked, it is natural for us to defend them. It may be another person or it may be we ourselves who call these things into question. We do the latter ourselves when we feel some misgivings or apprehension about the justification of our conduct, beliefs, or emotions. If one feels fully justified in the ways in which one has acted, if one deems one's beliefs and what one feels thoroughly reasonable, then the question of justifying them to oneself does not arise.

We have misgivings when we feel that our convictions are unsupported by reasons when they should be so supported, when they are backed by reasons but we regard those reasons as weak, or when we become aware of evidence that provides strong reasons against cherished convictions. A rationalization then is a form of justification prompted by a mixture of desire and fear such that the rationalizer tries to put his action, conviction, or emotion into a better light than it would otherwise appear to himself and to those significant others whose opinions matter to him. A rationalizer, as opposed to a liar, thinks that the justifications he produces are good ones. He does not produce justifications under the description: ''I am producing false justifications to fool others and myself.'' The enterprise is *prereflective:* it is prompted by motives that cannot be spelled out without destroying the enterprise itself. Its motives and structure can be made explicit but only in retrospect. It is like trying to forget something or someone. The projects of reflection necessarily frustrate this enterprise. The more carefully and attentively one formulates the ways and means whereby one is to forget something or someone, the more poignant are the recurring memories. Direct self-deception is indeed incoherent.

A related and easily recognizable strategy of self-deception is evasion. This often precedes rationalization, and its forms are woven together by our control over the direction of our attention. For example, if one finds that heart surgery is altogether too painful to watch, one can divert one's attention from it by directing one's gaze on the physique of the more attractive members of the surgical team. Ignoring the relevant facts or neglecting their import are forms of evasion whereby we distract ourselves from evidence that threatens our cherished convictions or undermines attitudes, feelings, commitments that occupy deep and important positions in the fabric of our life. The strategies of evasion are not necessarily self-deceptive. The blunt evader, if pressed, will admit what he believes, knows, or feels. He would rather not dwell on it. He would rather think about something else. In a case of self-deceptive evasion a person ignores evidence for *p*, so as to avoid the thought that *p* is true, a thought that would disturb him. If this thought recurs, the techniques of rationalization need to be resorted to for more effective self-defense.

Consider a frequent mode of self-deception that involves a change of belief. A person might get himself to give up a painful but well-supported true belief in favor of a pleasing but unreasonable belief that is false. Here is an instructive case of this sort of self-deceit:

> A shipowner was about to send to sea an emigrant ship. He knew that she was old, and not overwell built at the first; that she had seen many seas and climes, and often had needed repairs. Doubts had been suggested to him that possibly she was not seaworthy. These doubts preyed upon his mind, and made him unhappy; he thought this should put him to great expense. Before the ship sailed, however, he succeeded in overcoming these melancholy reflections. He said to himself that she had gone safely through so many voyages and weathered so many storms that it was idle to suppose she would not come safely home from this trip also. He would put his trust in Providence, which could hardly fail to protect all these unhappy families that were leaving their fatherland to seek for better times elsewhere. He would dismiss from his mind all ungenerous suspicions about the honesty of builders and contractors. In such ways he acquired a sincere and comfortable conviction that his vessel was thoroughly safe and seaworthy; he watched her depart with a light heart, and benevolent wishes for the success of the exiles in their strange new home that was to be; and he got his insurance-money when she went down in mid-ocean and told no tales.[18]

Such a shipowner is naturally described as having deceived himself. It is important to notice, however, the stage of the story when such a description is appropriate. One might wish to claim that self-deception is a conflict-state and therefore the person in self-deception experiences a conflict. Now our shipowner is, at one stage of the story, a person who is of two minds, as it were, about the condition of his ship. Doubts about the condition of the ship prey upon his mind; he experiences mental conflict. But should we say at this stage that he is self-deceived, or that he is deceiving himself? Of course not! It would be perfectly extraordinary to say so! At this stage the man is trying to make up his mind about the condition of the ship. He is even entertaining the thought of having it thoroughly repaired. So far he is quite above board; he has deceived no one, not even himself. So far he cannot even be said to have tried to deceive himself. It is at a further stage, when explaining away the conflict state, that it is natural to say, "He is deceiving himself"; and only when he has, by explaining away his doubts, "acquired a sincere and comfortable conviction," is it natural and appropriate to say that he has deceived himself.

It is important to notice that one is not even tempted to describe the self-deceived shipowner in 'paradoxical' ways, such as "He both believes and does not believe that the ship is seaworthy." He fulfills all the criteria that, one might suppose, are essential for a case of full-blooded believing. Roughly speaking these are, I think, three: (1) a psychological criterion, (2) a behavioral criterion, and (3) a 'logical' criterion. Our man has a feeling of conviction that p, and thus he fulfills the criterion I referred to as 'psychological.' He is disposed to act and speak as if p is true, and thus he fulfills the behavioral criterion. He produces reasons for p when challenged, and thus he fulfills what I have referred to as the 'logical' criterion. Now this is certainly not the belief that our man ought to have, but surely it is a belief that he does have. We have seen that philosophers have thought that there is a 'doxastic' paradox involved in self-deception; that the self-deceived person both believes and does not believe that p. But this is to misdescribe the person who has deceived himself. There seem to be no good reasons for saying that our shipowner, once he has deceived himself, believes that the ship is not seaworthy. It is quite obvious what he believes, viz., that the ship is seaworthy.

This is, of course, not to deny that the description "He believes that the ship is seaworthy and he does not believe it is so" has an application to the self-deception situation. There is a stage, as we have seen, where the cherished and favored belief is challenged—evidence is brought forth against it. The person in question sees where the evidence points, and he experiences conflict; he is plagued by doubt. It is at this stage that he can naturally be said to believe p and not to believe p. And this description is backed by good reasons, for the person in question does partially satisfy the criteria for both belief and disbelief. He says, thinks, and does things that genuinely conflict. Such a man is vacillating; he is dithering between two views.

It is at this stage that certain essential features, the dynamic aspects of self-deception, must be indicated. Indeed, it is true that our shipowner is at first in a state of conflict. Should he repair the ship? It needs repair, but it costs too much money. He is undecided and worried. We would not say he is self-deceived yet; nor is it likely that we would say that he is deceiving himself. To say of someone that he is self-deceived is not merely to say that he is in a certain state of mind; it also involves an appraisal as to how he got himself into that state of mind and how he sustains himself in it. To leave out the procedures whereby the self-deceiver makes himself believe something is to leave out an essential feature of self-deception. It is to ignore that self-deception contains essentially intentional or deliberate elements—actions—but, of course, is not wholly made up of these. These elements are best seen in the self-deceiver's reaction to the evidence brought against his cherished belief, a feature we might call 'quasi-rationality.'[19]

In this connection it is well to remind ourselves that only he who can play a game can be reasonably charged with violating its rules. Only he who can use and apply a set of procedures correctly can be intelligibly spoken of as misusing or abusing such procedures. Similarly, only he who knows how to apply and use the set of procedures involved in the language game we play with 'belief,' 'truth,' 'falsehood,' 'evidence' can be intelligibly charged with misusing or abusing such procedures. That is to say, the ascription of self-deception to someone presupposes that the person is a rational agent in a basic sense of 'rational.' A child has a lot to learn before he can be said to deceive others, for this presupposes (among other things) the skill to spy an advantage to be gained and the set of skills involved in trying to get someone to believe something that one thinks to be false, which, of course, involves knowing what would count as evidence for the proposition in question, arranging the evidence, etc. Deceiving oneself presupposes a certain general concern for 'rationality.' This is not to say that the person in self-deception is doing the rational thing. What the person in self-deception does involves a set of procedures that resembles what a person who is not self-deceived does when justifying and explaining his belief. The distinction I have in mind is made in ordinary language when people speak of someone's explaining and giving reasons for his point of view on the one hand, and when they speak of him explaining away and rationalizing on the other hand. The distinction between the pseudorationality involved in self-deception (and in some other-deception) and genuine rationality is by no means always clear-cut, but this does not mean that there are not many cases where it is possible to draw the line quite clearly between the two. The truth of the matter is that it is possible to distinguish between the two sets of procedures only when we view them in a larger context, only when we are in a position to assess them from a larger perspective. Being in such a position presupposes that one can correctly claim that one of the "players" (the one who rationalizes) has an axe to grind, has a personal stake in the matter at hand, while the person who is properly said to explain and justify his point of view does not.

We have seen then that the person who deceives himself argues, rationalizes, puts an "unnatural" interpretation on the evidence, explains away bits and pieces that do not fit his point of view. Bishop Butler has seen clearly this feature of the self-deception "situation." He remarks in his sermon "Upon Self-Deceit":

> And whilst they are under the power of this temper thought and consideration upon the matter before them has scarce any tendency to set them right: because they are engaged; and their deliberation concerning an action to be done, or reflection upon it afterwards, is not to see whether it be right, but to find out reasons to justify or palliate it; palliate it, not to others, but to themselves.[20]

Pseudorationality operates against the background of rationality. In cases in which we use the words and expressions "rationalize," "manipulate the evidence," "distort the evidence," "bolster a point of view," we assume a background in which it would have been possible to speak of "giving good reasons," "carefully weighing the evidence," "giving a natural interpretation to the evidence." Thus the idea of pseudorationality involved in self-deception presupposes that there is room for argument, rationalization, interpretation, etc. This feature enables us to delimit the sorts of things one can deceive oneself about and thus will further contribute to our understanding of the notion of 'self-deception.'

Such beliefs as "I am a human being," "I have a body," "I have sensations" leave no room for explaining away, manipulating, or distorting the evidence. It seems to me that there is no room here for self-deception either. Anyone who believes that he is not a human being, that, say, he is made of glass, or that, say, he is a pumpkin is not, it seems to me, self-deceived but deranged, mad.

Furthermore, take perceptual judgments of a basic sort. It is certainly possible to think (mistakenly) that there is a table in front of me. In this connection, we tend to think of hallucinations, perceptual distortions, and impairment of perceptual organs, but surely not of self-deception. Suppose that a housewife wants a refrigerator very badly, and fears the consequences of not having one. Suppose, further, that she claims to see one in her kitchen and behaves as if there were one. Surely, it would be quite out of place to speak of self-deception here. In self-deception there is the manipulation and twisting of the evidence at the level of inference and reasoning. There is no such possibility with regard to certain 'basic' propositions and perceptual beliefs.

This brings me to the question of the nature of the evidence in self-deception. Philosophers are apt to say the evidence against the proposition that a person deceives himself into believing must be "overwhelming"; must be "strong," or that the evidence must plainly be against the proposition that the self-deceiver believes. This is misleading, for the evidence in question obviously must allow the possibility of adjustment, coloring, manipulating, interpreting; otherwise, the very possibility of self-deception is ruled out. Suppose that a mother deceives herself into believing that her son is alive, in the face of evidence to the contrary. Suppose further that a few days later they bring the son's body home for burial—here the evidence can be said to be "overwhelming"—she still believes he is alive. (Exclude afterlife and religious beliefs from this story.) It would be inappropriate to talk of self-deception here. It would be natural to say, "The woman has been driven mad by the loss of her son." Consider the case of a man who believes that he is Napoleon. Now the evidence is "overwhelmingly" against such a belief. In certain situations and moments the man can be said to know that he is not Napoleon. Yet in certain other situations he believes that he is Napoleon. Self-deception has no application here. Such a man is suffering from a certain form of mental illness, delusions.

THE SELF AND ITS COMMITMENTS
IN SELF-DECEPTION

Philosophers do not seem to have paid much attention to the role that motives play in self-deception. It has been claimed, for example, that there is no incoherence in the idea of motiveless self-deception.[21] The argument for this appears to rest on the general principle that the motive for which something is done is not a proper part of an analysis of what is done. This general principle does not square with the facts. It seems to me that in some cases one of the criteria that we use for describing what is done has to do with the motives the agent is thought to have. A case in point is wishful thinking. Whether a person who jumps to conclusions is to be described as indulging in wishful thinking partly depends on the sorts of desires he has.

I wish to contend that there must be some reason for a man's failure to believe what he ought to believe if this is to count as a case of self-deceit. One can be self-deceived only about matters in which one has a personal stake. What one can be deceived about must link up with one's wants, hopes, fears and emotional needs. Consider the case of a man who deceives himself into thinking that his sick son's condition has improved. Suppose strangers become aware that our man holds this false belief. They may ask, "How can anyone be so blind?" It is explained to them that the boy is the only son and his father cannot envisage his own life without his son. Now the strangers might understand how a normally intelligent person like the man in question can come to believe and act the way he does. His beliefs and actions are made intelligible as self-deception, when the motive and the commitment are unearthed.

Now let us envisage a case where there is no relevant motive involved at all. Suppose that a perfect stranger to the father and the child is informed by the doctor as to the boy's condition. Also suppose that the stranger "doggedly" insists that the boy is getting better. It seems to me that it would be absurd to describe this as a case of self-deceit—mistaken judgment, stupidity, ignorance, cussedness perhaps—but not self-deceit. Similarly it is only when the desires and motives of the young man in love with Miss X become apparent that we are prepared to ascribe self-deceit. Once his emotional needs are unearthed, we see that his is not merely a case of mistaken judgment or of jumping to conclusions. In connection with our shipowner's case, it is difficult to see how a person who was utterly without moral scruples could plausibly be said to have deceived himself about the ship's seaworthiness. Our shipowner, through self-deception, tries to stifle and put to rest the voice of his conscience.

When faced with the task of choosing examples of self-deception, we have an inclination to be magnetized by those that involve intense desire or emotion expressive of the commitments of the self-deceiver. These intensely felt personal desires or emotions have the significance they do have in virtue of the deep commitments they reveal about the self-deceiver's conception of himself and his world. To the extent that a person thinks a matter to be trivial, to that extent his inclination to justify it to himself (or to others) is diminished, and, ergo, he is barely inclined to self-deception.

It seems to me that the objects of "strong" self-deception are precisely those commitments that constitute a person's sense of self-identity. These core commitments have deep importance for us because they determine how we see ourselves, how we stand to others, and they also shape the meaningfulness of our lives. Such deep commitments cannot be given up without a fight, without self-defense. The attempt to abandon such commitments instantaneously would result in acute pain and disintegration. Their severance must allow time for retrenchment, adjustment, and eventual acceptance. These forms of self-deception are occasions for self-transformation.

LOVE, JEALOUSY, AND THE PURSUIT OF SELF-KNOWLEDGE

That love and its shadow, jealousy, should provide fertile soil for self-deception and, as a consequence, for the pursuit of Socratic self-knowledge should hardly surprise us. Love is an intense form of attention whose focus is rather narrowly restricted to a woman: her beauty, her intelligence, her activities, her world. The yearning for reciprocity in love, once satisfied, transforms the lover, the beloved, and the world. Their world is a shared world, their identities, their conception of themselves are redefined by love itself. The beloved's virtues are larger than life, faults are rare, and if they do exist, they are ignored, dismissed, or minimized. The commitment in passionate love is so deep that it reconstitutes the persons in love; their life revolves around this commitment.

I do not wish to argue that love is itself a mode of self-deception. Rather, I want to depict how a person in love, once his own assurance of reciprocity is threatened, tries to preserve his treasured, if fragile, world, through the strategies of self-deception.

Consider the following case. A man, A, loves a woman, C, and she reciprocates his love. The man she loves has a diversity and richness of interests, which she comes to share and enjoy. He is sociable, and his friends become her friends, too. Their life is happy. Gradually A undergoes an alarming transformation. His romantic commitment to C acquires such a narrow focus, becomes so single-minded, that he begins to exclude many ingredients of their life that had made her so happy. As a result, their life becomes impoverished in dimension, and A becomes a mere skeleton of his former self. C is astonished, and her affection towards him cools and eventually ceases. Situations like the following are not uncommon. A and his wife, C, are at a party. C is absorbed in a conversation with Mr. B. A abruptly interrupts and insists that he and his wife have to go home. In the course of this, and for no apparently good reason, he makes rude and belittling remarks to Mr. B. Now suppose there is no real reason to go. He is not tired, he has no headache, he is not bored, etc. For that matter he has just had a stimulating conversation. Suppose that there is a history of this sort of conduct: whenever his attractive wife is giving a great deal of attention to another man and getting such attention in return, Mr. A "drops" his conversations and insists on going. It is plausible to say that Mr. A is jealous of his wife. Concerned friends decide to have it out with him and accuse him of being jealous. They bring up behavior of a possessive sort—hostile, offensive remarks, odd emotional displays, for example, anger with his wife on such occasions and hatred of the man he imagines to be his rival, conduct and feeling that seem to reveal his jealousy.

A is stunned and shocked, for he does not think of himself as the jealous sort, so he denies it and, to begin with, dismisses his friends' accusations. When this can no longer be done plausibly, he describes himself as protective and angry at his wife's reluctance to go. But on reflection and after some struggle with his pride, he realizes that it is not simply a case of protective and angry behavior. He knows very well that C is hardly the sort of person who needs protection in such circumstances, nor was his behavior merely an expression of anger at his wife's reluctance to go. It was a peculiar mode of anger, accompanied by a belief that he has an exclusive right to her attention and affection in virtue of their special relationship. Unless he believes that he has a special right to her company ("she belongs to him"), the idea of ascribing jealousy to him would be indistinguishable from mere irrational possessiveness.

But even this is not sufficient for the correct self-ascription of jealousy *propre*. The most interesting and complex cases, such as this one, involve the jealous person's perception of a threat to his world: the jealous person fears that he is being displaced in the affection, love, and friendship of the person who is the target of his jealousy. The alleged rival is hated precisely because he is suspected to be the recipient of those goods to which the jealous person feels he is exclusively entitled.

Now how does this connect up with the pursuit of self-knowledge? To begin with, why did A refuse to acknowledge his jealousy? His moral outlook may play an important role here. Suppose that his moral outlook is such that he thinks that jealousy is a bad thing. He holds that one ought not to think that one owns people or even that one has a special right to them in virtue of mutually agreed to relationships. This belief of his explains why he refuses first even to look upon his conduct and his feelings as amounting to jealousy. We may say that he has had an unconscious belief that his wife belongs to him, and that he was unconsciously jealous, but now he knows. How did he find out? With a little (or perhaps a lot of) help from his friends; by attending to his behavior, by taking seriously the import of what he has said or blurted out, by self-watching, if you will. Bizarre, apparently senseless behavior, slips of the tongue, the tone and purport of certain of his utterances and expressions of feelings were brought to A's attention, and after some struggle, he says, "I must have been jealous," and then avowing it, "I was jealous." Why the struggle? The reasons for this are often tied to our disinclination to self-ascribe what we hold to be defects of character, unworthy feelings, contemptible conduct. The image that we have of ourselves, our self-conception, is at stake here. Here we come face-to-face with the recognizable terrain of self-knowledge. This terrain, to say the least, is oversimplified and distorted by the classical Cartesian account of "knowledge of one's own mind" according to which such knowledge is so easy, so effortless, so immediately given "that there is nothing easier for me to know than my own mind."[22]

None of this is meant to deny that sometimes it is the complexity of our mental state, our remarkable lethargy, or uncharacteristic stupidity that explains our self-ignorance. After all, Socrates did not say that the examined life is simple, requires no effort or directed intelligence; he said only that the unexamined life was not worth living. In any event, the case of the jealous man is interesting if only because it involves such a complex mental state: love, wanting, hatred of another, threat to one's confidence, embarrassment before others. But these introspective discriminations are not accomplished in a vacuum. If they are to be successful, they must proceed with due attention to the context: to features of the situation one is in, to one's behavior, utterances and responses, to unfocused mental ingredients that have not been so far placed in a proper perspective.

Now I want to bring out into the open the different stages in the growth of self-knowledge as this is exhibited in the case of our jealous man and relate them to the "inferential" picture of self-knowledge.

There is the stage in which when confronted with evidence for the self-ascription of jealousy, he would look upon himself as his friends do and say: "I seem to be jealous; judging by my behavior, I must have been jealous." Here the "inferential" recipe for self-knowledge seems to be borne out: "the acts and manifestations which I notice in myself and do not know how to link up with the rest of my mental life must be judged as if they belong to someone else."[23] Again, "John Doe's ways of finding out about John Doe are the same as John Doe's ways of finding out about Richard Roe."[24] Our man stands back from himself, as it were, and asks himself, "If I were to observe this kind of behavior, talk, anger . . . in the case of someone else, would I say that he was jealous? And if I would in the case of another, why shouldn't I look at myself this way?" Looking at myself this way is one way of explaining my conduct and feelings.

Now comes the question, "Of the various ways of looking at myself, which is the right one?" Was I really jealous or did I merely appear so to others? Here the question "How do I know that I was really jealous?" has sense and a point. Here one can speak of "retrospection" and introspection—the calling up of memories of similar occasions, of unraveling the feelings one has had then but could not account for, of unearthing unacknowledged fears about thoughts of her loss, of trying to weave a coherent pattern of all these features of one's mental life that will enable one to say, "Now I know that I was jealous."

But why is self-knowledge thought to be so hard? It has been said that applying the method of inference to ourselves "is a proceeding to which we are not constitutionally disposed"; that some "special hindrance" interferes with our obtaining true knowledge of ourselves.[25]

Why then is there often this "constitutional" reluctance in this enterprise? Why is it that even though we become apprised of the facts, there is a struggle to accept them? Even though there may be knowledge about oneself, there may not be self-knowledge but only self-deception, evasion, or rationalization. The hardness here is not simply the hardness of fact finding. It is often, I suggest, the hardness of the moral life. In the pursuit of self-knowledge concerning our own motives, emotions, and beliefs, we encounter dearly held ideals and principles that we have violated. Racial prejudice, envy, jealousy, greed—stuff that we would rather eschew—are recognized as part of the eschewer. And this predicament brings tension, both emotional and intellectual—conflicting feelings in the emotional life and contradiction in the reflective life, a sense of shame in the moral life. And here the moral dimension of self-knowledge may reveal itself in its truly confessional form: "I have been thus and so, and I didn't realize it. But now I do and I resolve to transform myself."

Alas, by this time C's love for him has ceased entirely. All that remains is the residue of care, which is usually a provoking irritation to someone whose love is unrequited. C, precisely because she still cares for A, cannot bring herself to break the news to him. He notices C's cool behavior and her artificial airs towards him but explains them away as moodiness. Eventually C tells him that she no longer loves him and will try to find her own life. He refuses to accept this at face value: "She does not really know her own mind," "She is confused and needs a vacation." "Does she not admit that she still cares for me?" He focuses on gathering evidence for her love for him, trying to convince himself and, no doubt, trying to convince her, too. For a while he succeeds in convincing himself: his evasions and rationalizations work, and he has a comforting conviction of still being loved by C, but one day he comes to accept the loss of C; he sees a happy C in another man's company.

Now while his self-deception about being loved by C ceases, at this stage A may deceive himself concerning the past: he may deceive himself into thinking that C had not loved him at all. Consider this passage from Proust: "and love is so far obliged to find some justification for itself, some guarantee of its duration in pleasures which on the contrary, would have no existence apart from love and must cease with its passing."[26] I suspect something like this is true of loss of love, too. Sometimes loss of love in trying to find some explanation for itself denies the precondition for its existence: past love. It is a self-deceptive attempt to extirpate forms of disappointment and regret by denying their object. However, this is a case I shall not explore here.

Above, I produced two thought experiments, two examples of self-deception concerning deep passions and the gradual emergence towards self-knowledge. These examples are not to be regarded as mere aids to the understanding. Some may regard them and their somewhat byzantine detail tedious. However, I believe that our efforts to understand these passions, our sophisticated distortions thereof, and our pursuit of self-knowledge concerning them, are bound to be frustrated without a patient elaboration of the relevant contextual features and details.

It would be self-deceptive of me to say that I have offered or can offer a successful theory of self-deception if by this is meant a set of necessary and sufficient conditions for its correct ascription in any and every conceivable situation. I have my doubts whether it is fruitful or even possible to do this, given the richness and flexibility of our natural languages. What I have tried to do is to make us see how distinctive self-deception is by contrasting it with a variety of related notions; to sketch some significant features of the milieu, the frame of mind, the values and concerns and the relevant history of the self-deceiver. If this included excessive talk of what makes us tick, tainting the purity of the conceptual enterprise, so be it. Human beings are messy, deep, and mysterious. The phenomenon of self-deception just mirrors these facts.[27]

NOTES

1. The most sustained argument for the heretical view is M. R. Haight's book, *A Study of Self-Deception* (Atlantic Highlands, N.J.: Humanities Press, 1980). A more concise but perhaps less plausible "heretical" account is that of David Kipp. See his article "On Self-Deception" in *Philosophical Quarterly* 30 (1980): 305–317.

2. Haight, "Tales from a Black Box," in this volume.

3. Haight, *A Study of Self-Deception,* 129.

4. Kipp, "On Self-Deception," 315.

5. Jean-Paul Sartre seems to embrace this extreme thesis; see *L'Etre et le Néant* (Paris: Gallimard, 1943), translated into English by Hazel Barnes as *Being and Nothingness* (New York: Philosophical Library, 1956). Quotations and page references are from the translation.

6. Patrick Gardiner, *Proceedings of the Aristotelian Society* 70 (1969–70): 244.

7. This appears to be Alfred R. Mele's suggestion in "Self-Deception," *Philosophical Quarterly,* 33 (1983): 376.

8. See Daniel Dennett's *Brainstorms* (Montgomery, Vt.: Bradford Books, 1978), 307.

9. Aylmer Maude in an introduction to one of his translations of Tolstoy's novels in the Oxford *Little Classics* series.

10. Sartre, 87.

11. Haight, 108.

12. Ibid., 123.

13. Kipp, 314.

14. Haight, 109.

15. Ibid., 121.

16. Ibid., 120.

17. Ernest Jones, "Rationalisation," *Journal of Abnormal Psychology* (1908): 161.

18. W. K. Clifford, "The Ethics of Belief," in *Lectures and Essays,* ed. Leslie Stephen and Frederick Pollock (New York: Macmillan, 1879), 177–178.

19. It was Bishop Butler who pointed to this feature of self-deceit. See his sermon "Upon Self-Deceit," in Joseph Butler, *Works,* vol. 2, ed. W. E. Gladstone (Oxford: Clarendon Press, 1896). Hamlyn and H. O. Mounce also mention this feature of self-deceit. See their symposium "Self-Deception," in *Proceedings of the Aristotelian Society,* supp. vol. 45 (1971): 145–172.

20. Butler, 172.

21. T. M. Penelhum, "Pleasure and Falsity," in *American Philosophical Quarterly* 1 (1964): 88.

22. René Descartes in *Meditation II.* See p. 156 in *The Philosophical Works of Descartes,* trans. E. S. Haldane and G. R. T. Ross (Cambridge: Cambridge University Press, 1970).

23. Sigmund Freud, "The Unconscious," in *General Psychological Theory,* ed. Philip Rieff (New York: Collier Books, 1963), 120.

24. Gilbert Ryle, *The Concept of Mind* (London: Hutchinson, 1959), 153.

25. Freud, "The Unconscious," 120.

26. Marcel Proust, *Remembrance of Things Past: Swann's Way,* trans. Scott Moncrieff (London: Chatto and Windus, 1960), 4.

27. This essay builds on my earlier contributions to the philosophical literature on the topic of self-deception. I should like to thank the editors and publishers of *Analysis, Canadian Journal of Philosophy,* and *Canadian Philosophical Reviews* for permission to reprint or make use of in a revised form material first published in their journals. Thanks are due to my colleague H. H. Jack for discussing the topics of this paper with me.

Self-Deception and Rationality

Robert Audi

Self-deception is thought by some to be common and by others to be impossible. But even those who believe that it is common differ greatly in their conceptions of it. Most writers on the subject agree in this, however: that the topic of self-deception is a challenge both to philosophers and to psychologists. A central issue is whether self-deception is ultimately paradoxical. Part of the problem is that we apparently face a dilemma. If we conceive self-deception nonparadoxically, why is it so called? The basis for speaking of deception here is, prima facie, the idea that one somehow gets oneself to believe something one knows is not true. If we reject this description as hopelessly paradoxical, how are we to explain what it is to deceive oneself? On the other hand, if the concept of self-deception really is paradoxical, how useful can it be for descriptive or, especially, explanatory purposes? Can people be truly described as, for instance, believing something they know is not true? And if they can be, what should this lead us to expect about their behavior? Will they, as usual, tend to act on what they *believe*, or should we expect them to act on the contradictory of this proposition, which they *know* to be true? Or, if knowing a proposition to be true entails believing it, will they somehow act on both of these propositions, or neither? This paper is based on the view that despite these difficulties the concept of self-deception is both explicable without paradox and useful in understanding persons. This view can best be developed if we first note some central points about deception of one person by another. I begin with a paradigm: Iago's deception of Othello.

169

DECEPTION

Iago's deception of Othello is a piece of masterful maleficence. Step by step, Iago raises doubt, engenders suspicion, nurtures belief, and builds conviction. He plays up Desdemona's warmth toward Cassio, insinuates that her attentions to Cassio are improper, seduces Othello into believing that her pleas for Cassio's reinstatement belie her apparent fidelity, and finally, shows Othello the "ocular proof" he has demanded, in the form of the handkerchief Othello has given Desdemona, waved about almost mockingly by Bianca, Cassio's mistress. This is a paradigm of deception. We have the deceiver's production of misleading circumstances, including plausible evidence; his deceptive acts, such as false expressions of suspicion, and then lies; the actual infliction of the deception—here, taking Othello over the brink by leading him to believe that Desdemona is unfaithful; the state of deception thereby produced—Othello's falsely believing that she is unfaithful; and the reinforcement of this state by adding evidence and providing reaffirmation of the lie by words and deeds. Moreover, not only is false belief produced; it also supplants true belief. This is not strictly necessary for deception, but it seems common to the paradigm cases and is appropriate to any model of ordinary deception that is to guide an understanding of self-deception as a presumably analogous phenomenon.

The pattern of Iago's deception of Othello is all too familiar, and we understand it well. Iago deceives Othello by getting him to believe something which Iago knows is not true. When we speak of self-deception, however, there is far less understanding. How can one get oneself to believe something one knows is not true? And if one cannot, what analogy is left to warrant our speaking of self-deception as deception at all?

In preparing to answer these questions, let us imagine a different story, one in which Othello is self-deceived. Suppose that, as Iago claims to suspect, Othello really did have an affair with Emilia, and imagine that even after his marriage to Desdemona he retains an attraction, of which he is ashamed, for Emilia. As an upright man who loves his wife, he might well want to put his attraction for Emilia out of mind. If she were not around him, this might be generally easy; but since she is around him, he cannot simply keep the object of his shameful attraction out of mind. If he can get over the attraction, the problem will be solved. But suppose that he cannot, and that he senses this. We then have a situation in which his peace of mind might well be best served by coming to believe that the attraction has dissipated. For in that case, Emilia's coming to mind would be far less likely to be accompanied by painful or shameful thoughts. We have fertile ground, then, for self-deception. How might it proceed?

Surely we can find at least analogues of all the stages mentioned in describing Iago's deception of Othello. Othello might, e.g., play up, and often focus his attention on, his affection for Desdemona. He could note, and invite others to note, certain unattractive features of Emilia, and try to attend to these when he sees her. He could then, eventually, say to a *confidant* that he no longer feels attracted to her, and he could reinforce this avowal by appropriate actions, such as avoiding her company and devoting himself wholeheartedly to his wife. Now there is no reason to deny that this strategy could lead to uprooting the attraction and thus to a true belief that it is gone. But we are assuming that, for the time being at least, the attraction is inextirpable. It is still possible, of course, that Othello succeeds in producing a confident false belief that the attraction is gone, and has no second thoughts. He would then have deceived himself and would be in a state of *delusion* about his own emotions.

So far, however, he is not in a state of self-deception. The deceiver has dropped out of the picture; having produced a wholehearted delusion, he has completed his work. We have a case of one's *causing oneself to form a false belief.* This produces *a state of being deceived,* and not *a state of self-deception* or of *being disposed to deceive oneself.* What has been felt to be special about self-deception is that it apparently exhibits, in a single person, both deceiver and deceived. Thus, if Othello is in self-deception, we should find a kind of duality. He will sometimes act in the capacity of deceiver, e.g. by responding to incipient signs of his attraction for Emilia by directing his attention to her faults or to counterpart attractions of Desdemona. As deceiver, he in some sense knows the meaning of the impulses and feelings he refuses to countenance; as victim, he is simultaneously sincere in his denials, or dispositions to deny, that he is still attracted to Emilia. After all, when he affirms to a *confidant* that the attraction is gone, he speaks sincerely, and his consciousness is dominated by the thought of how attracted he is to Desdemona.

It certainly seems, then, that self-deception, and not merely the production of false belief in oneself, is possible. But how? And what role does such a strange phenomenon play in human life? Can self-deception be, for instance, rational, or is it more like an undeserved protection of an insecure self-image? These are the central questions to be treated in this paper. I shall start with an account of the nature of self-deception. Against that background, the longest section of the paper will explore the connections between self-deception and rationality. The last section will consider the explanatory and predictive power of the concept of self-deception, both in psychological investigation and in everyday life.

SELF-DECEPTION

There are many possible routes to understanding self-deception, and in the past two decades a large literature has grown up around the topic. It will be impossible to review that literature here, but it will be useful to describe some of the major variables that differentiate accounts of self-deception. With these before us, I can quickly introduce the view of self-deception that underlies this paper.

First of all, an account of self-deception should speak to what is often called the paradox of self-deception (though other paradoxes have been associated with it): that a self-deceiver believes something he knows is not true. A major distinction, then, is between accounts that embrace the paradox and those that do not and attempt to explain the crucial data without it. Second, some accounts make *acts* of self-deception primary and construe the *state* of self-deception in terms of them; other accounts do just the opposite. A third distinction is closely related to this: it is between accounts that conceive volitional concepts—such as willing and directing one's attention—as fundamental in self-deception, and those that conceive cognitive concepts—such as belief and knowledge—as fundamental. (There is actually a continuum between these two poles, and views on one side may have much in common with views on the other.) Fourth, an account may or may not make essential use of the notion of unconscious belief or of other unconscious elements; and fifth, it may or may not posit a split self or, more dramatically, two or more agents belonging to a single person.[1]

On the view underlying this paper, self-deception is not ultimately paradoxical, nor does it require positing multiple agents; and positively, it is best understood by taking the state of self-deception as primary and by making essential use both of cognitive concepts and of the notion of unconscious belief. On the other hand, the account attempts to explain why self-deception is ostensibly paradoxical, why it is natural to posit two or more agents to understand it, and how self-deceptive behavior and self-deceptive volition may be adequately conceived in a framework with a primary emphasis on states of cognition.

In outline, the account I propose (and have developed in earlier papers)[2] is this:

A person, *S*, is in self-deception with respect to a proposition, *p*, if, and only if:

(1) *S* unconsciously knows that not-*p* (or has reason to believe, and unconsciously and truly believes, that not-*p*);

(2) *S* sincerely avows, or is disposed to avow sincerely, that *p*; and

(3) *S* has at least one want which explains, in part, both why *S*'s belief that not-*p* is unconscious and why *S* is disposed to disavow a belief that not-*p*, and to avow that *p*, even when presented with what he sees is evidence against *p*.[3]

This account is meant to apply to paradigm cases, and it may not capture all the current admissible uses of 'self-deception.' Condition (3), moreover, may not be strictly necessary, but it seems important for understanding at least the paradigm cases of (states of) self-deception.[4] Many other comments and qualifications might be added,[5] but for our purposes it will be sufficient simply to show how the account might apply to the example of Othello, sketched above.

First, consider conditions (1) and (2). Given that Othello is an intelligent man who notices the signs of his continuing attraction to Emilia, and given his diverse efforts to put those signs out of his mind, it is plausible to suppose that he does in some way know that he in fact has the attraction. Second, since he is sincere in avowing that he does not have it, we cannot plausibly take the knowledge to be conscious. One could argue that he is not sincere, since he is, after all, lying to himself; but surely it is plausible to say that he is lying to himself, only because he is, at one level, apparently deceived. I suggest that, qua deceiver, he somehow gets himself to "believe," and to be disposed to utter without insincerity, what he knows is not true. He does not literally believe it, though it is natural to say that he "consciously believes" it, and perhaps he may be said to "half-believe" it. In any case, if we do not suppose that Othello is sincere in saying he is no longer attracted to Emilia, we are likely to assimilate self-deception to simple lying.

I do want to grant, however, that the sincere avowals of the self-deceiver are not manifestations of ordinary sincerity; for while they are not lies, they also do not express beliefs.[6] We may say that Othello "consciously believes" what he says; but in the attribution of beliefs, actions speak louder than words, and indeed the overall pattern of his words also does not support our ascribing to him the belief that he is no longer attracted to Emilia.[7] He not only exhibits embarrassment around Emilia, but lavishes unusual attention on Desdemona at the earliest opportunity thereafter and protests too much both regarding his attraction to Desdemona and concerning his immunity to the charms of

Emilia. We could, to be sure, attribute to him *both* an unconscious belief that he is still attracted to Emilia and a conscious belief that he is not.[8] But we need not say this, and if we do not, then the paradox of self-deception can be resolved.

Two further comments are needed before we apply the motivation condition of the account of self-deception to our example. One is that there is surely nothing in the concept of knowledge that renders unconscious knowledge impossible. Unconscious beliefs, for instance, may be justified by evidence (S may even grant that the evidence for p is strong, though he avows not-p—possibly citing counterevidence or intuition or faith as his justification); and clearly unconscious beliefs may be reliably produced. The second comment is simply that, as understood here, unconscious beliefs need not be deeply buried in a cavernous Freudian Unconscious Mind. They are simply not accessible to S without outside help or at least careful self-scrutiny.[9] They need only be sufficiently veiled from S to make his disavowals of them, and his avowals of their contradictories, sincere. But since they are inferable by others who observe S closely enough, he too may in principle come to know, through careful self-scrutiny, that he has them.

Concerning condition (3), we have already noted that Othello, after his marriage, wants to be a wholeheartedly devoted husband and to put his attraction for Emilia out of mind. This motivation could explain why he also wants to believe that this attraction is gone. That want in turn can partly explain why his belief that the attraction persists has not only been temporarily pushed out of consciousness, but veiled from it by the sort of self-deceptive behavior we have described. These same wants partly explain why he disavows the belief he unconsciously has, and sincerely affirms the contradictory proposition. Roughly, self-deceivers have one or more wants stemming from their preferred self-image or from some conception of themselves that is important to them, and wants of these sorts motivate behavior that veils from consciousness certain beliefs threatening the self-image or preferred self-concept.

If the suggested account of self-deception is sound, it provides a good basis for distinguishing self-deception from close cousins. Self-deception differs from a refusal to believe—to which it is similar in the way it leads S to explain away hostile evidence—in that S really does believe, unconsciously, the proposition which, often vociferously, he disavows. Self-deception differs from wishful thinking in that the self-deceiver does not believe the proposition he wants to believe.[10] It differs from lying in that, while S says something he does not believe, he says it sincerely. This is also why it differs from hypocrisy,[11] though behaviorally it may look like hypocrisy because of an incongruity between

174

what is said and what is done. Self-deception differs from self-induced delusion because, for one thing, it is not—in that way—a success: S still believes the proposition about which he has deceived himself. And self-deception differs from inconsistency in belief because, while S sincerely avows or is disposed to avow a proposition he believes is false, the avowal does not entail belief, though S may believe that it does (and at least does not consciously believe that it does not).

This last point indicates how the paradox of self-deception can be avoided: while it is *as if* S believed what he knows is not true, self-deception stops just short of this. Sincere avowal is normally sufficient for, though it does not entail, belief; and this implication is so pervasive that S's sincerely avowing that *p*, while unconsciously knowing it to be false, counts as his being sufficiently deceived to warrant our applying the term 'self-deception.' He *is* deceived in avowing it, since it is false; he is *self*-deceived because (for one thing) his own knowledge that *p is* false, together with motivation inclining him to cause himself to believe it, largely explains his avowing it.

There are other advantages of the proposed account of self-deception. In addition to avoiding the paradox and facilitating our drawing of the distinctions just made, the account explains some phenomena which, I believe, any good account of self-deception should explain. These phenomena are (1) the analogy with other-person deception, (2) the notion of refusing to admit something to oneself, (3) the notion of lying to oneself, (4) the patterns of behavior characteristic of self-deception, (5) the self-deceiver's capacity to respond to evidence, and (6) the various locutions, such as 'deceived oneself' and 'act of self-deception,' which indicate self-deception. The first three of these phenomena have been touched on above, but let me briefly elaborate.

Regarding the analogy with other-person deception, there are two main points of difference: there is just one person in self-deception; and secondly, despite appearances we do not have a belief of something known not to be true. There is, however, a certain dissociation in the self-deceiver, so that we have the agent qua deceiver and the agent qua deceived; and as suggested above, sincere avowal is such an important (though nonentailing) criterion of belief that it is rather as if S did believe the proposition with respect to which he is self-deceived.

As for (2), refusing to admit something to oneself is readily understood on my account of self-deception. Othello knows, deep down (unconsciously), that he is still attracted to Emilia, but he will not assent to this, even silently. Granted, ordinarily, when one refuses to admit something, one knows that one knows it, whereas the self-deceiver at most unconsciously knows, or unconsciously believes, that he knows (or believes) what he refuses to admit. But there may be exceptions to this generalization even in ordinary cases, and the disanalogy is in any event not major.

Concerning (3), we have already seen that the self-deceiver's avowals of what he knows is not true can be seen as lying to himself. But they are not ordinary lying, because they are sincere. Perhaps, however, the *self-deceiver is not sincere* in avowing them; they do, after all, represent a kind of self-manipulation, and they express, to himself as well as to others, something he does not believe. We may surely distinguish the overall sincerity of a person at a time, and the sincerity of a single avowal he makes at that time. It is only the latter that I maintain is sincere.

Much could be said about the patterns of behavior characteristic of self-deception (4), and I must be brief here. Above all, there should be behavior understandable in terms of three elements in my account (whether singly or in combination): by appeal to the relevant belief (e.g., that one is still attracted to Emilia), by appeal to its being unconscious, and by appeal to the want(s) that partly explain why it is unconscious. Consider Othello again. Because he knows that he is still attracted to Emilia, and because he wants to be wholeheartedly devoted to his wife, he avoids Emilia's company. Because this knowledge is unconscious, he explains his avoidance behavior in terms of such things as the undesirable characteristics of Emilia which he emphasizes in (for instance) backing up his avowal that he is no longer attracted to her. We typically have, then, both behavior attributable to the unconscious belief and behavior attributable to the desire to act in ways appropriate to the contradictory belief (or other opposed beliefs). The results can be highly variable, and it is doubtful that we should call any one pattern of behavior characteristic of self-deception. Broadly speaking, however, we should expect self-deceivers to exhibit behavior which they take to support the aspect(s) of their self-image or conception of themselves that the self-deception is in some sense designed to preserve or support, together with behavior revealing an unconscious belief whose content is (from the subject's point of view) at odds with that image or conception.

I come now to (5), the self-deceiver's capacity to respond to evidence. In my view, a self-deceiver's capacity to respond to evidence is in one crucial respect unimpaired: he need have no less tendency than anyone else to notice it, and what he actually believes, as opposed to what he sincerely avows, tends to accord with his sense of where the evidence points. Thus, in our example, Othello is aware of signs of his continuing attraction to Emilia; and like any normal person so close to the attraction, he knows he still has it. So far as this knowledge is a response to evidence, then (rather than a matter of noninferential self-knowledge), it shows a normal capacity to respond to evidence.[12] What is not entirely normal is that the resulting belief is unconscious. It may not be initially so; but where S is in self-deception, it is. Nor is it a fully normal reaction to explain away what one takes to be evidence for a proposition one believes. But note that even when S does explain it away, it may well be reinforcing the very unconscious belief whose preservation as unconscious is partly responsible for his explaining it away. Even here, however, it is precisely because S sees where the evidence points, and feels inclined to assent to what it supports, that he tends to explain it away. There is, in my view, nothing wrong with the inferential powers of self-deceivers, nor, necessarily, with their first-order belief formation processes. Their deficiency is mainly in the formation of second-order beliefs about what they do believe, and in the accompanying tendency to cover that up.

The last set of phenomena to be explained here is the locutions indicating self-deception (6). My presumption has been that the state of self-deception is most fruitfully taken to be fundamental, and my account is meant to explicate 'self-deception' in the state use. How, then, are we to account for the behavioral uses, especially 'deceiving oneself' and 'act of self-deception'? Imagine that, as a friend hears one say that one will patch up a breach with a loved one, she says, 'You're deceiving yourself.' If this is meant literally, it may be taken as calling the utterance an act of self-deception, not in the sense of an act *constituting* self-deception, but in the sense of one *manifesting* it. Self-deception, I believe, is never constituted by an act. That there are acts of self-deception no more entails that self-deception is ever so constituted than the existence of acts of compassion entails that compassion is sometimes an act. The term 'deceiving oneself' not only designates acts manifesting self-deception, but may also be used to refer to acts that are in some sense designed to produce, or are at least appropriate for producing, self-deception: such acts as explaining away certain evidence, putting certain thoughts out of mind, and making up arguments for the proposition one would like to believe. Here, too, if we understand the state of self-deception, we can account for behavioral uses of the term, and of related terms, by connecting them with the production, maintenance, or manifestation of the state.

We have seen, then, that by conceiving self-deception as constituted by (a) unconscious knowledge (or unconscious belief), (b) a disposition (usually realized) to avow sincerely the proposition unconsciously believed to be false, and (c) one or more wants that partly explain these things, we can distinguish self-deception from close cousins, explain many important phenomena which an account of self-deception should accommodate, and explicate the various central uses of the term. But there is another aspect of the topic on which, despite the large amount of literature concerning self-deception, much philosophical work remains to be done. I refer to the connections between self-deception and rationality. Is self-deception an intrinsically irrational state? And how does it affect the rationality of actions arising from it, or of the people who exhibit it? These are among the central questions of the next section.

RATIONALITY AND SELF-DECEPTION

It has been widely supposed that self-deception is not rational. It is easy to see why it often appears irrational. Recall our imaginary example. On the face of it, Othello does a number of things that seem significantly irrational: he uses himself as a means, fails to admit the force of the evidence, hides from the truth, and, by putting out of mind the attraction he would root out, undermines his capacity to solve the problem from which he is hiding. On the other hand, it is his own ends to which he uses himself as a means; and while he refuses to admit the force of the evidence, he does believe what it supports. We are, then, pulled in two directions. What needs to be said about the rationality of self-deception is by no means easily discerned. Moreover, it is not even clear what criteria of rationality should be used here. Let me, then, suggest some appropriate criteria and then proceed to apply them to some aspects of self-deception.

CRITERIA OF RATIONALITY

The most widely known standard of rationality of any kind is the maximization of expected utility criterion, according to which (in one version) an act is rational if and only if it has at least as much expected utility as any alternative the agent supposes he has.[13] The expected utility of an individual action is computed as follows: (a) determine what S takes to be its possible outcomes, the probability he attributes to each, and the subjective value (for him) of each outcome, using arbitrarily chosen numbers from negative to positive; (b) multiply the (subjective) probability of each outcome by its subjective value; and (c) add these products. This gives the action's expected utility. If we understand probability attributions in terms of beliefs and subjective utilities in terms of wants, then the maximization of expected utility view says roughly that, relative to S's beliefs, a rational action is at least as good as any alternative S supposes he has, in relation to satisfaction of his relevant wants.

Given our task here, this criterion is limited because it applies only to actions. But even apart from that, there are at least three reasons for rejecting it as it stands: (1) it takes no account of the rationality of the probability beliefs, or the wants, which form the basis of the utility calculations; (2) it is of narrow applicability because we very often simply do not have the requisite probability beliefs; and (3) it does not require that S act on the *basis* of the beliefs and wants in question. I have explained and defended these points elsewhere,[14] and will simply take them for granted and proceed to an alternative conception of rationality better suited for assessing self-deception. In any case, much of what is said about self-deception using that conception will also apply from the point of view of the maximization of expected utility conception and other notions.

What I propose is that we assess self-deception using a conception of rationality as *well-groundedness*. This conception is quite general and applies to all the key elements to be assessed here: beliefs, wants, and behavior. The conception is epistemic and is modeled on modest foundationalism.[15] To see the basic idea, consider beliefs first. Some are well-grounded directly—roughly, noninferentially—in experience, such as introspective and perceptual experiences. Others are well grounded indirectly, by virtue of being based on the former by chains of one or more sound inferences. We may conceive wants similarly, though there is more controversy about how to characterize sound foundational wants. I shall simply assume that it is rational (though perhaps defeasibly so) to want certain things—very notably one's own happiness—for their own sake. One could argue that this is because some things are obviously intrinsically *desirable*. Like Brandt,[16] one could also argue that this is because some intrinsic desires would survive cognitive psychotherapy—a kind of exposure of desires to facts and logic, designed to purge desires of irrationality.

Whatever we say here, if we can agree, as reflective people usually do, that (whatever else it may be rational to want intrinsically) it is rational to want one's own happiness intrinsically (and very strongly), and that wants for things clearly detrimental to this are prima facie irrational, we have the basis for quite far-reaching assessments of the rationality of human motivation and behavior. For instance, we can develop a useful strategy for assessing the rationality of actions. We may plausibly conceive it as a matter of how well-grounded they are, which in turn I take to be a matter of their connection to rational beliefs and rational wants. Roughly, S's rational actions are those which, on the basis of rational beliefs of his, contribute (or may be reasonably believed to contribute) toward fulfilling one or more of his rational wants, and are performed *on the basis of* the relevant wants and beliefs (otherwise they are rationally *groundable,* but not rationally *grounded*). This allows for some actions being more rational than others; but that seems appropriate: rationality (of actions as well as other things) is surely a comparative concept. Encapsulating this, we may simply say that a rational action is one performed for adequate reasons.

THE DIMENSIONS OF ASSESSMENT

We have seen that 'self-deception' applies to behavior as well as to the state of being self-deceived. We should then consider the rationality of both. Moreover, since the state may be long-standing, we must consider its rationality at a time; self-deception could be irrational at one time and rational at another. I also want to consider the bearing of self-deception on the overall rationality of the person. Let us formulate the questions to be pursued in each of these domains.

First, it seems plain that if a state of self-deception can be rational, it must be derivatively so. The crucial variables will be the person's circumstances and his rational beliefs and wants at the time. Clearly, one consideration is S's central belief, i.e., the unconscious one he does or would disavow. This belief usually constitutes knowledge, and as such it is normally quite rational.[17] But if it is merely a true belief for which S has some reason, it may not be highly rational, in which case, other things equal, S's self-deception is less rational than it would be. Other beliefs of S's are also relevant, particularly his beliefs about the consequences of believing he has the central belief or about the consequences of things being as that belief represents them to be. The rationality of S's beliefs about the evidence or grounds for p (the proposition which, as an expression of his self-deception, he sincerely but falsely avows), is relevant too. Similarly, the rationality of this want constituent of the self-deception, the want which partly explains why the central belief is unconscious, is important. So is the rationality of closely related wants, especially S's wants to be a certain kind of person. For instance, if his wanting to be a moral and generous person is rational, then other things equal, self-deception arising from this want has a mark in favor of its rationality not possessed by, say, self-deception arising from an irrational desire to be "masculine."

Regarding the behavior associated with self-deception, we must consider both acts that are in some sense aimed at getting one into self-deception, and those that arise out of it. In both cases an important factor is whether it would be rational to be self-deceived about the proposition in question; and in both the rationality of the wants and beliefs explaining the action is, as usual, of prime importance. The impact of self-deception on the rationality of a self-deceived person will depend on both the behavior to which the self-deception gives rise and the rationality of the state of self-deception itself.

I take these points about the assessment of self-deception to be largely neutral with respect to different views of rationality. For regardless of one's view of rationality, one will almost certainly want to assess the rationality of self-deception, and of related behavior, at least partly in terms of the variables just described. I now want to proceed to some specific theses about the rationality of self-deception. Other variables relevant to determining this will emerge as we proceed.

RATIONAL AND IRRATIONAL SELF-DECEPTION

That self-deception is not always an irrational state has already been suggested. Let us consider a case. Suppose that Jane is afraid of public speaking, yet needs to do it in her job. She knows she is moderately successful at it, yet she does less well than she should at it because of her fear. She tries to overcome the fear, but neither practice nor self-expostulation succeeds. She realizes, however, that it is the thought of the fear, more than the fear by itself, which impairs her performance. Clearly, then, it is reasonable for her (much of the time) to put the thought of it out of her mind. To do this she might occupy her mind with positive thoughts so far as possible, and might seek the company of supportive, admiring colleagues. Now suppose this strategy works a bit too well, and that Jane becomes "convinced" that she is not afraid, with the result that she performs better as a public speaker. I am assuming that the fear has remained (if diminished), and that she unconsciously knows she has it. This knowledge might be sustained, say, by her noticing—then dismissing—her trembling, and by her avoiding, and realizing that she avoids, public speaking engagements whenever she can.

Is Jane's self-deception an irrational state? Is it, e.g., like a desire to do something one knows one does not even enjoy, or like a belief which one nurtures despite clearly overwhelming evidence? It surely need not be. Suppose that the crucial want is to see herself as highly competent. Acknowledging a somewhat debilitating fear is at odds with this and not only reminds her that her goal is not realized, but reduces the degree to which she *is* competent—and to be competent is of course another thing she wants. Does her self-deception involve any irrational belief? In my view, it does not involve her believing that she is unafraid and certainly not her having contradictory beliefs. She may have the false second-order belief that she does not any longer believe she is afraid; but if her self-deception is embedded in enough supporting behavior, that belief may not be irrational: it could be based in part on considerable observation of her own behavior. (I am assuming that a belief of this sort could well be partly based on [presumably tacit] inference, since Jane might realize that in such a matter she should look objectively at herself.) It is true that Jane will sincerely but falsely say she is unafraid; but in doing so she is not lying, hence not violating her moral standards about honesty. Moreover, it could be that her being in self-deception helps her to realize a number of rational wants that are important to her (professionally and personally) and does not produce conflicts in her belief system. Furthermore, nothing we have assumed entails that her self-deception is *ineradicable by exposure to relevant evidence,* nor even that it has an excessively high *threshold* for *evidential eradication.* She might, e.g., be quite capable of emerging from her self-deception if a credible friend presented her with appropriate evidence of it. To be sure, this is largely a matter of how rational a *person* she is, but it also bears on the status of her self-deception. If all this is so, it is plausible to conclude that her self-deception is not irrational and indeed is to some degree rational. I do not take this to imply that there is no ''strategy'' available to her that is *more* rational (though that may be conceivable if certain further details are added to the example). The case is simply meant to illustrate how self-deception can be *one* rational outcome of attempts to solve a serious problem.

What the case seems to show, then, is roughly this: self-deception can be rational if it advances, better than readily available alternatives, the person's rational wants; does not embody or produce irrational beliefs, wants, or actions, at least not in a way that outweighs its contribution to realization of the person's rational wants; and does not have an excessively high threshold of evidential eradication. How often this happens and how often self-deception which meets these conditions will *continue* to do so are empirical questions. It takes no empirical inquiry, however, to see that over time rational self-deception can cease to be rational. Imagine, e.g., that Jane begins to take on public speaking assignments for which she should see she is unprepared. This might occur where her knowledge that she is still afraid is threatening to surface, and as a result she acts vigorously, but foolishly, in line with her avowals that she is unafraid. Here the tail wags the dog: she acts against, and not simply in spite of, her knowledge that she is still afraid, and either on an irrational belief that she can do certain assignments, or at least against good evidence that she cannot. This is where an understanding friend, previously content to let the self-deception pass, might want to intervene and bring her fear, and the consequences of keeping the knowledge of it veiled, to light.

What has just been illustrated is the irrationality of self-deception in virtue of its having *extreme consequences*, however few. Self-deception may also be irrational for other reasons. One is by virtue of *pervasive effects*, even if they are minor. Consider a man who has deceived himself about his wife's fidelity. If, day in and day out, he acts so as to keep his knowledge of the truth veiled, then his being self-deceived, even if it saves his marriage, could be ruining his life. He might, e.g., fill his mind with distracting thoughts to the point that his work is impaired, avoid half his friends, and alienate the others with inflated talk about his wife's goodness. His self-deception is not rational.

Furthermore, self-deception may cause *cognitive disorder*. If, for instance, our man were sufficiently desperate, he might offer foolish rationalizations of his wife's cool behavior towards him, begin to accept clearly inconsistent stories from her, and loosen his standards of evidence in general to the point that his thinking is impaired. This is presumably a kind of case in which self-deception can become evidentially ineradicable.

Self-deception might also cause *motivational imbalance*. Even if none of the consequences described above occurred, our man could become so obsessed with wanting to believe his marriage is stable, and steadily to see it as such, that he does not concentrate well on his work nor order his activities so as give priority to his rational wants, such as to meet his obligations toward his children as opposed to keeping his wife at home. No one consequence of this imbalance need be extreme, but the overall efforts of such self-deception could be very serious.

There are other ways in which self-deception can be irrational, but perhaps enough has been said to provide a sense of how it is to be assessed in terms of the variables I have proposed as primary. Let us now proceed to the rationality of the behavior associated with self-deception.

The Rationality
of Self-Deceptive Behavior

If we begin with acts that manifest self-deception, such as sincere avowals of the proposition the self-deceiver unconsciously knows to be false, it naturally occurs to one that if the self-deception generating them is rational, they are well-grounded and inherit its rationality. But this is at most a reasonable presumption to which there are many exceptions. Recall Jane. If she has just been presented with obviously overwhelming evidence that she is still afraid, her sincere avowal that she is not is not rational. Moreover, suppose she can see that her career depends on fearlessly addressing a certain group or not addressing it at all, feels afraid, and can see that if she says she is not afraid she will be committed to giving the speech. Here, even given the rationality of her self-deception, her avowing that she is unafraid would presumably not be rational. It is not that she must suddenly cast off her self-deception; the point is that this time she should admit the fear she feels (perhaps saying it is unusual) rather than be carried over the brink by her self-deception.

This shows that while the rationality of the self-deception from which an act arises is relevant to the rationality of the act, there is no simple connection. The point can also be illustrated by *ir*rational self-deception's giving rise to a rational act. Thus, the desperately self-deceived husband might, in keeping his self-deception veiled, treat the man he unconsciously believes is his wife's lover warmly when the latter visits her in the hospital where she is quite ill. If the husband's concern to keep his wife calm, and his adherence to good manners, are also important in motivating his warmth, then in exhibiting the warmth he is acting rationally.

We must also note cases where the unconscious knowledge (or unconscious true belief) in self-deception largely explains an action. For here, whether the self-deception is rational or not, S is acting on knowledge or on a true belief for which he has some reason. Such actions have a significant mark in favor of their rationality, though they are certainly not necessarily rational. Suppose, e.g., that the husband we have described has to decide whether to agree to his wife's leaving him to join a woman friend for a pleasure trip. If his unconscious knowledge that she is unfaithful leads him to believe (unconsciously) that she will use the occasion to meet her lover, then his refusing to agree, on the basis of that knowledge, might be rational (as self-protective, let us say). To be sure, this is not the sort of action we think of as arising from self-deception—since here it is the agent qua non-deceived who acts. But the central belief in S's self-deception is crucial in his motivation, and the action is of a kind self-deception sometimes seems to cause. Its rationality is thus of interest here. Granted S might feel a need to rationalize it, given his frequent praises of her merits; and in rationalizing he might act irrationally, e.g. by offering silly excuses. But that is a different point and we need not resist it.

To judge the rationality of self-deceptive action, then, we must consider both its circumstances and the rationality of the total set of motivating wants and beliefs. What we find is that the distinction between rational and non-rational action cuts across the distinction between actions arising from rational self-deception and those arising from irrational self-deception. Both sorts of action may or may not be well-grounded; and since the self-deceiver typically has (unconscious) knowledge, actions crucially motivated by that, together with one's normal self-protective wants, usually are at least minimally rational.

Similar considerations apply to behavior that produces or is meant to produce self-deception, such as putting the thought that p (say, that one is afraid of public speaking) out of mind, exposing oneself selectively to evidence against p, and seeking the company of those who reinforce one's tending to disavow p. We can best analyze such behavior if we divide it into two categories: those actions performed in order to put the thought that p out of mind, or even in order to become self-deceived with respect to p; and those which are of the sort that can be expected to contribute to one or the other of these results, but are not performed in order to do so. Both sorts are such that discerning observers would call them attempts to deceive oneself, or beginning to deceive oneself, or, perhaps, spinning a web of self-deception.

Regarding acts of the first sort, which we might call *intentional self-deceptive efforts*, a crucial point has already been made: self-deception itself can be rational. Recall Jane. Her self-deception was rational. Imagine that instead of sliding into it she made a decision to try to become self-deceived about her fear of public speaking. She might then have done a number of things in order to bring this about, such as putting certain thoughts out of mind, concentrating on her strengths as a speaker, recalling her successes in public speaking, and seeking comments on her speaking from people who she knows admire it. How are we to assess the rationality of all these acts? Notice first that if her being in self-deception concerning her fear of public speaking is rational, then the decision to try to get into it is prima facie rational. There might be preferable alternatives for realizing the same end, i.e., doing her job competently. And the consequences of carrying out the decision might be foreseeably bad. But these and other defeating factors need not occur, and when they do not, the decision may be rational. Similar points apply to the actions performed in order to become self-deceived. Does S have preferable alternatives? Are these actions detrimental to S, e.g. by preventing his maintaining realism about himself *in general* or weakening his standards of evidence in general, or alienating friends who cannot bring themselves to play along? Such effects would be common in attempts to put oneself in self-deception. But they need not always arise, and we can imagine a rational decision to become rationally self-deceived, carried out by minimal steps, most of which are rational behavior.

185

Nonintentional self-deceptive efforts are more difficult to assess. These are actions which, even if intentional, are not performed in order to contribute to producing self-deception but are the sort that usually do contribute to producing it. Thus, Jane may put her fear of public speaking out of mind because the fear is unpleasant, and may recall to mind compliments on a speech of hers because doing so is pleasant. These acts may contribute to her becoming self-deceived, but that alone does not make them less than rational. Suppose, however, that she knows, and judges, that she must not become self-deceived about her capacities (because it will harm her, let us say). Then she might, after a time, resist such acts. If they then occurred, against her better judgment, she herself might justly regard them as irrational. If they occurred repeatedly and eventually produced self-deception, it too would presumably be irrational. Since she judged (on the basis of knowledge) that she ought not to become self-deceived in this case, and might remain convinced that she should not be, we can even regard the case as *akratic self-deception*. To be sure, she would not consciously know she is in it, but her being in it is still in opposition to her will, and the rational thing for her to do is to resist the behavior it produces, such as excessive exposure to biased judges of her speaking.

We should also consider actions which contribute to self-deception yet are not intentional at all. Some of these are unintentional, e.g., accidentally misreading a word with the result that one's audience laughs heartily, thereby contributing to one's self-deception about oneself as a speaker. Such behavior is of no special interest here, however, because unintentional actions are presumably not rational, though they may belong to *types*, such as amusing one's audience, which are a rational kind of thing to do.[18] There are, by contrast, things one does by (or in) doing something intentionally, such that one consents to doing them but does not do them intentionally (Bentham called these obliquely intentional). Suppose, e.g., that, to conduct some routine business, Jane meets with a colleague who raves, obviously excessively, about the ease and high quality of her public speaking. If she knows he will rave about her latest speech, then even in seeing him in order to conduct routine business she is consentingly and nonintentionally exposing herself to something favorable to self-deception about her fear of public speaking.

How should we assess the rationality of such an act? It will not do to say that if the set of intentional *base acts*, i.e., intentional acts by, or in, the performance of which *S* performs the nonintentional act, is rational, then so is the latter. Here the base act is conducting the routine business. Now we can easily imagine that another colleague who would not excessively rave about Jane's speaking is equally accessible for the same routine business. Then, assuming she does or should realize that exposing herself to the raving is a bad thing for her, the rationality of her conducting business with the raver is not sufficient to render rational her nonintentional exposure to something favorable to her self-deception. There are two important points here: one is that rationality is not necessarily transmitted from an intentional action to all the nonintentional actions generated by it; the other, implicit in the example, is that the irrationality of one's doing something nonintentionally can even undermine the rationality of intentionally doing something that will generate the former. Thus, if Jane's exposing herself to the raving is sufficiently irrational, it may cease to be rational for her to conduct the routine business with the colleague who will do it.

Both points have moral counterparts. It may be prima facie right for one to render aid to a depressed student, but not for one (even nonintentionally) to miss an appointment in so doing; and the latter could be so morally objectionable that one's rendering aid would be on balance quite wrong. If this were not so, then if we could somehow manipulate ourselves so that we do terrible things only as nonintentional side effects of intentional acts that are prima facie right, all manner of evil deeds would be permissible. Neither morality nor rationality comes so cheap.

What emerges, then, is that there are at best few simple generalizations we can make about the rationality of behavior associated with self-deception. It tends to be irrational, but it need not be. It must be judged partly in the light of whether the self-deception it manifests, or to whose production it is favorable, is rational; and partly in the light of S's rational beliefs and wants, and his circumstances (particularly as they bear on what it is rational for S to believe and want). All of these elements, I believe, may be understood in terms of rationality conceived as well-groundedness. What has been said only begins to show how the well-groundedness conception applies to these elements, but perhaps it indicates some major directions for further inquiry. In any case, there is one other area we should briefly address in connection with the rationality of self-deception, namely how self-deception bears on the rationality of persons. Let us explore this.

Self-Deception and the Rational Person

A paradigmatically rational person might be expected to be free of self-deception. This at least applies to such people in fairly fortunate life circumstances. But if self-deception can be rational, a rational person can surely be self-deceived about some things at least some of the time. On the other hand, self-deception is prima facie nonrational, and rational persons can surely be expected not only to have limited self-deception, but to conduct themselves in a way that makes unlikely their becoming irrationally self-deceived. Moreover, when they are in self-deception, they can be expected to exercise certain kinds of rational control over themselves. Let us consider these points in turn.

A rational person generally does not hide from unpleasant truths, nor distort evidence, nor seek to obtain a biased sample of the evidence. It is easy to see how this accords with deep-seated wants common in such people, such as the want to lead a happy and fulfilling life. The result of these tendencies in rational persons is a natural resistance to self-deception. Special circumstances may make self-deception a rational option for such persons, but this is not normal for them. Moreover, there is such a thing as minor self-deception on a minor matter. If Kate likes her students and wants them to like her, then she may rationalize hostile behavior by one of them as due to insecurity and become self-deceived regarding his affection for her. But we are talking of one student in one course, and little if anything of significance need turn on Kate's self-deception. If, in addition, we suppose the evidence to be somewhat ambiguous, so that it is only because Kate is so insightful that she knows, deep down, that the student does not like her, then even if her self-deception is not rational it detracts little from her rationality as a person. Here is one way, then, that a quite rational person can be self-deceived.

Now consider a rational person who is in self-deception. What should we expect? With Kate, for instance, we would not expect irrational behavior, such as doing important things that presuppose the boy's affection (say, trusting him to go beyond the call of duty in acting as a class leader). We would also not expect her to have a great emotional stake in the self-deception, e.g. to be such that she is seriously upset upon hearing evidence against her sincere avowals of his affection. This in turn suggests that we would not expect the self-deception to be so deeply *entrenched* that it cannot be eliminated by careful self-scrutiny. Similarly, we would not expect it to be *multiply layered*, covered by camouflage of (e.g.) rationalization supported by a system of false beliefs and steadfast relations to people who help maintain the self-deception.

As all this suggests, rational agents monitor themselves to some degree, do not normally build up a multiply layered network of deception, and have a good capacity for acquiring self-knowledge and eliminating their false beliefs about their own cognition and motivation.

Thus, if Kate were faced with a situation in which it is important to see clearly how the student really feels about her, we would expect her to be able to respond appropriately. If, for instance, he lodged a grade appeal case against her, we would expect her to reassess his feelings about her and, if the evidence warrants it, to give up saying that he likes her and to make use of her knowledge that he does not. An irrational person, by contrast, might be unable to accomplish this.

We may conclude, then, not that rational persons are never self-deceived, but that they are less often so than nonrational persons, seldom if ever in irrational self-deception, and far less likely either to behave irrationally as a result of self-deception or to remain in it when evidence pulls hard at the veil between their consciousness and what they unconsciously know. Their self-deception, if any, is likely to be minor, and the actions it generates are likely to be monitored. It is in good part because such monitoring is both possible and normally expectable in rational persons that they are often morally criticizable for getting into self-deception, for remaining in it, or for acting out of it.[19] This is not to suggest that rational actions and dispositions are equivalent to moral ones; the point is simply that what is expectable conduct in a rational person is the sort of thing whose performance—or omission—it is appropriate to evaluate morally. In any case, as often as self-deception exhibits both irrationality and associated behavior that deserves moral criticism, it can occur in a rational person and need not lead to irrational or morally deficient behavior.

SELF-DECEPTION AS AN
EXPLANATORY AND PREDICTIVE CONCEPT

Our discussions have strongly associated self-deception with the paradigmatically action-explaining concepts of believing and wanting. We have also noted how self-deception gives rise to actions (overt and covert). Is it an explanatory concept, and what predictive powers might it have? In answering these questions I shall consider only explanatory and predictive power regarding actions and conscious states. I want to begin with a distinction between directly and obliquely explanatory concepts.

Let us call a concept *directly explanatory* if appeal to it in attempting to explain something can indicate just why the thing in question occurred (or is the case). Believing and wanting, at least where an appropriate instance of one is taken in the context of an appropriate instance of the other, are directly explanatory. We can, e.g., explain just why Jane visited her supportive colleague by citing her wanting to hear him rave about her speech. I call a concept *obliquely explanatory* when appeal to it only indicates the sort of explanation available for the thing in question, but not just why it occurred. A concept may, of course, be directly explanatory relative to one sort of thing—say, actions—and obliquely explanatory relative to another—say, personality traits. (We may also want to relativize to contexts, since the explanatory capacity of a concept may vary with the context in which it is appealed to in order to explain something.) The crucial difference may be that directly explanatory concepts are, and obliquely explanatory concepts are not, such that their attribution (in typical contexts) is sufficient to subsume the phenomenon to be explained under a particular explanatory generalization.[20] If we make the further assumption that self-deception does not figure in the relevant generalizations, then we might also want to say that its explanatory power is *derivative* from that of one or more other concepts, as well as oblique.

Now self-deception, I believe, is obliquely explanatory, at least relative to actions and to most other phenomena one might reasonably hope to explain by appeal to it. Suppose that, in answer to 'Why is Jane listening to that clearly insincere flattery?' someone says, 'It's because of her self-deception about her fear of public speaking.' This tells us that, speaking loosely, some ego need explains her behavior, but not what need it is. We would thus know what sort of explanation to look for, but not what explanation(s) in the relevant range to regard as applicable. A direct explanation, by contrast, would be, 'She wants to believe the sorts of things he is saying,' or 'It helps her satisfy her desire to keep out of mind her unconscious knowledge that she is really afraid of public speaking.' It may of course be a very short step from oblique to direct explanation. This is one reason why oblique explanatory power is significant. Still, it is important to see that the concept of self-deception is not directly explanatory.

It will be apparent from these points that the predictive power of the concept of self-deception is highly limited. Even if we know with respect to what proposition S is self-deceived, we are not generally in a good position to predict what he will do or just how he will feel upon (say) being given evidence against the proposition. Granted, even when we know S's wants and beliefs and their relative strengths, we often cannot predict his behavior precisely—if only because his circumstances may be unpredictable. But the situation is worse if all we know is that S is self-deceived with respect to p. For all that, there are general expectations we may form. Self-deception often leads to vacillation: for there is the influence both of the knowledge that p and of the sincere avowals that not-p, or at least of the desire to act in accord with those avowals. Self-deception also tends to generate cognitive dissonance, in the sense of a felt incongruity among one's propositional attitudes.[21] So we can expect efforts to explain away apparent inconsistencies and to rationalize some behavior. There will also be a tendency to keep evidence against p out of mind and to find entertaining it, or having the thought of not-p, unpleasant. Moreover, in a very general way, a person's being in self-deception, particularly multilayered self-deception on an important matter, suggests a tendency to protect oneself.

One way to put some of this is to say that the concept of self-deception is more interpretive and diagnostic than predictive. To be sure, a good diagnosis puts one in a good position to predict, at least where the illness and the patient's circumstances are well understood; and this, I think, is often the case with self-deception. For one can often discover the want constituent in the deception, the central (unconscious) belief, and related motivation, and frequently the person's approximate circumstances are known: Moreover, one can often tell a good deal about a person from knowing the sort of thing about which he is self-deceived. The usefulness of the concept of self-deception, in psychology and everyday life, and in one's own case as well as that of others, is not to be underestimated.

CONCLUSION

On the account of self-deception proposed in this paper, to be self-deceived with respect to a proposition, p, involves both being disposed to avow it sincerely and knowing unconsciously that it is false. More specifically, the self-deceiver unconsciously knows p to be false (or, with some reason, unconsciously and truly believes it to be false), sincerely avows it or is disposed to avow it sincerely, and has at least one want which in part explains (among other things) why his belief that not-p is unconscious. This account resolves the paradox of self-deception, preserves a strong analogy with other-person deception, and enables us to distinguish self-deception from close cousins. By placing self-deception largely in the domain of beliefs and wants, it also facilitates the assessment of the rationality both of self-deception and behavior associated with it. I have taken states of self-deception to be fundamental, both in explicating the concept and in connecting self-deception and associated behavior with rationality. In part because self-deception, as conceived here, typically embodies knowledge and represents, at one level, a normal response to evidence, it is not always irrational. Indeed, under special circumstances self-deception can play a useful role in the psychic economy of a rational person. Its rationality may be evaluated, I have argued, in terms of the well-groundedness of the wants and beliefs constituent in it and of related wants and beliefs of the subject. It turns out that in certain cases a person may have rational beliefs and wants in relation to which both self-deception and various actions contributing to it or arising from it are rational. These are special cases, however; typically, neither self-deception nor the associated behavior is rational. The concept does, however, have a good measure of explanatory and diagnostic power. Indeed, if we do not adequately understand it, then we lack an important element in understanding not only rationality and irrationality, but the human agent in general. This paper is meant to contribute to those tasks.[22]

NOTES

1. For accounts that embrace the paradox see Amélie Oksenberg Rorty, "Belief and Self-Deception," *Inquiry* 15 (1972), especially 393–396, and "Self-Deception, Akrasia and Irrationality," *Social Science Information* 19 (1980), especially 914–915; and Jeffrey Foss, "Rethinking Self-Deception," *American Philosophical Quarterly* 17 (1980), especially 241–242. For a detailed account that makes acts of self-deception and volitional concepts primary, see Herbert Fingarette, *Self-Deception* (London: Routledge and Kegan Paul, 1969). Accounts making essential use of unconscious belief are less common than the other sorts I have mentioned, but (in addition to my own view) D. W. Hamlyn's "Self-Deception," *Aristotelian Society,* suppl. vol. 15 (1971), may be an instance. He says, e.g., that "the self-deceiver has to make himself unconscious or unaware of what he really knows" (p. 57). It should be added that while most writers on self-deception who do not embrace the paradox hold that self-deception is possible, one might, like M. R. Haight in *A Study of Self-Deception* (Sussex: Harvester Press, and Atlantic Highlands, N.J.: Humanities Press, 1980), hold that because of this paradox, self-deception taken literally is impossible. See especially chap. 2. Regarding the view that self-deception involves a divided self, there is quite a range of positions from strong views to the effect that a kind of multiple personality is involved to the modest claim (made below) that self-deception involves a kind of dissociation. Cp. Fingarette, *Self-Deception,* 129, on self-deception as involving a splitting off of "a nuclear, dynamic complex."

2. I refer mainly to my "Epistemic Disavowals and Self-Deception," *The Personalist* 57 (1976): 378–385, and "Self-Deception, Action, and Will," *Erkenntnis* 18 (1982): 133–158.

3. Audi, "Self-Deception, Action and Will," 137.

4. A good case for the importance of wanting in self-deception is made by Kent Bach in "An Analysis of Self-Deception," *Philosophy and Phenomenological*

Research 41 (1981). In other respects, however, his view of self-deception differs markedly from mine.

5. For a number of the needed comments and qualifications see ''Self-Deception, Action, and Will,'' especially 135–143. A point worth adding here is that while the self-deceiver's sincere avowal typically goes against evidence he has, one can be self-deceived in avowing something (such as that one disbelieves a certain proposition) where one is going against, not *evidence*, but noninferential knowledge (say, that one does believe the proposition in question). Many writers on self-deception have talked as if self-deception were always partly a matter of somehow going against one's evidence, but that seems too strong (and is not entailed by my account).

6. Sincerity is partially explained, and this claim is defended, in ''Self-Deception, Action, and Will,'' 138–140.

7. For an account of believing which supports these points see my paper ''The Concept of Believing,'' *The Personalist* 53 (1972).

8. This line is taken by Alfred Mele in ''Ordinary Self-Deception,'' forthcoming in *The Philosophical Quarterly;* my own view of the matter is defended in ''Self-Deception, Action, and Will,'' 138–142.

9. The relevant notion of unconscious belief is discussed in ''Self-Deception, Action, and Will,'' 137–138. It may help, however, to say here that the sense in which *S*'s unconscious belief is not accessible to him except under special conditions is roughly that apart from them he cannot come to know (at least not consciously) that he has it.

10. For a different view of the relation between self-deception and wishful thinking, see Jon Elster, *Sour Grapes: Studies in the Subversion of Rationality* (Cambridge: Cambridge University Press, 1983). He says, e.g., that ''the substitution of wishful thinking for self-deception is a step toward the elimination of the Freudian unconscious as a theoretical entity—a highly desirable goal'' (p. 152). This is a good place to say that no such entity is presupposed by the limited use of unconscious beliefs in this paper.

11. For detailed explication of hypocrisy, see Béla Szabados, ''Hypocrisy,'' *Canadian Journal of Philosophy* 9 (1979). There are, of course, other phenomena that might be confused with self-deception. A strange but noteworthy one is Anton's Syndrome, in which trauma in the visual cortex produces sudden blindness, yet *S* does not know he cannot see and makes excuses for, e.g., bumping into things. My account gives the intuitively correct result, I think: that because (among other things) there is no evidence of knowledge of the blindness, *S* is not self-deceived. For discussion of the case see Patricia Smith Churchland, ''Consciousness: The Transmutation of a Concept,'' *Pacific Philosophical Quarterly* 64 (1983).

12. One's knowledge that one has a belief can be based both on a noninferential relation to it and a grasp of evidence for one's having it. Self-deception may exhibit such mixed grounds, but may also arise around knowledge not based on evidence (a point often missed in the literature).

13. For discussion of the maximization of expected utility view of rational action see Carl G. Hempel's treatment of rational action in his *Aspects of Scientific Explanation* (New York: Macmillan, 1965).

14. In ''Rationality and Valuation,'' forthcoming in the Theory and Decision Library in a collection edited by Gottfried Seebass and Raimo Tuomela.

15. See ibid. and "An Epistemic Conception of Rationality," *Social Theory and Practice* 9 (1983), for development of this idea and references to contrasting views.

16. See R. B. Brandt, *A Theory of the Good and the Right* (Oxford: Oxford University Press, 1979), e.g. p. 11. I have critically evaluated Brandt's criterion of rationality in "An Epistemic Conception of Rationality," cited in note 15. For other views of rationality see, e.g., William Dray, *Laws and Explanations in History* (Oxford: Oxford University Press, 1957); John Rawls, *A Theory of Justice* (Cambridge: Harvard University Press, 1971), especially sections 25 and 63–65; and Kurt Baier, "The Social Source of Reason," *Proceedings and Addresses of the American Philosophical Association* 47 (1977).

17. One reason it need not be maximally rational, or even very highly rational, is that apparently one can know on the basis of reliably produced belief even when one has some reason to doubt the proposition in question, or at least one can know on the basis of far less than optimal justification.

18. One might put the point by saying that unintentional actions for which one has good reasons are merely *rationalizable* in terms of those reasons, not *rational* on the basis of them. This distinction is developed and defended in my "Rationalization and Rationality," forthcoming in *Synthese*.

19. Moral responsibility in these three kinds of cases is discussed in detail in "Self-Deception, Action, and Will," 148–154. Some of the parallels between the rationality of self-deception and related phenomena and, on the other hand, their morality, are instructive. For further discussion of moral issues connected with self-deception see Mike W. Martin, *Morality and Self-Deception* (mimeographed).

20. For an account of some explanatory generalizations in which wanting and believing figure see my paper "The Concept of Wanting," *Philosophical Studies* 21 (1973). As I have suggested, at least much of the explanatory power of the concept of self-deception is derivative from that of believing or wanting or both together.

21. For what is perhaps the classical statement of the theory of cognitive dissonance see Leon Festinger, *A Theory of Cognitive Dissonance* (Stanford, Calif.: Stanford University Press, 1975). The theory has been influential and there have been many versions. Here I offer a liberal interpretation of the concept simply for illustrative purposes.

22. For helpful comments on earlier versions of the material in this paper I want to thank John King-Farlow, Eric Kraemer, John Longeway, and Mike W. Martin.

Self-Formation and the Mean (Programmatic Remarks on Self-Deception)

John King-Farlow and Richard Bosley

Let the world choose men of glass and snow
That melt in the burning ordeal:
Tomorrow's sun will cast them down and fill the sea.
The salamander and I never eat anything but fire,
And the children of our suffering shall remain
Even until the end of the earth's despair.

INTRODUCTION

It was the beginning of the world's despair when Eve lost her faith in deceiving herself. She had only to match the serpent's suggestions with a creatively human response. She had only to liven her own wits and deceive herself, rather than letting a reptile fool her with grubby little paradoxes of power against omnipotence. (''Ye shall be as gods.'') Not yet being a fallen creature, she had many means in any context to protect herself other than by craftily disarranging her thoughts. But it would have been so easy to pretend to herself and her tempter that she was, say, strictly carnivorous on Mondays; she could not abide the texture of apples and other fruit until after Tuesday's dawn prayers with Adam. (''You could come and join us in singing Jehovah's praise. He often reveals his countenance to us at sunrise.'') Only the last nine words need be the truth. There are some points, we would agree with God and the Devil, where deception and self-deception repeat the kiss of Judas. (Too many philosophers ignore other points and contexts in their eagerness to call all self-deceptions sick or evil.)

Indeed, Eve might have shuffled her words and earnestly pressed the serpent to follow her homewards, away from the Tree of the Knowledge of Good and Evil. After all, he could stiffen his back and make up a foursome at bridge with the Creator and His two new tenants. Eve might have done the human race's first glorious deed, turning back the monotonous sounds of evil and temptation by all but sincerely offering some such bizarre counterproposal.

The serpent might well have scurried away. With more imaginative uses by mankind's ancestors of self-deception and grace, there need have been no Fall from Eden. Humanity could have remained in Paradise.

As self-deceiving and imagination can bring about so much power for human flourishing, it is hardly miraculous that they can achieve no less for establishing what is diabolical and morally intolerable. In *Sophie's Choice* William Styron has searched profoundly for an example of great, innovative evil. Styron takes us through hundreds of pages of Sophie's reminiscences about torture, humiliation, and mass execution in Poland and East Germany during the Second World War. Most of the evildoing soon becomes as monotonous and drab as it was vile. Finally, Styron depicts a profoundly gifted Nazi doctor. Prevented by his family from becoming a priest, he is torn between, first, a desire to prove a perfect God's nonexistence through a new feat of astonishing inhumanity, and, second, a rebellious believer's aim to play Lucifer—to smite a perfect God with a stroke of unbelievably inhuman devilry. The nameless doctor watches hordes of non-Aryan children led mechanically off to the ovens. Then he conjures up for himself the sharply innovative device of asking a Polish mother to choose the life of *one*, and only one, of her two children. (Styron appears not to perceive consciously that this is a brilliant conversion to evil of the novelty and imagination shown in 'The Judgment of Solomon.') Eve could usefully exercise self-deception by persuading herself, for the sake of good, that she had a more attractive pastime to offer the serpent. The nameless medical officer could hope to achieve the sense of realizing his clashingly satanic and his all but atheist projects—or what would be as near as man could come to perfect evil in contradiction. But he needed a highly original form of self-deception or the only result would be fresh floundering in stale sins. Styron writes:

> No sin! He had suffered boredom and anxiety, and even revulsion, but no sense of sin from the bestial crimes he had been party to, nor had he felt that in sending thousands of the wretched innocent to oblivion he had transgressed against divine law. All had been unutterable monot-

ony. . . . Was it not supremely simple, then, to restore his belief in God, and at the same time to affirm his human capacity for evil. . . . But first a great sin. One whose glory lay in its subtle magnanimity—a choice. After all, he had the power to take both. This is the only way I have been able to explain. . . .[1]

Self-deception is heterogeneous. But the present net brings in a number of interestingly similar fish. Let us roughly diagnose many cases of self-deception in this way. The agent may well be aware, and admit to himself quite consciously, that he allows himself to be led into doing good or evil by those he considered more clever, more highly placed by the government or more qualified by some sort of authority in his earlier background. Lest he come to feel paralyzed by warring perceptions, he chooses to let certain blandishments on the good or evil side affect him more strongly. The agent may now take a particularly virtuous or vicious step forward. He may use a mechanism of self-deception with an especially generous and creative inner light to make an obviously dangerous temptation much weaker—or with notably original but evil-seeking force to make a monstrous novelty possible. So Styron's doctor wants to make himself believe and not believe all at once in God. He wants to feel the northern Christian's guilt of 'infinite' proportions, so that he may once more believe that he possesses a real option both between proof and disproof *and* between faith and rejecting the companionship of God. Such thought and deeds of truly inspired self-deception are, one might guess, among the least easily predictable modes of persons' reactions to the world.

More should be said of profound, creative self-deception in the reaching of self-fulfillment. When Julius Caesar announced that he would rather be first man in the village than second man in Rome, he probably appeared to most readers over the centuries *just* to be making clear an instructive fact about the psychology of the most determined competitors in realpolitik. Perhaps Caesar was. But in an episode of *Buddenbrooks*, which Thomas Mann set in Hanseatic merchants' Germany about eighteen hundred years later than Caesar's death, the author lets the shrewd, if sometimes confused, mind of Antonia take up Caesar's point and relate it for her embittered uncle's sake to an ideal of wise and constructive self-deception:

> Oh, we are travelled and educated enough to realize that the limits set to our ambitions are small and petty enough, looked at from outside and above. But everything in this world is comparative, Uncle Gottwold. Did you know one can be a great man, even in a small place; a Caesar even in a little commercial town on the Baltic? But that takes

imagination and idealism—and you didn't have it, whatever you may have thought yourself.[2]

What is Antonia saying? Let a person's *idealism* and *imagination* be directed to finding a career and family life in a community, however large or small, where native and instilled gifts of leadership may be channeled to match that community's values and one's own. Let the idealism and imagination (and vanity) search out and feed on the values of this community so that one is all the more greatly fulfilled by forms of leadership that are harmonious with this chosen group's traditions. And finally let that idealism and that imagination be directed to half-consciously repairing what is seen as flawed or evil in the community, with its own historical materials and without despair of its lasting, intrinsic worth.

We have begun this investigation of self-deception by pointing, as often only literature and other arts can let one point, that is, pointing at extremes of good and evil in some cases that fall within a Family of Families of Meanings. Such a Family of Families includes terms like "Deceive oneself," "Con oneself," "Confuse oneself," "Trick oneself," "Throw sand in one's own eyes," "Practice hypocrisy against oneself," "Make a mistake and bear at least some responsibility for it," "Lie in the soul," "Turn a blind eye," "Repressing her own pride," "Avoid putting 2 and 2 together," "Manipulate one's own good nature," and so on. But we started with such prickly moral teachers as the authors of the early chapters of Genesis, then with Mann and Styron, in order to drive home from the start our belief that self-deception is not necessarily an evil. It is a human power or potency—a potency *for* Good or Evil.

The most interesting and discussable types of self-deception are usually those that allow what is intrapersonal and less intelligible to be understood in terms of metaphors of the interpersonal. Let someone ask, "But what is this *'self'* of self-deception that performs feats of solitaire against a person?" We ask, "What is so mysterious about talk of interpersonal and relatedly intrapersonal conflicts?"

Since 1962 our writings on self-deception have been largely directed at the two philosophers who are to be thanked most justly and warmly for keeping interest in self-deception alive: Professor Herbert Fingarette of the University of California, Santa Barbara, and the late Jean-Paul Sartre. Unfortunately, both men's efforts to stress the importance of self-deception in human thought and action result in a great deal of superfluous guilt-mongering. "Guilt" and "self-deception" are simple to understand—all but univocal: guilt feelings must be the result of authentic guilt; self-deception must be a sign of moral guilt (Sartre, or early Fingarette), psychological illness (late Fingarette), or both (later Fingarette). From the standpoint of the ideals that we shall be discussing, both Sartre and Fingarette are profoundly misguided. The Bibliography indicates where our original attacks first appeared.

DEFECT AND EXCESS

Sartre and Fingarette, however interesting, are not rivals in ethical and psychological perception to a Plato or an Aristotle, nor to a Confucius or a Siddhartha Buddha. Happily for our purposes, there is a revival of interest in the ancient world, not least in Aristotle's ethical theory. We intend to make some use of his concepts and teachings—in particular, those involved in the Doctrine of the Mean. Certain questions that bear on self-deception can usually be posed in terms of Aristotle's moral tenets. Indeed, we shall see that, while other forms of self-deception remain, there is a potential infinity of essentially culpable forms of self-deceiving related to forms of the Mean. Further, we shall draw on Hellenism to create and employ a developmental view of human life, a view based to some extent on both Plato and Aristotle. Our goal here, of course, is not strict exegesis. But we do attach much importance to the continuity and breadth of our human tradition, so we shall finally be casting glances at similarly old and influential concepts of the Mean in Chinese philosophy.

There is an old premise that should be laid before the reader at the beginning: that truth itself is a Mean. For example, Thomas Aquinas writes that among the virtues of the speculative intellect, the Mean will be truth itself. To miss the Mean of truth is to go wrong, and being quite deceived (embracing falsehood without reservations) is one way of going completely wrong. The view that truth is best understood in a great many cases as a Mean helps orient our essay and, in the manner of classical philosophy, invites certain questions. (If some modern philosophers can only bear to think of *truthfulness* as a Mean, let them follow us *mutatis mutandis*.)

Four questions naturally open a classically oriented discussion of self-deception. The first is "What is self-deception?" An answer to the question provides a new path for discussion. Our answer here will anticipate a good deal of what is to follow. Our answer depends upon Aristotle's account of the Mean: to hit the Mean is to go right. To fall short of it is to accept and endorse a defect, and to exceed it is to be in excess. Self-deception, whenever it is popularly and rightly understood in context to be *undesirable,* is of two sorts: one of defect and one of excess. When one is asked for a testimony, one swears an oath informed by this question: "Do you swear to tell the truth, the whole truth and nothing but the truth?" One is asked for the truth, that is, for speech faithful to the Mean. One is asked to avoid two ways of straying from the Mean. First, there is defect: that is, not clearly telling the whole of what is relevant truth. Second, there is excess: that is, erecting an alternative to the truth, or misstating it, or encasing the truth dishonestly in irrelevant and distracting additions. Excess, too, is an alternative that must eventually be set aside and eliminated if the speaker is to return to the Mean. One form of self-deception arises when we do not or will not face certain things and admit them; another, when we fabricate an alternative to reality, or use a cloak of irrelevant truths or deceptive methods of truthful reporting to conceal what is the Truth in the context.

Two Mean-centered forms of self-deception can be discerned in English idioms that depend, on the one hand, upon the sense of sight and, on the other, upon that of hearing. One can be blinded both because of a defect of light and also because of an excess of light. We have the anonymous saying: "Love is blind; friendship closes its eyes." Falling in love may move one to close one's eyes, hoping to escape the possibility of discerning faults in another. Exercise of the will to close one's eyes in this way and to keep them closed has its active and passive sides. One wills, it might be said, to paralyze one's will. One opts to be a 'passive agent' of self-deception. It may be said behind one's back: "He's blinded himself to her faults." One becomes a 'passive agent' of the deception because one has contrived and is set to go on contriving that the soul should have too little light. On the other hand, an exposure to an excess of light can destroy sight just as effectively. For one can also be dazzled and so blinded. In "To Night" Shelley writes:

> Blind with thine hair the eyes of Day;
> Kiss her until she be wearied out,
> Then wander o'er city, and sea, and land,
> Touching all with thine opiate wand—
> Come, long-sought!

One can flee the Mean and, therefore, at least half-consciously choose to come too close to a source of light. One can blind oneself in this way and, bedazzled, tell oneself a story that usurps the place reserved by reality for its own story telling. Feeling shame at having persecuted Ukrainian children in one's schooldays, one can seek out the *shattering* evidence for Stalin's destroying three million Ukrainians in 1933 by creating an artificial famine. One's sense of one's own responsibility is conveniently overwhelmed, at least for a while. Having harmed one's family by borrowing and not returning ten thousand dollars, one can take a job where the picture of man's fiscal cruelty to man is dazzling, all but overpowering. And so on.

Description in the matter of sight becomes metaphor in the service of reason, for the seat of self-deception is not sight and/or any form of sense perception but rather speech and thought (to which we shall shortly turn). Greek epistemology depends for its basic expression upon analogies with seeing and visual images. Plato, in particular, writes as though self-perfection through knowledge of universals is a special kind of seeing. Given such a historical tradition, it doubtless took great thinkers to mark a systematic distinction between seeing and knowing and, in general, between sense-perception and thought. Sophocles has Tiresias accuse King Oedipus of seeing but not knowing; Tiresias himself, being blind, knows, seeing not. But there are ripe conditions of perception in which reason flourishes most. No one supposes he can tell what color something is when he faces either too little or too much light. And so one can blind reason. That is, one can blind oneself either by placing oneself in a position to receive too little light or to be kept in blissful ignorance by too much.

Let us turn from the modality of sight to that of hearing. One can be deaf both because of a defect of sound and also because of an excess of sound. Jonathan Swift writes in "Dingley and Brent":

> They never would hear,
> But turn the deaf ear,
> As a matter they had no concern in.

One can refuse to listen and so deceive oneself. One can also arrange to receive too much sound and be deafened. Description in the matter of hearing, to adapt an earlier remark, becomes metaphor in the service of reason. If we had to choose either sight or hearing as a foundation for reason, Aristotle would turn from Plato and advise us to choose hearing; there would be, he remarks, a more acute and generally better intelligence. But in so many cases we are prepared to attribute equal severity to these parallel accusations of self-deception: "You've blinded yourself" and "You can't hear what is being said."

Having dealt in earlier writings with the polymorphic approach to the 'whole,' open-ended class of self-deceivings and with a 'Parliamentary' approach to many, we are now employing the doctrine of the Mean. We hope to use it as a path to understanding a great host of cases in a manner imparting historical depth.

We have undertaken to introduce four questions. The first concerns what self-deception is. An introductory answer is that we speak here of two kinds of self-deception, one of defect and one of excess. The second question is wherein one can be self-deceived. We answer, it is possible to be deceived in speech and thought. Here our intuitions divide on a point. Only one of us believes that, in early human development, speech is prior to thought. Thus we divide over the belief that it makes no sense to attribute *deception* and *self-deception* to prelinguistic children. Nevertheless, we both agree on the importance of a view of human growth that more easily attaches itself to the *first* position, and that is what we shall principally follow here. Very well, then, let us say that the earlier subject of quasi-adult deception is one or another form of verbal process, whether sermon, letter to the editor, soliloquy, conversation, or lecture. In very early childhood there is incipient speech without a parallel course of thought and awareness. Parallel awareness, rather, is an offshoot of growing speech. Some interesting forms of self-deception are to be found under this label of early speech-given awareness: talking oneself or allowing oneself to be talked into forms of defect and excess.

The third question was how one comes to be self-deceived. In light of the answer to the second question, it is evident that the third question may want placing twice over: first, How can one talk oneself into deception? And second, How can one think oneself into deception? We want an explanation that looks to a certain end: a moment of speech or thought that falls short of or exceeds the Mean. Coming to that end is either an instantaneous jump or a process. It is easier for philosophy to understand the second, leading oneself little by little to a first moment of full or complete deception, than it is to understand the first, jumping straight into deception. We shall consider examples in a moment. Suppose that there is a process leading to deception. There are distinguishable mechanisms that supply the needs of that process, depending upon whether the process ends in a form of defect or in one of excess, for it is one thing to keep truth from oneself by turning a more and more myopic or 'selectively blind' eye; it is another to work up a hefty tale, which is capable of squeezing out a competing story that happens to be the truth.

The fourth question, finally, is what the consequences are likely to be where a case of self-deception stands among those best illuminated by reference to the Mean. The last question rounds off an introduction to our theme about such kinds of self-deception, for the first two questions ask for an account of what self-deception is; the third asks for an explanation of the causes, and the fourth for an account of the likely or necessary consequences. The fourth strikes us as particularly important, for it would seem that self-deception can lead both to great good and also to great evil. The question is also important in light of the literature of our theme. Must use of the term "self-deception" in cases most relevant to the Mean be judgmental, morally critical? On the one hand, if relevantly expressing and pursuing truth is an intellectual virtue, a case of 'immoderate' or Mean-defying self-deception involves a pair of vices. In that case, of course, to use the term "self-deception" is not wholly to describe! It is far more to judge and probe. We would, therefore, not praise someone with immoderate intentions of being self-deceived. We would, perhaps, be prepared to forgive him in the light of special consequences. But pardon is not praise.

On the other hand, it should be repeated, there are other cases where the use of self-deception is not to be construed simply as a deviation from the Mean. Moderate or Mean-respecting intentions can sometimes be the roots of self-deceit. Dreyfus remained sane on Devil's Island, through years of unjustified imprisonment. If his moral and soldierly ideals prompted him to make himself believe that he would be found innocent and released "any day now," and if such beliefs proved empirically to him that they did prevent a slide into madness, then why not speak of this as virtuous in itself *and* in its consequences? But the reader will have recognized from this introduction, and from common experience, such a wealth of cases where self-deception is a (moral) defect or (immoral) excess that our critical points can be easily understood as applying to a *limited infinity* of possible cases and kinds of cases. Self-deceptions as sins against the Mean are potentially infinite.

CHILDREN: A BUTLERIAN STAGE

SOME MODES OF DEPENDENCE

Let us speak of an ordinary and threefold division: childhood, maturity and old age. Within this framework an obvious question arises: What kinds of change and stability are required if the evolving person is to stay within the Mean of general human goodness?

In this and the next section we shall touch on the four following types of relation between two distinct persons A and B. (Whether or when to call a live fetus a distinct person *we* cannot tell.)

(i) The first mode is one of *single dependence*. A is a helpless young child and B is his widowed parent. For life, early training, and early education, A must rely entirely on B. But soon there is quite a richness of respects in which the child needs support from a parent *and* from many others. As his life becomes vigorous, his training thorough, and his education deep, he becomes fit for other modes of dependence, its complements and opposites.

As his life develops, the moral relevance and extent of the first mode are found to be narrowing. But we ought not to think of that first mode's pertinence as merely evaporating. Nor should we even desire its disappearance. There is a Mean and a virtue of duly accepted single dependence. Its subject-range in childhood is wide, then narrow in maturity and middle years, but once again wide in old age. Even great power in those central years does not exclude occasions of return to single dependence. He who seeks an invitation from busier, more conventionally successful people of his acquaintance, crudely dropping hints of appreciation and submission if he is asked, must be prepared to accept Procrustean hospitality, fit in style for an infant. But, of course, the acceptance of so many warmer invitations and favors from an equal also implies one's willingness to embrace a measure of single dependence while the occasion of the other's hospitality or favor giving lasts. Surely this is most typically so when the guest willingly and knowingly places himself into the hands of another. Both host and guest who hit the contextual Mean can exhibit two sides to the virtue of *trusting*. The one proves himself ready to act in fullness of trust, the other responds by showing himself just as fully deserving of trust.

(ii) A second mode of relationship is *mutual dependence*. There are respects in which even a child can be and doubtless wishes to be someone on whom others may depend, for he or she would wish in turn to be trusted, and the soul of an adult wants the practice of trusting. Perhaps defect and excess are equally easy: trusting too little and trusting too much. (We consider this in the next section.) Training and education make it possible to take up a trade or a profession. One's practice of a trade or profession offers support to others while one depends oneself upon the practice; as a doctor, one person supports another as a patient. But the two people move from that relation to one of mutual dependence: capitalist or socialist, the doctor now depends upon the patient in part for his livelihood. As a doctor he gives. As a wage-earner he takes. (There *can* be a fair exchange: neither doctor nor patient need damn himself by exploitation.)

The shift to mutual dependence and reciprocity is a shift to a profoundly human and important mode of being related. One instance of the mode we find in friendship and love. Another is revealed in devotion to fairness in exchange. To be wholly incapable of pursuing (and blessing) such fairness as a welcome rule is to be estranged beyond rational cooperation. It is to have become in the full measure incapable of community. Just to be *largely* incapable of wanting to act as a fair man in mutual dependence is to be a social deceiver on a grand scale or to flee others as a recluse. In either case, one will probably need self-deception to make such a human commitment to such an inhuman project bearable to maintain. Some who are now called psychopaths or megalomaniacs may be Napoleonic exceptions. But a good life is in large part a life which moves well through cycles of trust and reciprocity.

(iii) A third mode of relationship is *single independence:* one agent gives support. The first and the third modes are, taken together, parts of the second. There are nevertheless two possibilities: either there is a transition from the first to the third, or one is performing two parts of a whole. With respect to the first case, there is a long transition from a person's first depending upon parents to the stage where he is no longer a child (or even a provider), but an aged (largely resourceless) parent. He must depend upon his children or the state bureaucracy. Here it is plain there is little or no mutual dependence. And with respect to the second, a full exchange involves A's now depending upon B and B's now depending upon A.

In practice it is difficult to tell whether to speak of a transition or just of two parts of a whole. Consider: conversation offers many people an occasion for mutual aid and inspiration. Yet some make no benevolent connections as they appear to converse. They let a conversation lapse into turn taking at soliloquy. (Each may avoid noticing clearly that this is helped by self-deception's cozy feel.)

(iv) A fourth mode of relationship is *mutual independence.* At its worst C affects to *argue* with D, for example, but again they trade soliloquies. C would be showing no interest in persuading D with reasons and arguments related to D's own views. Nor would either be seeking reasons from the other that would end his machine-like isolation. In less egocentric cases of mutual independence a certain distance and independence are established and respected. Our treatment of reciprocity in this essay tends to be warm and enthusiastic; that accorded to mutual independence, and to chilly modern notions of freedom, is usually more cautious and restrained. And yet a full human life does require changes to and from many forms of mutual independence. There are obviously enriching instances of freedom and self-reliance within the span of the Mean. But the pitch of our culture's voice needs lowering. Too often it serves to praise freedom and self-reliance as pretexts for renouncing any ties of love, family feeling, conscience and fairness in exchange, or even neighborly benevolence and friendship. Too often it fosters self-deception and hypocrisy about such ties.

We turn next to self-deception and the Mean in early childhood. We turn to them, that is, prepared to give a special stress to what is mainly single dependence and how it may normally make moral consciousness possible.

Now consider the manifold of self-deception as it pertains to dependence and independence in the early years of many humans. As the young child's command of language grows, he begins to grasp certain principles. At least, he does if heredity and environment have been healthy and generous.

(A) The child is aware of a ubiquitous web of dependence upon kindly elders. They are very gradually, but obviously, helping him to become less dependent. Thanks to them he is becoming better able to make his own imprint on his surroundings as he chooses. Their actions, even if they temporarily thwart his desires, keep him feeling secure and happy. At least some of the time he can somehow grasp that when adults thwart or punish him, it is his own desires for more pleasure and no more pain, for love, security, and control of his world, that are being served.

With this perception comes an increasing division between his ideas, *first*, of what is merely *frightening*, what is likely just to bring harm, pain, deprivation; *second*, of what warrants *guilt feelings* or fair claims to a reward. The bulb of human morality has put forth a fragile shoot, essential to the formation of a rational self. Still earlier, an infantile Mean had crudely delineated the span of 'Lack' or 'Not enough.' This, too, was frightening, painful or pleasureless, but it did not yet need to suggest the prospect of guilt feelings being added. On the other side of this moral-free, hedonic Mean there was the span of what often seemed tempting, intensely pleasant, a boon to curiosity, far from frightening, a new source of power and control. But in that realm there was likely to be a rapid tumble into nauseating excess (with foul odors of mouth, stomach, and throat). There was likely to be physical pain or harsh reactions from normally comforting adults. Though often overruled by curiosity and other attractions, primitive hopes of keeping to a very agreeable path between lack and excess began to form. Interest in language fortified these hopes. And it led, with better understanding of punishments and rewards, encouragement and disapproval, to the later founding of belief in a protoethical Mean.

(B) The protoethical Mean is flanked on one side by roughly what Bishop Butler would call blind desires for particular states and objects. (Eighteenth-century philosophers' psychology was not all fatally image ridden.) Such desires are defective in terms of self-love and self-interest.

To give in to such 'selfishness' is to hide from single dependence. On the Mean's other side lie what Butler would take to be cerebrally clever, but excessive projects of self-love and self-interest. Such projects are often exploitations of single dependence. They may be projects willfully aimed at inflicting pain on other persons or animals. Or they may be projects willfully aimed at something harmless in itself, but obviously involving harm to other persons' feelings or belongings. In ordinary language we call such doings *selfish*. (Or course, these and other forms of selfishness can go on being linked with evil self-deception for later decades.)

By now the child has begun to dread the prospect of straying too far into either span of either extreme and being seen to do so. Being caught in the realms of too little and too much self-love goes with the dreaded prospect of evoking *moral* censure from his protectors. Then the terror brought by *guilt feelings* may follow. And so a nearly helpless child, who is fortunate in his genes and lucky in his elders, comes by ethical ways to appreciate his dependence on others. This and further linguistic growth can strengthen his first vision of a Mean in a moral world.

(C) In his early linguistic years this child begins to recognize that he and even those on whom he most depends will all incur responsibility by performing certain acts of speech. The notions of correct reporting, telling fairy stories, playing on ambiguities, lying, failing to deliver what was undertaken in speech, joking, acting in charades with wild claims, etc., take hold with the expanding of his internal lexicon, grammar, and syntax. For example, an uncle promises this child that he will *give* the child a *new* toy within one hour. The uncle goes to the child's room, where he picks up a very new toy which the child already owns. He gives it to his nephew exactly sixty minutes after undertaking to give him a new toy. The youngster protests violently that, in effect, this is a shoddy trick; it is as if the uncle has lied to him. The uncle then presents a new model tank, bought that very morning, and gives it to him. Now the protester may well accept the first use of "new" and "give" as a delightful way of using ambiguity for playing honest tricks on others. He hastens to try out the "super joke" and its analogues on his sister and neighboring playfellows. If he is kind and morally clever, he takes care not to play this joke in a way that will create long or intense expectations in others, as his uncle did with him. He learns limits of tolerable deception.

This child feels the tug of at least three ethical beliefs. *First*, he must not prolong or overdo the trick with others, because, unlike his uncle, he has no gift to offer that will cancel out the sense of grievance that can be aroused by the slightest excess. (Missing a Mean?) *Second*, since he is

207

a child and not an adult, his playing the joke on other children does not warrant their feeling of grievance to the same extent. It is more deserving of acceptance by these youngsters as something funny, for they do not yet depend on their fellow children in the ubiquitous ways they do on adults. (Hitting a Mean?) *Third*, by parity of reasoning it is usually nothing like as serious to deceive other children on purpose, as it is to lie, mislead, or cause confusion in dealing with the adults who nurture him. The exceptions tend to come in cases where the child knows or strongly believes that 'his' adults would deplore his deceiving other adults or other children in various types of circumstance. (Keeping to a Mean?)

The importance of what we have described as *development* (B) in (possible or probable) moral formation lies mainly in its creating a sense of special obligation to those upon whom the young human depends almost entirely. From the start of that sense with the development of speech many a child can form a simple, but very relevant, attachment to a Mean. And from this, in turn, a partly conceptual and moral, rather than a purely instinctive, kind of loving and love-evoking agency can emerge in normal humans. Soon, if not always, such a child actively grasps that those upon whom he most depends for his needs also depend upon a good number of causes for their happiness. They too have legitimate needs. The child observes that various deeds will be rewarded by joy for himself. He will sooner or later infer that his own sayings and doings can produce the reward of cheering, consoling, delighting, or otherwise meeting the needs of *adults*, as well as other children. The rigid, mechanical father or mother may be cheered most by the offspring's mechanical, systematic obedience or conformity from cradle to grave. (Think again of some characters in Mann's *Buddenbrooks*.) On the other hand, many parents will be far more cheered, if the youngster's obedience is fair and not perfect, but he somehow notices how to help in cheering them up, in making them feel deeply loved, in making them believe in their own worth more keenly, and the like. The early Mean between too little self-interest and too much comes to be viewed as not just a matter of "avoiding expressly forbidden extremes." True moderation in self-love includes active responses to the needs of those on whom one most depends. Not to respond with affection to dependence, love, and nurture is another way of falling into the guilt-ridden span of excessive self-interest.

Whether all remotely rational thought in humans must begin with acquiring speech, what we have called 'development (C)' may also be essential to moral progress for an instructive range of girls and boys. In learning vocabulary, grammar, and typical speech acts, largely from hearing adults converse, the child becomes acquainted with some foundations of *communal* values. At least tenuous notions of truthfulness, implication, intelligibility, negation, relevance, correct formation, and validity are 'internalized' at an early age. Before serious schooling, many of the young can manage to understand the uncle's trick first as a violation of truthfulness and unfair use of ambiguity, then as a fair joke with an altered backdrop. The whole family, at all levels of age, largely follows various communal rules and values connected with the language. It becomes evident that those rules and values are not freely mutable creations of the family, 'private' to the family as an isolated unit. If he is thinking, while very young, of the community and its language as the *only* ones, the older child can begin to form ideas of obligations and right goals for members of his whole community, embracing many families. But in this idea of his community and language as the *only* ones, lie the seeds of *universal* moral concepts, of rules and values that all sane beings beyond the cradle should obey. (If his community is the *only* one, then *its* values are those of all mankind.) And when the child learns of other communities with different languages, his sense of the superiority of *his* community and its language may be chauvinistically intensified. At the same time, however, he is likely to develop the belief that speakers in any human community remotely worth its social salt must respect truthfulness, promise keeping, and uttering intelligible constructions in speech along with other values. Adults, especially, in foreign groups must all belong to a Linguistic Kingdom of Ends or fail to be truly human.

What, then, of self-deception at this early stage of normal human development? Even now the range of conceivable forms is wide and heterogeneous. But the points we have been introducing about the possible kinds of early Mean make some forms especially clear. Think of a young human who is tempted, as if by songs from Sirens or Lorelei, to explore the realm of the Golden Risk—the area of what seems riskily tempting and especially challenging, although it is not yet specifically forbidden by those on whom he depends. Consider what may have to remain metaphoric for our purposes here: talk of Thought and Inner Speech monitoring and advising each other. A child sees fruit on a dangerous tree that he might be able to climb. He can somehow contrive to bring down from a shelf a tempting can of paint. He advances towards a neighbor's large and snarling dog, which is chained to a veranda. He experiences curiosity and blind desire to handle, possess, or master *this* beast or object in his vicinity. Compare again Bishop Butler's famous contrast between blind particular desires untamed by self-love and goals arising from rational self-interest. Such desires prompt the child to talk himself out of the reasonable caution of self-interest. Maybe he already *thinks* that the project is somewhat frightening and imprudent, but from such belief there may come the main impetus for the particular desire. Thought, insofar as it is cautious, self-interested thought, must somehow be 'talked out' of impeding the glorious adventure. Inner speech is yammering: the project is not expressly forbidden; at the top of the tree there must be immense pleasure and proof of power; every other available project is boring: "if the thing isn't done now, I may never get another chance."

What are the sources of this inner speech which is aimed at using deceit for anesthetizing prudent and self-interested thoughts? Whatever the cerebral sources of what we may consider here as self-interested thoughts and serpentine inner speech, we must once more leave in part to the future of neurology—or to new revelations about Souls or Selves. The fact is that inner conflicts of such kinds can and do occur in a host of young humans. The fact is that with the grasp of language comes the possibility of gulling, conning, and manipulating oneself to go against one's more prudent, self-interested thoughts. And good sense can be made of many such examples by saying that here is a normal, healthy speaker of an early age who has some prudential and even some moral sense of duty to himself and his parents, but who allows himself to be lured into the realm of the Golden Risk. He half-knowingly violates his understanding of a Mean. On other occasions, thought and self-interest may be too greatly provoked by such a project; their more effective means of gulling and conning, added to comment on hard facts, may enable young virtues to succeed in neutralizing such irrational and shabbily 'selfless' promptings of desire.

But what of his Fall from this Mean in the other direction? What of pursuing an *excess* of self-interest, rather than permitting a *defect?* Reflect on new elements of moral knowledge that can be used to support both Good and Evil. (i) There is the evolving realization that even one's "god-like" parents have communal or universal obligations. These occasionally appear to transcend even some of the "holy" rights of parents whose dependents have great duties to obey them. (ii) There is, as was seen before, the growing insight that even "god-like" parents have needs to which their own young children can best minister: some small degree of *reciprocal* dependence has appeared. (iii) Again, there is the beginning of the idea that any human being, great or small, is subject to something communally greater; a parent may be god-like, rather than "God"-like. Hence their dependents may have some rights as fellow humans. (iv) These three factors, with or without the added force of unlucky or unseemly incidents in the family, easily combine to arouse at least a slight suspicion. "Could all adults, even my own parents, sometimes make mistakes?"

What is the price of these four and other such indispensable elements in the self-formation of an early moral being? The price is that even the highly dependent boy or girl now develops or discovers a great treasure house of moral pretexts, moral excuses, moral alibis, moralistic lies, and pseudomoral evasions. Here the biblical notion of The Tree of Knowledge of Good *and Evil* fits a religious or secular notion of humans as fallen beings rather well. In advancing as a moral agent, the typical human almost inevitably acquires great powers and temptations to deceive. Now the still so greatly dependent kind of partly free agent can motivate himself to place his sense of self-interest above duties, gratitude, love, the reality of dependence, and reciprocal powers for doing or receiving what creates harmony or joy. He can make himself believe that he is not so very dependent. ("I don't need *them*"!) The child who thinks too much of his own self-interest is guilty of Pride. The child who thinks too little of it is less fully human, but closer to human innocence.

All the same, as we have stressed from the start of this essay, such a loss of innocence may lead to new virtues in a fallen creature. Motivating objects from the new treasure house of ethical pretexts and excuses may be used by the young agent to persuade himself to keep his feet on the middle path. But that belongs to potentially more noble and morally helpful uses of self-deception.

ADOLESCENTS: A PLATONIC STAGE

If a lion could speak, we might well understand his forecasts of the weather. But if he could not convey to us what would be cases of excess or defect for his tastes and nature, we might not understand him as a fellow mammal and fellow agent. The prelinguistic child, who already recognizes when his drink is too hot or cold for comfort, is easily enabled by language and adult guidance to move from the purely hedonic to the protoethical Mean. Certainly he feels conflicting desires, but when he makes the rudimentary start of human Selfhood, of sometimes backing choices with intelligent deliberation, we have viewed that Self as weak, but essentially single.

The Self of what we shall call *adolescence* is essentially divided by its conflicts. Some precocious children reach the stage of adolescence very early, and some prodigies may even bypass it. A great many who are adults, in terms of years, remain perpetual adolescents in terms of psychic reality. This stage involves and exhibits self-deception most clearly. (We must repeat that our *synthetic* a priori sketches are meant to fit only a good number, not all of the heterogeneous humans and self-deceptions in this or other possible worlds. We remain here more concerned with evils in self-deceit, but we continue to reject the assumption of Fingarette and others that it is essentially, hence always, undesirable. As we have written extensively before on the phenomena that we associate here with adolescence, this section will be much compressed.)[3]

Plato could envisage in the following way an ideal Council of a few Guardians given a special task. The oldest Guardian with most wisdom and experience of the problems chairs the sessions. All are familiar with objective values, the Forms. But all have slightly different views of how best to apply their certainties about Being to this partly unintelligible world of Becoming. After respectful exchanges, backed by knowledge and fair, rational argument, they easily agree on an excellent policy, satisfying them all from all their perspectives. Let us say that for Plato a *Rational Group Mean* has been partly discovered and partly created. These Guardians are not only wise, but accordingly have the same primary values, and practically the same ordering of preferences for ways of dealing with the surds of Becoming.

In the *Republic* Plato shows by similes what he thinks of actual Assemblies in the Athenian and other Greek democracies. It is as if a ship had an experienced and nautically mediocre captain, who is strong, but somewhat deaf and myopic, and otherwise too unimpressive to keep his ignorant crew of conflicting rascals in order. He must try to reason or beg or wheedle in order to get some of their attention. At times he can contribute to a compromise between his nautical expertise and the turbulent clash of their arbitrary urges. At times a faction manipulates him.[4]

If we may put loosely implied words in his mouth, Plato would say: ''In this case there is a far less than rational decision, constituting a *Common Mean*, a compromise between what ought to be done and what busybodies are content to do. In the case where the ignorant sailors drown their captain and hold an assembly by themselves, we may suppose that an ambitious, unusually intelligent, and attractive fellow, with a limited sense of responsibility, will preside over the meeting as an appealing, but nautically ignorant, leader. He will skillfully play off rivals against each other to the point of general exhaustion. Then he can try out various compromises on the crew, pretending that most of them have already endorsed these compromises—or that they embody the highest wisdom of several sailors prominent in the debate. By such a mixing of true reasoning with lying, misleading, and sophistry he gets them to agree to a policy that he considers the best of a mad lot—and something likely to strengthen his own power. The crew thus arrive at a *Mob Mean*. That is, each of a sufficiently large number of them believes (a) that the policy is not defective with regard to his own interests and preferences, and (b) that the policy is not excessively good for others, especially not those whom he presently most dislikes. But such a democratic leader may not last very long. Other ambitious sailors may start playing their own deceitful tricks against the leader. They will change the preferential rankings, the alliances of groups and individuals once loyal to him."

The mentally and morally sound human being who arrives at adolescence is committed, thanks to good rearing and good experience, to a spectrum of healthy values. Among them one would expect to find such obvious examples as truthfulness, promise keeping, respect for those who are loving and honest, readiness to help and forgive, acceptance of obligations in cases of single and mutual dependence, fairness in exchange, care about his own and others' due measures of freedom, and much else. Insofar as he thinks and acts with these values as ones highly ranked among his guides for dealing with the world, let us say that his *Master Self* is in command. The Master Self, when largely unchallenged, seeks to pursue an *Objective Mean* across a space of increasing temptation. He seeks, for example, to be neither stingy nor extravagant (given his family's resources), to be properly frank but sensitive to others' feelings, to accept and enjoy his new role as a sexually excitable being, while taking care to preserve his time and strength for many relevant goals. That is, he wants to do what is morally right ('simpliciter'). He understands that to include ample scope for enjoyment, affection, achievement, and increased freedom, but he is one Self in a Nation of Selves.

Heredity and environment do not leave matters so simple. His matured body and added liberties often make him vulnerable to external and internal promptings. They call on him to neglect the Objective Mean, or even his well-being and very existence. Externally, there are fresh opportunities to gratify himself by wounding himself or others. There are people who urge him to ''seize happiness,'' to ''have your fun right away.'' There are far more chances to act unobserved and to lash out against anyone or anything he presently happens to detest. The list is long. Internally, there is the fact that he has remembered and stored a wide number of orderings of preference.

And so he remembers his own changes of orderings when certain desires and emotions 'carried him away' in his childhood. He remembers the very different kinds of orderings he had attributed to actual people he had met in the flesh or to possible people learned about through tales, television, malicious gossip. The uses of hypnotism, electrodes and "truth drugs" can show that such a young person's brain has stored an enormous amount of "memories," of events *interpreted* by him as the observer from a very early age. Stored with many of these interpreted events are different rankings taken to have been held in context by himself or others. Certain of these internalized rankings, perhaps those most easily allied to presently intense desires and emotions, become in cerebral and motivating reality very like members of an assembly of heterogeneous persons, each of whom tries to form enough alliances to guide the adolescent's aims and behavior. Call them *Personae.*

Confronted by these Personae as possible allies, rivals, and enemies, the Master Self grasps that mental realpolitik or plain, practical realism makes the exclusive pursuit of an Objective Mean impossible in numerous contexts. (The adolescent is not sufficiently 'integrated.') Sometimes an analogue of a Rational Group Mean can be worked out, when only closely allied Personae are aroused, and the Objective Mean is almost reached. More often the Master Self will have to engage in tomfoolery and horse trading to create a Collective Mean that is not too far from an Objectively sound policy.

Thus the Master Self comes to resemble a modern Prime Minister or President. His Cabinet Members are normally his trusted allies, yet they have ambitions and preferential orderings of their own. He must 'carry' his Cabinet with him, if there is to be any closeness in his nation to respect in context for an Objective Mean. He and the Cabinet must then carry both the Assembly and, at times, the larger group of electors. Under pressures of weariness, bewilderment, disgust, excessive desire for popularity or a minor goal, etc., the Master Self may *'allow'* itself for a time to be pushed in directions it has usually opposed. ("I couldn't help it.")

The initial commitment to honest reasoning and fairly honest tomfoolery causes on occasions too much discomfort or too many an *impasse:* the Master Self, like some once exemplary leaders, may let itself be 'forced' to resort to the least honest and most ignorant thoughts and tricks of its opponents. Eventually such Machiavellian habits may whittle away at the Master Self's nobler preferences. The adolescent's decisions, in such an onrush of self-deception, can change to illustrating the Mob Mean of addicts, parasites and greedily inconsistent meddlers in other peoples' lives.

ADULTS: ARISTOTLE AND CONFUCIUS[5]

B: You see I have brought two scholars together, one from the East and one from the West. You are too polite to contradict one another. I have read you my essay on self-deception. You are too polite to contradict me.

A: C is a Confucian, and I am an Aristotelian. We may be polite; we are not *too* polite.

C: Not too anything, I hope.

A: At the beginning of your essay you listed four questions. Tell us again what they are; perhaps we can help you answer them.

B: The first is, "What is self-deception?"

A: Your first question asks for the essence of self-deception. You alter it to ask for an essence of much self-deception, the essence where what lies *within* a person is particularly like something *between* people. You know that we answer such questions by locating a genus, then a species and by distinguishing the species from other species of the genus. You get off to a good start; for you give an answer *(looking at the Confucian and smiling)* in terms of our beloved Doctrine of the Mean. You hold before· yourself three sovereign genera: those of defect, the Mean, and excess. You then come to the appropriate genus: truth as a Mean. Flanking that Mean are two kinds of falsity: one of defect and one of excess.

B: I'm glad we got our discussion off to a good start.

A: Let us turn to appropriate species within the three genera of Falsity, Truth, and Falsity. The appropriate species of Truth we can call self-enlightenment; flanking that species are two species of self-deception.

B: Self-enlightenment?

A: Yes, self-enlightenment.

B: Our discussion is about self-deception and nothing else.

A: Are you in flight from extremes without being equally in pursuit of the Mean?

B: Come now. We are modern philosophers.

C: Confucius says it is not enough to love humanity; one must also hate inhumanity. A discussion of self-deception is worthless unless we know what Mean to love.

B: Is it not possible to warn ourselves against self-deception without first heeding a call to self-enlightenment?

A: No one understands an opposite without understanding its opposite or opposites. Doesn't Plato say that in order to understand non-being we need to understand being?

B: Doubtless he does.

A: Then let us equally try to understand self-enlightenment and two species of self-deception.

B: What distinguishes one species from another species of a genus of Falsity? For not every instance of Falsity is one of self-deception.

A: Etiology. An account of the differentia is an account of the cause. To be self-deceived is to experience defect or excess twice: once with respect to the effect and once with respect to the cause. With respect to the effect one says or believes something that is false. Hence the classification of self-deception as a species of Falsity.

B: And would you also say that to be self-enlightening is to experience the Mean twice: once with respect to the effect and once with respect to the cause? With respect to the effect one says or believes something that is true, hence the classification of self-enlightenment as a species of Truth.

A: The parallel accounts are fine. May I continue?

B: Yes, of course.

A: With respect to the cause there is defect or excess of will or feeling; mention of such defect or excess is part of the justification or the explanation of passing into Falsity. Defect of will and excess of passion so weaken reason that one goes wrong.

B: I see you are anxious to turn to a subject dear to Aristotelians: weakness of the will.

A: Not anxious, but interested. But let us come back to the subject.

C: I should not like to rush from the first inquiry. According to my friend's answer to your question, he who is self-enlightened or self-deceived must accept a certain kind of explanation of the situation where he finds himself. Along the causal trail he will find two causal factors: will and passion. The person who finds himself on the Mean of Truth will also find that his will and passion also lie on the Mean. With respect to issues that powerfully move us, he has steered a course between defect and excess. If he is a mature adult and has found the Way, his feelings provide a finely graded sounding board for his reason, which has itself been finely tuned. His soul can change from moderate shame to moderate anger without blocking his reason and burdening his will. We can practice the five constant virtues of humanity, justice, wisdom, loyalty, and propriety. His emotions, becalmed and becalming, provide a resting place for his reason.

But with respect to the person who becomes self-deceived we find that will and passion, too, have missed the Mean: perhaps his will was insufficiently strong; his passions, excessively strong. A weak will and strong passions lead him close to the edge of the Mean. He thinks, "I can live here without losing my way." As he moves closer to the edge, the edge appears to recede from him, giving him room for further wandering. To the person in excess the edge of excess is a mirage appearing to recede, providing him with ever more room on the Mean.

B: Yes. And this shows that he has in fact left it long behind.

C: He is now self-deceived. His will and passion have undermined his reason. His own will and passion are leading his reason astray. Therefore I say: Cultivate will and passion so that reason finds Truth.

Only he who lives well within the Mean can see its borders. Strong passion carries him away from the center. If will consents to passion, they conspire against reason. That conspiracy points ahead to self-deception; for such a person will lead himself into believing that the borders to defect and excess lie where they only appear to lie. For true self-deception arises at the end of a causal trail laid down by the will and twisted by passions out of joint with the Mean.

B: I see that you are just as anxious as our Aristotelian friend to discuss weakness of the will. I thought we were to return to the subject; we seem unable to leave it. So perhaps I shall ask you now for an example that fully illuminates what you have been saying.

C: Like the Aristotelians, we cherish anger in moderation, but anger easily slips away from moderation and helps work the illusion of which I have been speaking, the illusion of the shifting boundary. The angrier one becomes, the more scope one gives oneself for becoming still angrier—scope which still appears to lie *on* the Mean. The more a man of weak will allows himself expression of anger, the more he gives license of self-deceit; for he believes he can turn back; he believes he is in control; he believes he is making things clear. In fact, what he is doing is creating the illusion of being able to turn back, of being in control and of making things clear.

B: Moderate and righteous anger, I agree, enlivens and strengthens reason. But how does one know where the border lies? How can one start distinguishing the Mean from excess?

C: It is often hard and sometimes impossible to know the boundaries. My Taoist friends are right to teach self-cultivation with fluid imagery. Distrust those who offer fixed rules and principles. We must hope for a good and just community in which to learn where, roughly, the boundaries lie. But I teach you this: too much anger and too much shame create the illusion of the drifting boundaries that create ever more room for excess to breed excess. Is anyone more profoundly self-deceived than he who, deeply injured and mistreated, thinks he can justly act as police, jury, judge, and executioner?

B: That question, I'm sure, answers itself.

A: We should perhaps return to the four questions of your essay.

B: I am satisfied that the first, what a crucial kind of self-deception is has been answered well enough in relation to some proper back grounds. The second was this: Wherein can one deceive oneself?

A: From our accounts an answer to the second question is evident: on can deceive oneself wherein one can go wrong, provided a certain causa story can be told. In the telling of that story there must be room fo prominent mention of will and passion.

B: Fine. The third question was how one comes to deceive oneself. see that the third question has been answered in the course of answer ing the first one. The third question leads to puzzlement, for som people have tried to think about self-deception as a kind of lying t oneself.

C: And do they think about self-enlightenment as a kind of self-truth telling?

B: Most of us don't think about self-enlightenment at all. We're self possessed with our risks.

A: Let us linger over the third question. In response to the secon question I remarked that a certain causal story can be told, a story tha makes prominent mention of will and passion. When one is put upon path leading to Falsity, will and passion either avert awareness an reason or pervert them with irrelevant matter and lies: in the first cas they underpower and in the second they overpower reason. In the firs case she fails to see clearly what she sees. In the second, she use disguises with the aim of almost forgetting what she knows.

B: And the fourth question was what the consequences are of self deception. According to my essay some are good and some are bad

A: And we are bound to agree with you.

B: There is one small question remaining. Do we still have time for it

C: I do. What is it?

B: Of the three possibilities of self-formation that we have bee discussing, the best is self-enlightenment. There are two inferior ways o self-formation. My question to you is this: Which species of self deception is worse: to keep the Truth from oneself or put a usurping an false story in the place reserved for a true story? Which is worse: not t face Reality or to put a false face on Reality?

A: It is difficult to tell. If we look to the consequences, either species o going wrong may have fruitful offspring.

C: But if we look to a journey, the aim of which is reaching the Mean, i is not difficult to tell. The wisdom of the East has a counterpart amon Platonists and Aristotelians: Risk defect. My Taoist friends say: ''Henc the Sage eschews excess, eschews extravagance, eschews pride.''

A: Plato, also, argues that it is better to receive too little in being treated unjustly than it is to take too much in treating another unjustly. But for what kind of reason could you order the species of self-deception as you do?

C: Not to think or speak at all is to think or speak defectively; it is to do too little, and that defect is self-deception. Hovering on the edge of envy, pained, withholding honor, withholding a thought of just deserts, and withholding congratulations are defective. But this species is less bad than the second extreme: distorting an account of someone's success, diminishing and falsifying his reputation. I say the first is less bad for this reason: defect can be made good by advancing. One can perhaps come to grips with pain and advance a bit further towards the Mean, but a return from excess is harder labor. There is fresh pain in tearing away the false story and trying to get a true one to grow. Return from excess doubles the Way home. And so I say it is better to err by underdoing than by overdoing; for by overdoing we are apt to get the opposite of what we really want.

I do not recommend trying to face every painful situation immediately and all at once. If there is terrible loss and terrible failure, we can approach facing them only little by little. But it is better to make one's way from defect than it is from excess.

B: And not give oneself a story at all?

C: Not at the beginning. One should first dream or imagine the outline of a true story but only in part and gradually.

B: You say the Mean is broad. If one makes one's way to the border and crosses it, could one well rest there?

C: The wise will not rest there, as you know. For he who risks self-deception the most is the one who persists in residing at the edges or trampling on the borders of the Mean.

CONCLUSION

Our dialogue closes with questions as well as answers. This is as it should be. Our subtitle promised programmatic remarks about certain forms and roles of self-deception in the central human business of self-formation. We hope to have provided a sound conceptual basis for understanding. We focused on cases where the *intrapersonal* is most like the *interpersonal*, on some crucial functionings of self-deception in human growth. But "self-deception," we remain convinced, is so Protean a term that projects of composing a single definition of *all* its senses must arise from a simplistic, Procrustean analysis. Such projects cannot fit a continuing evolution, let alone a limited infinity.

Narrow analyses in the literature, that lay essentialist stress on catch terms like "Mauvaise Foi" or "Spelling Out," can blind readers to deep, but varied, truths about human nature. At one extreme there is defective attention to examples that do not match a preconception. At the other extreme, some who try imitating the later Wittgenstein will pile up packages of disconnected snapshots. In this essay we have sought to keep closer to a Mean. We have applied notions of *Many-a-Mean* and of *Variation-in-Dependence* to the central human business of Self-Formation. This policy strikes us as providing a stretch of truly luminous central ground, at least broad enough for one contribution to the exciting interdisciplinary volume that Mike Martin has undertaken to bring out. Let there be light from many perspectives and directions!

NOTES

1. William Styron, *Sophie's Choice* (New York: Bantam Books, 1980), 593.

2. Thomas Mann, *Buddenbrooks* (New York: Vintage Books, 1961), 215–216.

3. See especially: John King-Farlow, "Self-Deceivers and Sartrean Seducers," *Analysis* 24 (1963): 131–136; "Philosophical Nationalism: Self-Deception and Self-Direction," *Dialogue* 17 (1978): 591–615; and "Akrasia, Self-Mastery and the Master Self," *Pacific Philosophical Quarterly* 62 (1981): 47–60.

4. Plato, *Republic*, in *The Collected Dialogues of Plato*, ed. Edith Hamilton and Huntington Cairns (Princeton, N.J.: Princeton University Press, 1963), sections 488B–489B.

5. Cf. Richard Bosley, *On Truth* (Washington, D.C.: University Presses of America, 1982), 90 and *passim*.

PART IV
PURSUING PARADOX:
AMBIGUITY AND SKEPTICISM

Introduction

Mike W. Martin

People believe that their reason governs words. But words turn and twist the understanding.

—Francis Bacon, *Novum Organum*

Writing as a prophet of modern science, Francis Bacon distinguished four main sources of error, or what he called "idols." Idols of the Tribe are false conceptions resulting from limitations in perceptual and reasoning ability inherent in the human race. Idols of the Theater are sophistries conveyed by speculative systems, which provide little more than imaginative plays for the stage. Idols of the Cave are errors generated within the darkened cavern of the individual mind as it refracts and garnishes truth according to personal biases. Most troublesome of all, however, are Idols of the Marketplace, misunderstandings built into the everyday language with which we think and talk. Common words embody common sense, and common sense is often based on unrefined understanding or even superstition. Closer to our own time, Ludwig Wittgenstein also cautioned us about how models and assumptions embedded in language may handicap our understanding.

These warnings need to be taken seriously in reflecting on expressions like "self-deception" and "lying to oneself." As we have seen, these expressions conjure up analogies with interpersonal deception that may or may not prove fruitful. Could it be that such locutions are more misleading than helpful in understanding the perplexing phenomena to which they are applied? Each of the authors in this part believes that the term "self-deception" is not only misleading, but in its literal sense implies a contradiction.

Kenneth J. Gergen is especially concerned with the unconscious self-deception hypothesized by Freud. His attack on it is three-pronged. First, he contends that there is no solid experimental evidence establishing that unconscious activities exist and keep mental contents from entering consciousness. Because behavior is always ambiguous, there is room for psychoanalysis to explain it in terms of unconscious purposes, but these interpretations are merely imposed without firmly warranted inferences dictated by hard fact. Nor has recent controlled experimentation been decisive in proving the simultaneous presence of the main components of self-deception: a conscious disposition (belief, desire, etc.), an opposing unconscious disposition, and a defense process explaining how the conscious disposition motivates the person to keep the unconscious disposition out of consciousness.

Second, Gergen asserts that future research in principle cannot provide evidence proving the existence of self-deception. For self-deception requires what is impossible: self-contradictory combinations of beliefs and impulses. (Here Gergen seems to merge explicitly contradictory states—for example, the simultaneous belief and nonbelief that p, or the simultaneous desire and absence of desire that p—and states of ambivalence—for example, believing p and also believing not-p, or desiring p and desiring not-p.)

Third, a careful attempt to make sense of unconscious defense requires postulating an unnecessarily elaborate system of theoretical structures and processes. For example, one must hypothesize "subceiving" sensing devices operating below conscious perception, registering the contents of both consciousness and unconsciousness. This criticism is related to but developed with more precision than Sartre's objections to Freud in the chapter of *Being and Nothingness* entitled "Bad Faith." But whereas Sartre goes on to distinguish different degrees of self-consciousness (e.g., "pre-reflective" versus "reflective" self-consciousness), Gergen rejects any dual-level consciousness as itself requiring unnecessary postulates of mental machinery.

In the second half of his essay, Gergen seeks to explain why a concept riddled with so many difficulties has played such an important role in contemporary psychology and everyday discourse. He suggests that the notion of self-deception is based on primitive folk beliefs about the human mind, or the "ethnopsychology" of our culture. Its primary function in that context is not merely to describe and explain (or misdescribe and pseudoexplain), but to license a special type of evaluation of conduct. It allows us to hold people responsible for acting under self-deception, since their deception is supposedly willful and voluntary, while simultaneously to excuse or forgive them as not blameworthy, since they did not have full consciousness of what they are deceived about. While belief in self-deception can be a useful myth or superstition that helps us live with one another without excessive blaming, it can become a potent rhetorical weapon when used by professional therapists and others holding positions of authority. Labeling a patient a self-deceiver can be the initial step in controlling interpretations of whole realms of allegedly unconscious behavior supposedly inaccessible to patients themselves.

M. R. Haight concurs that self-deception in a literal sense is impossible since it requires that a person be split into a deceiver who has knowledge readily available to consciousness, and also a victim of deception who is unable to be conscious of the same knowledge. If this schism were present in one person it would have to involve a split personality, one part of which has access to the other's consciousness, but not vice versa. That would in fact amount to two 'selves' in a way different from one self's deceiving itself, as "self-deception" implies. (Also see Haight's book, *A Study of Self-Deception.*)

Unlike Gergen, Haight points out that the term "self-deception" can be metaphorically applied to forms of behavior that writers on self-deception have often had in mind. For example, 'self-deceivers' might know something that they are motivated not to become conscious of on occasions when recollection would normally be expected. Haight calls this "buried knowledge" and contrasts it with "free knowledge," which readily enters consciousness. So-called self-deceivers also fail or even refuse to admit things to themselves, sometimes things they have buried knowledge about. They may also lie or pretend to others (the aspect of Haight's earlier writing that Szabados emphasized in his criticisms); engage in obsessive daydreaming, motivated forgetfulness, and ignoring; or make oblique remarks about what they have buried knowledge of (as in jokes, irony, or metaphor). The point of all these strategies is to enable a person to act as if some truth accessible to him or her were false in order to pursue a desired course of conduct.

Nevertheless, it generates moral confusion to refer to such behavior with the literally contradictory expression "self-deception." This typically inconsistent behavior is ambiguous to begin with, and a self-contradictory label invites unchecked moral improvisation in holding people responsible or not responsible, guilty or blameless.

Haight presses the problem of ambiguous behavior with an illustration adapted from Anita Loos's *Gentlemen Prefer Blondes.* When Lorelei

Lee killed Mr. Jennings, (1) was she momentarily blanked out, as she claims, either because of (1a) a shock-induced automaton-like trance, or (1b) a loss of consciousness motivated by anger or revenge? Or (2) did a dissociated conscious state appear (of the sort described by the psychologist William McDougall), whether owing to (2a) sheer shock, or (2b) motivation by an aspect of her normal personality, or (2c) the action of a dissociated personality (making Lorelei a full-blown split personality of the sort studied by Morton Prince)? Or (3) was Lorelei at least partially aware at the time of what she did and perhaps a victim of her own confusion about her unconscious motivations ("Freud's story")? Or (4) was she grasping any available rationalization to avoid responsibility ("Sartre's story")? Or (5) was she refusing to avow the impulses that led to the act ("Fingarette's story")? Or (6) was she cynically lying to cover up the callous act of a sociopath?

Moral terms are applied with normal undivided people in mind as paradigms. The inner splits and absence of "free knowledge" involved in self-deception make it impossible to form accurate moral judgments, and the mind of the self-deceiver is largely a morally unfathomable "black box." Yet even the behavior of undivided people is ambiguous, a difficulty that leads immediately to general philosophical skepticism about the possibility of knowing about other people's minds. We cannot even tell whether people are ever free from causal determinism in a manner that would warrant holding them morally responsible.

David Kipp construes literal self-deception as the impossible feat of getting oneself not to know something that one really does simultaneously know or suspect. What is *called* "self-deception" is actually only ignorance or interpersonal pretense—indeed, either *sincere* ignorance, *dishonest* pretense, or some combination thereof. In sections 1, 5, and 6 of his paper (which might be read together before reading the essay straight through), Kipp develops the view that most self-deceivers sham beliefs in order to keep others from discovering something about them which they themselves know and can bring to consciousness. Thus most 'self-deception' is a special case of interpersonal deception, distinguished by the motive of fear of being known by others. It is related to inauthenticity: treating conventional truths and values of one's society as the decisive basis for one's self-image, motivated by fear of heeding the call of one's own conscience.

In the main body of the essay, Kipp explores psychological factors that historically generated widespread shamming of the sort he portrays, and he also sketches the ideological origins of the concepts of self-deception, authenticity, and weakness of will. In section 2 he argues that the notion of weakness of will as traditionally conceived in Christian thought (''Christian fideism'') is itself incoherent as Socrates foreknew (''Socratic rationalism''). Weakness of will presupposes that the human mind is divided into reason, will, and passion, and that unthinking passion tempts reason not to perform its proper function of guiding will. But what one's reason dictates on a given occasion—that is, what one's judgment is about how one ought to act—is revealed by one's actions, and it is senseless to hypothesize a blind passion that somehow intervenes between reason and the act one's will performs. Christianity also defends what Kipp sees as the further absurdity that religious belief and love can be generated by pure acts of will, in response to commandment, even when an individual's reason sees insufficient warrant for them. As Christianity came to dominate society, this latter doctrine helped create an enormous pressure on people whose reason did not incline them to embrace Christianity. The upshot was large-scale self-protective sham: in order to gain the security of solidarity with the group and also out of resentment against people who rejected the Christian message, many people acted as if they believed the Christian message, without really believing it.

In section 3 it is argued that resentment-based hypocrisy also underlies the ideologies of modern mass movements (''Modern collectivism''). Mass society derides elitism and genuine individualism. In fact it attacks the belief in objective values, those warranted by good reasons rather than by mere passion. Kipp avers that the irrational (because self-contradictory) idea of self-deception arose as part of this debunking of reason, for it is essentially the idea that passion and will can manipulate beliefs independently of a person's reason.

In section 4 Kipp more directly indicates his concern for autonomously based individuality (''Modern individualism'') and traces its roots to Nietzsche, Kierkegaard, and especially Heidegger. Authentic individuals shape their identities and commitments without domination by the 'crowd.' They do so amidst the universal human anxiety in confronting death and living by personal conscience. Failures to be authentic are ultimately the result of ignorance and cowardice under the influence of the crowd (a view congruous with Kipp's earlier emphasis on Socratic rationalism). Sartre's obsession with literal self-deception represents a confused distortion of Heidegger's insights and is itself the product of *ressentiment* and sham.

The trenchant skepticism defended in these three essays invites and should provoke a rereading of the earlier essays. Yet it should not be assumed that it is incompatible with all of that earlier material. For one thing, Gergen, Haight, and Kipp take it for granted that ''literal'' self-deception should be understood (and then criticized as self-contradictory) by applying a strict analogy with interpersonal deception. They hold that the self-deceiver must both know and not know, believe and not believe, be conscious and not conscious, etc., in ways that are impossible. But there are other ways to approach the analogy with interpersonal deception, such as those mentioned in the General Introduction, and there are other ways of defining what "literal" self-deception is. Most of the earlier writers understood "literal" self-deception to be whatever the expression is standardly used to refer to. Using their approach, Haight and Kipp could be viewed as granting the existence of standard cases of self-deception, even though they differ over what those cases are. In part, then, disagreements about "literal" self-deception are merely verbal, and in part are conceptual and empirical disputes over how to analyze a certain range of human behavior. Beneath some of the apparent skepticism are disagreements of the same sort the earlier authors displayed.

Nevertheless there remain fundamental new questions raised in these final three essays, the response to which will depend on one's view of human nature and one's view of what can be known. For example, Haight raises ultimate questions about freedom and responsibility, and both Haight and Gergen disturbingly challenge the extent of possible knowledge about human conduct. Kipp is equally provocative in apparently claiming that people can be ignorant or engage in pretense but never be willfully evasive in how they form their beliefs. (I say "apparently" since his central notion of "conscious pretense" may be broad enough to cover both self-conscious pretense and pretense that one refuses to acknowledge to oneself or evades belief in.)

Whatever one's verdict on these deeper issues, these final essays provide a sobering caution about potential abuses in uncritically charging particular individuals with self-deception. Gergen is surely right that allegations of self-deception are at least sometimes based on power-seeking attempts to dominate others. Kipp seems to me justified in seeing bitter ressentiment beneath Sartre's general indictments of self-deceivers. And Haight and Gergen insightfully identify genuine difficulties in accurately grounding explanations and evaluations of ambiguous behavior.

The Ethnopsychology
of Self-Deception

Kenneth J. Gergen

It is difficult to ascertain the earliest origins of the concept of self-deception. During the past several decades, however, psychoanalytic terminology has ceased to be the rarefied argot of a professional clique and has entered full force into the public language. This proliferation of analytic concepts into the common vernacular[1] has meant that self-deception, a key characteristic of all Freudian mechanisms of psychic defense, has become widely accepted as a fundamental constituent of mental life. It is not unusual to hear others (but seldom oneself) portrayed as "fooling themselves," "lying to themselves," "not facing the truth about themselves," or otherwise engaging in various forms of self-dissemblance. And too, such discourse has increased the common accessibility to other descriptive forms in which one's psyche is said to be divided against itself. The Marxist concepts of "false consciousness," in which one is superficially committed to a system antithetical to one's more basic nature, and "self-alienation," in which one lives an impoverished emotional life cut away from one's true and natural potential, continue to possess strong rhetorical value. Concepts of "inner conflict," "man against himself," and "inauthenticity" are also rendered the more felicitous by the entry of self-deception into the common vernacular.

For those within the psychoanalytic profession, and presumably within the educated laity, there has been little question of the existence of self-deception. For the former group it is assumed to be an integral part of one's psychic defenses, to be a critical constituent of normal (although not thereby desirable) personality make-up. All people defend themselves against their natural impulses; defenses are erected to prevent such impulses from reaching consciousness. Psychoanalysis is devoted in large measure to opening the conscious mind to that which is hidden but truly desired, in effect, to reduce the magnitude of self-deception. With such assumptions more or less taken for granted by the psychoanalytic profession, there is little reason for the laity to suppose otherwise. They are left clinging to the uncomfortable hope that most of their major emotional, moral, and political investments do not rest on the quicksand of self-deception.

Yet, precisely what is the warrant for the assumption of self-deception? In what manner is the concept grounded? In particular, is there reason to believe that there is an empirical basis for the concept? The two major ways in which empirical grounding has been sought leave little room for confidence. In the therapeutic domain the analyst does not so much discover or locate instances of self-deception as he or she employs the concept as an interpretive lens for determining "what there is." Given the ambiguities of meaning in the normal accounts people make of their lives, an analyst should encounter little difficulty in "finding" that virtually all analysands are self-deceived in one manner or another. And, by the same token, support can be garnered from life history data for virtually any alternative theory of human action. To find that one can derive support for a given theory from case history material speaks far less to the empirical validity of the theory than to the interpretive skills of the theorist.

Being discontent with ambiguities surrounding case history interpretation, investigators have attempted to explore self-deception in more systematically controlled circumstance. For example, Sackeim and Gur[2] report a negative correlation between scores on a self-deception questionnaire measure and three self-report psychopathology scales; the more self-deceived the individual, the less likely to report psychopathology. Mont, Zurcher, and Nydegger[3] found that more self-deceived individuals reported less insecurity, less authoritarianism, higher self-esteem, and a stronger set toward repression. Yet, results such as these also leave one with little confidence. In particular, the manner in which self-deception is to be isolated for study remains deeply problematic. For self-deception to be located, one must minimally have access to (1) a conscious disposition (belief, motive, intent), (2) an unconscious disposition antithetical to that which is conscious, (3) some form of defense whereby the existence of the conscious disposition provides the grounds for the unconscious disposition remaining in this state. There are no studies known to this writer that have successfully assessed all three components. Perhaps the most ambitious attempt was made by Gur and Sackeim in 1979.[4] However, the methodology has subsequently been shown to be problematic.[5] More fundamentally, none of these components is transparently available for observation; each must be inferred from behavioral activity. Yet, there is no apparent limit (save the limits of human creativity) to the number of interpretations that can be made of the psychological basis of any given action.[6]

In order to clarify the psychological basis for an action, one may turn to other behaviors of the person. However, the psychological basis of these, too, must be inferred. Each attempt at clarification must inevitably make use of other actions, the meanings of which themselves are subject to inferences unwarranted except through other inferences. In effect, all inferences to the unseen realm of the mind (whether conscious or not) receive their warrant from the network of associated inferences one chooses to make. What has appeared in the hands of behavioral scientists as sound empirical support for the concept of self-deception is found, on closer inspection, to be a series of associated interpretations without objective anchor.

We thus find ourselves at the present juncture with a concept of compelling interest, profound ramifications, and broad social and professional utility. Yet we can find little or nothing in the way of an objective warrant for the concept. Can we anticipate the emergence of an objective grounding through future research? And if not, what is to be made of the concept? Should it be relegated to the status of folk myth and barred from serious discourse about the world? Or, might there be other important functions for the concept that do not rely on its empirical warrant? In the pages that follow I shall propose that future research cannot, in principle, provide an objective grounding for the concept. There are conceptual impediments that prevent the term from acquiring such credibility. As these conceptual issues are elaborated, it will further be seen that self-deception is best regarded as a constituent of the culture's ethnopsychology, that is, its system of common beliefs about "the mind" and its functioning. As will finally be proposed, the concept plays a vital role within the culture as an illocutionary device— an implement through which discourse alters social patterns.

THE PROBLEMATICS OF SELF-DECEPTION

Although the concept of self-deception has entered effortlessly into common discourse, one should not conclude that the term is thereby without difficulties in terms of its logical entailments or implications. Frequently employed concepts may often lead to incoherence, obfuscation, or illogicality within the larger system of meaning in which they are embedded. Such problems have been revealed, for example, in treatments of "the mind,"[7] beliefs,[8] sense data,[9] and self-conception.[10] Such problems lie at the analytic rather than the empirical level. That is, such problems emerge when one examines the implications of committing oneself to a given term for other things one either must or cannot say within the existing discourse conventions. For example, such conventions generally prevent one from speaking of reason as a form of emotion or intentions as deterministically governed; and if one is to speak of the "velocity of free falling bodies," one has committed oneself by implication to such terms as "space," "time," "mass," "height," and so on. As we unpack the conceptual implications of the term self-deception, we find the results particularly problematic. Three major problems demand our attention.

THE PARADOX OF ·SELF-DECEPTION

For scholars pursuing the problem of self-deception the most notorious obstacle to analytic progress has been variously termed the paradox of self-deception. The crux of the paradox is located in Demos's statement that self-deception "entails that B believes both P and not-P at the same time."[11] This statement may be translated into more psychodynamic terms by saying that "an individual possesses both an impulse (wish, goal, desire) and does not possess such an impulse (or possesses its negation)." Yet, as is readily apparent, such formulations are logically incoherent: To "believe P" is by definition a state of eschewing "not-P"; or, to say that a person possesses a given impulse is in itself an assertion that the impulse is not absent. The concept thus leads to an assertion that is logically prohibited.

Various attempts have been made to dissolve the paradox. Demos's own stance is similar (though not identical) to Freud's in that his solution depends on differentiating among levels of consciousness. A belief in "P" can exist at one level of consciousness, while a belief in "not-P" is sustained at another. A person can "focus attention" on one disposition (focal consciousness) while failing to attend or notice its contradiction within peripheral consciousness. Yet, as critics such as Canfield and McNally,[12] Penelhum,[13] Siegler,[14] and Fingarette[15] have justly argued, once this move has been made, the term "self-deception loses its capacities to designate a uniquely interesting aspect of mind. Rather, such longstanding terms as "ignorance," "forgetfulness," being "carried away by one's arguments or pretenses," and the like would be wholly adequate descriptions. There would be no need for the term self-deception. (See also Haight's analysis, this volume, of "buried" knowledge.)

As Bach[16] has pointed out, it is important to distinguish the term self-deception from processes of "failing to see," "thinking in ignorance," or "illogical thinking." More must be implied. Indeed, more is implied by theorists and practitioners in the psychoanalytic tradition. Specifically, there is an added motivational component: One of the dispositions (beliefs, wishes, etc.) is actively *pushed* or *thrust* from the conscious or focal state into the unconscious. In effect there are motivational defenses against the material reaching consciousness. The individual actively engages in such processes as repression, active evasion, "counter-cathexis," and so on, in order to block the contradictory impulse from awareness.

THE PROBLEMATICS OF PSYCHIC DEFENSE

Although the more dynamic account of self-deception is desirable as a means of avoiding the twin problems of paradox and redundancy, this option creates as many problems as it solves. Among the most prominent is the classic issue of "subception." Generally, the capacity to notice or perceive threatening events is identified with the state of consciousness. Such events are registered in consciousness, and corrective action is initiated. One consciously notices the oncoming tram and intentionally steps aside. Yet in the case of self-deception we have corrective action (the erection of defenses) occurring without conscious awareness of the impulses (beliefs, desires) against which defenses are erected. (To argue that there was awareness of the unconscious would recapitulate the problems described above.) The result is that the theorist is logically pressed into developing yet another form of consciousness, one that perceives or registers the undesirable impulses of the unconscious, sets defenses in motion, but does not report its activities to conscious awareness. In effect, one must posit a subceiving agency operating below the level of conscious awareness, yet serving the interests of the conscious mind.

Many theorists have been justifiably concerned over taking this theoretical step. The acceptance of an unknown (and virtually unknowable) level of mind, namely the Freudian unconscious, already commits one's theory to a dangerous romanticism in which the mysteries of the unknown achieve prominence over that which is known. Now to add a third level of functioning, an awareness of the unknown that does not itself report to the known, seems further to threaten the intelligibility of the theory. What limits are to be placed over the characteristics attributed to the nether region of the mind? Is the door being opened to an endless and ultimately self-defeating array of exotic entities? Will the discipline find itself asking how many impulses are dancing at the foot of an action? And indeed, such reservations are legitimate. For if one does embrace the concept of subception, several additional theoretical constructs quickly follow on its heels. Specifically, the theorist must be prepared to furnish the subceiving process with, among other things:

a. A sensing device enabling it to be informed of the contents of the unconscious.

b. A conceptual apparatus that enables these contents to be classified (e.g., threatening, nonthreatening).

c. A storage and retrieval system that enables these contents to be recalled on necessary occasions.

d. A sensing device enabling it to be informed of the status of the conscious mind (in order that its dispositions be honored).

e. A conceptual apparatus, memory bank, and retrieval system that enables understanding of and adjustments to the commitments of the conscious mind.

f. A logical processing device or comparator that enables it to understand which contents of the unconscious are antithetical to the commitments of the conscious.

g. A command center that activates the defensive maneuvers.

h. A feedback device that enables it to retain control over the defensive maneuvers.

i. A storage and retrieval system necessary for the proper operation of the command system.

Such theoretical prospects seem both staggering and prohibitive.

THE IDENTIFICATION OF MENTAL STATES

Should one be willing to accept the conceptual ramifications of embracing the concept of self-deception, there is one additional hurdle of some significance. The problem is not specific to the issue of self-deception; rather, it is of general import. However, it is one which becomes increasingly critical as one adds layers and multiple mechanisms and processes to the compendium of the mind. The question is how to identify the constituents of the mental arena: to differentiate among the contents, so as to identify what is and is not the case, to know when there has been a recurrence of an event of a particular kind, or to be able to say when one event has ceased and another begun? To appreciate the magnitude of the problem we can confine ourselves to the most transparent level, that of available consciousness. If the difficulties encountered at this level are severe, their magnitude will only be compounded as one turns to assay the more opaque regions of the unknown.

How is the process of identifying mental contents to proceed? We have previously seen that the observer is in a disadvantageous position in this regard. The inference that any given indicator measures or stands for a given mental event depends on assumptions that can be warranted only by reference to other indicators, the use of which depends on making further unwarranted inferences. It is in this vein that my colleagues and I[17] have attempted to demonstrate that virtually any item from any standardized measure of personality can be used as evidence for virtually any underlying personality trait, along with its negation. Common interpretive skills, along with a pervasive flexibility in interpretive rules, enable us to draw from people's avowals an immense range of inferences regarding the state of their minds. In effect, behavioral data serve much as blank slates that permit the investigator to inscribe the theoretical message of his or her choosing.

Do we improve matters if we shift to the level of the actor? Are actors capable of reporting accurately on the state of their mental life? Are they, by virtue of their "living their own consciousness," able to distinguish among its constituents? German mentalist theory of the nineteenth century was committed in large measure to the assumption that persons could be trained to report with accuracy on their mental conditions. The classic method of introspection was an outgrowth of this assumption. It remained unclear to many theorists whether there were not powerful processes that operated at a nonconscious level (not to be equated with Freud's unconscious). For example, both Helmholtz and Wundt speculated about a process of "unconscious inference," which could give rise to a consciousness of results—although itself beyond consciousness. This latter line of thinking has been revitalized in recent psychological inquiry by Richard Nisbett and his colleagues,[18] who argue that people do not generally have access to the processes that engender varying states of consciousness but are conscious only of the resulting products. For example, we may be able to bring to consciousness a little used name, but the process of memory itself is beyond the ken of consciousness. Yet this line of work has been criticized on a variety of grounds,[19] and it remains unclear whether it can be sustained.

More direct confrontations with the assumption of mental accessibility are available.

1. *Process in search of itself.* To say that one is aware of one's intentions or can identify one's own psychological states more generally forces theoretical speculation to the border of incredulity. Such a conclusion would entail a concept of mind in which psychological process would be forced to turn reflexively upon itself and identify its own states. Rather than a single stream of consciousness, one would be forced into a mental dualism in which one level of process (an "inner eye") acted as a sensing and recording device, and a second process furnished the stuff to be sensed and recorded. Such a dualism is sufficiently awkward that one is invited to consider how such a peculiar construction might have acquired such broad credibility. It seems most plausible in this case that the assumption of "internal perception" is a reconstructed form of the traditional metaphor for "external perception." The latter view is based on a subject-object dichotomy: A subject apprehending the character of the external object. The popular model of "internal perception" appears to represent a projection of this view into the covert world. A justification for this displacement is much in need.

2. *Internal perception as self-biased.* If one can perform the theoretical circumlocution necessary to justify an internal dualism, one faces a second problem of no less magnitude. Specifically, if both the sensing process and the sensed data are constituents of the same psychological structure, what safeguards (if any) could be placed over misperception? Could the processes one hoped to identify not hinder or distort the very task of identification itself? On what grounds could one argue that internal processes do not operate in this way?

3. *The ambiguous properties of psychological states.* A third difficulty emerges when one inquires into the properties of mental states that would enable them to be identified. What is the size, shape, color, sound, or smell, for example, of an intention, a thought, a motive, a desire, a need, or a hope? Even the questions seem ill conceived. If one closes one's eyes, sits in silence, and turns one's attentions inward, what entities or states does one encounter? It is this fundamental ambiguity of internal states that stimulated the early work of Schachter and Singer[20] on the social definition of emotions. Such work strongly suggested that the identification of emotional states is subject to wide-ranging contextual influence. The extensive work on the reattribution of emotional states,[21] along with more extensive accounts of the social construction of emotion and motivation,[22] further suggests that accounts of internal states are neither informed nor corrected by observation of the states themselves.

SELF-DECEPTION
AS ILLOCUTIONARY IMPLEMENT

At this juncture we find that the concept of self-deception is on shaky ground indeed. As the preceding discussion indicates, if the concept is not to lead to logical incoherence, it commits the theorist to a Byzantine architecture of the mind. And regardless of which of these choices is made, there is no apparent way of anchoring the term either in observables or in conscious experience. How then is the concept to be regarded? Should it be scratched from the contemporary vocabulary of person description? Is it merely foolish and misleading talk? An answer to such questions is suggested by the earlier discussion of the ambiguity of experience. There it was ventured that characterizations of the mind get their bearing, not from experience of the mind itself, but from the cultural conventions of understanding. The language of self-understanding is generated, not from the character of the self, but from the metaphors, tropes, figures, and other conventions of common discourse. In effect, the concept of self-deception is a constituent of the culture's ethnopsychology—or system of folk beliefs about the nature of human functioning at the psychological level.

This perspective is rendered the more compelling as one surveys the psychological vernaculars of other cultures and/or times. As anthropological inquiry suggests, there are broad variations among cultures in the kinds of mental predicates ascribed to human beings. For example, emotion terms within many Oceanic peoples, including the Samoans,[23] Pintupi Aborigines,[24] and the Ifaluk,[25] are used, not as a means of reporting on internal states, but as statements about a relationship between a person and an event (or another person). The Marquesans possess a complex system of allocating various emotions to bodily parts;[26] for example, envy lies in the belly, disgust resides in the eyes. Many cultures view the self, not as possessing agency in voluntary control, but as being an object under the control of external events or beings.[27] Such variability in psychological discourse is again underscored when one turns to studies of earlier periods of history. The Aristotelian conception of mental life[28] differed markedly from that outlined by Descartes in *Les Passions de l'Ame,* or later by William James in his *Principles of Psychology.* As Marshall[29] has proposed, the dominant metaphor of the mind has shifted over the centuries from water, to the tablet, to the library or storehouse, to the machine.

Of course, regardless of time or culture, virtually all such mental elements or processes are subject to the kinds of warranting problems outlined above. Neither observer nor actor possesses means of furnishing objective anchors for the terms in question. Their warrant seems derived principally from social usage. Thus it is to social process that we must look for an understanding of how the concept of self-deception came to acquire its capacity to render human action intelligible, and how it functions in contemporary society.

THREE MOMENTS
OF PSYCHOLOGICAL ASCRIPTION

Although a full answer to the question of social function is beyond the scope of this paper, significant headway can be made. However, such inquiry depends at the outset on an understanding of the person description process. Let us thus consider briefly three significant aspects of psychological terminology in the understanding of persons. To say that such terms "render human action" intelligible does not take us far enough. There are many vocabularies of intelligibility. One can account for behavior by referring to biological processes, the physical or social environment, the social system that the person inhabits, and so on. Why is a vocabulary of psychology necessitated? As explained more fully elsewhere,[30] psychological predicates seem required in part as a means of solving the pragmatic problem of describing entities in continuous, protean-like movement. Because descriptive terms cannot be used practically to index the ever-changing complex of behavioral movements, a dispositional (or psychological) language is invoked to refer to goals or the end points of action sequences. In effect, if persons are to be described, one must rely on inner dispositional terms to do so. This sets the stage for what may be viewed as the first moment of psychological ascription: It enables one to index or label ongoing activity.

Yet the deployment of "inner state" or dispositional terms to speak of human actions simultaneously inbues this terminology with a second function. Such terms not only name the action but they also designate its source. That is, they not only "describe"; they also furnish an explanation for the behavior. For example, to describe someone's behavior as acquisitive also furnishes a first-order explanation for the action. That is, the person must possess an underlying disposition one might call an acquisitive intention, need, motive, or the like. Should the underlying source not be an acquisitive disposition of some variety, then it would be inappropriate by definition to describe the behavior as acquisitive. If the underlying disposition were a hunger for power or a need for security, we would not wish to call the behavior acquisitive, but security seeking or a power ploy.

The third moment of psychological ascription follows closely upon the second. As we have seen, descriptions of human actions simultaneously offer an explanation of these actions. Yet, explanations of an action simultaneously designate a potential target of praise or blame. To say that a person "aggressed" is, by definition, to attribute to him or her an intention to aggress. Yet, to attribute an intention to aggress is also, by Western standards, to hold the person responsible for the action. He or she may justifiably be punished or condemned. In the same way someone who was said to be "helping" others might, because the description simultaneously attributes responsibility for the action, be praised or rewarded as a result. In effect, psychological terminology necessarily becomes implicated in the process of moral sanctioning. Descriptions serve as explanations, and explanations as moral designators.

SELF-DECEPTION AND THE POSSIBILITY OF RESPONSIBLE IRRESPONSIBILITY

Given these three aspects of psychological discourse more generally, we can return to the case of self-deception. As is rapidly discerned, this term functions at all three levels. First, on the descriptive level, we may speak of people's actions as self-deceived. We may believe that a person's current passion is in marked contrast to his long-enduring life patterns, and conclude that his actions are an instance of self-deception. At the same time, this designation informs us of the psychological basis of the conduct. Self-deceived action must, by definition, be the result of a process by the same name. And, finally, to say that one is "self-deceived" is to say something about one's moral character. Precisely what this message is, and indeed, the chief social significance of the concept, deserves special attention.

As we have seen, person description generally operates in such a way as to hold persons responsible for their actions. To describe thus tends to render the person vulnerable to praise and blame (positive and negative social sanctions). Of course, people frequently wish to avoid negative sanctions, and current discourse conventions furnish one major means of deflection. In particular, one may adopt an alternative vocabulary of explanation, namely that which traces the source of the activity to the environment. The discourse conventions permit the individual to fall back on accounts that place the cause of the action (and thus the blame) on external situations. "They made me do it," "The circumstances were beyond my control," and "I was a victim of circumstance'' are all common means of removing the locus of behavioral cause from the psyche to the environment.

Yet these two vocabularies—the one placing blame on self and the other on the environment—are also insufficient for many purposes. For example, at times the blaming agent him- or herself may be part of the situation, and it would be tactically obtuse for the actor to shift blame in this direction. In other cases the blaming agent may feel sympathy for the actor and search for a means to reduce the punishment that would otherwise be administered. Or there may be no easy means available at times to show how the environment is at fault. A form of accounting is thus needed in which the responsibility for the action remains within the actor but which would not simultaneously evoke blame. Various mental predicates have been used to meet this need. The terminology of the emotions furnishes an array of candidates, as do such terms as need, drive, and want. In each case the terms trace the source of action to the individual (he or she is responsible for the behavior), but blame or censorship can be muted. We can say, ''I couldn't help it, I was overcome by anger (or passion, grief, etc.).'' Or we can say, ''I needed it so much that I couldn't think straight,'' or ''My want was so intense that I couldn't help it.'' Yet, this range of terms is only partially successful in achieving its joint goals of retaining yet denying responsibility. In Western culture the rhetorical force of such terms has been blunted by the counterclaim that the normal person can and should generally maintain responsible control over his or her emotions, needs, wants, drives, etc. In the modern courtroom it is difficult to be excused for a ''crime of passion''; the individual who allows passion to overcome his or her principles is viewed as morally inferior. In short, a plea for exoneration on the basis of emotion has only limited utility.

We may now appreciate what would appear to be the chief cultural value of the concept of self-deception. Like perhaps no other integer within contemporary discourse, it enables the individual to be held responsible for his or her actions, but simultaneously holds the person blameless. The individual is responsible inasmuch as he or she voluntarily originates the action in question, but is forgiven to the degree that the voluntary system was misled, influenced, or otherwise constrained by mental events obscured from consciousness. The concept of self-deception is thus a wonderfully economic and effective means of solving an important array of social problems. This particular role has been fulfilled by other terms in previous historical periods. In early Greek civilization madness was traced to the influence of the gods on the individual.[31] The culture was not to be held responsible for the aberrant conduct; it was the individual's responsibility. Yet, because the gods were the source of the problem, the individual was beyond censure. Similarly, within the history of Christianity, it was long possible (and remains so today in certain circles) to view problematic or bizarre actions as the result of Satan's inhabiting the person's body. Again, such a conceptualization enabled the individual to be held responsible, but in a compassionate way. Belief in the effects of the gods and Satan has declined, and there has been little effective replacement within the language of human responsibility. The concept of self-deception fills precisely this much valued function.

To underscore the significance of this addition to the contemporary lexicon of understanding, we need only turn to modern practices of jurisprudence. Only within the present century has it become possible to argue on grounds of objective fact that the guilty should be nurtured instead of punished. In particular, if the case can be made that the individual's actions were driven by inner forces beyond conscious reach (self-deception), hospitalization may replace prison as the preferred mode of treatment. The insanity defense, with its strong reliance on the concept of self-deception (or its close associates), has become a celebrated if not notorious form of judicial maneuvering.

SELF-DECEPTION
AND THE ACQUISITION OF POWER

In its creation of a category of "responsible but forgiven," the concept of self-deception may be viewed as a vital cultural resource. Yet its role is not limited to this domain. One other prominent function deserves final attention. As is broadly recognized, language is an implement of inestimable power in human affairs. Properly patterned language may move people to their greatest deeds of courage, or their most dastardly acts of inhumanity. Because of its power, there has been lively competition over the centuries in maximizing voice, that is, in ensuring that one's favored language patterns come to predominate or prevail. Although there are many crudely mechanical means of securing voice (e.g., publishing a newspaper, censorship by force, advertising), one of the more sophisticated and pervasive means is through deploying ancillary language patterns. In particular, linguistic means may be sought for justifying one kind of voice over another. Rationale may be furnished as to why certain voices are more legitimate than others—religious voices, royal voices, mystical voices, rational voices, scientific voices, and so on.

The concept of self-deception proves, in the contemporary arena, to be a valuable rhetorical means of acquiring social power. This power is derivative rather than generic. That is, it depends in large measure on the development of the more fundamental warrant of objectivity, as it has been elaborated particularly within the past century. The culture now furnishes those who lay special claims to objectivity (e.g., scientists, doctors) a disproportionate degree of voice. Their definitions of reality are trusted, and the behavioral implications of their constructions thus embraced. The psychiatric profession, because of its close association with medicine, has fallen heir to this favored status. Its terminology comes to acquire the character of objectivity; those who are professionally trained to deploy the terminology command wide-ranging respect for the objectivity of their opinions. The behavioral implications of their judgments (e.g., judgments of insanity, mental disorder, emotional disorder, etc.) have broad and sometimes substantial effects. (Anyone who has been detained in a mental institution has experienced directly the physical instantiation of such judgments.)

In this light we find that the concept of self-deception is a potent weapon in the arsenal of social control. When one is positioned to use the term with authority, he or she is capable of ruling on the legitimacy of another's conduct, and can anticipate that his or her suggestion for remedial treatment will be adopted. For example, when a psychiatrist informs a man that he is deceiving himself, the individual will typically be led to distrust his manifest commitments, and to suspect that they are merely a subterfuge for underlying dispositions of an opposing character. The devout must be prepared to admit faithlessness; the debauched, an underlying strength of character; the optimistic, a deep-seated pessimism; and so on. And as life decisions follow, the client is forced by his or her capitulation at the rhetorical level, to rely on the therapist's judgment as to the proper steps to be taken. In effect, anyone granted the warrant to ascribe self-deception to others possesses a powerful fulcrum for changing patterns of human conduct. The extent to which the society has benefited or been ill served by the granting of this warrant is a matter for continued concern.

NOTES

I am indebted to Stephen Fisher for his assistance in preparing the present manuscript.

1. Serge Moscovici, *La Psychanalyse; Son Image et Son Public: Étude sur la Representation Sociale de la Psychanalyse* (Paris: P.O.F., 1961).

2. Harold Sackeim and Ruben Gur, "Self-Deception, Other-Deception and Self-Reported Psychopathology," *Journal of Consulting and Clinical Psychology* 47 (1979): 213.

3. J. K. Mont, L. A. Zurcher, and R. V. Nydegger, "Interpersonal Self-Deception and Personality Correlates," *Journal of Social Psychology* 103 (1977): 91.

4. Ruben Gur and Harold Sackeim, "Self-Deception: A Concept in Search of a Phenomenon," *Journal of Personality and Social Psychology* 37 (1979): 147.

5. W. Douglas and K. Gibbins, "Inadequacy of Voice Recognition as a Demonstration of Self-Deception," *Journal of Personality and Social Psychology* 44 (1983): 589.

6. Kenneth Gergen, *Toward Transformation in Social Knowledge* (New York: Springer-Verlag, 1982); and Kenneth Gergen, Alexandra Hepburn, and Debra Comer, "The Hermeneutics of Personality Description," unpublished manuscript, 1983.

7. Jeff Coulter, *The Social Construction of the Mind* (New York: Macmillan, 1979); and Gilbert Ryle, *The Concept of Mind* (London: Hutchinson, 1949).

8. Rodney Needham, *Belief, Language and Experience* (Chicago: University of Chicago Press, 1972).

9. John Austin, *Sense and Sensibilia* (London: Oxford University Press, 1962).

10. Kenneth Gergen, "Theory of the Self: Impasse and Evolution," in *Advances in Experimental Social Psychology,* ed. Leonard Berkowitz (New York: Academic Press, in press).

11. R. Demos, "Lying to Oneself," *Journal of Philosophy* 57 (1960): 588.

12. J. Canfield and P. McNally, "Paradoxes of Self-Deception," *Analysis* 21 (1961): 140.

13. T. Penelhum, "Pleasure and Falsity," in *Philosophy of Mind,* ed. S. Hampshire (New York: Harper and Row, 1966).

14. F. A. Siegler and R. Demos, "On Lying to Oneself," *Journal of Philosophy* 59 (1962): 469.

15. Herbert Fingarette, *Self-Deception* (Atlantic Highlands, N.J.: Humanities Press, 1969).

16. K. Bach, "An Analysis of Self-Deception," *Philosophy and Phenomenological Research* 41 (1981): 352.

17. Gergen, Hepburn, and Comer, "The Hermeneutics of Personality Description."

18. Richard Nisbett and Nancy Bellows, "Verbal Reports about Causal Influences as Social Judgments: Private Access versus Public Theories," *Journal of Personality and Social Psychology* 35 (1977): 613; and Richard Nisbett and Timothy D. Wilson, "Telling More Than We Can Know: Verbal Reports on Mental Processes," *Psychological Review* 84 (1977): 231.

19. John Sabini and Maury Silver, *The Moralities of Everyday Life* (London and New York: Oxford University Press, 1982); and John Shotter, "Telling and Reporting: Prospective and Retrospective Uses of Self-Ascriptions," in *The Psychology of Ordinary Explanations,* ed. C. Antaki (London: Academic Press, 1981).

20. Stanley Schachter and Jerome Singer, "Cognitive, Social and Physiological Determinants of Emotional State," *Psychological Review* 62 (1962): 121.

21. Ben Harris and John Harvey, "Self-Attributed Choice As a Function of the Consequence of a Decision," *Journal of Personality and Social Psychology* 31 (1975): 1013; Ellen Langer and J. Roth, "Heads I Win, Tails It's Chance: The

Illusion of Control as a Function of the Sequence of Outcomes in a Purely Chance Task," *Journal of Personality and Social Psychology* 32 (1975): 951; J. E. Luginbuhl, Douglas Crowne, and J. P. Kahan, "Causal Attributions of Success and Failure," *Journal of Personality and Social Psychology* 31 (1975): 86; and C. Mynatt and S. J. Sherman, "Responsibility Attribution in Groups and Individuals: A Direct Test of the Diffusion of Responsibility Hypothesis," *Journal of Personality and Social Psychology* 32 (1975): 1111.

22. James Averill, *Anger and Aggression* (New York: Springer-Verlag, 1983); and C. Wright Mills, "Situated Actions and Vocabularies of Motive," *American Sociological Review* 5 (1940): 904.

23. E. Gerber, "The Cultural Patterning of Emotions in Samoa" (Ph.D. diss., University of California, San Diego).

24. F. Myers, "Emotions and the Self: A Theory of Personhood and Political Order among Pintupi Aborigines," *Ethos* 7 (1979): 343.

25. Catherine Lutz, "The Domain of Emotion in Ifaluk," *American Ethnologist* 9 (1982): 113.

26. John Kirkpatrick, "Some Marquesan Understandings of Action and Identity," in *Approaches to Ethnopsychology,* ed. G. M. White and J. Kirkpatrick (in press).

27. Paul Heelas, "The Model Applied: Anthropology and Indigenous Psychologies," in *Indigenous Psychologies,* ed. P. Heelas and A. Lock (London and New York: Academic Press, 1981).

28. A. K. Griffin, *Aristotle's Psychology of Conduct* (London: Williams and Norgate, 1931).

29. J. C. Marshall, "Minds, Machines and Metaphors," *Social Studies of Science* 7 (1977): 475.

30. Gergen, *Toward Transformation in Social Knowledge.*

31. R. Padel, "Madness in Fifth-Century (B.C.) Athenian Tragedy," in *Indigenous Psychologies,* ed. P. Heelas and A. Lock (London and New York: Academic Press, 1981).

Tales from a Black Box

M. R. Haight

Freud once remarked that the idea of infantile sexuality would come as no surprise to nursery maids, though it left the intellectual world aghast. In the same way valets and confidential secretaries probably have never doubted that human beings can in some way or other deceive themselves, but philosophers have on the whole been slow on the uptake. How can we for so long have ignored so interesting a phenomenon?

The trouble may have been that self-deception, even more than infant sexuality, has disturbing implications if we take it seriously. No real deception within oneself can happen—I maintain—unless one is split, in a way that, if real, menaces important traditional axioms and sentimentalities. The split must be both in agency and cognition; and I think not even the Greek tradition that gave us the Socratic Paradox and Aristotle's study of *akrasia* contemplated quite so much.[1] But even accounts which make self-deception less than a full deception are unsettling, if they come anywhere near doing justice to what we see. So what we see may have seemed too alien to our ways of thinking to think about, in the study if not in the real world.

I think we owe it (again) to Freud that the idea became at last less alien. He gave us an intellectually recognized system according to which people may be divided against themselves both cognitively and in volition, and therefore able after a fashion to deceive themselves. And now the philosophical interest and importance of self-deception and a flock of related issues have become too visible to ignore, whether we follow Freud or attack him or forget him. Sartre's discussion of bad faith (which he defines like self-deception as ''a lie to oneself'')[2] is a case in point. If he is to save his main moral thesis—the total accountability of a consciousness, or Being-for-Itself—he *must* find a way to dismiss Freud's (or any comparable) "split" theory; and so he tries to do, and thinks he does. It forces him to an account of bad faith that is confused by any standard and, I would say, self-contradictory when analyzed: enough to make an old-fashioned Rationalist abandon the whole idea. But that is one thing he cannot do.

I shall have to say again briefly here some things I argue at length in a book.[3] I shall start with a point I have already mentioned: that self-deception—if it is really deception—can happen only when one is split into a deceiver who is not deceived, and a victim who is not the deceiver. If there is no such split, the "victim" will know all that the "deceiver" knows about what is in question, including the fact that the "deceiver" hopes to fool the "victim" and how the "deceiver" hopes to do so. In such conditions the lie (as Sartre says) destroys itself. But my reason for saying this is not Sartre's: that consciousness is translucent—no part of it can be blocked off from any other—and any such deceiver and victim must both be conscious. On the contrary, I am sure that the dissociation of knowledge is possible.[4] I call such knowledge *buried* as opposed to *free:* terms that I have coined so as to avoid near-equivalents that evoke other people's theories. I may have buried knowledge of some truth (T) when (i) I have at some time learned it, and (ii) nothing like a damaged brain now makes me forever unable to recall it, and yet (iii) I do not recall it, when recollection is to be expected. We may find out later that my knowledge was buried, not lost, if in time I do recall it; though people might also sometimes be able to infer it from how I behave. My point is simply that a deceiver must know freely something that his or her victim cannot know, unless the knowledge is buried; for deception consists of deliberately suppressing a truth, or making one's victim believe that it is false. If I (the deceiver) have no access to my own knowledge that T, we can fairly say only that I mislead my victim unintentionally about it if (somehow) I make the knowledge equally inaccessible to him or her, or make him or her believe a thing I could sincerely believe myself. "Believe" here, by the way, must be taken in the epistemological or cognitive sense. Mere action or feeling—as in "I know Granny is dead, but I can't really believe it yet"—is not enough: the doctor who breaks the news of death with a tranquilizer, to delay its emotional recognition, is no deceiver.

Of course there is a weak sense of "deceive" which will allow unintended misleading. ("This fly deceives predators by being colored like a wasp.") And of course a dispositional term like "believe" is slipperier in what it does or does not entail than are dispositional terms like "bursts if you stick a pin in it." Such thoughts may seem to suggest ways round the paradox of *literal self*-deception, which Sartre never escapes; but I think a careful analysis must always show that there really is none.

This leads to the linguistic observation that we should either understand the "self" in "self-deception" as figurative (not truly reflexive, since in fact one part deceives another), or the "deception," or both: no trouble unless we, like Sartre, object to all theories that allow a split that will make sense of this. The real difficulty is not what he suggests: that the only adequate story contradicts itself; it is that for any observable case, too many adequate stories contradict each other. The more imaginative we are about human possibilities, the more we shall find. For each individual occasion some will seem likely, which at other times would not; but I think it logically inevitable that several we cannot fairly rule out will entail incompatible moral judgments.[5] I think it is this conflict that inspires us to describe the people involved with a self-contradiction. We need not mean quite that, though. One may coin a term because it feels right somehow, without working out whether one means it literally.

The rival diagnoses are about what is going on in that black box, the self-deceiver's mind, and the moral judgments. His or her behavior is ambiguous between them. On the other hand its general aim may be clear thoughout; I would describe any self-deceiver's project in the same way. It is *to behave (so far as one can) as though some manifest truth were false, because this allows one to act in a way that otherwise seems impossible.*[6] So far as one can; often such action entails, in an oblique way, just the knowledge one will not admit. ("I must know the truth very exactly *in order* to conceal it more carefully.")[7] The nature of that otherwise impossible-seeming action, the motives or reasons for it, the character and state—from moment to moment—of the self-deceiver and (importantly) the supporting cast—all may affect the thinking that underlies this. It may range, I think, from a deep burial of the forbidden but influential truth (again call it T)—so that most of oneself really is deceived about it—to mere lying, meant only to deceive other people.

This last manifestation might seem strange, because the first lie we think of here is probably *that T is false.* It seems an absurd lie when T is, *ex hypothesi,* obvious. But really another lie is in question: it is *that the liar believes* T to be false, or *is not aware*—in spite of the evidence—that T is true. If this works as a lie, it must usually make people feel the liar is also (somehow) *self*-deceived. But it may often not need to succeed precisely as a lie—that is, by suggesting some definite story. For I think that the liar's essential aim—as always, when a self-deceiver faces an audience—

is to make people accept, or at least not hinder, what she or he wants to do. Short of making them believe something false, mere bullying or bewildering could be enough; and a really implacable pretense can do either or both.[8]

Between these extremes may lie innumerable maneuvers toward the same end. T must be officially disregarded, however unofficially vital it may be; but this hidden vitality may lead to many kinds of tortuous T-expression. I shall mention two here, to give a sample:[9] obsessive daydreaming "as if" T were true, which one dismisses as only daydream; and stating T—to oneself, sometimes even to others—in a code that seems safe. It might be a poem in metaphor, say, or a joke. One must feel able to trust the other people (if any) not to make an issue of it; and—this is important—one must feel that *this* way of saying it (without specifying what "it" is) will not force one to act appropriately. I shall also mention one important variation in the kind of lie that may be behind self-deceptive behavior. Its form is as I have already described; but it is acted out, not from choice, but by compulsion.

Some readers of my book seemed to pick out that one tactic, the somewhat obscurely motivated lie, as my whole or main account of self-deception. No; surely many other things may happen instead, though they may also make the lie more plausible at another time. It might not be incredible in theory that self-deceivers were always pretending that something happened, when in fact it never did. People who tell Santa Claus stories to children do this. All we need is an accepted myth. Or in theory, self-deceivers might not always be pretending; but when they do, they pretend a myth: literal self-deception or (what comes to the same thing) Sartrean "bad faith." But experience and the reports of many intelligent and honest-seeming individuals have convinced me that neither of these is the case. One part of oneself does sometimes deceive another. We fail to remember or to notice the utterly relevant and obvious, for some just as obvious purpose. Other more complicated things may happen too. Only the project stays the same.

I think such ways of avoiding reality typically involve some division within oneself (except when one simply lies without compulsion); though this may not always be cognitive, or cognitive in a straightforward way. And wherever divisions in awareness, feeling, or action are possible, familiar philosophical problems turn up in new shapes to puzzle our judgments; especially the moral judgments we may feel forced and yet unable to make of self-deceivers. Beside the Other Minds problem,[10] which, outside the study, we generally forget—a Split or Extra Mind problem may appear that seems harder to forget and that can arise, disturbingly, about oneself as well as about other people.

Beside the free-will/determinism issue—which I for one can neither forget nor resolve, outside the study or in it[11]—we may find others inspired by a suspicion that we carry hidden puppeteers within us, and so on. In the rest of this paper I want to consider some of the issues involved when we try to adapt our usual standards to judge those we think may be divided against themselves. Although she only looks like a self-deceiver from certain angles, the case of Lorelei Lee and Mr. Jennings could be an example.

> So Mr. Jennings helped me quite a lot and I stayed in his office about a year when I found out that he was not the kind of gentleman that a young girl is safe with. I mean one evening when I went to pay a call on him at his apartment, I found a girl who really was famous all over Little Rock for not being nice. So when I found out that girls like that paid calls on Mr. Jennings I had quite a bad case of histerics and my mind was really a blank and when I came out of it, it seems that I had a revolver in my hand and it seems that the revolver had shot Mr. Jennings.[12]

Suppose that I (Lorelei) claim—and really act as though I believed—that my mind was a blank when I shot Mr. Jennings. The trouble starts here, because whatever doubts people might have, nobody—not even an eye-witness—can fairly contradict this. I *say* that I remember nothing (and therefore must have acted like an automaton). In the circumstances it is quite credible, at least, that I had an emotional shock. Other people—occasionally people known to be honest and *compos mentis*—claim stories like mine now and then. And finally (and this is the crux) what I did would not have been done by the sweet girl I claim to be, if she had been conscious and in control. The author of *Gentlemen Prefer Blondes* may unfairly give my game away to her readers, first by suggesting in several ways that I am not so sweet and later by making me tell the truth about the Jennings incident. (See below.) But no one in Little Rock at the trial would have such an insight. In that situation, to deny my story is to prejudge me: the prosecution's job but no one else's. If instead we start from scratch, a lot of different things could be true, and the right verdict varies with them.

    (1) Maybe my mind *was* a blank, entirely, when Mr. Jennings got shot. No part of me was aware of anything. Even in this case the issue is not quite simple, because different stories are possible about motive. They entail different pictures of me which, if not moral judgments strictly, come very close: considerations that should not affect whether you blame or punish or exonerate me but that might well, and wisely, affect Mr. Henry Spoffard's

eventual choice of me as a wife, or anybody's choice of me as a children's nurse. In fact, whether my story is true or a lie, I seem to have told the one that washes me cleanest:

(1a) I blacked out and acted automatically, *purely* because of the shock of my awful discovery. It made me go wrong, as a machine might. We cannot blame whatever it was of me that shot Mr. Jennings (call it K, for "killer"): one does not for example blame a computer struck by lightning, if it then does something disastrous. And all the rest of me, it seems, had no part in the shooting at all.

My "histerics" might appear suspiciously well-directed, if this is my story. Why shoot Mr. Jennings instead of (say) flailing about, making a noise? Where did I get the revolver? But we could account for that, and exonerate me, by pointing out that this is quite a plausible disruption of several programs a nice Arkansas girl might have about her: for example, shooting at a villain to save her honor. (The gun was in my bag.) Ideally, too, all trace of the disruption has now vanished: I am my sweet self again.

But a blanked mind might have been useful too—even necessary, for a girl with inhibitions—if I had really *meant* to shoot Mr. Jennings. This suggests other possible stories, even if the mental blank was real. For example:

(1b) an anger-and-revenge program (call it K, too) blacked out the conscious "me" so as to get on with the job. Or the blackout was caused by my shock, but K used it. K's behavior (we may suppose) was still automatic: no part of me was aware that it was happening. So nobody and nothing seem precisely to blame. On the other hand if I had such a program anywhere about me, waiting for a shock to set it off, I am less lovely than in story (1a). Apart from making me potentially a danger to know, K has no doubt already affected what I am: colored my thoughts about people (I do tend to *imagine* shooting them dead whenever they cross me) and—through such thoughts or without them—in small "safe" ways biased what I do. It may be really why I carry a revolver.

A further refinement: if my blacked-out inhibitions included moral ones, I am a nicer girl than if they were only prudential. (Probably. Certain moral principles might be nastier than none at all.) Interpretation (1b) by the way illustrates a point I have made before about self-deception: we seem to expect more of that concept than of deception in the "weak" sense between two parts of oneself. Both (1a) and (1b) would be this; and provided we knew they were what was happening, we would not normally use "self-deception" of either.

These are (more or less) psychoanalytic stories; and many others of that form might fit the externals. It would depend on what I was like. But instead of any one of these tales, we could postulate several ''McDougall'' stories:[13] different cognitively if in no other way. It might be that

(2) the shooter, K, was a *conscious* ''splinter,'' still awake when all other awareness had gone. It had enough autonomy to aim and fire at Mr. Jennings. My (Lorelei's) experience of doing this—a thing that did not exist in the earlier stories—is unknown to the main conscious ''me.'' All ''I'' remember is seeing Mr. Jennings with his guest, and then Mr. Jennings bleeding on the floor. If we parallel (1a) and make me as nice as possible, then

(2a) K appeared, and acted so regrettably, only (once again) because a shock temporarily disrupted my real nature. This passed, and K is now no more, except perhaps for a buried memory. But if we follow (1b), then

(2b) in *some* form the conscious shooter of Mr. Jennings was already part of me. It may never before have been a conscious part; or it may have been conscious before, but never cognitively split off: those daydreams of shooting anyone who crossed me. (Compare ''B'' of McDougall's/Morton Prince's ''BCA.'')[14] In fact until the shock and again after the shooting, the story could be exactly like (1b). K might also, while consciously aiming and firing, have been guided only *un*consciously by those parts of the project that make it attempted murder, in revenge. (I seem to have hit the lung, probably aiming for the heart: see below.) A cat will scratch if you make a feint at it; assuming the cat is conscious, maybe K experienced the act like that: a natural movement without moral coloring. Or it may have seemed equivalent to a slap, because its deadliness was not part of the experience; or like killing a fly, not a person; or target shooting. Once we postulate consciousness, we may posit different parts of the project which it might affect. In theory, it might even be that

(2c) K was (most unusually) a full dissociated personality in action, ''Eve Black'' to ''my'' ''Eve White,''[15] with a past and probably a future; aware of all the issues including the fact that if ''I'' knew, ''I'' would condemn the shooting and try to stop it. Typically K would disagree articulately: Mr. Jennings deserved to be shot, for betrayal.

If (2c) turned out to be true, ''I'' could still protest: ''*That* Lorelei isn't me! I know nothing about her! I hate what she did! You can't hold her against me!'' Fair enough, but the best of a bad job. Killer-Lorelei lives too near, and is not a desirable connection. (2c) however assumes so rare a condition that its main use is oblique: to help us understand the other possibilities by comparison. For example, if we want to choose between "Freud" and "McDougall" stories, we need what (2c) provides, but not the other cases, or hardly ever the others. We must be able to identify K, the part that did the shooting, independently of that shooting's outward appearance; and also independently of my statement that my mind was a blank. For these fit either version (in the McDougall cases my mind would not really have been altogether blank, but that is how it would seem to the ''me'' that reports it). And in (1a), (2a), and (1b), K's identity seems fixed entirely by these things, so far as we can know. (2b)-stories would usually be the same: I think they could only, perhaps, provide something better in a few special cases where K was a borderline near-personality. Again this seems a thing we cannot usually expect, if indeed one can distinguish such a case from (2c).

But consciousness, we usually think, is what permits memory. Memory can sometimes, given a few physical conditions,[16] establish both a person's presence and consciousness at some past time. (The FitzDolphin Doggerel is told only by the earl to his presumptive heir, on the heir's seventh birthday. A strange man has turned up who claims *he* is the real earl: the present earl's elder brother who vanished in Africa in 1937.) It might also establish the "presence," that is, consciousness, of a particular personality. And even if K were less than a personality, K's experience of the shooting—if K had one—might have left a record, buried from "me." Suppose you hypnotize me and unearth it, so that I (Lorelei, incorporating "me") can tell you how it was. You check my story with witnesses, if any, also fingerprints, footprints, entry and exit wounds. I have got it right. Does that not vindicate McDougall, at least in this case? No. Especially where abnormalities such as hypnosis and "histerics" are concerned, we should not trust our usual ideas about memory. There seems no reason a priori why we might not have unearthed the record of *un*conscious behavior. It might feel unlike a usual memory; but so might the first example. It might feel the same. The *content* could be the same in every detail whether I took it in consciously or not; for consciousness is that mode of thinking about a certain content which makes one's thinking into experience. It cannot be part of the content itself.

Furthermore, if we are interested mainly in moral verdicts on the affair, we should remember that (i) ''I''—the main conscious self—am guiltless in all these stories; and (ii) as I said above, the emotional and intellectual content of K's whole project, as it works itself out, may be the same whether anyone or anything experienced it or not.[17] Its role in my overall nastiness or niceness therefore should, on the face of it, be the same in either case. And (iii) if we are after something to punish or blame, consciousness does make K in (2b) more like a moral agent, but only in one way. What we really need to know is whether this K can choose between different courses of action—the old free-will problem with one of the new twists. And that, I think, is an impossible question, because "choose" in this context is messy beyond all logical tidying up. If we define it behaviorally, we lose the element that interests us: the *sine qua non* of a moral agent, whatever this may be. One could in theory simulate any series of K's "choices" (or anybody's), using only determined sequences and perhaps some random ones. Nor does it matter that these "choices" are goal-directed and involve a rational use of symbols: consider a chess-playing computer. Again if we define it negatively, we shall never get there: "Choice is acting without this constraint and this and this . . ."; the set is open-ended. The only other possible way I think is to try a paradigm, but this either begs the question or rejects it. "Choice is how moral agents make their moves, when they act in that capacity." Our paradigm? Of course a normal, whole human being. *Yes, but what else will do?*

Sartre would say "any consciousness," but he gives no reason that makes sense to me. And if he were right, the question would not arise, for his theory of consciousness will allow no K, unconscious or conscious, to exist. It is true that the only kind of K we are likely to accept at once as a moral agent is a personality: B of "BCA" or Eve Black; and this is perhaps the only kind we would also accept at once as conscious. But we should not therefore assume that the second condition establishes the first. An Eve Black is more like a whole person than a lesser "splinter" is in every way, perhaps; certainly in more than the evidence of consciousness. Until we can specify better what makes our paradigm moral agent into a paradigm, *any* extrapolation from it, so far as we can tell, may go out of bounds. The only thing we can safely say is that the farther we go, the more we risk being wrong.

So even if we could tell them apart when we met them, there might be nothing to prefer, evaluatively, between an unconscious K and a conscious one; or between any two that are conscious of different selections from the same program. And this seems true whether we are evaluating someone generally (would I be good for the children?) or assessing guilt (should I—or any part of me—be punished for shooting Mr. Jennings?). Nevertheless if you ask people which they prefer, they tend to say—without being sure why—that a conscious incubus seems worse than one like it in all other ways, but unconscious.

For any particular pair this now seems like prejudice (or aesthetic taste). But it could stem from an intuition worth considering: that the more a thing is emotionally and intellectually like a whole person, the likelier it is *both* to be conscious *and* to have power for good or ill in the world. I am assuming that it has a human-type body (or such a body has it). If so, the chance that either of a similar pair of Ks is conscious will become greater, as both (equally) become more dangerous. Above some level or beyond some scope there might always be consciousness. This is another issue than whether our dangerous being—animal, vegetable, or mineral—is a moral agent. I think we have some hope of knowing what it means; perhaps even of deciding for or against it.

How, though? If I say a paradigm definition of "choice" (of the moral sort) is no use when we consider K, if I find the very issue incoherent, why do I not say that "Can K be conscious?" is an impossible question too? For we also take a normal whole human being as our paradigm here, I think. At least one strong tradition, the behaviorist, would find little to choose between them. (The "power" or "danger" question seems different: something one would decide—as far as anything can be decided—operationally, in terms of goals and behavior. But I shall not go into that here.) If, as I maintain, there may be no external difference between cases (1a) and (2a), or (1b) and (2b), is it not really nonsense trying to distinguish them?

If it is, not only my Lorelei stories so far (and a few more to come) but my general account of self-deception seem to be at risk. But I think it is not, for the following reasons.

First, though we may sometimes use a paradigm to define "conscious," it is not an unanalyzed paradigm. We can explain what it is about a normal, whole human being that we mean, when we say that she or he is conscious. And if we do not do so in terms of any specific thought content, or any specific physical or mental state, that is because it would be a logical mistake rather like the mistake of treating "exists" as a predicate. "Lorelei exists" tells us nothing about Lorelei's nature. The name might stand for a color or a car model (the 1984 Ford Lorelei) or the latest thing physicists predicate of quarks. What it does is tell us that, if it is true, there is in the world *something* we may truly say of Lorelei: "Lorelei has a hatchback" for example. "Lorelei is conscious"— to borrow Nagel's expression (his longer one, which I prefer)[18]— "Lorelei is conscious" tells us that, if it is true, there is something which it is like, for Lorelei, to be Lorelei. If we use "conscious" in the actual sense, there is such a thing now; if dispositionally, there is such a thing now and then, while Lorelei survives. And if we cannot point these things out to each other, we can at least point out Lorelei—though that is not yet enough to answer the objections of behaviorists.

We can also use this way of putting it to spell out what it would be for a "splinter" K to be cut off cognitively from Lorelei's "me." There is something that it is like for Lorelei to be "me," and this is distinct from what it would be like for Lorelei to be K. (I do not identify Lorelei with "me" or with K here; I predicate them of her.) We distinguish "me" from K by content: by definition, "I" took in no impression and keep no record of shooting Mr. Jennings. K (consciously or unconsciously) did the first; and if a record was made, did both. If hypnosis later makes "me" aware of K's record, there will then be—now and then—something that it is like for Lorelei to be "me" playing back what K recorded. And finally, if K was ever conscious, there was for that time something that it was like for Lorelei to be K. If K was not conscious, there never was.

Not long ago, many English-speaking philosophers felt bound to say, "But your account of 'conscious' is in language. Language is only correct or incorrect insofar as it follows rules. Rules must be formulated, learned, and used by reference to public criteria. It must therefore be something *outside* the black box you think you mean by 'the mind,' which allows you correctly to assert or deny that there is something it is like for Lorelei to be Lorelei, or to be K, or to be anything." To which, notoriously, the traditional answer is: not if I am Lorelei. "But this would mean you use one rule when you say anybody else is conscious (of shooting a gun, say) and a different one—if it is a rule at all—when you say *you* are. That is to misunderstand the nature of language."[19]

It is surely right to insist that communication depends on consistency; *inter alia*, first-, second-, and third-person ascriptions of a term must in some essential sense use it the same way. And surely we have a successful working vocabulary for experience: I mean terms such as "itch" and "what it feels like to shoot an Arkansas lawyer." If any of our uses of such terms seem anomalous, this must be an illusion and must be explained. But we must also explain why those uses that the logical-behaviorist redescribes, because "they cannot work in the way we think," are the very ones we usually think go to the heart of the matter: not only many first-person ascriptions, but many that the significantly termed "omniscient author" of fiction makes in the other forms.

Our traditional *rationale* for experience-language has sometimes led to exaggerated claims for introspection. But I think that in itself, when spelled out, it is not only acceptable but inevitable, if we are to be consistent. It rests on two principles that we all, including the behaviorists, seem to need: (i) *no event is uncaused* (at the macroscopic level, anyway) and (ii) *like causes have like effects* (and *vice versa*). We decide what they are by noting correlations that suggest, confirm, falsify general theses. To do this we must to some degree trust our memory for experiences, without always using public criteria to identify them. As Ayer points out,[20] to find public criteria for one experience we must rely on others; and we cannot check ad infinitum. Furthermore if—as it seems—we live by learning *from* experience how to react *to* experience, survival entails not just eventual, but quick, identification. If (i) and (ii) do not fit private events, this is inexplicable.

The alternative is to suppose that we do not really learn from, act on, or react to experience. Not even epiphenomenalism is allowed—that is, the thesis that all mental events are caused by physical events, but never *vice versa*. For even epiphenomenalism assumes a correlation between types of public and types of private events, which it seeks to explain; and if we cannot rely on memory, we cannot identify types of private events so as to correlate them.

This is the stuff that skeptical arguments are made of. Compare Russell's "For all we know the world—just as it is—might have come into being five minutes ago."[21] Since evidence is not proof, it might not even be evidence. This steel-hard egg may really be no reason at all for thinking that the water has boiled thirty minutes, not five; and similarly this apparently familiar agony may be no reason for thinking that a jellyfish has stung me again, even if it comes with an experience I seem to remember as to how a jellyfish looks. I find skeptical arguments meaningful and unanswerable, so far as they go. But they are never arguments for a rival theory—a five-minute world, or a world where subjective and objective do not tally; for by an exactly parallel argument our usual theory—so far as we can tell—might be true.

Each set of private events is necessarily inaccessible to more than one person. (Like Nagel, I do not understand anyone who claims that private events do not exist.) But logical-behaviorists, like the rest, will use (i) and (ii) to cope with other inaccessibilities; for example the one that inspired Russell's argument, the fact that the past is necessarily out of reach. Altogether—and given that we do not abandon *all* theory, which is *always* vulnerable to skepticism—there simply seems no good reason to be inconsistent about (i) and (ii) when we think of experience, in the teeth of intuition and with no better theory in view.[22]

If (i) and (ii) hold, we have linguistic rules that fit all ascriptions of experience. Principles (i) and (ii) allow me to assume that if you—being human too—are attacked by the same kind of jellyfish, your experience will be like mine. "What it feels like to be stung by a black-dotted jellyfish" may then legitimately stand for a peculiar quality of agony. Principles (i) and (ii) justify my using the effects and causes of an experience to fix a reference to it, as we fix the reference to a past event by its effects.[23] Thus I can learn the words for it from other people; but this does not mean I must have any public criterion when I use them again later. Principles (i) and (ii) also justify a rival reference fixer for later occasions: memory. (Naturally we may have problems in particular cases if reference fixers disagree; this is not fatal.) A thick network of simile confirms all this. "Like being lashed by electric nettles" I have said, of the black-dotted-jellyfish sting; and other victims (who knew nettles and whips and electric shocks) said "YES!"

A fortiori "conscious"—meaning that a subject has some, but no specified, experience—will therefore not mean something outside the black box; will not be meaningless; and we will ascribe it to others when they show what we think are (public) causal correlatives of experiences. (These need not be only behavioral; they can be physiological, too.) By principle (ii) we should know the correlatives of human experience best; so it makes sense if we take as paradigm a normal human being. But (ii) also gives us the chance to argue for or against extrapolations: a bat? a computer, if it behaved like HAL in Arthur C. Clarke's *2001*? a "splinter"? We may well decide of a given case or class of cases that the evidence is inconclusive: I have said that I think this is true of most postulated "splinters." But because we are talking about evidence, not what it is evidence for, the distinction between "There is something it is like for Lorelei to be K" and "There is no such thing" is still real. Since physiology may yield causal correlatives when behavior does not, we might even still learn to distinguish them in practice.

"Freud" and "McDougall" stories seem to be the only types in which "My mind was really blank" may be both literal and sincere. But there are also the mental states that might go with a lie. Some of these, too, would leave me innocent and sweet; others not guilty, but less admirable; still others guilty, or otherwise bad, in varying degree. The least harmful story would as usual be that the shock threw me out of control, so that I moved in ways quite foreign to my nature. With distress, I now remember this happening: my mind was not a blank. But I am not articulate enough to describe how it really was and am afraid of being misunderstood or not believed. And I am sure of one thing: I was as helpless as if story (1a) had been true. So I tell that, as a metaphor for the truth. Or I have a very blurred memory of what happened, and I tell (1a) as a metaphor for *that*. It is the kind of story I may come to believe more firmly as I tell it, however; and I might also suspect this before I start, and do it partly in the hope of a more comfortable inner state as well. You may blame me for attempted self-deception if so, because here you have a standard-looking moral agent trying to *make* a split. (Note that if it succeeds, ''self'' is still not reflexive: Forgetful-Lorelei does not know what I, her deceiver, have concealed from her.) Or I may feel that although this once, as I quite well remember, I felt and acted like a murderess, it cannot be typical of me: I so much disapprove of violence. Story (1a) surely gives a fairer picture of the *real* me. (A Sartre story.[24]) This shades into: I cannot admit that my sweet image of myself—by which I have lived for so long—is broken. So now I lie because I can see no way to go on, except to behave as if the unthinkable were not so. This is like a Fingarette story, and as Fingarette points out, it is the person with moral scruples who gets into this kind of mess, not the whole-hearted scoundrel.[25]

In fact nearly all the ''split'' stories split me along lines drawn by moral tension. One may conceive of splits where fear or obsessive prudence replaces conscience, but we tend to think they are less typical. If so, it seems that we may add yet another kind of contrariness to our impression of self-deceptive behavior, one I have not spelled out before. Too many possible stories fit in every case, and they lead to incompatible moral judgments; but most of these stories on their own also divide the individual into better and worse components that are at war. It makes fair judgment doubly difficult.

The wholehearted scoundrel or sociopath is the main exception to this. The time has come to unmask Lorelei. Worn out by the logistics of a double life which leaves her no time for sleep, she goes to see Dr. Freud in Vienna.

> Dr. Froyd . . . seems to know how to draw a girl out quite a lot. I mean I told him things that I really would not even put in my diary. So then he seemed very very intreeged at a girl who always seemed to do everything she wanted to do. So he asked me if I never wanted to do a thing that I did not do. For instance did I ever want to do a thing that was really vialant. . . . So then I said I had, but the bullet only went in Mr. Jennings lung and came right out again. So then Dr. Froyd looked at me and looked at me . . . and it really seems as if I was quite a famous case.

You may also wonder how Little Rock judged Lorelei, without the help of Dr. Freud. In its way, this, too, illustrates the ambiguity of possibly split behavior. The District Attorney called Lorelei names she really would not put in her diary, and ''all the time he was calling me all those names . . . he really thought I was.'' And yet, faced with exactly the same Lorelei, ''The gentlemen in the jury all cried when my lawyer pointed at me and told them that they practically all had had either a mother or a sister. So the jury was only out three minutes and then they came back and acquitted me.''

NOTES

1. For a short discussion of the Socratic Paradox, related to self-deception: M. R. Haight, *A Study of Self-Deception* (Sussex: Harvester Press; Atlantic Highlands, N.J.: Humanities Press, 1980). For one on *akrasia* in Aristotle: J. L. Ackrill, *Aristotle the Philosopher* (Oxford: Oxford University Press, 1981), 145 ff. Aristotle's discussion of *akrasia* (''weakness of will'') is mainly in *Nichomachean Ethics*, bk. 7.

2. Jean-Paul Sartre, *L'Etre et le Néant* (Paris: NRF/Gallimard, 1943), translated into English by Hazel E. Barnes as *Being and Nothingness* (London: Methuen, 1947). All quotes and page numbers refer to this translation. The definition of bad faith as a lie to oneself appears on p. 48. Sartre's theory (spelled out mainly in *Being and Nothingness* and illustrated in many of his novels and plays) cannot adequately be summed up in a footnote. For a longer critical discussion see Haight, *A Study of Self-Deception*, chap. 5. But—leaving aside his arguments—here are a few conclusions that he seems to think may be derived a priori from an understanding of what it is to be a consciousness or ''Being-for-Itself'':

(a) All motivated behavior is conscious.

(b) Consciousness is translucent.

(c) Consciousness entails freedom: a Being-for-Itself is always responsible for its (that is, her or his) actions.

(d) This freedom and responsibility to which we are ''condemned'' is what bad faith typically tries to deny. But since a Being-for-Itself must *know* it is free, to do this is to try to lie to oneself; and (a) and (b)—which add up to the thesis that cognitive dissociation is impossible—doom any such project from the start.

(e) Bad faith nevertheless exists, because ''the nature of consciousness simultaneously is to be what it is not and not to be what it is'' (*Being and Nothingness*, 70).

3. Haight, *Study of Self-Deception*.

4. Ibid., especially chap. 2.

5. Ibid., chap. 9.

6. Ibid., chap. 6.

7. Sartre, *Being and Nothingness*, 49.

8. Haight, *Study of Self-Deception*, 111 ff. A good example is Emily Brontë's last illness, as reported by her sister Charlotte. The relevant letters and journals are quoted in Margaret Lane, *The Brontë Story* (London: Fontana, 1969).

9. For more examples: Haight, *Study of Self-Deception*, especially chap. 6.

10. A traditional formulation of this might be: ''Since I have no direct access to any mind but my own, how can I ever know for sure that other people have (conscious) minds at all? Or if they have, how can I ever be sure what they are thinking?'' A Split or Extra Mind problem arises when we add ''—or how far the 'main' mind knows all a person's thoughts?''

11. Haight, *Study of Self-Deception*, 147 ff.

12. Anita Loos, *Gentlemen Prefer Blondes* (London: Brentano, 1926), 48–49. Later quotes are from pages 155–156, 51, and 49.

13. See, for example, William McDougall's *Outline of Abnormal Psychology* (London: Methuen, 1926), passim. McDougall suggests that dissociations that a Freudian would see as unconscious are in fact split-off *conscious* thought. He was much influenced here by Dr. Morton Prince's studies of multiple personality: clear evidence (it would seem) that this kind of split can happen.

14. Morton Prince, *The Unconscious: The Fundamentals of Human Personality Normal and Abnormal* (New York: Macmillan, 1921), 545–663; McDougall, *Outline of Abnormal Psychology*, 287–289. "B" was one of the dissociated personalities from whose case McDougall extrapolates down to lesser "splinters." She was aware of the thoughts of the other personality, "A," but would not acknowledge either "A's" thoughts or acts as her own. "C" is the label given to the whole woman before "B" split off, and the only thoughts of "C's" which "B" would acknowledge were certain recurring daydreams of rebellion and escape.

15. Or "B" to my "A." "Eve" is described in C. H. Thigpen and H. Cleckley, "A Case of Multiple Personality," *Journal of Abnormal and Social Psychology* (January 1954), 135–151—*inter alia*. The case and other sources are discussed in Haight, *Study of Self-Deception*, 33 ff. and 133 ff.

16. Bernard Williams, *Problems of the Self* (London: Cambridge University Press, 1973), 15 ff.: memory alone is not enough without physical continuity.

17. The "Freud *versus* McDougall" issue is discussed in Haight, *Study of Self-Deception*, 36 ff. Some accounts of emotion might rule out an emotion that is not felt, as absurd. What I mean by unconscious emotion—anger, say—is a physical (mainly brain) process, whose intentional aspect is the same as that of anger one feels (e.g., it is directed against the same person), and whose effect on behavior is similar (e.g., it makes one shoot Mr. Jennings). Happily we have, in computers, not only theoretical but real grounds for supposing that there can be intentional, goal-directed processes that are not conscious.

18. Thomas Nagel, "What Is It Like to Be a Bat?" *Philosophical Review* (October 1971). The title is an example of his shorter (and more ambiguous) formulation.

19. The locus classicus for this approach is Ludwig Wittgenstein, *Philosophical Investigations* (New York: Macmillan, 1953), sections 288 ff. and 293 ff.

20. A. J. Ayer, "Could Language Be Invented by a Robinson Crusoe?" in *The Private Language Argument*, ed. O. R. Jones (London: Macmillan, 1971), 53 ff.

21. See, for example, his treatment of this suggestion in "On the Experience of Time" and "Sensation and Imagination," *Monist* (1915): 224 and 34–35.

22. This is, of course, a version of the "argument from analogy," *locus classicus* chap. 12 of J. S. Mill, *An Examination of Sir William Hamilton's Philosophy* (London: Longman's, Green, 1865). It has often been criticized, but where criticism succeeds, I believe that it is directed against the claim that Mill's argument disposes of the *skeptical* "Other Minds" problem. Since I think *no* positive theory is proof against skeptical arguments of this sort, I make no such claim.

23. A "reference fixer" identifies a subject for reference on a given occasion, but it is not self-contradictory to deny it of that subject. See Saul K. Kripke, "Naming and Necessity," in *Semantics and Natural Language*, ed. Davidson and Harmon (Dordrecht: Reidel, 1972), 274 ff.

24. Compare the pederast in *Being and Nothingness*, 63–64: "It frequently happens that this man, while recognizing his homosexual inclination, while avowing each and every particular misdeed which he has committed, refuses with all his strength to consider himself *'a paederast'*. His case is always 'different', peculiar; there enters into it something of a game, of chance, of bad luck. . . ."

25. Herbert Fingarette, *Self-Deception* (London: Routledge and Kegan Paul, 1969). His theory is discussed in Haight, *Study of Self-Deception*, chap. 7. (See also this volume, "Alcoholism and Self-Deception.") Self-deception occurs when an individual is drawn into some "engagement in the world" that "in part or in whole, the person cannot avow as *his* engagement, for to avow it would apparently lead to such disruptive, distressing consequences as to be unmanageably destructive to . . . that currently achieved synthesis of engagements which is the person" (87). "Having paid due attention to the element of spiritual cowardice and inner warfare in the movement into self-deception, we must also appreciate that this . . . presupposes a person with a certain integrity" (139–140).

Self-Deception, Inauthenticity, and Weakness of Will

David Kipp

SELF-DECEPTION: INTRODUCTORY CONSIDERATIONS

This study aims to clarify the nature of so-called 'self-deception' by tracing the psychological, historical, and ideological connections that exist between it and the closely related notions of 'inauthenticity' and 'weakness of will.' Behind the study is a basic conviction that literal self-deception, or literally 'deceiving' oneself, is impossible, and that 'self-deceivers' are really either sincerely ignorant or strategically dishonest about whatever they *seem* to have 'deceived' themselves into not knowing. Most characteristically, they appear concerned to uphold an acceptably esteemed social image, steadfastly shamming belief that things are 'so' in order to stave off what they regard as an intolerable loss of face that would result from admitting (to others) that things are 'not so.'[1] Although the correctness of this conviction is not presupposed by the present study, the results of the study will lend support to the conviction. In any event, because the phenomenon called 'self-deception' may not actually *be* what its name literally *suggests*, the term 'self-deception' will be used as a name for the phenomenon, while the term 'literal self-deception' will be used to identify what that name questionably suggests about the phenomenon (i.e., that people can somehow 'deceive' themselves into not knowing, or only half-knowing, something that they know, or suspect, but find unpleasant).

The need for a study of the present sort is suggested by the fact that both self-deception and Existentialist inauthenticity seem somehow bound up with attaching undue importance to other people's opinions about oneself, and by the fact that Sartre's apparent conflation of self-deception and inauthenticity invites reflection on Heidegger's earlier—and perhaps more characteristically Existentialist[2]—theory of inauthenticity. More directly, however, it is suggested by the fact that both Sartrean self-deception and Heideggerian inauthenticity are closely related to the traditional problem of 'weakness of will.' Just as self-deceivers are thought to be too 'weak' to face what they 'know' to be true, so the inauthentic are thought to be too 'weak' to become the selves that they 'know' they ought to be. Hence, it seems advisable to begin any exploration of the links between self-deception and inauthenticity with an exploration of the problem of weakness of will. Although this beginning exploration may appear, initially, somewhat protracted, it is crucial to uncovering the roots of the problems of self-deception and inauthenticity, and its various steps will ultimately lead straight into these problems.

Here it should be noted that the dramatis personae of the following analyses include things called Socratic rationalism, Christian fideism, Modern collectivism, and Modern individualism. These are obviously 'generalizations,' intended to signify nothing more than characteristically predominant aspects of the complex intellectual and historico-cultural orientations concerned. Their precise meanings, beyond those conveyed by common usage and by dictionary definitions of their substantive terms, must be left to emerge in context. Also, the interconnections among these broad orientations are historically 'dramatized' in an obviously oversimplistic way, so as to throw into clearer relief the centrally relevant *psychological* structures that underlie them. Throughout, psychological and historical factors are interrelated in mutually illuminating ways, but the burden of the argument is carried by the former.

WEAKNESS OF WILL, SOCRATIC
RATIONALISM, AND CHRISTIAN FIDEISM

In its traditional context, the problem of weakness of will presupposes a threefold division of the psyche into faculties of passion, will, and reason. Passion includes the totality of 'irrational' impulses associated with the body, such as instincts, drives, emotions, or sensual pleasures and pains; will implies a separate, 'volitional' agency capable of translating the results of rational decisions and projects into appropriate personal actions; and reason includes the various 'intellectual' abilities associated with the mind, such as thought, cognition, memory, imagination, or self-consciousness. Further, the problem presupposes the view that reason naturally directs an overall, personal pursuit of the 'good,' which ultimately derives its various concrete strivings from 'knowledge'-based evaluative thought, and that will naturally subserves reason's evaluative assessments, i.e., conforms its volitional allegiance to them as soon as they are made or changed.

Now, the problem of weakness of will arises from the widespread belief that people can often be 'tempted' by passion into acting in ways clearly opposed both to their reason's assessment of what they 'ought' to do and to what they themselves later insist they 'really' wanted, and tried, to do. Under the assumption that will naturally aligns itself with reason, there seem to be only two ways of explaining such cases: either the people concerned have not accurately described their relevant experiences (whether through lack of discrimination or lack of honesty) or they are to be seen as victims of weakness of will. Historically, what may be called 'Socratic rationalism' favored the first explanation, claiming that such actions are, in fact, always immediately preceded by concrete rational evaluation that they 'ought' to be done. (For example, the difference between the captured spy who finally betrays secrets under increasingly severe torture and the one who remains silent until death is not that the former's will was weak and the latter's strong, but that the former's rational evaluation of what he ought to do finally changed once the suffering reached a certain intensity, while the latter's did not.) On the other hand, what may be called 'Christian fideism' favored the second explanation, assuming that weakness of will was both possible and frequent. But why was that?

For Socratic rationalism, the faculty distinguished as reason was 'natural' reason, whose proper function was to discover and follow 'evident' truth solely according to its own lights; while for Christian fideism, that faculty was 'mere' reason, whose proper function was to accept and subserve 'revealed' truth as embodied in Christian dogma. Thus Christian fideism required reason to adopt certain guiding assumptions not in consequence of rational evidence, or 'grounded' belief, but in consequence of religious faith, or 'willed' belief. The cosmological myth that anchored Christian morality was to be 'believed' through willing to believe, just as God, one's neighbor, and one's enemy were to be 'loved' through willing to love; consequently, 'weakness of will,' especially under temptation by the passion of pride or vanity, was primarily to blame for failures to believe or to love as commanded. Christian fideism, then, obviously had its use for the notion of weakness of will. But how intelligible is such a notion?

From a Socratic-rationalist viewpoint, one must deny not only the possibility of weakness of will, but also the very existence of will as a faculty possessing independent 'decisional' power, i.e., power to give or withhold 'assent' to rational evaluations (or to anything else). Reason itself 'decides' or 'concludes,' not through an act of will (or quasi will), but through undergoing an experience of 'being decided' or 'being forced to conclude' by what it recognizes as the 'truth' about situationally relevant facts and values, i.e., by as much relevant 'knowledge' as is accessible to it at the time. What one introspectively experiences as the phenomenon of will is merely a 'felt' quality of the degree of certainty behind rational evaluations and of the degree of directness and acceptance of the self-expressive flow of rational evaluations into appropriate actions.[3] There is no such thing as 'will' that might interpose independent decisional force between rational evaluation and action, nor can the specifically characteristic experience of rational cognition be regarded as an 'action' that will (or anything else) performs. Hence, even if will could somehow determine action independently of rational evaluation, cognitions or beliefs, not being actions, could not be determined by it, and 'willed' belief would remain impossible. For Socratic rationalism, then, both Christian 'faith' and Christian 'weakness of will' are clearly unintelligible. But could they perhaps be made intelligible from another, more Christian viewpoint?

If the assumption that will naturally subserves reason is denied, so that will might be presumed capable of independently determining belief or action, it is hard to see what could enable will to 'choose' beliefs or actions contrary to those indicated by rational cognition or evaluation. 'Choosing' seems to require 'rational' processes of entertaining, understanding, remembering, comparing, and evaluating, without which will would be 'blind'; but how could will avail itself of reason without necessarily arriving at reason's relevant choices? If, however, will is thought somehow to possess a 'reason' of its own, then will and reason cannot be seen as two complementary 'faculties' within an autonomous psyche, but must be seen as two autonomous 'subpsyches' within one brain; and the whole problem of the relation between will and reason recurs within each of them, rather than being at all resolved. If, alternatively, will is thought of, not as being able to 'choose,' but as somehow simply able to 'express itself' compellingly through contrarational belief or action, then what is 'expressed' could hardly be just empty 'will,' but would have to be some particular passion that informs will, such as Nietzschean will-to-power or Dostoevskian will-to-caprice. But if will could thus be informed sometimes by reason and sometimes by passion, yet cannot itself be either reason or passion, what is the point in worrying about will at all? Rather than being something that could independently 'decide' between reason and passion, it would be little more than an inert psychical 'funnel' through which either reason or passion would flow down into belief or action. But if the irrelevance of will is the logical outcome of the attempt to deny that will naturally subserves reason, the notion of weakness of will hardly seems likely to become intelligible. What, then, is to be said about the state of affairs that weakness of will was meant to explain?

Retreat could always be made, of course, to Socratic rationalism, which sees reason as able to take existing passions into account when making its ultimately decisive evaluative choices, and which sees 'regrettable' choices as resulting from a kind of 'weakness of reason' known as error or ignorance. But might not Christian fideism still find some way to reformulate itself intelligibly regarding the issue in question?

If the notion of weakness of will is a logical dead end, and if recourse to a kind of weakness of reason leads back to Socratic rationalism, then Christian fideism must apparently have recourse to weakness of passion. 'Willing' to believe or to love thus becomes 'wanting,' or passionately desiring, to believe or to love, and failures to believe or to love as commanded are caused by a comparative weakness of Christian passion in the face of some other, 'tempting' passion. Christian faith and love are thus both 'installed' and 'defended' by Christian passion, and the life of the soul is to be seen, not as a struggle to separate truth from error, but as a struggle to defend Christian passion from tempting passion. Yet just how intelligible is that 'struggle'?

Here it is necessary to ask just what 'leads' the struggle, and how. If Christian passion is only one among many competing passional 'upsurges' in the psyche, and if reason remains at best a helpless, irrelevant 'spectator,' then Christian passion is thrown back upon its own inherent strength, and nothing can 'struggle' to defend it. Either it is inherently strong enough to prevail over competing passions or it is not, and any seeming 'struggle' is but the dance of a puppet on passional strings pulled by God or fate. If, on the other hand, real struggle is to be possible, as Christian fideism generally presupposes, it has to be 'led' by the belief that Christian passion 'ought' to prevail, and such belief has to be 'grounded' independently of the concrete successes and failures of Christian passion (since tying it to those successes and failures would make it a mere epiphenomenon of a pulled 'puppet string'). This, however, amounts to saying that Christian passion could be 'defended' (against competing passions) only on the basis of properly rational belief. Thus Christian-fideist recourse to the notion of weakness of passion, like that to the notion of weakness of will, leads ultimately back to Socratic rationalism. But where does that leave the Christian-fideist notions of 'willed' belief (in the Christian cosmological myth) and of 'willed' love (of God, one's neighbor, and one's enemy)?

From a Socratic rationalist viewpoint, it seems inherently impossible to believe that one 'ought' to believe something that one does not independently recognize as believable, or to believe that one 'ought' to love something that one does not independently recognize as lovable. Despite the grammatical ambiguity that surrounds the verbs 'believe' and 'love' (and that reflects the natural self-expressive flow of cognition into action), the indispensably characteristic bases of the psychical states that those verbs refer to are not actively 'performed,' but are passively 'undergone.' One can, however, 'wish' to be able to believe or to love something because one does believe or love something else; for example, if one believes that one is a great painter, one may wish to be able to believe that one is not going blind; or if one loves flying in airplanes, one may wish to be able to love working as an airline steward. This kind of 'wishing' is not random fantasy, but arises from rational belief that the wished-for state of affairs would, if actual, serve as a means to realizing or preserving something that one believes 'ought' to be. Christian fideism, of course, would hardly characterize itself as mere 'wishful thinking' of this sort. But then what else could it possibly be? Inevitably, if not unexpectedly, 'self-deception' suggests itself as the only remaining answer. Hence, it is necessary to probe a bit more deeply into the 'logic' of Christian fideism.

'Enlightened' people today often assume that Christian fideism, though clearly absurd to the sophisticated mind, was able to captivate the masses by a uniquely effective mixture of emotional and rational persuasion. The emotional persuasion took the form of a cosmological myth calculated to instill both strong desire for believing in it and strong fear of not believing in it; man's natural fear of death and longing for happiness were offered the hope of eternal life and heavenly bliss, while man's natural abhorrence of suffering was confronted with the threat of eternal damnation. The rationalized persuasion, however, was somewhat more subtle. First, all the things whose reality was essential to the credibility of the cosmological myth were carefully situated outside the scope of (normal) earthly experience: God was given transcendent existence beyond the sky, while Heaven, Hell, and the Last Judgment were relegated to a future after death or at the end of time. Thus a cosmological state of affairs was proclaimed that was either true or not true, that was inherently such as to make the question of its truth or nontruth a matter of intense human interest, but that was also inherently such as to preclude all (normal) 'this-worldly' verification of its truth or nontruth. Then the point was urged that, although the proclaimed state of affairs could not (now) be certainly 'known' to be true, it also could not (now) be certainly known to be not true; and this was conjoined to the point that the proclaimed state of affairs, quite reasonably, demanded, not knowledge-based belief, but rather 'willed' belief, or 'faith.' Finally, those points were hedged round with hints at a practical-minded, Pascalian-Jamesian logic of risk-taking prudence (i.e., the claim that one has really nothing to lose, and possibly everything to gain, by opting for Christian belief and acting accordingly).

Now, if 'willed' belief is actually impossible (as suggested earlier), what Christian-fideist 'faith' seems to demand is not that one actually *believes* that the Christian myth is true, but rather that one *hopes* that it is true and *acts as if* it were true. The Christian myth, after all, served to anchor a certain socio-moral code, and since socio-morality is less a matter of true belief than of right action, what counted most was how 'believers' *acted*, and not how they *believed*. Further, if 'willed' belief is actually impossible, yet if 'believers' are nevertheless commanded to will it, then it follows that they can do nothing but to will as much of what directly relates to the commanded belief as lies within their power, namely, *acting as if* they believed it. If, however, will inevitably subserves reason (as suggested earlier here), this means that those who act 'as if' they believe must still rationally believe that they 'ought' to act in that way. Given the sort of weaknesses that natural reason is prone to, the combination of emotional and rationalized persuasion that was sketched out in the preceding paragraph may often have sufficed to produce actual rational belief in such an 'ought.' However, it seems highly unlikely that Christian fideism could have succeeded so impressively as a world-historical phenomenon solely on the basis of persuasion of that sort. Thus it is necessary to probe beyond Christian fideism's other-worldly rationale, and to ask what sorts of this-worldly attraction it may have held for the faithful.

Obviously, one such attraction is a kind of 'existential' security that comes from collective solidarity under a clearly defined and authoritatively administered moral code (or 'way of life'). Another, originating in what Nietzsche and Scheler have diagnosed as 'resentment,'[4] is a kind of socio-moral vengeance that can be wrought upon the envied powerful and successful 'elite' of this world. Regardless of whether the Christian myth is true, acting as if one *believes* it to be true provides not only a face-saving excuse for those who must accept inferiority and impotence as their lot in this world, but also a resentful strategy for depriving the 'elite' of whatever pleasure or pride they may take in their position, and for intimidating them into a state of self-doubting guilt instead; in short, the weak and the insignificant of this world are praised as the truly good and blessed, while the strong and the significant are promised that they will 'get theirs' in the afterlife. Probably, as Nietzsche claimed, the second of these two this-worldly attractions is the key to Christian fideism's success as a world religion. Also, it clearly qualifies as an example of 'self-deception' in the sense given to that phenomenon in the opening paragraph of this study.

Inasmuch as exploration of the problem of weakness of will has ultimately led to an uncovering of self-deception at the core of Christian fideism, three important points about that self-deception should be noted. First, it is a mistake to assume that Christian fideist self-deception was *literal* self-deception in the modern irrationalist sense; instead, it was a conscious socio-moral strategy originating in a rationally perceived 'ought' on the part of both Church authorities and 'believers.' Second, what that strategy amounted to was a decision to compromise the integrity of the natural connection between belief and action by resorting to *hypocrisy* as a means to supposedly overriding *moralistic* ends. For the Church, whose socio-moral ambitions were un-Socratically vast, the important thing was not that people should be left to arrive at whatever beliefs their natural reason led them to, but that as many people as possible should be led to act in accordance with the Christian moral code. For 'believers,' whose sense of resentment fed on their sense of the injustice of their own lot in the world, shamming belief in the Christian myth was a (self-perceived) way of partly redressing the worldly moral balance. Third, the connection between Christian fideism and the problem of weakness of will now appears in a new light: rather than resulting from an inability of something called 'will' to effect what one 'really' believed one 'ought' to do, Christian-fideist 'moral lapses' typically resulted from privately or exceptionally indulging one's *real* moral beliefs, as opposed to publicly and generally pretending to endorse one's 'as if' (Christian) moral beliefs. With these points on record, the next step is to explore the problem of just what links, if any, can be discovered between Christian fideism and the modern irrationalist notion of self-deception.

SELF-DECEPTION, CHRISTIAN FIDEISM, AND MODERN COLLECTIVISM

Despite the incoherence of Christian fideism's demands for 'willed' belief and 'willed' love, and despite the irrationalism of its implicit (moralistically motivated) corrupting of the natural connection between belief and action, it retained a Socratic-rationalist belief in the objectivity of truth, and also presented a surface appearance of endorsing the Socratic-rationalist view that right belief leads to right action. The Christian moral code and the Christian myth were both presumed objectively true, and the emphasis on the need for 'willed' belief in them implied, as its surface justification, that right belief (regardless of whether installed through rational evidence or through will) would necessarily incline the—unfortunately sometimes 'weak'—will to right action. Because of this lingering element of Socratic rationalism, and because of the official Church's overcomfortable alliance with the worldly status quo, Christian fideism was destined to be overthrown (from within) by a radicalized version of the very sort of strategic hypocrisy, or 'self-deception,' that it had originally devised to win the allegiance of the masses.

If 'believers' could achieve the (self-perceived) moral end of inflicting face-saving socio-moral 'revenge' upon the elite of this world by feigning belief in certain authoritatively proclaimed, but personally unknowable, states of affairs, why should they stop there? Could they not do even better by setting *themselves* up as authoritative proclaimers of all sorts of states of affairs that they did not really believe true, but that they could *act as if* they believed true in order to achieve (self-perceived) 'moral' ends? And could not their sheer numerical superiority, as the 'massed' many over the 'elite' few, guarantee that anything they (collectively) *pretended* to believe true would have to be accepted as *being* true?[5] Aside from the bothersome fact that the elite already possessed a disproportionately large degree of available worldly power, the main obstacle to this creeping mass moral megalomania was posed by the notion of 'objective truth' that was central to both Christian fideism and Socratic rationalism (although rationally defensible only by the latter). In the course of attempting to overcome this obstacle, an increasingly unstable Christian fideism ultimately metamorphosed into what may be called 'Modern collectivism.'

Basically, an expedient revision of both the Socratic-rationalist and the Christian-fideist views of the psyche was undertaken. If Socratic rationalism had supposed that reason governs passion and will by subjecting passion to knowledge-based evaluative processes whose adjudications will naturally subserves; and if Christian fideism had pretended that will governs reason and passion by both installing 'belief' against reason and defending 'belief' against passion; then Modern collectivism needed to pretend that passion governs reason and will by 'dictating' independent passional ends that reason cannot but seek means for realizing and that will cannot but carry out. In taking this

position on the psyche, of course, Modern collectivism implicitly acknowledged that its 'belief' in the position was dictated by its own
passion and not by reason; yet it persistently churned out 'reasoned'
propaganda to support its claim that 'reasonings' about such matters
were only passion-dictated 'rationalizations.'

Modern collectivism's first task was to discredit the 'divine authority' that grounded objective truth in the Christian-fideist context. It
accomplished this by rationally exposing the inadequacy of the bases for
belief in the Christian myth, all the while pretending not to know that
(its own previous) Christian-fideist 'belief' was not real belief, but
shammed strategy, and thus covering up its own intent to radicalize that
strategy. Then it drew a distinction between the Church authorities and
the 'believers,' linking the authorities to the Socratic-rationalist aspects
of Christian fideism, and portraying them as deceitful oppressors who
had devised Christian fideism in order to trick 'believers' into accepting
as 'objective truth' certain fictions that served only the interests of the
'elite.' The 'believers,' meanwhile, were linked to the volitional-pas-
sional aspects of Christian fideism, and were portrayed as right-feeling
citizens, with legitimate moral grievances and aspirations, who had long
allowed themselves to be taken in by Christian fideism, but who would
now have to look for more 'earthly' means of obtaining moral redress.

The next task was to ensure that the way back to Socratic rationalism was effectively barred by a similar discrediting of the 'rational
authority' that grounded objective truth in the Socratic-rationalist context. As Socratic-rationalist reason was primarily associated with ultimate values and moral ends (and as Modern collectivism needed to
enlist 'instrumental' or 'technical' reason in its new-found moral strategy), 'values' and moral ends were distinguished from 'facts' and moral
means, and the Socratic-rationalist view that reason could disclose
objective truths about the former pair was pronounced absurd. Did not
Socratic-rationalist reason itself subserve an overall, passionate pursuit
of 'the good'? Was not 'the good' a meaninglessly empty notion until it
was informed by some more concrete passion, such as love of pleasure,
power, or rationality? Were not rational 'truths' totally ineffective until
reason itself was 'chosen' by passion, and were not passionate choices
of irrational 'truths' just as valid as a passionate choice of reason? Worse
yet, was not the foremost advocate of Socratic rationalism, namely
Plato, clearly an elitist oppressor whose motives for seeking to ground
objective truth in rational authority were as deceitfully manipulative as
those of the Christian-fideist authorities?[6] Finally, after having been so
cruelly tricked, in the name of so-called objective truth, by the Church
authorities, could self-respecting 'believers' ever again allow themselves

to be deprived of their 'natural' right to their *own* truths about values and moral ends?

Having thus apparently discredited objective truth in favor of 'passionate' truth, Modern collectivism needed to find some means for ensuring that the former 'believers' would not simply degenerate into anarchic 'free-thinkers,' but would all pretend, as a 'massed' many, to believe the same, strategically anti-elitist, things (about man, values, and moral ends). For this purpose, nothing was more suitable than a slightly revised version of the old Christian myth, which had already proven its psychological strength, and which the recently disillusioned 'believers' would still be psychologically predisposed to.[7] Heaven was brought down to earth, but kept unknowable by being located in an indefinitely far-off 'Utopian' future. God, too, was brought down to earth, but kept unknowable as the unseen director of human history, who 'revealed' his will solely through the beliefs and actions of his new 'chosen people' (the massed many). The Last Judgment, also brought down to earth, was presented as already underway, with the massed many winning ever-increasing success in their historical struggle to wreak 'divine justice' on the elite few. Finally, those who hesitated to pretend belief in the Collectivist myth were threatened with the special earthly 'Hell' of relentless persecution at the hands of the 'faithful.' Thus, the psychologically crucial inducement to 'belief' in the Collectivist myth was a greatly radicalized version of the old Christian-fideist appeal to the all-too-human passion of 'resentment,' along with a radicalized emphasis on the time-worn tactic of group-enforced intimidation of nonbelievers. Also, the old Christian-fideist notion of 'willed' belief was rehabilitated as a call for 'commitment' to the cause, while Pascalian-Jamesian 'risk-taking' prudence was appealed to through the prospect of 'getting with the strength' in a great historical battle.

Once again, then, massed 'believers' rallied round a new religious myth that they could not know to be true, and could only hope to be true, yet could *act as if* they believed true because they rationally concluded, on (self-perceived) 'socio-moral' grounds, that they 'ought' to act in that way. Interestingly enough, the sort of moral behavior encouraged by the Collectivist myth was neither Socratic-rationalist 'minding one's own business' nor Christian-fideist 'turning the other cheek,' but rather self-righteous social aggression according to belief in '(my) right needs might' that masks itself as belief in '(my) might makes right.' But how do all these things bear upon the modern irrationalist notion of self-deception?

First of all, just as the notion of weakness of will is a characteristically Christian-fideist one, the notion of literal self-deception is a characteristically Modern-collectivist one; hence, there is reason to suspect that it plays some part in the whole 'logic' of Modern collectivism. Further, since the logic of Modern collectivism closely parallels that of Christian fideism, and since both self-deception and weakness of will carry connotations of moral frailty, there is reason to suspect that self-deception, like weakness of will, serves to explain 'moral lapses' in a way that both appears consistent with the relevant 'myth' and tends to conceal the real nature of the 'lapses.' Could this be so?

Although Socratic rationalism was almost as much the bane of Christian fideism as of Modern collectivism, Christian fideism's ultimate reliance on 'objective truth,' and on the idea that right action follows from right belief, prevented it from making an open assault on reason from the side of passion (hence its 'sidestepping' approach through the ambiguities of 'will'). Modern collectivism, however, made just such an assault, pretending to believe that reason is nothing but a 'technical' servant of passion, that all actions are 'motivated' by some irresistibly strong passion, and that claims to be motivated by rational insight into 'objective truth' (about ultimate values or ends) are mere 'rationalizations,' i.e., authoritarian attempts to force others to accept as true one's own peculiar passionate prejudices. This total assault on reason was necessary because the more the elite few came under pressure from the massed many, the more they would have to rely (like all beleaguered minorities) on general respect for objective truth if they were to defend whatever rights and privileges they claimed to be 'deserving' of. Also, overthrowing respect for objective truth would encourage the view that anyone's 'own truth' was as good as anyone else's, and thus that differences of opinion about 'truth' were in principle 'resolvable' only by majority rule. Hence, if the massed many could effectively discredit reason, and also maintain effective solidarity of strategically pretended 'belief,' the elite few could eventually be brought to their knees.

Now, for Modern collectivism, 'moral lapses' occurred whenever people refused to pretend belief in the Collectivist myth because they did not find that myth reasonable. Such people were anathematized as partisans of the elite few, and were accused of being motivated by the despicable passions of selfishness and cowardice. Because they were basically 'selfish,' they needed to think that they were better than everyone else, and that they should have all the 'blessings' of this world for themselves; and because they had now been exposed for what they were to the massed many, who had begun to exact their just revenge, they had been seized by cowardly fear and were trying to worm out of their fate. Thus their whole emphasis on reason, and on the supposedly 'objective' truths that might entitle certain people to special rights and privileges, was merely a passion-dictated rationalization aimed at duping the massed many into mistaking selfishness for superiority and cowardice for 'reasonableness.' But does this Modern-collectivist linkage of 'moral lapses' to 'rationalization' in any way imply linking them to self-deception?

The answer depends on whether the so-called rationalizers are presumed to be themselves taken in by their rationalizations. On the surface, the logic of the Modern-collectivist strategy amounts to a diversionary projecting onto 'nonbelievers' of the very sort of strategically pretended belief that underlies Modern collectivism itself; that, however, would mean that nonbelievers *know* that they are motivated by selfish and cowardly passions, and that they contrive and deploy their rationalizations with fully conscious deceptive intent. In fact, if nonbelievers could *not* be depicted as knowingly and intentionally perpetrating their rationalizatons, or as somehow being 'responsible' for them, it would be difficult constantly to stoke the moral fires that preserved effective solidarity among the massed many. On the other hand, depicting nonbelievers as fully aware, at the rational level, of what they were doing had the disadvantage of making reason look far too respectably central and all-knowing, which could threaten the plausibility of the Modern-collectivist view of the psyche. Moreover, as Modern collectivism knew that its own view was really false, and that reason would not often lead nonbelievers to doubt the correctness of their nonbelief, a way of sabotaging reason from the 'inside,' as well as just attacking it from the outside, seemed desirable. The obvious answer to these problems was the notion of literal self-deception, according to which nonbelievers could be depicted as both responsibly knowing, and yet irrationally not knowing, that their rationalizations were mere inventions of selfish and cowardly passions.

Formulated originally as Marxian 'class consciousness,' then given psycho-socially ambiguous but welcomely irrationalist support as Nietzschean will-to-power and Freudian 'unconscious desire,' this notion of literal self-deception succeeded quite well in shaking the self-confidence of many rationalistic 'nonbelievers,' whose rationalistic critical powers were often outstripped by devotion to (self-perceivedly) 'open-minded' self-suspicion. Today, formulated as Sartrean-Freudian self-deception, the notion is widely debated by those with vested Modern-collectivist interests in proving that the phenomenon exists, and by those whose natural Socratic-rationalist sympathies have grown either honestly self-suspicious or heroically self-castigating. Consistently with Modern-collectivist strategy, the few who protest that the phenomenon is unintelligibly self-contradictory, and could not possibly exist, tend to be accused of serving vested Socratic-rationalist interests (which mask deeper elitist-oppressive interests), and are thenceforth largely ignored. Meanwhile, Modern collectivism itself, increasingly confident over its successes as a socio-moral strategy, moves towards strengthening the manipulative-oppressive power of its notion of self-deception by redefining it as 'sickness of reason,' i.e., mental illness, thereby arrogating to the new Modern-collectivist elite a pretended 'duty' to 'care for' self-deceivers, i.e., nonbelievers in the Collectivist myth, by confining them to insane asylums.[8] But lest all this seem unduly digressive, if not rashly dramatic, the question about the relation between self-deception and inauthenticity should be brought up here.

INAUTHENTICITY, MODERN INDIVIDUALISM, AND HEIDEGGER VS. SARTRE

As noted at the beginning of this study, both Sartrean self-deception and Heideggerian inauthenticity are closely related to the traditional problem of weakness of will. For the most part, the foregoing analysis of the links between Christian-fideist weakness of will and Modern-collectivist self-deception also pertains to the problem of inauthenticity. This is because the notion of inauthenticity was formulated as part of a Modern-individualist reaction to the Modern-collectivist strategy. Although perhaps the definitive theorist of inauthenticity is Heidegger, he was preceded by Nietzsche and Kierkegaard, both of whom deplored what they saw as the increasingly tyrannical self-deification of the 'herd' or the 'crowd,' i.e., the massed many, in modern society. For all three thinkers, existential inauthenticity was epitomized by the 'crowd,' which sought false security through conventional truths and values designed to flatter its own mediocrity, and instinctively persecuted those who it feared were capable of realizing 'higher' truths and values. Authenticity, on the other hand, was epitomized by a minority of rare, outstanding individuals, who sought to live by integrating independently certified (though not self-willed) truths and values into the concrete potentialities of their own uniquely 'personal' selves, situations, and destinies. In effect, then, inauthenticity serves to explain Modern-individualist 'moral lapses,' just as weakness of reason, weakness of will, and self-deception served to explain Socratic-rationalist, Christian-fideist, and Modern-collectivist ones. But is it, too, as unintelligible as the latter two of those three notions turned out to be?

For Heidegger, inauthenticity is a kind of socially grounded 'original sin' that everyone is necessarily born into, and that even the authentic can sometimes fall back into, but that the authentic must constantly strive to reclaim themselves from. When the massed many allow themselves to remain totally inauthentic, this is because they react to a certain psycho-metaphysical 'anxiety' by seeking existential security in the crowd. Unable to bear the task of responsibly constituting their 'own' lives in full view of the mysteriousness of their existence and the 'nothingness' of their deaths, they seek to 'drown out' the call of their 'conscience' by fleeing into the everyday distractions of life in the crowd.

Now, inasmuch as self-deception is often presumed to be motivated by anxiety (about what one knows of oneself), one might suspect that inauthenticity is a form of self-deception. But if one could somehow 'deceive' oneself about the 'call' of one's conscience, there would be no need to 'drown it out' or to 'flee' from it;[9] again, to 'flee' from some danger that one feels incapable of coping with is not to 'deceive' oneself about it, but to respond logically (if mistakenly or unheroically) to it;[10] and finally, being all too well aware of one's own anxious incapacity to cope with authenticity would fit in with one's tending to resent the courageous authentic individual. Thus, inauthenticity seems more like weakness of will than like self-deception: one's conscience calls one to something that one 'ought' to do, but one is 'tempted' by the passion of anxiety to act against that 'ought.' Unlike the case of Christian fideism, the disobeyed 'ought' originates in one's own conscience (i.e., in a kind of 'higher self') rather than in Church-mediated 'divine' authority, but like the case of Christian fideism, there is a problem about why one disobeys. This apparent similarity between weakness of will and inauthenticity might seem confirmed by Heidegger's linkage of inauthenticity to a lack of 'determination' or 'decisiveness' that suggests a lack of 'will-power.'

In fact, however, Heideggerian inauthenticity is more like Socratic-rationalist ignorance than like weakness of will. His word for 'determination' or 'decisiveness' (*Entschlossenheit*) literally means 'unclosedness,' and is directly linked by him to the disclosedness of *truth (Erschlossenheit)*.[11] Thus, although he speaks of cowardice,[12] choice,[13] and willing[14] in connection with being inauthentic or authentic, he ultimately sees 'closedness of truth,' or ignorance, as responsible for the inauthentic, cowardly flight from conscience. The 'higher' part of oneself intimates that one 'ought' to become authentic, but if one disobeys, it is because the totality of truth that is 'open' to one presents authenticity as so threatening that one finally believes one 'ought' to flee from confronting it. (In part, Heidegger's very diagnosis of inauthenticity is an attempt to dispel the ignorance that keeps people trapped in inauthenticity, i.e., an attempt to "become a 'conscience' for others.")[15] To be sure, Heidegger is not a Socratic rationalist, and he even seems to implicate rational thought in inauthentic failures to respond to conscience;[16] but he also seems to regard such thought as a symptom of inauthentic ignorance based on truths and values from the crowd (i.e., it carries cognitive weight because one *is* inauthentic, and if one is also somehow *kept* inauthentic because it carries cognitive weight, one is kept that way unintentionally and ignorantly). Still, the way to Heideggerian authenticity runs through cognitive 'insight' into the truth about oneself and one's situation, and Heidegger regards the nature of one's actions as following from the nature of one's beliefs.[17] But if Heidegger's notion of inauthenticity is not tied to a notion of literal self-deception, how does it happen that Sartre equates inauthenticity with literal self-deception?

What Sartre regards as literal self-deception he actually calls 'bad faith.' This he describes as a 'lie to oneself,' or an intentional 'project' that enables one to hide a displeasing truth from oneself.[18] Although explicitly aware of the puzzling paradoxicality of this notion, and after giving a persuasive critique of any attempt to justify the notion in Freudian terms,[19] he nevertheless assumes that bad faith is possible, and proposes to explore some concrete examples of it in order to show how the psyche must be constituted if people are to be capable of such a thing.[20] These examples are always carefully *described* in a question-begging way favorable to his own theoretical perspective, and they remain unconvincing; but there is no need to discuss them in detail here, because he admits that they all *could* be interpreted as instances of 'lying' (aimed at deceiving others, but not oneself).[21] In the end, the crux of the matter, as he sees it, is that bad faith is 'faith,' or a problem of 'belief'; and by 'belief' he means "the adherence of being to its object when the object is not given or is given indistinctly."[22] Obviously, this is very much like what was called 'willed' belief in the earlier discussion of Christian fideism, and Sartre would surely view such 'willed' belief as an example of his 'bad faith.' But how intelligible is his notion of bad faith?

First, on the crucial matter of how one can supposedly implement a project of bad faith without necessarily being self-aware in a way that would preclude successful realization of the project, Sartre clarifies nothing, but simply compounds the original paradoxicality of the problem by introducing notions of a self-causing causedness and of an actively effected passive undergoing.[23] Second, his analysis of the supposedly self-deceptive 'logic' behind bad faith reveals merely the age-old tactic of using an excessively fastidious (theoretical) skepticism to undermine the notion of rationally justified belief so that one can claim (practical) freedom to choose, or to 'will,' to believe anything at all. But that 'logic' is usually recognized as a merely pretended rhetorical strategy, and (as with his interpretatively 'loaded' examples of bad faith) his claim that those in bad faith contrive to fool *themselves* by such logic is at best question begging. Finally, his attempt to make a polemical virtue out of his admission that those in bad faith are *not* able to 'hide' their skeptical strategy from themselves, and that ''bad faith does not succeed in believing what it wishes to believe,''[24] seems a convenient play upon ambiguity of the very sort that he attributes to bad faith. Hence, although Sartre's notion of bad faith contains an intelligible strategic core not unlike the one in the Christian-fideist notion of 'willed' belief, and although it implies that authenticity is primarily a matter of adhering to rationally justified, rather than 'willed,' belief, it contributes nothing at all towards making intelligible a notion of literal self-deception. It seems worth asking, however, why Sartre would go to such tortuous lengths to try justifying such a notion.

In contrast to Heidegger, Sartre is a moralistically obsessed 'man of resentment,' who fumes with indignation at 'cowards' or 'hypocrites,' and even resorts to dismissing people as ''scum'' for the sin of trying to show that their existence is necessary.[25] Resentful of the moral authority of others (Socratic-rationalist, Christian-fideist, or secular-bourgeois), he sets out to overthrow it by proclaiming that there are no 'objective truths' about values and morals; however, equally obsessed with condemning others on the basis of his own moral authority, he sets out to devise a substitute for the very moral criteria he has overthrown. His substitute is the notion of 'bad faith,' which he employs as a socio-moral strategy in much the same way that Modern collectivism employs the notion of self-deception. Not *what* one chooses, but *how* one chooses, becomes the new criterion for the morality of action; hence, an authentically 'free' choice to massacre one's enemies is 'good,' while a choice in 'bad faith' to tolerate or forgive one's enemies is 'bad.' Further, whether or not people's choices are regarded as having been made in bad faith depends entirely upon Sartre's supposed ability to peer directly into the souls of others.[26] If any of those he condemns protest that their choices were not made in bad faith, this, he retorts, is only what one would expect of 'self-deceptive' bad faith; if, on the other hand, they protest that they are morally innocent because they were 'deceived' by bad faith, he retorts that bad faith is an intentional project that one responsibly effects upon oneself. Thus, although Sartre began his career as a Modern-individualist sympathizer, his relatively early doctrine of 'bad faith' already points in the direction of his later turn to

Modern collectivism. In any case, it is Heidegger, and not Sartre, who is the definitive theorist of Modern-individualist 'inauthenticity.'

SELF-DECEPTION AND INAUTHENTICITY

Is it true, then, as suggested at the outset of this study, that both self-deception and inauthenticity are somehow bound up with attaching undue importance to other people's opinions about us? In the case of self-deception, one secretly knows (or suspects) oneself to lack some quality that one wants other people to believe one possesses; hence, one shams beliefs consistent with one's possessing that quality in the hope of deceiving the others into thinking that one possesses it (or at least confidently believes oneself to possess it). Moreover, as distinct from merely harboring opportunistic hopes of obtaining some 'practical' advantage from one's deceit, one characteristically fears becoming known by the others as the self that one is, because this would amount, in one's own view, to being 'existentially' devalued by the others. Immersed in a social game whose rules are the conventional truths and values of a certain group, one regards the others as primarily authoritative about what one 'ought' to be and about what one is 'worth,' and one identifies oneself primarily with whatever 'social image' one can create and sustain in the eyes of the others. In the case of inauthenticity, on the other hand, one is aware both that one's conscience calls one to be the author of one's self and that the call of conscience is too frightening to obey; hence, one declines to obey, and immerses oneself in the secure familiarities and distractions of living by the conventional truths and values of the crowd. In fearing authenticity, however, one characteristically fears the change that it would produce in one's relation to the crowd, whose meaning-bestowing authority would suddenly be lost to one, and whose previously supportive attitude towards one would suddenly become hostile. Insofar as one meets with reasonable acceptance from the crowd, one tends to remain at the level of mere inauthenticity; but insofar as one fears rejection or humiliation by the crowd, one tends to descend to the level of self-deception. On the whole, then, it seems that inauthenticity naturally predisposes to self-deception, and that the inauthentic remain existential 'cowards,' while self-deceivers become existential 'liars,' because both types attach great importance to the (self-perceived) role played by other people's opinions in constituting their own 'existential' reality, i.e., the worth of their selves and the meaningfulness of their lives.

Usually, those who inquire into self-deception tend to regard the self-deceiver as a muddled, morally incompetent 'misfit' surrounded by a group of clear-sighted, morally mature people who care and who could, if only the misfit would listen to them, administer all the corrective truths that the misfit needs. Inquiry into inauthenticity, however, has the useful effect of suggesting a reversal of that situation, with the 'normal' group being regarded as a muddled, morally incompetent 'crowd,' and the 'authentic' individual, as a clear-sighted, morally mature 'outcast.' Similarly, whereas inquiry into self-deception suggests that the self-deceiver uses apparent self-deception as an instrument of manipulative defense (against the group), inquiry into the links between self-deception and inauthenticity suggests that the group uses self-deceptively shammed belief in literal self-deception as an instrument of manipulative aggression (against the individual). On both sides, notably, this self-deceptive shamming transcends mere interest-serving deceit by virtue of the predominantly 'socio-moralistic' nature of what is at stake, i.e., 'existentially' deep-rooted matters of face, self-esteem, or (self-perceived) justice.

SELF-DECEPTION:
CONCLUDING OBSERVATIONS

Now, although none of the points that have been covered so far suffice to refute the possibility of literal self-deception, they do suggest, first, that instances of alleged self-deception can be readily accounted for, quite nonparadoxically, as instances of sincere ignorance, strategic pretense, or both; and second, that the two-faced paradoxicality of the notion of literal self-deception is remarkably well suited to furthering the interests of irrationalistic moral disfranchisement of rationalistic 'dissidents' (whether individuals or social minorities). In view of these results, it seems worth asking just how, if at all, the possibility of literal self-deception could be proved or disproved.

As far as the outside observer can tell, behavior that appears to issue from self-deception could always, in fact, issue from mere shamming; hence, inferential attributions of self-deception that are based on observation of other people are inherently question begging. This suggests that knowledge of the possibility of self-deception would have to be introspectively based, i.e., one would have to experience self-deception within oneself. But would that be possible? Seemingly, self-deception could not succeed without simultaneously 'covering its tracks' in such a way as to preclude introspective awareness of its existence; and to say that one would obviously be both aware and not aware of its existence is still to beg the question. But might not one somehow be able to 'wake' from the spell of a self-deceptive project, and to become aware, 'after the fact,' that one had cast such a spell on oneself? Both error and dream, for example, are states that one recognizes oneself as having been in only after one 'wakes' from them. However, neither error nor dream, unlike self-deception, are 'projects' that one might effect in oneself; rather, both are things that one passively 'falls into.' (Although one may intentionally effect the project of putting oneself in a state favorable to 'falling asleep,' the falling itself happens, if it does, of itself, and tends to be prevented, rather than effected, by trying to 'make' it happen.) Finally, might one not be able to infer, after noticing certain inconsistencies in one's past behavior yet feeling introspectively certain that one was not a shammer, that one must have been in self-deception? The problem here is that the very act of *noticing* the past inconsistencies, as such, introduces an element of new *knowledge,* so that a question remains about whether the inconsistent past behavior did not, in fact, result from mere *ignorance* (that the behavior was inconsistent). Even if such behavior could sometimes be interpreted as having been in one's 'interest,' or as 'unconsciously motivated,' this need not be more than coincidental, and remains largely irrelevant until one can provide a credible account of how the alleged unconsciousness of the 'motivation' was effected through properly 'self-deceptive' intent. Hence, it seems as if the very nature of literal self-deception puts it hopelessly beyond being either introspectively experienced in oneself or reliably inferred from the behavior of oneself or others.

If, however, the very possibility of establishing the reality of self-deception is so questionable, there is dubious justification for proceeding (like Sartre and most current theorists) by dogmatically assuming the reality of self-deception, and then trying to conceive a 'model' of the psyche that would show how self-deception is possible. For if, in fact, self-deception is *not* possible, this approach would tend to generate nothing but increasingly subtle exercises in misexplanatory fantasy. Rather, one should start with the most adequate model of the psyche that one can conceive of on all other available evidence, and then try to determine whether, and how, self-deception would be possible on that model.

Again, even if literal self-deception were, in fact, possible, there is a problem about whether it could ever be 'explained' in anything but a question-begging way. When conceptual paradoxes of a similar sort are able to be usefully 'explained,' this is because the paradox is really only apparent, and can be shown to disappear under closer examination. For example, it appears paradoxical to say that all people are inalienably free and that inauthentic people renounce their freedom, but the paradox can be explained by showing that one can freely decide (in the inalienable sense) to renounce one's freedom (in a secondary sense) by allowing other people to make one's (other) decisions for one. Similarly, one might resolve the apparently paradoxical claim that the same surface is both black and white by showing that parts of it are black and other parts white; but then the paradox is resolved by explaining that the notion of the 'same surface' is not really to be taken literally. If, however, one dogmatically assumes that the same surface *can* literally be both black and white, and then presumes to 'explain' how this is possible, one would seem foredoomed to merely perpetuating the original paradoxicality in one's 'explanations.' For example, one might (quite ingeniously) reason that black is the absence of all colors, that white is the reflection of all colors, that what reflects colors does not retain them, that white is thus black 'underneath,' that surfaces have no separate 'underneaths,' and thus that white surfaces are also black. The original paradoxicality would simply recur in the notion of a surface that both has and does not have an underneath,' however, and nothing would have been resolved or explained. Unfortunately, this futile perpetuation of an original paradoxicality seems to crop up in even the cleverest attempts to explain how literal self-deception is possible.

If, then, the existence of literal self-deception is as difficult to prove or to disprove as the existence of God (although Sartre is prepared to 'believe' in the former but not in the latter), if those who like to accuse others of self-deception are no less 'morally' suspect than those who are accused by others of self-deception, and if 'aggressive' accusations of self-deception by the group can be illegitimately bolstered through the principle of 'might makes right,' while 'defensive' resorts to self-deception by isolated individuals can be readily 'laughed off' by anyone, there seems to be something pointless, and even worrying, about accusing people of self-deception. If one wishes to convince others that they are wrong or deluded about something, nothing morally respectable can be gained by arrogating mental and moral soundness to oneself alone; rather, one should seek to dispel what may be sincere ignorance, or to expose what may be strategic pretense, by attempting to illuminate the 'truth' through rational evidence. Quite possibly, such an attempt may have the unexpected, but salutary, effect of illuminating one's own ignorance; and even if it fails to convince the supposedly deluded, the moral example provided by adhering to reason may be more important than anything obtainable by resorting to accusations of self-deception.

As suggested, in their own ways, by both Socrates and Heidegger, one might well conclude that something like the 'philosophical' life, in which one attempts to pursue and to certify 'truth' independently of the fashions and pressures of the 'crowd,' offers the only escape from a life of 'existential' alienation within the crowd. In the case of self-knowledge or self-deception, for example, the qualities of 'self' that one possesses or shams are themselves understood, as is the notion of 'self,' only in the vague, unanalyzed, and unsystematized senses attributed to them by the crowd. But just what *are* things like 'courage,' 'vanity,' or 'honesty,' and just what *is* a 'self'? Might one's 'real' self turn out to be simply the totality of one's 'values'? Would self-knowledge then presuppose knowing what one really values? Would that be possible without knowing what 'value' is? Or that, in turn, without knowing what 'being' is? Would all this point one (with Socrates) towards 'the form of the Good'? Or perhaps (with Heidegger) towards 'the meaning of Being'?

NOTES

1. See my essay "On Self-Deception," *Philosophical Quarterly* 30 (1980): 305–317, which arrives at these conclusions by analyzing both the word and the concept and by elucidating the phenomenon of ostensibly self-deceptive behavior as encountered in everyday life.

2. Although Sartre is more closely identified than Heidegger with the term 'Existentialist,' Heidegger is more closely representative of the movement that began with Nietzsche and Kierkegaard.

3. Similar views on 'will' are developed in Max Scheler's theory of the psyche. See, for example, his *Formalismus in der Ethik und die materiale Wertethik,* 5th ed. (Bern-Munich: Francke Verlag, 1966), 87–89, 200, 569.

4. The main relevant texts are Nietzsche's *Jenseits von Gut und Böse* (1886) and *Zur Genealogie der Moral* (1887) and Scheler's (final version of an earlier study) *Ressentiment im Aufbau der Moralen* (1915). While Scheler is more concerned than Nietzsche to rescue the possibility of resentment-free Christian belief, there is no reason to think that he identifies this with popular-historical Christianity or with fideism. Still, it is as theorists of the *phenomenon* of resentment that both thinkers are noted here.

5. Compare José Ortega y Gasset, *The Revolt of the Masses* (London: Unwin Books, 1961), 80; and Emil L. Fackenheim, *Metaphysics and Historicity* (Milwaukee, Wisc.: Marquette University Press, 1961), 5–7.

6. The antirationalist force of rhetorical questions like these is spurious, although this claim cannot be argued here. A central relevant point, however, is that human beings can no more escape being 'rational' than they can escape having brains.

7. Essential reading on this still insufficiently appreciated aspect of Modern collectivism is Karl Löwith, *Meaning in History* (Chicago: University of Chicago Press, 1949). See especially the comments on Marxism on pages 44–45.

8. The frequent attempts by Modern-collectivist sympathizers to dismiss Heidegger's philosophy as symptomatic of 'schizophrenia' are to the point here.

9. See Martin Heidegger, *Sein und Zeit*, 12th ed. (Tübingen: Max Niemeyer Verlag, 1972), 184.

10. Ibid., 185–186.

11. Ibid., 297.

12. Ibid., 266.

13. Ibid., 268.

14. Ibid., 270–271.

15. Ibid., 298.

16. Ibid., 274, 296.

17. Ibid., 300.

18. See Jean-Paul Sartre, *Being and Nothingness* (New York: Washington Square Press, 1966), 89.

19. Ibid., 90–96.

20. Ibid., 96.

21. Ibid., 112.

22. Ibid., 112.

23. Ibid., 112.

24. Ibid., 115.

25. See Walter Kaufmann, ed., *Existentialism from Dostoevsky to Sartre*, rev., exp. ed. (New York: New American Library, 1975), 366.

26. See the section on "The Look" in Sartre, *Being and Nothingness*, 340–400.

About the Contributors

ROBERT AUDI is Professor of Philosophy at the University of Nebraska, Lincoln. He earned a B.A. from Colgate University and his M.A. and Ph.D. degrees from the University of Michigan. A recipient of several grants from the National Endowment for the Humanities, he has conducted two NEH Seminars for College Teachers and directed an NEH Summer Institute on Human Action. He has also served as chair of the American Philosophical Association's Committee on Career Opportunities. His main research areas are epistemology and action theory, and his many articles include a number of essays on self-deception and related topics in epistemology and philosophy of mind.

RICHARD BOSLEY was born in Corinne, Utah, and holds a B.A. in Greek from the University of Utah, an M.A. in philosophy from the University of California, Berkeley, and a Ph.D. in philosophy from the University of Göttingen. He is now Professor of Philosophy at the University of Alberta in Edmonton. He has published papers on logic and on the history of philosophy, as well as the books *Aspects of Aristotle's Logic* (1975) and *On Truth* (1982). He is currently working on a book on the Doctrine of the Mean.

BENZION CHANOWITZ received his Ph.D. in social-personality psychology from the Graduate Center, City University of New York. Currently he is a Postdoctoral Fellow in Psychology at Harvard University and a Research Associate in the Program in Psychiatry and the Law at Massachusetts Mental Health Center, Harvard Medical School. He has published a number of articles in scholarly journals and books.

JOEL COOPER is Professor of Psychology at Princeton University. He also served as Assistant and Associate Professor at Princeton after receiving his Ph.D. in social psychology from Duke University. He is the author of articles and chapters in social psychology focusing on attitudes, attitude change, and cognitive dissonance. He is also coauthor of *Understanding Social Psychology*.

HERBERT FINGARETTE is Professor of Philosophy at the University of California, Santa Barbara. He was Romanell–Phi Beta Kappa Professor of Philosophy, 1983–84; President of the American Philosophical Association, Pacific Division, 1976–77; Gramlich Lecturer on the Philosophy of Human Nature, Dartmouth College, 1978; Evans-Wentz Lecturer in Oriental Religions, Stanford University, 1977; and William James Lecturer in Religion, Harvard University, 1971. His publications include: *The Self in Transformation, On Responsibility, Self-Deception, The Meaning of Criminal Insanity, Confucius: The Secular as Sacred*, and *Mental Disabilities and Criminal Responsibility* (with A. F. Hasse).

KENNETH J. GERGEN is Professor of Psychology at Swarthmore College. After receiving his Ph.D. at Duke University he was Assistant Professor at Harvard University. He is the author or editor of ten books, including *The Concept of Self* (1971), *The Self Concept: Advances in Theory and Research* (1981, with M. Lynch and A. Norem-Heibeisen), and *Toward Transformation in Social Knowledge* (1982). He has been a recipient of a Guggenheim Fellowship and a Fulbright Research Fellowship.

DANIEL T. GILBERT earned his bachelor's degree at the University of Colorado and his master's at Princeton University, where he is currently a doctoral candidate working with Edward E. Jones. His primary research is in inference errors and person perception, with emphasis on persons' tendencies to underestimate their roles in evoking other people's behavior. He has been a National Science Foundation Fellow and a winner of the University of Colorado Outstanding Graduate Award (1981). He is widely published as a science fiction writer.

MARY ROWLAND HAIGHT is Lecturer in the Department of Philosophy, University of Glasgow, Scotland. She was born in California, read Greats at Oxford, did graduate work at Berkeley, and earned the B.Phil. in philosophy at Oxford. Her publications have been primarily in aesthetics and the philosophy of psychology, and include *A Study of Self-Deception* (1980).

JOHN KING-FARLOW, B.A., M.A. (Oxford), A.M. (Duke), Ph.D. (Stanford), is Professor of Philosophy at the University of Alberta. A founding editor of the *Canadian Journal of Philosophy*, he has been president of the Canadian Philosophical Association. He is also a former officer in the Royal Air Force and a published poet. He has served on the faculties of ten universities and colleges in the United States, Britain, and Canada. His books include *Reason and Religion* (1969), *Faith and the Life of Reason* (1972), *Self-Knowledge and Social Relations* (1978), and also English- and French-Canadian anthologies.

DAVID KIPP received degrees from Pennsylvania State University (B.A., English; M.A., philosophy) and Flinders University (Ph.D., humanities) and also studied at the universities of Freiburg and Basel (philosophy, psychology, German literature) and the University of Melbourne (history and theory of fine arts). A poet (*The Colourless Eye*, 1968), translator (*Selected Poems of Gertrud Kolmar*, 1970), literary theorist (*Poetic Truth*, 1975), frequent contributor to philosophical journals, and former Lecturer in Philosophy at Murdoch University, he is currently Honorary Research Fellow in Philosophy at La Trobe University.

ABOUT THE CONTRIBUTORS

ELLEN LANGER received her Ph.D. from Yale University and is currently Professor of Psychology at Harvard University. She is also a member of the Division on Aging of the Faculty of Medicine at Harvard. Currently she is completing a book on mindlessness/mindfulness theory and editing a book on new end points to human development. Her most recent book is *The Psychology of Control*.

MIKE W. MARTIN is Associate Professor of Philosophy at Chapman College. His Ph.D. is from the University of California, Irvine (1977), and his B.S. and M.A. degrees are from the University of Utah. A recipient of two fellowships from the National Endowment for the Humanities, he also was given a Matchette Foundation Award and a Graves Award for teaching in the humanities. He has published on self-deception, autonomy, humor, literature, and applied ethics; he is coauthor of *Ethics in Engineering* (1983); and he is currently completing a monograph on morality and self-deception.

C. R. SNYDER is Professor of Psychology and Director of the Graduate Training Programs in Clinical Psychology at the University of Kansas. After receiving a B.A. from Southern Methodist University and M.A. and Ph.D. degrees from Vanderbilt University, he was a Fellow in Medical Psychology at the University of California Medical Center, San Francisco. In addition to publishing sixty articles, he is author of *Comparisons* (1974) and coauthor of *Uniqueness: The Human Pursuit of Difference* (1980) and *Excuses: Masquerades in Search of Grace* (1983).

BÉLA SZABADOS is Associate Professor of Philosophy at the University of Regina. Born in Hungary in 1942, he attended elementary school in Hungary and Austria and high school in Montreal. He studied philosophy in Montreal, Toronto, and Calgary, and received M.A. and Ph.D. degrees from the University of Calgary. His publications include many articles on self-deception.

TIMOTHY D. WILSON is Associate Professor of Psychology at the University of Virginia. He received his Ph.D. in psychology in 1977 from the University of Michigan. His research has been in the area of social cognition, with a focus on the limits of people's ability to report on their mental processes and internal states. His essays include (with Richard E. Nisbett) "On Telling More Than We Know: Verbal Reports on Mental Processes" and "The Halo Effect: Evidence for Unconscious Alteration of Judgments" (1977).

Bibliography

Ackrill, J. L., ed. *Aristotle the Philosopher.* Oxford: Oxford University Press, 1981.

Adler, Alfred. *The Individual Psychology of Alfred Adler.* Edited by Heinz L. Ansbacher and Rowena R. Ansbacher. New York: Harper and Row, 1964.

Adorno, Theodor W. *The Jargon of Authenticity.* Translated by Knut Tarnowski and Frederick Will. Evanston, Ill.: Northwestern University Press, 1973.

Allport, Gordon W. *Personality: A Psychological Interpretation.* New York: Holt, Rinehart and Winston, 1937.

Ammerman, Robert R. "Ethics and Belief." *Proceedings of the Aristotelian Society* 65 (1965): 257–266.

Anderson, Thomas C. *The Foundations and Structure of Sartrean Ethics.* Lawrence: Regents Press of Kansas, 1979.

Anscombe, G. E. M. "Pretending." In *Philosophy of Mind,* edited by Stuart Hampshire. New York: Harper and Row, 1966.

Aquinas, St. Thomas. *Summa Theologiae.* Vol. 25. New York: McGraw-Hill, 1969.

Aristotle. *Nicomachean Ethics.* In *The Basic Works of Aristotle,* edited by Richard McKeon. New York: Random House, 1968.

Armstrong, David M. *Belief, Truth and Knowledge.* Cambridge: Cambridge University Press, 1973.

Aronson, Elliot. "The Theory of Cognitive Dissonance: A Current Perspective." In *Advances in Experimental Social Psychology,* edited by Leonard Berkowitz, vol. 4. New York: Academic Press, 1969.

Audi, Robert. "The Concept of Believing." *The Personalist* 53 (1972): 43–62.

———. "The Concept of Wanting." *Philosophical Studies* 21 (1973): 1–21.

———. "The Epistemic Authority of the First Person." *The Personalist* 56 (1975): 5–15.

———. "An Epistemic Conception of Rationality." *Social Theory and Practice* 9 (1983): 311–334.

———. "Epistemic Disavowals and Self-Deception." *The Personalist* 57 (1976): 378–385.

———. "The Limits of Self-Knowledge." *Canadian Journal of Philosophy* 4 (1974): 253–267.

———. "Rationalization and Rationality." *Synthese*. Forthcoming.
———. "Self-Deception, Action and Will." *Erkenntnis* 18 (1982): 133–158.
———. "Weakness of Will and Practical Judgment." *Nous* (1979).
Austin, John. *Sense and Sensibilia*. London: Oxford University Press, 1962.
Averill, James. *Anger and Aggression*. New York: Springer-Verlag, 1983.
Avorn, Jerry, and Ellen Langer. "Induced Disability in Nursing Home Patients: A Controlled Trial." *Journal of the American Geriatrics Society* 30 (1982): 397–400.
Ayer, Alfred J. "Could Language Be Invented by a Robinson Crusoe?" In *The Private Language Argument*, edited by O. R. Jones. London: Macmillan, 1971.
Bach, Kent. "An Analysis of Self-Deception." *Philosophy and Phenomenological Research* 41 (1981): 351–370.
———. *Exit Existentialism: A Philosophy of Self-Awareness*. Belmont: Wadsworth, 1973.
Baier, Kurt. "The Social Source of Reason." *Proceedings and Addresses of the American Philosophical Association* 47 (1977).
Bandura, Albert. *Aggression: A Social-Learning Analysis*. Englewood Cliffs, N.J.: Prentice-Hall, 1973.
———. *Social Learning Theory*. Englewood Cliffs: Prentice-Hall, 1977.
Becker, Ernest. *The Denial of Death*. New York: Free Press, 1975.
Beehler, Rodger. "Moral Delusion." *Philosophy* 56 (1981): 313–331.
Bem, Daryl. "Self-Perception Theory." In *Advances in Experimental Social Psychology*, edited by Leonard Berkowitz, vol. 6, pp. 1–62. New York: Academic Press, 1972.
Bennett, David H., and David S. Holmes. "Influence of Denial (Situation Redefinition) and Projection on Anxiety Associated with Threat to Self-Esteem." *Journal of Personality and Social Psychology* 32 (1975): 915–921.
Berglas, Steven, and Edward E. Jones. "Drug Choice as a Self-Handicapping Strategy in Response to Non-Contingent Success." *Journal of Personality and Social Psychology* 36 (1978): 405–417.
Berkowitz, Leonard. *Social Psychology*. New York: Holt, Rinehart, and Winston, 1980.
Berkowitz, Leonard, James A. Green, and Jacqueline R. Macaulay. "Hostility Catharsis and the Reduction of Emotional Tension." *Psychiatry* 25 (1962): 23–31.
Billson, Marcus K. "Inside Albert Speer: Secrets of Moral Evasion." *Antioch Review* (1979): 460–474.
Bok, Sissela. *Lying*. New York: Vintage Books, 1979.
———. *Secrets*. New York: Pantheon Books, 1982.
———. "The Self Deceived." *Social Science Information* 19 (1980): 923–935.
Bosley, Richard. *Aspects of Aristotle's Logic*. Assen: Van Gorcum, 1975.
———. *On Truth*. Washington, D.C.: University Press of America, 1982.
Boyers, Robert. "Observations on Lying and Liars." *Review of Existential Psychiatry* 13 (1974): 150–168.
Branden, Nathaniel. *The Disowned Self*. New York: Bantam Books, 1973.
Brandt, Richard B. *A Theory of the Good and the Right*. Oxford: Oxford University Press, 1979.
Brenner, Charles. *An Elementary Textbook of Psychoanalysis*. Garden City, N.Y.: Anchor Books, 1974.
Broad, C. D. *The Mind and Its Place in Nature*. London: Routledge and Kegan Paul, 1962.

Brock, Timothy C., and Arnold H. Buss. "Dissonance, Aggression and Evaluation of Pain." *Journal of Abnormal and Social Psychology* 65 (1962): 197–202.
———. "Effects of Justification for Aggression and Communication with the Victim on Postaggression Dissonance." *Journal of Abnormal and Social Psychology* 68 (1964): 403–412.
Brown, Robert. "Integrity and Self-Deception." *Critical Review* 25 (1983).
Burish, Thomas G., and B. Kent Houston. "Causal Projection, Similarity Projection, and Coping with Threat to Self-Esteem." *Journal of Personality* 47 (1979): 57–70.
Burnyeat, Myles F. "Belief in Speech." *Proceedings of the Aristotelian Society* (1967–68): 227–248.
Burrell, David, and Stanley Hauerwas. "Self-Deception and Autobiography: Theological and Ethical Reflections on Speer's *Inside the Third Reich*." *Journal of Religious Ethics* 2 (1974): 99–117.
Butler, Joseph. "Upon the Character of Balaam," "Upon Self-Deceit," and Sermon 3 of the *Six Sermons*. In *The Works of Joseph Butler*, edited by W. E. Gladstone, vol. 2. Oxford: Clarendon Press, 1896.
Byrne, Donn E. *The Attraction Paradigm*. New York: Academic Press, 1971.
Byrne, Donn E., G. D. Baskett, and L. Hodges. "Behavioral Indicators of Interpersonal Attraction." *Journal of Applied Social Psychology* 1 (1971): 137–149.
Campbell, C. A. "Towards a Definition of Belief." *Philosophical Quarterly* 17 (1967): 204–220.
Camus, Albert. *The Fall*. Translated by Justin O'Brien. New York: Vintage Books, 1956.
Canfield, John V., and Don F. Gustavson. "Self-Deception." *Analysis* 23 (1962): 32–36.
Canfield, John, and Patrick McNally. "Paradoxes of Self-Deception." *Analysis* 21 (1961): 140–144.
Carrier, James G. "Misrecognition and Knowledge." *Inquiry* 22 (1979): 321–342.
Carver, Charles S., and Michael F. Scheier. *Attention and Self-Regulation: A Control-Theory Approach to Human Behavior.* New York: Springer-Verlag, 1981.
Catalano, Joseph S. "On the Possibility of Good Faith." *Man and World* 13 (1980): 207–228.
Cavell, Stanley. "The Avoidance of Love: A Reading of King Lear." In *Must We Mean What We Say?* New York: Scribner, 1969.
———. *The Claim of Reason*. Oxford: Oxford University Press, 1979.
Champlin. T. S. "Double Deception." *Mind* 85 (1976): 100–102.
———. "Self-Deception: A Problem about Autobiography." *Proceedings of the Aristotelian Society*, suppl. vol. 53 (1979): 77–94.
———. "Self-Deception—A Reflexive Dilemma," *Philosophy* 52 (1977): 281–299.
Chanowitz, Benzion, and Ellen Langer. "Knowing More (or Less) Than You Can Show: Understanding Control through the Mindlessness-Mindfulness Distinction." In *Human Helplessness: Theory and Applications*, edited by J. Garber and M. E. P. Seligman. New York: Academic Press, 1980.
———. "Premature Cognitive Commitment." *Journal of Personality and Social Psychology* 41 (1981): 1051–1063.
Chisholm, Roderick M., and Thomas Feehan. "The Intent to Deceive." *Journal of Philosophy* 74 (1977): 143–159.

Churchland, Patricia Smith. "Consciousness: The Transmutation of a Concept." *Pacific Philosophical Quarterly* 64 (1983).

Cioffi, Frank, and Peter Alexander. "Symposium: Wishes, Symptoms and Actions." *Proceedings of the Aristotelian Society* 48 (1974): 97–134.

Clair, M. S., and C. R. Snyder. "Effects of Instructor Delivered Sequential Evaluative Feedback upon Students' Subsequent Classroom-Related Performance and Instructor Ratings." *Journal of Educational Psychology* 71 (1979): 50–57.

Clifford, William Kingdon. "The Ethics of Belief." In *Lectures and Essays of W. K. Clifford*, edited by Leslie Stephen and Frederick Pollock, vol. 2. London: Macmillan, 1879.

Cohen, E. A., D. N. Gelfand, and D. P. Hartmann. "Causal Reasoning as a Function of Behavioral Consequences." *Child Development* 52 (1981): 514–522.

Collingwood, Robin G. *The Principles of Art.* New York: Oxford University Press, 1958.

Collins, Arthur W. "Unconscious Belief." *Journal of Philosophy* 66 (1969): 667–680.

Cooley, Charles H. *Human Nature and the Social Order.* New York: Scribner's, 1902.

Cosentino, Dante A. "Self-Deception without Paradox." *Philosophy Research Archives* 6 (1980): 443–465.

Coulter, Jeff. *The Social Construction of the Mind.* New York: Macmillan, 1979.

Cronin, R. G. "A Definition of Believing." *Auslegung* 4 (1977): 122–132.

Croyle, Robert T., and Joel Cooper. "Dissonance Arousal: Physiological Evidence." *Journal of Personality and Social Psychology* 45 (1983): 782–791.

Daniels, Charles B. "Self-Deception and Interpersonal Deception." *The Personalist* 55 (1974): 244–252.

Darley, John M., and George R. Goethals. "People's Analyses of the Causes of Ability-Linked Performances." In *Advances in Experimental Social Psychology*, edited by Leonard Berkowitz, vol. 13. New York: Academic Press, 1980.

Darley, John M., and Charles Huff. "Person Perception as a Kuhnian Process: A Paradigm-Based Model of Attribution." Department of Psychology, Princeton University. Photocopy.

Davidson, Donald. "Paradoxes of Irrationality." In *Philosophical Essays on Freud*, edited by Richard Wollheim and James Hopkins. Cambridge: Cambridge University Press, 1982.

Davis, Stephen T. "Wishful Thinking and 'The Will to Believe.'" *Transactions of the Peirce Society* (1972): 231–245.

Deci, Edward L., and Richard M. Ryan. "The Empirical Exploration of Intrinsic Motivational Processes." In *Advances in Experimental Social Psychology*, edited by Leonard Berkowitz, vol. 13, pp. 39–80. New York: Academic Press, 1980.

Demos, Raphael. "Lying to Oneself." *Journal of Philosophy* 57 (1960): 588–595.
———. "What Is It That I Want?" *Ethics* 55 (1945): 182–195.

Dennett, Daniel C. *Brainstorms.* Montgomery, Vt.: Bradford Books, 1978.

Descartes, René. *Meditations.* In *The Philosophical Works of Descartes*, translated by E. S. Haldane and G. R. T. Ross. Cambridge: Cambridge University Press, 1970.

De Sousa, Ronald B. Review of *Self-Deception* by Herbert Fingarette. *Inquiry* 13 (1970): 308–321.

———. "Self-Deceptive Emotions." *Journal of Philosophy* 75 (1978): 684–697. Reprinted in *Explaining Emotions*, edited by Amélie Oksenberg Rorty. Berkeley: University of California Press, 1980.

Deutsche, Eliot. "Personhood and Self-Deception." Chap. 1 in *Personhood, Creativity and Freedom*. Honolulu: University of Hawaii Press, 1982.

Dewey, John. *Human Nature and Conduct*. New York: Modern Library, 1957.

Dilman, Ilham. "Is the Unconscious a Theoretical Construct?" *Monist* 56 (1972): 313–342.

———. "The Unconscious." *Mind* 68 (1959): 446–473.

Dilman, Ilham, and D. Z. Phillips. *Sense and Delusion*. New York: Humanities Press, 1971.

Douglas, W., and K. Gibbins. "Inadequacy of Voice Recognition as a Demonstration of Self-Deception." *Journal of Personality and Social Psychology* 44 (1983): 589–592.

Drengson, Alan. "Critical Notice of H. Fingarette, *Self-Deception*." *Canadian Journal of Philosophy* 3 (1974): 142–147.

Dyke, Daniel. *The Mystery of Selfe-Deceiving*. London, 1630. Department of Special Collections, University of California, Los Angeles, Library.

Eck, Marcel. *Lies and Truth*. New York: Macmillan, 1970.

Edgley, Roy. *Reason in Theory and Practice*. London: Hutchinson University Library, 1969.

Ekman, Paul, and Wallace V. Friesen. "Detecting Deception from the Body or Face." *Journal of Personality and Social Psychology* 29 (1974): 288–298.

———. "Nonverbal Leakage and Clues to Deception." *Psychiatry* 32 (1969): 88–106.

Eliot, T. S. *The Complete Poems and Plays*. New York: Harcourt, Brace and World, 1962.

Ellenberger, Henri F. *The Discovery of the Unconscious*. New York: Basic Books, 1970.

Elster, Jon, ed. *The Multiple Self*. Cambridge: Cambridge University Press, forthcoming.

———. *Sour Grapes: Studies in the Subversion of Rationality*. Cambridge: Cambridge University Press, 1983.

———. *Ulysses and the Sirens*. Cambridge: Cambridge University Press, 1979.

Erdelyi, Matthew. "A New Look at the New Look: Perceptual Defense and Vigilance." *Psychological Review* 81 (1974): 1–24.

Exdell, John, and James R. Hamilton. "The Incorrigibility of First Person Disavowals." *The Personalist* 56 (1975): 389–394.

Exline, R. V. "Visual Interaction: The Glances of Power and Preference." In *Nebraska Symposium on Motivation*, edited by James K. Cole. Lincoln: University of Nebraska Press, 1971.

Faber, Frederick. *Self-Deceit*. Wallingford, Pa.: Pendle Hill, 1983.

Factor, R. Lance. "Self-Deception and the Functionalist Theory of Mental Processes." *The Personalist* 58 (1977): 115–123.

Falk, W. D. "Morality, Self, and Others." In *Morality and the Language of Conduct*, edited by Hector-Neri Castañeda and George Nakhnikian. Detroit: Wayne State University Press, 1965.

Fazio, Russell H., and Mark P. Zanna. "Direct Experience and Attitude-Behavior Consistency." In *Advances in Experimental Social Psychology*, edited by Leonard Berkowitz, vol. 14. New York: Academic Press, 1981.

Festinger, Leon. *The Theory of Cognitive Dissonance.* Stanford, Calif.: Stanford University Press, 1957.

———. "A Theory of Social Comparison Processes." *Human Relations* 7 (1954): 117–140.

Fingarette, Herbert. "How an Alcoholism Defense Works under the ALI Insanity Test." *International Journal of Law and Psychiatry* 2 (1979): 299–322.

———. "Legal Aspects of Alcoholism and Other Addictions: Some Basic Conceptual Issues." *British Journal of Addiction* 76 (1981): 125–132.

———. *The Meaning of Criminal Insanity.* Berkeley: University of California Press, 1974.

———. *On Responsibility.* New York: Basic Books, 1967.

———. "The Perils of *Powell:* In Search of a Factual Foundation for the 'Disease Concept of Alcoholism.'" *Harvard Law Review* 83 (1970): 793–812.

———. "Philosophical and Legal Aspects of the Disease Concept of Alcoholism." (A Comprehensive Analytical Review of the Scientific and Legal Literature.) In *Research Advances in Alcohol and Drug Problems,* edited by Reginald G. Smart, vol. 7. New York: Plenum Press, 1983.

———. *Self-Deception.* London: Routledge and Kegan Paul; New York: Humanities Press, 1969.

———. *The Self in Transformation.* New York: Basic Books, 1963.

Fingarette, Herbert, and Ann F. Hasse. *Mental Disabilities and Criminal Responsibility.* Berkeley: University of California Press, 1979.

Flew, Anthony. "Parapsychology: Science or Pseudo-Science?" *Pacific Philosophical Quarterly* 61 (1980): 100–114.

Foss, Jeffrey. "Rethinking Self-Deception." *American Philosophical Quarterly* 17 (1980): 237–243.

Fox, Michael. "On Unconscious Emotions." *Philosophy and Phenomenological Research* 34 (1973): 151–170.

Frankel, Arthur, and Melvin L. Snyder. "Poor Performance Following Unsolvable Problems: Learned Helplessness or Egotism?" *Journal of Personality and Social Psychology* 36 (1978): 1415–1423.

Frenkel-Brunswik, Else. "Mechanisms of Self-Deception." *Journal of Social Psychology* 10 (1939): 409–420.

Freud, Anna. *The Ego and the Mechanisms of Defense.* New York: International Universities Press, 1974.

Freud, Sigmund. *The Standard Edition of the Complete Psychological Works.* Translated by James Strachey. London: Hogarth, 1953–66.

Fromm, Erich. *Beyond the Chains of Illusion.* New York: Simon and Schuster, 1962.

Fuller, Gary. "Other Deception." *Southwestern Journal of Philosophy* 7 (1976): 21–31.

Gardiner, Patrick. "Error, Faith and Self-Deception." *Proceedings of the Aristotelian Society* 70 (1969–70): 221–243. Reprinted in *The Philosophy of Mind,* edited by Jonathan Glover. New York: Oxford University Press, 1976.

Gardner, M. Robert. *Self Inquiry.* Boston: Little, Brown, 1983.

Gazzaniga, Michael S. "Right Hemisphere Language Following Brain Bisection: A 20-Year Perspective." *American Psychologist* 38 (1983): 535–536.

Gazzaniga, Michael S., and Joseph E. LeDoux. *The Integrated Mind.* New York: Plenum Press, 1978.

Gergen, Kenneth J. *The Concept of Self.* New York: Holt, Rinehart and Winston, 1971.

———. "The Social Construction of Self-Knowledge." In *The Self, Psychological and Philosophical Issues*, edited by Theodore Mischel. Oxford: Blackwell, 1977.

———. "Theory of the Self: Impasse and Evolution." In *Advances in Experimental Social Psychology*, edited by Leonard Berkowitz. New York: Academic Press, in press.

———. *Toward Transformation in Social Knowledge*. New York: Springer-Verlag, 1982.

Gergen, Kenneth J., Alexandra Hepburn, and Debra Comer. "The Hermeneutics of Personality Description." Department of Psychology, Swarthmore College. Typescript.

Gide, André. *The Counterfeiters*, with *Journal of "The Counterfeiters."* The novel translated by Dorothy Bussy, the journal translated and annotated by Justin O'Brien. New York: Modern Library, 1955.

Gill, Merton M. *Topography and Systems in Psychoanalytic Theory*. New York: International Universities Press, 1963.

Glover, Jonathan. "Freud, Morality and Responsibility." In *Freud: The Man, His World, His Influence*, edited by Jonathan Miller. London: Weidenfeld, 1972.

———. *Responsibility*. London: Routledge and Kegan Paul, 1970.

Goffman, Erving. *Frame Analysis*. New York: Harper and Row, 1974.

———. *Interaction Ritual: Essays on Face-to-Face Behavior*. Garden City, N.Y.: Doubleday, 1967.

———. *The Presentation of Self in Everyday Life*. Garden City, N.Y.: Doubleday, 1959.

———. *Relations in Public*. New York: Basic Books, 1971.

Greenwald, Anthony G. "The Totalitarian Ego: Fabrication and Revision of Personal History." *American Psychologist* 35 (1980): 603–618.

Grene, Marjorie. "Authenticity: An Existential Virtue." *Ethics* 62 (1952): 266–274.

Griffin, A. K. *Aristotle's Psychology of Conduct*. London: Williams and Norgate, 1931.

Gur, Ruben C., and Harold A. Sackeim. "Self-Deception: A Concept in Search of a Phenomenon." *Journal of Personality and Social Psychology* 37 (1979): 147–169.

Guthrie, Jerry L. "Self-Deception and Emotional Response to Fiction." *British Journal of Aesthetics* 21 (1981): 65–75.

Guttentag, M., and C. Longfellow. "Children's Social Attributions: Development and Change." In *Nebraska Symposium on Motivation*, edited by Charles B. Keasey. Lincoln: University of Nebraska Press, 1977.

Haight, M. R. *A Study of Self-Deception*. Sussex: Harvester Press; Atlantic Highlands, N.J.: Humanities Press, 1981.

Hall, Edward T. *The Hidden Dimension*. New York: Doubleday, 1966.

Hamilton, Lee. "Role Play and Deception: A Re-examination of the Controversy. *Journal for the Theory of Social Behavior* 6 (1976): 233–250.

Hamlyn, D. W. "Self-Deception." *Proceedings of the Aristotelian Society* 45 (1971): 45–60.

———. "Unconscious Intentions." *Philosophy* 66 (1971): 12–22.

Hampshire, Stuart. "Sincerity and Single-Mindedness." In *Freedom of Mind and Other Essays by Stuart Hampshire*. Princeton, N.J.: Princeton University Press, 1971.

———. *Thought and Action*. New York: Viking Press, 1959.

Harris, Ben, and John Harvey. "Self-Attributed Choice as a Function of the Consequence of a Decision." *Journal of Personality and Social Psychology* 31 (1975): 1013.

Harvey, John H., Ben Harris, and Richard D. Barnes. "Actor-Observer Differences in the Perceptions of Responsibility and Freedom." *Journal of Personality and Social Psychology* 32 (1975): 22–28.

Harvey, Van A. "Is There an Ethics of Belief?" *Journal of Religion* 49 (1969): 41–58.

Hastie, Reid. "Schematic Principles in Human Memory." In *Social Cognition: The Ontario Symposium*, edited by E. Tory Higgins, C. Peter Herman, and Mark P. Zanna, vol. 1. Hillsdale, N.J.: Erlbaum, 1981.

Hausman, Carl R. "Creativity and Self-Deception." *Journal of Existentialism* 7 (1967): 295–308.

Hawthorne, Nathaniel. *The Complete Novels and Selected Tales of Nathaniel Hawthorne*. New York: Modern Library, 1937.

Heelas, Paul. "The Model Applied: Anthropology and Indigenous Psychologies." In *Indigenous Psychologies*, edited by P. Hellas and A. Lock. London: Academic Press, 1981.

Hegel, Georg W. F. *The Phenomenology of Mind*. Translated by J. B. Baillie. New York: Harper Torchbooks, 1967.

Heidegger, Martin. *Being and Time*. Translated by John Macquarrie and Edward Robinson. New York: Harper and Row, 1962.

Hellman, Nathan. "Bach on Self-deception." *Philosophy and Phenomenological Research* 44 (1983): 113–120.

Henry, Jules. *On Sham, Vulnerability, and Other Forms of Self-Destruction*. New York: Vintage books, 1973.

———. *Pathways to Madness*. New York: Vintage Books, 1973.

Hochschild, Arlie R. "Emotion Work, Feeling Rules, and Social Structure." *American Journal of Sociology* 85 (1979): 551–575.

Hofstadter, Douglas R., and Daniel C. Dennett. *The Mind's I: Fantasies and Reflections on Self and Soul*. Toronto: Bantam, 1982.

Holmes, David S. "Dimensions of Projection." *Psychological Bulletin* 69 (1968): 248–268.

———. "Projection as a Defense Mechanism." *Psychological Bulletin* 85 (1978): 677–688.

Holmes, David S., and B. Kent Houston. "The Defensive Function of Projection." *Journal of Personality and Social Psychology* 20 (1971): 208–213.

Horney, Karen. *Neurosis and Human Growth*. New York: Norton, 1950.

Ibsen, Henrik. *The Wild Duck*. Translated by Dounia B. Christiani. New York: Norton, 1968.

Ichheiser, Gustav. "Misunderstandings in Human Relations: A Study in False Perception." *American Journal of Sociology* 55 (1949): Part 2.

James, William. *The Principles of Psychology*. 2 vols. New York: Dover, 1950.

Johnson, Samuel. *Works*. Edited by A. Murphy. Vol. 2. London: Bentley, 1823.

Jones, Edward E. *Ingratiation*. New York: Appleton-Century-Crofts, 1964.

———. "The Rocky Road from Acts to Dispositions." *American Psychologist* 34 (1979): 107–117.

Jones, Edward E., and Steven Berglas. "Control of Attributions about the Self through Self-Handicapping Strategies: The Appeal of Alcohol and the Role of Underachievement." *Personality and Social Psychology Bulletin* 4 (1978): 200–206.

Jones, Edward E., and Keith Davis. "From Acts to Dispositions: The Attribution Process in Person Perception." In *Advances in Experimental Social Psychology,* edited by Leonard Berkowitz, vol. 2. New York: Academic Press, 1965.

Jones, Edward E., and Richard deCharms. "The Organizing Function of Interaction Roles in Person Perception." *Journal of Abnormal and Social Psychology* 57 (1958): 155–164.

Jones, Edward E., and Harold B. Gerard. *Foundations of Social Psychology.* New York: Wiley, 1967.

Jones, Edward E., and Victor A. Harris. "The Attribution of Attitudes." *Journal of Experimental Social Psychology* 3 (1967): 1–24.

Jones, Edward E., and Richard E. Nisbett. "The Actor and the Observer: Divergent Perceptions of the Causes of Behavior." In *Attribution: Perceiving the Causes of Behavior,* edited by Edward E. Jones et al. Morristown, N.J.: General Learning Press, 1972.

Jones, Edward E., and Thane Pittman. "Toward a General Theory of Strategic Self-Presentation." In *Psychological Perspectives on the Self,* edited by Jerry Suls, vol. 1. Hillsdale, N.J.: Erlbaum, 1982.

Jones, Ernest. "Rationalisation." *Journal of Abnormal Psychology* (1908).

Jones, S. C. "Self and Interpersonal Evaluations: Esteem Theories vs. Consistency Theories." *Psychological Bulletin* 79 (1973): 185–199.

Jordan, James N. "On Comprehending Free Will." *Southern Journal of Philosophy* 11 (1973): 184–201.

Joseph, R. "Awareness, the Origin of Thought, and the Role of Conscious Self-Deception in Resistance and Repression." *Psychological Reports* 46 (1980): 767–781.

Kant, Immanuel. *The Doctrine of Virtue.* Translated by Mary J. Gregor. Philadelphia: University of Pennslyvania Press, 1964.

Karniol, R., and M. Ross. "The Development of Causal Attributions in Social Perception." *Journal of Personality and Social Psychology* 34 (1976): 455–464.

Kassin, Saul M., and Mark R. Lepper. "Oversufficient and Insufficient Justification Effects: Cognitive and Behavioral Development." In *The Development of Achievement Motivation,* edited by J. Nicholls. Greenwich, Conn.: Jai Press, in press.

Kauber, Peter, and Peter H. Hare. "The Right and Duty to Will to Believe." *Canadian Journal of Philosophy* 4 (1974): 327–343.

Kaufmann, Walter. *Discovering the Mind.* 3 vols. New York: McGraw-Hill, 1980–81.

————, ed. *Existentialism from Dostoevsky to Sartre.* New York: New American Library, 1975.

————. *The Faith of a Heretic.* Garden City: Anchor Books, 1963.

————. *Nietzsche,* 4th ed. Princeton, N.J.: Princeton University Press, 1974.

Keen, Ernest. "Suicide and Self-Deception." *Psychoanalytic Review* 60 (1973–74): 575–585.

Kellenberger, J. "The Death of God and the Death of Persons." *Religious Studies* 16 (1980): 263–282.

Kelley, Harold H. "Attribution in Social Interaction." In *Attribution: Perceiving the Causes of Behavior,* edited by Edward E. Jones et al. Morristown, N.J.: General Learning Press, 1972.

————. "Attribution Theory in Social Psychology." In *Nebraska Symposium on Motivation,* edited by David Levine, vol. 15. Lincoln: University of Nebraska Press, 1967.

———. "The Process of Causal Attribution." *American Psychologist* 28 (1973): 107–128.

Ketchum, Sara Ann. "Moral Redescription and Political Self-Deception." In *Sexist Language,* edited by Mary Vetterling-Braggin. Totowa, N.J.: Littlefield, 1981.

Kierkegaard, Søren. *Either/Or.* Translated by Walter Lowrie. 2 vols. Princeton, N.J.: Princeton University Press, 1959.

———. *Fear and Trembling* and *The Sickness unto Death.* Translated by Walter Lowrie. Garden City, N.Y.: Anchor Books, 1954.

———. *Purity of Heart Is to Will One Thing.* Translated by Douglas Steere. New York: Harper Torchbooks, 1956.

King-Farlow, John. "Akrasia, Self-Mastery and the Master Self." *Pacific Philosophical Quarterly* 62 (1981): 47–60.

———. "The Concept of Mine." *Inquiry* (1964).

———. "Critical Notice of Herbert Fingarette's *Self-Deception.*" *Metaphilosophy* 4 (1973): 76–84.

———. "Deceptions? Assertions? or Second-String Verbiage?" *Philosophy* 56 (1981): 100–105.

———. "'Mine' and the Family of Human Imaginings." *Inquiry* (1969).

———. "Philosophical Nationalism: Self-Deception and Self-Direction." *Dialogue* 17 (1978): 591–615.

———. "The Sartrian Analysis of Sexuality." *Journal of Existential Psychiatry* (1962).

———. "Self-Deceivers and Sartrian Seducers." *Analysis* 23 (1963): 131–136.

———. *Self-Knowledge and Social Relations.* New York: Science History Publications, 1978.

King-Farlow, John, and William N. Christensen. *Faith and the Life of Reason.* Dordrecht: D. Reidel, 1972.

King-Farlow, John, and Lorraine Code. "Bonne Foi/Mauvaise Foi, Sincérité et Espoir." *Dialogue* 12 (1973): 502–514.

King-Farlow, John, and Fred W. Hagen. "Recent Texts in Philosophy." *Massachusetts Review* (1964). Includes a review of Herbert Fingarette's *Self in Transformation.*

King-Farlow, John, and D. W. Hunt. "Reflections on the Fall." *Scottish Journal of Theology* (1982).

King-Farlow, John, and J. M. Rothstein. "Thoughts, Acts and Authentic Guilt." [Reply to Fingarette's "Real Guilt and Neurotic Guilt."] *Archiv für Philosophie* (1964).

Kipp, David. "Aphorisms." *Independent Journal of Philosophy* 3 (1979): 61–69.

———. "On Self-Deception." *Philosophical Quarterly* 30 (1980): 305–317.

Kirkpatrick, John. "Some Marquesan Understandings of Action and Identity." In *Approaches to Ethnopsychology,* edited by G. M. White and J. Kirkpatrick. In press.

Kittay, Eva Feder. "On Hypocrisy." *Metaphilosophy* 13 (1982): 277–289.

Kleinke, Chris L. *Self-Perception: The Psychology of Personal Awareness.* San Francisco: W. H. Freeman, 1978.

Kohlberg, Lawrence. "Moral Development and Identification." In *Child Psychology,* edited by H. Stephenson. Chicago: University of Chicago Press, 1962.

Kopp, Sheldon. *An End to Innocence: Facing Life without Illusions.* New York: Bantam Books, 1981.

Kovar, Leo. "The Pursuit of Self-Deception." *Review of Existential Psychology and Psychiatry* 13 (1974): 136–149.

Kuhn, Thomas S. *The Structure of Scientific Revolutions.* Chicago: University of Chicago Press, 1962.

Kun, A. "Development of the Magnitude-Covariation and Compensation Schemata in Ability and Effort Attribution of Performance." *Child Development* 48 (1977): 862–873.

Laing, R. D. *The Divided Self.* Baltimore, Md.: Penguin, 1973.

Lang, Berel. "The Neurotic as Moral Agent." *Philosophy and Phenomenological Research* 29 (1968): 216–231.

Langer, Ellen J. "Rethinking the Role of Thought in Social Interaction." In *New Directions in Attribution Research,* edited by John H. Harvey, William Ickes, and Robert F. Kidd. Hillsdale, N.J.: Erlbaum, 1978.

Langer, Ellen J., and Anne Benevento. "Self-Induced Dependence." *Journal of Personality and Social Psychology* 36 (1978): 886–893.

Langer, Ellen J., Arthur Blank, and Benzion Chanowitz. "The Mindlessness of Ostensibly Thoughtful Action: The Role of Placebic Information in Interpersonal Interaction." *Journal of Personality and Social Psychology* 36 (1978): 635–642.

Langer, Ellen, Lawrence Perlmuter, Benzion Chanowitz, and Robert Rubin. "Two New Applications of Mindlessness Theory: Aging and Alcoholism," 1984. Department of Psychology and Social Relations, Harvard University. Typescript.

Langer, Ellen J., and J. Roth. "Heads I Win, Tails It's Chance: The Illusion of Control As a Function of the Sequence of Outcomes in a Purely Chance Task." *Journal of Personality and Social Psychology* 32 (1975): 951.

Latané, Bibb, and John M. Darley. "Bystander Apathy." *American Scientist* 57 (1969): 244–268.

———. "Group Inhibition of Bystander Interventions in Emergencies." *Journal of Personality and Social Psychology* 10 (1968): 215–221.

———. *The Unresponsive Bystander: Why Doesn't He Help?* New York: Appleton-Century-Crofts, 1970.

Latané, Bibb, and Judith Rodin. "A Lady in Distress: Inhibiting Effects of Friends and Strangers on Bystander Interaction." *Journal of Experimental Social Psychology* 5 (1969): 189–202.

Lazarus, Richard S. "Cognitive and Coping Processes in Emotion." In *Stress and Coping,* edited by Alan Monet and Richard S. Lazarus. New York: Columbia University Press, 1977.

Lee, Vernon. *Vital Lies.* 2 vols. London: John Lane, 1912.

Lemmon, E. J. "If I Know, Do I Know That I Know?" In *Epistemology,* edited by Avrum Stroll. New York: Harper and Row, 1967.

———. "Moral Dilemmas." *Philosophical Review* 71 (1962): 139–158.

Leon, Philip. *The Ethics of Power.* London: Allen and Unwin, 1935.

Lepper, Mark R., and David Greene, eds. *The Hidden Costs of Reward.* Hillsdale, N.J.: Erlbaum, 1978.

Lepper, Mark R., David Greene, and Richard E. Nisbett. "Undermining Children's Intrinsic Interest with Extrinsic Reward: A Test of the 'Over-justification' Hypothesis." *Journal of Personality and Social Psychology* 28 (1973): 129–137.

Linder, Darwin, Joel Cooper, and Edward Jones. "Decision Freedom as a Determinant of the Role of Incentive Magnitude in Attitude Change." *Journal of Personality and Social Psychology* 3 (1967): 245–254.

Linehan, Elizabeth A. "Ignorance, Self-Deception and Moral Accountability." *Journal of Value Inquiry* 16 (1982): 101–115.

Linsky, Leonard. "Deception." *Inquiry* 6 (1963): 157–169.

Locke, John. "Of Enthusiasm." In *An Essay on Human Understanding,* vol. 2. New York: Dover, 1959.

Lord, Charles G., Lee Ross, and Mark R. Lepper. "Biased Assimilation and Attitude Polarization: The Effects of Prior Theories on Subsequently Considered Evidence." *Journal of Personality and Social Psychology* 37 (1979): 2098–2109.

Lovejoy, Arthur O. *Reflections on Human Nature.* Baltimore, Md.: Johns Hopkins Press, 1961.

Lynch, Mervin, Kenneth J. Gergen, and Ardyth A. Norem-Hebeisen, eds. *The Self-Concept: Advances in Theory and Research.* Boston: Ballinger, 1981.

McDougall, William. *Outline of Abnormal Psychology.* London: Methuen, 1926.

McGinnies, Elliot. "Emotionality and Perceptual Defense." *Psychological Review* 56 (1949): 244–251.

McGuire, William J. "A Contextualist Theory of Knowledge: Its Implications for Innovation and Reform in Psychological Research." In *Advances in Experimental Social Psychology,* edited by Leonard Berkowitz, vol. 16. New York: Academic Press, 1983.

MacIntyre, Alasdair. *The Unconscious.* New York: Humanities Press, 1958.

Mandler, George. *Mind and Emotion.* New York: Wiley, 1975.

Mannison, D. S. "Lying and Lies." *Australasian Journal of Philosophy* 47 (1969): 132–144.

Marcel, Gabriel. *Homo Viator: Introduction to a Metaphysic of Hope.* New York: Harper and Row, 1951.

Marks, Charles E. *Commissurotomy, Consciousness, and Unity of Mind.* Cambridge: MIT Press, 1981.

Markus, Hazel. "Self-Schemata and Processing Information about the Self." *Journal of Personality and Social Psychology* 35 (1977): 63–78.

Martin, Mike W. "Demystifying Doublethink: Self-Deception, Truth, and Freedom in *1984.*" *Social Theory and Practice* 10 (1984): 319–331.

———. "Factor's Functionalist Account of Self-Deception." *The Personalist* 60 (1979): 336–342.

———. "Immorality and Self-Deception." *Dialogue* 16 (1977): 274–280.

———. "*Invisible Man* and the Indictment of Innocence." *CLA Journal* 25 (1982): 288–302.

———. *Moral Perspectives on Self-Deception.* (1984) Department of Philosophy, Chapman College. Orange, Calif. Typescript.

———. "Morality and Self-Deception: Paradox, Ambiguity, or Vagueness?" *Man and World* 12 (1979): 47–60.

———. "Sartre on Lying to Oneself." *Philosophy Research Archives* 4 (1978): 1–26.

———. "Self-Deception, Self-Pretense, and Emotional Detachment." *Mind* 88 (1979): 441–446.

Mayo, Bernard. "Belief and Constraint." In *Knowledge and Belief,* edited by A. Phillips Griffith. Oxford: Oxford University Press, 1967.

Mead, George Herbert. *Mind, Self, and Society.* Chicago: University of Chicago Press, 1934.

Mehrabian, Albert. *Nonverbal Communication.* Chicago: Aldine-Atherton, 1972.

Meiland, Jack W. "What Ought We to Believe? or The Ethics of Belief Revisited." *American Philosophical Quarterly* 17 (1980): 15–24.

Mele, Alfred R. "Self-Deception." *Philosophical Quarterly* 33 (1983).

———. "Self-Deception, Action and Will: Comments." *Erkenntnis* 18 (1982): 159–164.

Merleau-Ponty, Maurice. *Sense and Non-Sense.* Translated by Herbert L. Dreyfus and Patricia A. Dreyfus. Evanston, Ill.: Northwestern University Press, 1964.

Midgley, Mary. *Wickedness: A Philosophical Essay.* Boston: Routledge and Kegan Paul, 1984.

Milgram, Stanley. "Behavioral Study of Obedience." *Journal of Abnormal and Social Psychology* 67 (1963): 371–378.

———. *Obedience to Authority.* New York: Harper and Row, 1975.

———. "Some Conditions to Obedience and Disobedience to Authority." *Human Relations* 18 (1965): 57–76.

Miller, Dale T., and Michael Ross. "Self-Serving Biases in the Attribution of Causality: Fact or Fiction?" *Psychological Bulletin* 82 (1975): 213–235.

Millham, J., and R. W. Kellogg. "Need for Social Approval—Impression Management or Self-Deception?" *Journal of Research in Personality* 14 (1980): 445–457.

Mills, C. Wright. "Situated Actions and Vocabularies of Motive." *American Sociological Review* 5 (1940).

Milo, Ronald D. *Immorality.* Princeton, N.J.: Princeton University Press, 1984.

Miri, Mrinal. "Self-Deception." *Philosophy and Phenomenological Research* 34 (1974): 576–585.

Mischel, T. "Understanding Neurotic Behavior: From 'Mechanisms' to 'Intentionality.'" In *Understanding Other Persons,* edited by T. Mischel. Totowa, N.J.: Rowman and Littlefield, 1974.

Molina, Fernando. *Existentialism As Philosophy.* Englewood Cliffs, N.J.: Prentice-Hall, 1962.

Monts, J. Kenneth, A. Louis, and Rudy Nydegger. "Interpersonal Self-Deception and Personality Correlates." *Journal of Social Psychology* 103 (1977): 91–99.

Morgan, M. "The Overjustification Effect: A Developmental Test of Self-Perception Interpretations." *Journal of Personality and Social Psychology* 40 (1981): 809–821.

Morris, Phyllis Sutton. "Self-Deception: Sartre's Resolution of the Paradox." In *Jean-Paul Sartre,* edited by Hugh J. Silverman and Frederick A. Elliston. Pittsburgh: Duquesne University Press, 1980.

Mortimore, G. W., ed. *Weakness of Will.* London: Macmillan, 1971.

Mounce, H. O. "Self-Deception." *Proceedings of the Aristotelian Society* 45 (1971): 61–72.

Moustakas, Clark E. "Honesty, Idiocy, and Manipulation." In *Readings in Humanistic Psychology,* edited by A. Sutich and M. Vich. New York: Free Press, 1969.

Mullen, John Douglas. *Kierkegaard's Philosophy: Self-Deception and Cowardice in the Present Age.* New York: New American Library, 1981.

Murphy, Arthur Edward. "The Moral Self in Sickness and in Health." In *The Theory of Practical Reason,* edited by A. I. Melden. La Salle, Ill.: Open Court, 1964.

Murphy, Gardner. "Experiments in Overcoming Self-Deception." *Psychophysiology* 6 (1970): 790–799.

———. *Outgrowing Self-Deception.* New York: Basic Books, 1975.

Murphy, Gardner, and Wendell M. Swenson. "Outgrowing Self-Deception." *American Journal of Psychiatry* 133 (1976).

Myers, Donald G., and J. Ridl. "Can We All Be Better Than Average?" *Psychology Today* 12 (1979): 89–98.

Mynatt, C., and S. J. Sherman. "Responsibility Attribution in Groups and Individuals: A Direct Test of the Diffusion of Responsibility Hypothesis." *Journal of Personality and Social Psychology* 32 (1975).

Needham, Rodney. *Belief, Language and Experience.* Chicago: University of Chicago Press, 1972.

Neisser, Ulric. "John Dean's Memory: A Case Study." *Cognition* 9 (1981): 1–22.

Nemiah, John C. *Foundations of Psychopathology.* New York: Aronson, 1973.

Neu, Jerome. *Emotion, Thought and Therapy.* Berkeley: University of California Press, 1977.

Niebuhr, Reinhold. *The Nature and Destiny of Man.* Vol. 1. New York: Scribner, 1964.

Nietzsche, Friedrich. *Basic Writings of Nietzsche.* Edited and translated by Walter Kaufmann. New York: Modern Library, 1968.

———. *The Use and Abuse of History.* Translated by Adrian Collins. Indianapolis, Ind.: Bobbs-Merrill, 1957.

———. *The Will to Power.* Translated by Walter Kaufmann. New York: Vintage Books, 1968.

Nisbett, Richard, and Nancy Bellows. "Verbal Reports about Causal Influences as Social Judgments: Private Access versus Public Theories." *Journal of Personality and Social Psychology* 35 (1977).

Nisbett, Richard E., and Lee Ross. *Human Inference: Strategies and Shortcomings in Social Judgement.* Englewood Cliffs, N.J.: Prentice-Hall, 1980.

Nisbett, Richard E., and Timothy D. Wilson. "The Halo Effect: Evidence for Unconscious Alteration of Judgments." *Journal of Personality and Social Psychology* 35 (1977): 250–256.

———. "Telling More Than We Can Know: Verbal Reports on Mental Processes. *Psychological Review* 84 (1977): 231–259.

Oates, Joyce Carol. "The Impostors." *Review of Existential Psychiatry* 13 (1974): 169–183.

Olafson, Frederick. *Principles and Persons: An Ethical Interpretation of Existentialism.* Baltimore, Md.: Johns Hopkins, 1967.

O'Neill, Eugene. *The Iceman Cometh.* New York: Vintage Books, 1957.

Ortega y Gasset, José. *The Revolt of the Masses.* New York: Norton, 1960.

Orwell, George. *1984.* New York: New American Library, 1961.

Palmer, Anthony. "Characterizing Self-Deception." *Mind* 88 (1979): 45–58.

———. "Self-Deception: A Problem about Autobiography." *Proceedings of the Aristotelian Society,* supp. vol. 53 (1979): 61–76.

Paluch, Stanley. "Self-Deception." *Inquiry* 10 (1967): 268–278.

Paskow, Alan. "Towards a Theory of Self-Deception." *Man and World* 12 (1979): 178–191.

Pears, David. "Freud, Sartre and Self-Deception." In *Freud*, edited by R. Wollheim. Garden City, N.Y.: Anchor Books, 1974. Earlier version published as "The Paradoxes of Self-Deception." *Teorema* (1974): 7–24.

———. "Motivated Irrationality, Freudian Theory and Cognitive Dissonance." In *Philosophical Essays on Freud*, edited by R. Wollheim and J. Hopkins. Cambridge: Cambridge University Press, 1982.

———. *Motivated Irrationality*. New York: Oxford University Press, 1984.

Penelhum, Terence, W. E. Kennick, and Arnold Isenberg. "Symposium: Pleasure and Falsity." *American Philosophical Quarterly* 1 (1964): 81–91.

Peterman, James. "Self-Deception and the Problem of Avoidance." *Southwestern Journal of Philosophy* 21 (1983): 565–574.

Peyre, Henri. *Literature and Sincerity*. New Haven, Conn.: Yale University Press, 1963.

Phillips, D. Z. "Bad Faith and Sartre's Waiter." *Philosophy* 56 (1981): 23–31.

Piaget, Jean. *The Moral Judgment of the Child*. New York: Free Press, 1965.

Pole, David. "The Socratic Injunction." *Journal of the British Society for Phenomenology* 2 (1971): 31–40.

———. "Virtue and Reason." *Proceedings of the Aristotelian Society* 48 (1974): 43–62.

Price, H. H. *Belief*. New York: Humanities Press, 1960.

Prince, Morton. *The Unconscious: The Fundamentals of Human Personality, Normal and Abnormal*. New York: Macmillan, 1921.

Proust, Marcel. *Swann's Way*. Vol. 1 of *Remembrance of Things Past*, translated by C. K. Scott Moncrieff. New York: Vintage Books, 1970.

Pugmire, David. " 'Strong' Self-Deception." *Inquiry* 12 (1969): 339–346.

Quattrone, George, and Amos Tversky. "Causal versus Diagnostic Contingencies: On Self-Deception and the Voter's Illusion." *Journal of Personality and Social Psychology* 46 (1984): 237–248.

Rank, Otto. *Truth and Reality*. Translated by Jessie Taft. New York: Norton, 1978.

Rapaport, David. *The Structure of Psychoanalytic Theory: A Systemizing Attempt*. New York: International Universities Press, 1960.

Reid, Thomas. *Essays on the Active Powers of the Human Mind*, essay 5, chap. 4. Cambridge: MIT Press, 1969.

Reik, Theodor. *Listening with the Third Ear*. New York: Arena Books, 1972.

Reilly, Richard. "Self-Deception: Resolving the Epistemological Paradox." *The Personalist* 57 (1976): 391–394.

Ricoeur, Paul. *Freud and Philosophy: An Essay in Interpretation*. Translated by Denis Savage. New Haven, Conn.: Yale University Press, 1970.

Rieff, Philip. *Freud: The Mind of the Moralist*. London: Gollancz, 1959.

Riess, Marc, and Barry R. Schlenker. "Attitude Change and Responsibility Avoidance As Modes of Dilemma Resolution in Forced-Compliance Situations." *Journal of Personality and Social Psychology* 35 (1977): 21–30.

Rivière, Jacques. *The Ideal Reader*. New York: Meridian Books, 1960.

Robinson, Jonathan. *Duty and Hypocrisy in Hegel's "Phenomenology of Mind": An Essay in the Real and Ideal*. Toronto: University of Toronto Press, 1977.

Rogers, Carl R. *Client-Centered Therapy: Its Current Practice, Implications and Theory*. Boston: Houghton Mifflin, 1951.

———. "A Theory of Therapy, Personality, and Interpersonal Relationships as Developed in the Client-Centered Framework." In *Psychology: A Study of a Science*, edited by S. Koch, vol. 3. New York: McGraw-Hill, 1959.

Rorty, Amélie Oksenberg. "Adaptivity and Self-Knowledge." *Inquiry* 18 (1975): 1–22.

———. "Akrasia and Conflict." *Inquiry* 23 (1980): 193–212.

———. "Akratic Believers." *American Philosophical Quarterly* 20 (1983): 175–183.

———. "Belief and Self-Deception." *Inquiry* 15 (1972): 387–410.

———. "Self-Deception, Akrasia, and Irrationality." *Social Science Information* 19 (1980): 905–922.

———. "The Transformation of Persons." *Philosophy* 48 (1973): 261–275.

Rorty, Richard. "Incorrigibility as the Mark of the Mental." *Journal of Philosophy* 67 (1970): 419–420.

Rosenthal, A. M. *Thirty-Eight Witnesses.* New York: McGraw-Hill, 1964.

Ross, Lee. "The Intuitive Psychologist and His Shortcomings: Distortions in the Attribution Process." In *Advances in Experimental Social Psychology,* edited by Leonard Berkowitz, vol. 10. New York: Academic Press, 1977.

Runciman, Walter G. "False Consciousness." *Philosophy* 44 (1969): 303–313.

Russell, J. Michael. "Reflection and Self-Deception." *Journal for Research in Phenomenology* 11 (1981): 62–74.

———. "Saying, Feeling, and Self-Deception." *Behaviorism* 6 (1978): 27–43.

Rychlak, Joseph F. *Discovering Free Will and Personal Responsibility.* New York: Oxford University Press, 1979.

Ryle, Gilbert. *The Concept of Mind.* New York: Barnes and Noble, 1949.

———. *Dilemmas.* Cambridge: Cambridge University Press, 1980.

Sabini, John, and Maury Silver. *Moralities of Everyday Life.* New York: Oxford University Press, 1982.

Sackeim, Harold A., and Ruben C. Gur. "Self-Deception, Other-Deception, and Self-Reported Psychopathology." *Journal of Consulting and Clinical Psychology* 47 (1979): 213–215.

———. "Self-Deception, Self-Confrontation, and Consciousness." In *Consciousness and Self-Regulation: Advances in Research and Theory,* edited by Gary E. Schwartz and David Shapiro. New York: Plenum Press, 1978.

Santoni, Ronald E. "Bad Faith and 'Lying to Oneself.'" *Philosophy and Phenomenological Research* 38 (1978): 384–398.

———. "Sartre on 'Sincerity': Bad Faith? or Equivocation?" *The Personalist* 53 (1972): 150–160.

Sarbin, Theodore, and William C. Coe. "Hypnosis and Psychopathology: Replacing Old Myths with Fresh Metaphors." *Journal of Abnormal Psychology* 88 (1979): 506–526.

Sartre, Jean-Paul. *Anti-Semite and Jew.* Translated by George J. Becker. New York: Schocken, 1965.

———. *Being and Nothingness.* Translated by Hazel E. Barnes. New York: Washington Square Press, 1966.

———. "Existentialism Is a Humanism." In *Existentialism from Dostoevsky to Sartre,* edited by Walter Kaufmann. New York: New American Library, 1975.

———. *No Exit and Three Other Plays.* Translated by Stuart Gilbert and Lionel Abel. New York: Vintage Books, 1949.

Saunders, John Turk. "The Paradox of Self-Deception." *Philosophy and Phenomenological Research* 35 (1975): 559–570.

Schachter, Stanley, and Jerome Singer. "Cognitive, Social and Physiological Determinants of Emotional State." *Psychological Review* 62 (1962).

Schadler, Margaret, and Beverly Ayers-Nachamkin. "The Development of Excuse-Making." In *Excuses: Masquerades in Search of Grace,* edited by C. R. Snyder, Raymond L. Higgins, and Rita J. Stucky. New York: Wiley, 1983.

Scheff, Thomas J. *Being Mentally Ill: A Sociological Theory.* Chicago: Aldine, 1971.

Scheler, Max. *Ressentiment.* Edited by Lewis A. Coser and translated by William W. Holdheim. New York: Schocken, 1972.

Schiller, Ferdinand Canning Scott. *Problems of Belief.* New York: Doran, 1924.

Schlenker, Barry R. "Translating Actions into Attitudes: An Identity-Analytic Approach to the Explanation of Social Conduct." In *Advances in Experimental Social Psychology,* edited by Leonard Berkowitz, vol. 15. New York: Academic Press, 1982.

Schopenhauer, Arthur. *The World as Will and Representation.* Translated by E. F. I. Payne. Vol. 2, Chap. 19. New York: Dover, 1966.

Scott-Taggart, M. J. "Socratic Irony and Self Deceit." *Ratio* 14 (1972): 1–15.

Shafer, Roy. *A New Language for Psychoanalysis.* New Haven, Conn.: Yale University Press, 1976.

Shapiro, Gary. "Choice and Universality in Sartre's Ethics." *Man and World* 7 (1974): 20–36.

Shaw, M. E., and H. T. Reitan. "Attribution of Responsibility as a Basis for Sanctioning Behavior." *British Journal of Social and Clinical Psychology* 8 (1969): 217–226.

Shklar, Judith. "Let Us Not Be Hypocritical." *Daedalus* 108 (1979): 1–25. Published in a revised version in Judith N. Shklar, *Ordinary Vices* (Cambridge: Harvard University Press, 1984).

Shlien, John M. "A Client-Centered Approach to Schizophrenia." In *Psychotherapy of the Psychoses,* edited by Arthur Burton. New York: Basic Books, 1961.

Shoemaker, Sydney. *Self-Knowledge and Self-Identity.* Ithaca, N.Y.: Cornell University Press, 1963.

Shope, Robert K. "Freud on Conscious and Unconscious Intentions." *Inquiry* 13 (1970): 149–159.

Shotter, John. "Telling and Reporting: Prospective and Retrospective Uses of Self-Ascriptions." In *The Psychology of Ordinary Explanations of Social Behavior,* edited by Charles Antaki. London: Academic Press, 1981.

Shrauger, J. Sidney. "Responses to Evaluation As a Function of Initial Self-Perceptions." *Psychological Bulletin* 82 (1975): 581–596.

Sidgwick, Henry. "Unreasonable Action." *Mind* 11 (1893): 174–187.

Siegler, Frederick A. "An Analysis of Self-Deception." *Nous* 2 (1968): 147–164.

———. "Demos on Lying to Oneself." *Journal of Philosophy* 59 (1962): 469–475.

———. "Lying." *American Philosophical Quarterly* 3 (1966): 128–136.

———. "Self-Deception." *Australasian Journal of Philosophy* 41 (1963): 29–43.

———. "Self-Deception and Other Deception." *Journal of Philosophy* 60 (1963): 759–764.

———. "Unconscious Intentions." *Inquiry* 10 (1967): 251–267.

Skolnick, Paul. "Reactions to Personal Evaluations: A Failure to Replicate." *Journal of Personality and Social Psychology* 18 (1971): 62–67.

Smith, Adam. "Of the Nature of Self-Deceit." In *The Theory of Moral Sentiments.* New York: Kelley, 1966.

Smith, Holly, "Culpable Ignorance." *Philosophical Review* 92 (1983): 543–571.

Smith, Timothy W., C. R. Snyder, and Mitchell M. Handelsman. "On the Self-Serving Function of an Academic Wooden Leg." *Journal of Personality and Social Psychology* 42 (1982): 314–321.

Smith, Timothy W., C. R. Snyder, and Suzanne Perkins. "The Self-Serving Function of Hypochondriacal Complaints: Physical Symptoms as Self-Handicapping Strategies." *Journal of Personality and Social Psychology* 44 (1983): 787–797.

Smoot, William. "The Concept of Authenticity in Sartre." *Man and World* 7 (1974): 135–148.

Snyder, C. R., and Mark S. Clair. "Does Insecurity Breed Acceptance? Effects of Trait and Situational Insecurity on Acceptance of Positive and Negative Diagnostic Feedback." *Journal of Consulting and Clinical Psychology* 45 (1977): 843–850.

———. "Effects of Expected and Obtained Grades on Teacher Evaluation and Attribution of Performance." *Journal of Educational Psychology* 68 (1976): 75–82.

Snyder, C. R., and J. R. Endelman. "Effects of Degree of Interpersonal Similarity on Physical Distance and Self-Reported Attraction: A Comparison of Uniqueness and Reinforcement Theory Predictions." *Journal of Personality* 47 (1979): 492–505.

Snyder, C. R., Raymond L. Higgins, and Rita J. Stucky. *Excuses: Masquerades in Search of Grace*. New York: Wiley, 1983.

Snyder, C. R., and Randy J. Shenkel. "Effects of 'Favorability,' Modality, and Relevance on Acceptance of General Personality Interpretations Prior to and after Receiving Diagnostic Feedback." *Journal of Consulting and Clinical Psychology* 44 (1976): 34–41.

Snyder, C. R., Randy J. Shenkel, and Carol R. Lowery. "Acceptance of Personality Interpretations: The 'Barnum Effect' and Beyond." *Journal of Consulting and Clinical Psychology* 45 (1977): 104–114.

Snyder, C. R., and Timothy W. Smith. "Symptoms as Self-Handicapping Strategies." In *Integrations of Clinical and Social Psychology*, edited by Gifford Weary and Herbert L. Mirels. New York: Oxford, 1982.

Snyder, Mark, Elizabeth D. Tanke, and Ellen Berscheid. "Social Perception and Interpersonal Behavior: On the Self-Fulfilling Nature of Social Stereotypes." *Journal of Personality and Social Psychology* 35 (1977): 656–666.

Snyder, Melvin L., Robert E. Kleck, Angelo Strenta, and Steven J. Mentzer. "Avoidance of the Handicapped: An Attributional Ambiguity Analysis." *Journal of Personality and Social Psychology* 37 (1979): 2297–2306.

Solomon, Robert. *The Passions*. Notre Dame: University of Notre Dame Press, 1983.

Speer, Albert. *Inside the Third Reich*. Translated by Richard Winston and Clara Winston. New York: Avon Books, 1971.

Springer, Sally P., and Georg Deutsche. *Left Brain, Right Brain*. San Francisco: Freeman, 1981.

Stern, Laurent. "On Make-Believe." *Philosophy and Phenomenological Research*. 28 (1967–68): 24–38.

Sullivan, Harry Stack. *The Interpersonal Theory of Psychiatry*. New York: Norton, 1953.

Swann, William J., and Stephen J. Read. "Self-Verification Processes: How We Sustain Our Self-Conceptions." *Journal of Experimental Social Psychology* 17 (1981): 351–372.

Sykes, Gresham M., and David Matza. "Techniques of Neutralization: A Theory of Delinquency." *American Sociological Review* 22 (1957): 664–670.

Szabados, Béla. "Butler on Corrupt Conscience." *Journal of the History of Philosophy*, October 1976.

———. "Fingarette on Self-Deception." *Philosophical Papers* 6 (1977): 21–30.

———. "Freud, Self-Knowledge and Psychoanalysis." *Canadian Journal of Philosophy*, 1982.

———. "Hypocrisy." *Canadian Journal of Philosophy* 9 (1979): 195–210.

———. "The Morality of Self-Deception." *Dialogue* 13 (1974): 25–34.

———. Review of M. R. Haight's *A Study of Self-Deception*. *Canadian Philosophical Reviews* (1982): 259–263.

———. "Rorty on Belief and Self-Deception." *Inquiry* 17 (1974): 464–473.

———. "Self-Deception." *Canadian Journal of Philosophy* 4 (1974): 51–68.

———. "Wishful Thinking and Self-Deception." *Analysis* 33 (1973): 201–205.

Tedeschi, James T., ed. *Impression Management Theory and Social Psychological Research*. New York: Academic Press, 1981.

Tesser, Abraham, and Jennifer Campbell. "Self-Definition and Self-Evaluation Maintenance." In *Social Psychological Perspectives on the Self*, edited by Jerry Suls and Anthony Greenwald, vol. 2. Hillsdale, N.J.: Erlbaum, 1983.

Tesser, Abraham, and Del Paulhus. "The Definition of Self: Private and Public Self-Evaluation Management Strategies." *Journal of Personality and Social Psychology* 44 (1983): 672–682.

Tesser, Abraham, and Jonathan Smith. "Some Effects of Task Relevance and Friendship on Helping: You Don't Always Help the One You Like." *Journal of Experimental Social Psychology* 16 (1980): 582–590.

Tetlock, Philip E., and Ariel Levi. "Attribution Bias: On the Inconclusiveness of the Cognition-Motivation Debate." *Journal of Experimental Social Psychology* 18 (1982): 68–88.

Thigpen, Corbett H., and Hervey M. Cleckley. "A Case of Multiple Personality." *Journal of Abnormal and Social Psychology* (1954): 135–151.

Tolstoy, Leo. *Anna Karenina*. New York: New American Library, 1961.

———. *The Death of Ivan Ilych*. In *Great Short Works of Leo Tolstoy*. Translated by Louise and Aylmer Maude. New York: Harper and Row, 1967.

Trilling, Lionel. *Sincerity and Authenticity*. Cambridge: Harvard University Press, 1971.

Tversky, Amos. "Self-Deception and Self-Perception." In *The Multiple Self*, edited by Jon Elster. Cambridge: Cambridge University Press, forthcoming.

Tversky, Amos, and Daniel Kahneman. "The Framing of Decisions and the Rationality of Choice." *Science* 211 (1981): 543–558.

———. "Judgment under Uncertainty: Heuristics and Biases." *Science* 185 (1974): 1124–1130.

Vaihinger, Hans. *The Philosophy of "As-If."* Translated by C. K. Ogden. New York: Barnes and Noble, 1952.

Walker, A. D. M. "The Ideal of Sincerity." *Mind* 87 (1978): 481–497.

———. "Sartre, Santoni and Sincerity." *The Personalist* 58 (1977): 88–92.

Warner, C. Terry, and Terrance D. Olson. "Another View of Family Conflict and Family Wholeness." *Family Relations* (1981): 493–503.

Warner, Richard. "Deception and Self-Deception in Shamanism and Psychiatry." *International Journal of Social Psychiatry* 26 (1980): 41–52.

Wason, P. C., and J. St. B. T. Evans. "Dual Processes in Reasoning?" *Cognition* 3 (1975).

Welles, Jim. "The Sociobiology of Self-Deception." *Human Ethology Newsletter* 3 (1981): 14–19.

Wells, L. Edward, and Gerald Marwell. *Self-Esteem: Its Conceptualization and Measurement.* Beverly Hills, Calif.: Sage, 1976.

Wetzel, C. G., Timothy D. Wilson, and J. Kort. "The Halo Effect Revisited: Forewarned Is Not Forearmed." *Journal of Experimental Social Psychology* 17 (1981): 427–439.

White, Alan R. *Attention.* Oxford: Blackwell, 1964.

Wicker, Allan W. "Attitudes versus Actions: The Relationship of Verbal and Overt Behavior Responses to Attitude Objects." *Journal of Social Issues* 25 (1969): 41–78.

Wicklund, Robert. "Self-Focused Attention and the Validity of Self-Reports." In *Consistency in Social Behavior: The Ontario Symposium,* edited by Mark P. Zanna, E. Tory Higgins, and C. Peter Herman, vol. 2. Hillsdale, N.J.: Erlbaum, 1982.

Wild, John. "Authentic Existence." In *Introductory Readings in Ethics,* edited by William K. Frankena and John T. Granrose. Englewood Cliffs, N.J.: Prentice-Hall, 1974.

Wilkes, Kathleen V. "Consciousness and Commissurotomy." *Philosophy* 53 (1978): 185–199.

Williams, Bernard. *Problems of the Self.* Cambridge: Cambridge University Press, 1973.

Williams, John N. "Believing the Self-Contradictory." *American Philosophical Quarterly* 19 (1982): 279–285.

Wilshire, Bruce. "Self, Body and Self-Deception." *Man, and World* 5 (1972): 422–451.

Wilson, Catherine. "Self-Deception and Psychological Realism." *Philosophical Investigations* 3 (1980): 47–60.

Wilson, Timothy D. "Strangers to Ourselves: The Origins and Accuracy of Beliefs about One's Own Mental States." In *Attribution in Contemporary Psychology,* edited by John H. Harvey and Gifford Weary. New York: Academic Press (in press).

Wilson, Timothy D., Dana Dunn, Jane Bybee, Diane Hyman, and John Rotondo. "Effects of Self-Reflection on Attitude-Behavior Consistency." *Journal of Personality and Social Behavior* 47 (1984): 5–16.

Wilson, Timothy D., Jay Hull, and Jim Johnson. "Awareness and Self-Perception: Verbal Reports on Internal States." *Journal of Personality and Social Psychology* 40 (1981): 53–71.

Wilson, Timothy D., P. S. Laser, and Julie I. Stone. "Judging the Predictors of One's Own Mood: Accuracy and the Use of Shared Theories." *Journal of Experimental Social Psychology* 18 (1982): 537–556.

Wilson, Timothy D., G. Daniel Lassiter, and Julie I. Stone. "Regulated versus Unregulated Nonverbal Behavior in Social Interaction: Evidence for Limited Access to Mental States." (1983) Department of Psychology, University of Virginia. Charlottesville. Typescript.

Wilson, Timothy D., and Patricia W. Linville. "Improving the Academic Performance of College Freshmen: Attribution Therapy Revisited." *Journal of Personality and Social Psychology* 42 (1982): 367–376.

Wilson, Timothy D., and Richard E. Nisbett. "The Accuracy of Verbal Reports about the Effects of Stimuli on Evaluations and Behavior." *Social Psychology Quarterly* 41 (1978): 118–131.

Winters, Barbara. "Believing at Will." *Journal of Philosophy* 76 (1979): 243–256.

Wittgenstein, Ludwig. *Culture and Value.* Translated by Peter Winch. New York: Blackwell, 1980.

———. *Philosophical Investigations.* Translated by G. E. M. Anscombe. 3d ed. New York: Macmillan, 1953.

Wollheim, Richard, ed. *Freud: A Collection of Critical Essays.* Garden City, N.Y.: Anchor Press, 1974.

———. "Wish Fulfillment." In *Rational Action,* edited by Ross Harrison. Cambridge: Cambridge University Press, 1979.

Wollheim, Richard, and James Hopkins, eds. *Philosophical Essays on Freud.* Cambridge: Cambridge University Press, 1982.

Wylie, Ruth C. *The Self-Concept: Theory and Research on Selected Topics.* Vol. 2, rev. ed. Lincoln: University of Nebraska Press, 1979.

Young, Robert. "Autonomy and the 'Inner Self.'" *American Philosophical Quarterly* 17 (1980): 35–43.

Zajonc, Robert B. "Feeling and Thinking: Preferences Need No Inferences." *American Psychologist* 35 (1980): 151–175.

Zanna, Mark P., and Joel Cooper. "Dissonance and the Pill: An Attributional Approach to Studying the Arousal Properties of Dissonance." *Journal of Personality and Social Psychology* 29 (1974): 703–709.

Zemore, Robert, and T. Greenough. "Reduction of Ego Threat Following Attributive Projection." *Proceedings of the 81st Annual Convention of the American Psychological Association* 8 (1973): 343–344.

Zimbardo, Philip G., and Shirley Radl. *The Shy Child.* New York: McGraw-Hill, 1981.

Zimmerman, Burke K. "Self-Discipline or Self-Deception?" *Ethics and Values in Health Care* 2 (1977): 120–132.

Zuckerman, Miron. "Attribution of Success and Failure Revisited, or: The Motivational Bias Is Alive and Well in Attribution Theory." *Journal of Personality* 47 (1979): 245–287.

Zuckerman, Miron, Bella M. DePaulo, and Robert Rosenthal. "Verbal and Nonverbal Communication of Deception." In *Advances in Experimental Social Psychology,* edited by Leonard Berkowitz, vol. 14. New York: Academic Press, 1981.

Zuckerman, Miron, D. T. Larrance, N. H. Spieget, and R. Klorman. "Controlling Nonverbal Cues: Facial Expressions and Tone of Voice." *Journal of Experimental Social Psychology* 17 (1981): 506–524.

Index

Adam and Eve, 195–196
Adler, Alfred, 4, 6
adolescence, 141, 211–214
agency, impaired in self-deception, 53–54, 55–56, 59, 62–64
akrasia. *See* weakness of will
alcoholism and use of alcohol, 20–21, 32–34, 52, 54–67, 87; causes of, 56–57; definition of, 57–58; is it a disease? 45–46, 52, 54–67; loss of self-control in, 53–56, 58; and self-handicapping behavior, 45–46, 87, 131; therapy for, 58–59, 63–64
alienation from oneself, 53, 61–62, 228. *See also* self-divided
Allport, Gordon, 36
ambiguity and vagueness: of behavior, and skepticism, 72, 98–99, 113, 224–225, 229–230, 233–235, 246–258 passim; of behavior, self-generated, 71, 86–88; and cognitive schemas, 78–80; of values, 32, 43–44
anger, 33, 61, 111–112, 217
anorexia, 117–118
anxiety, 12, 41, 54, 61, 85, 91, 95–96, 226, 275
Aquinas, Saint Thomas, 11, 199
Aristotle, 22, 141, 199, 201, 215–219, 236
attention and inattention, selective, 71, 96–97, 152, 156–160, 166, 231. *See also* language, and consciousness; mindless vs. mindful behavior
attribution theory, 82–83, 88, 99–101, 104, 111–114, 235

authenticity, 23, 62, 138, 225–226, 228, 261–282 passim; Heidegger's definition of, 274–275; Sartre's definition of, 10, 261–262
authority: Milgram's experiments on, 40; parental, 203–204, 206–211; religious, 263–267; to speak for one's engagements, 53
autonomy, 10, 59, 62–63. *See also* freedom; individualism
avowal, 21, 33, 52–54, 61–64, 140, 173–175, 191
Ayer, A. J., 255

Bach, Kent, 26 n.42, 192–193 n.4, 232
Bacon, Francis, 222
bad faith, 223, 244–245, 247, 276–277. *See also* Sartre, Jean-Paul
Bandura, Albert, 37
Becker, Ernest, 8, 50 n.46
behaviorism, 4–5, 253–255
beliefs. *See* self-deception paradoxes, of contradictory beliefs *and* of willful belief
Bem, Daryl, 83, 101
beneffectance bias, 75–76, 80
Bentham, Jeremy, 186
Berglas, Steven, 86–87
Berscheid, Ellen, 83
brain, two hemispheres of, 102
Branden, Nathaniel, 12, 25 n.7
Brandt, R. B., 179
Brontë, Emily, 258 n.8
Buddenbrooks (Thoman Mann), 197, 208

311

INDEX